Baedeker

Paris

How to use this book

Following the tradition established by Karl Baedeker in 1844, sights of particular interest, outstanding buildings, works of art, etc. as well as good hotels are indicated by one or two stars as follows: especially worth attention ★, outstanding ★★.

To make it easier to locate the various places listed in the "A to Z" section of the Guide, their co-ordinates on the large city map are shown in red at the head of each entry.

Only a selection of hotels, restaurants and shops can be given; no reflection is implied therefore on establishments not included.

In a time of rapid change it is difficult to ensure that all the information given is entirely accurate and up-to-date, and the possibility of error can never be entirely eliminated. Although the publishers can accept no responsibility for inaccuracies and omissions, they are always grateful for corrections and suggestions for improvement.

Preface

This guide is one of the new generation of Baedeker guides. Illustrated throughout in colour they are designed to meet the needs of the modern traveller. They are quick and easy to consult, with the principal sights described in alphabetical order, and practical details and useful tips shown in the margin. The information is presented in a format that is both attractive and easy to follow.

The subject of this guide is the French capital Paris, together with places of particular interest in the area. The guide is in three parts. The first part gives a general account of the city, its population, economy, transport and development, a comprehensive survey of art and culture, famous people and a history of the city. A brief selection of quotations and some suggested itineraries lead into the second part, in which the principal sights of tourist interest in the capital and in the surrounding area are described. The third part contains a variety of

Jardin and Palais du Luxembourg in the heart of the French capital

practical information designed to help visitors find their way about and make the most of their stay. Both the sights and the practical information sections are listed in alphabetical order.

The new Baedeker guides are noted for their concentration on essentials and their convenience of use. They contain numerous specially drawn plans and colour illustrations; and at the end of the book is a large map making it easy to locate the various places described in the "A to Z" section of the guide with the help of the co-ordinates given at the head of each entry.

Contents

Baedeker Specials

Beauty on

"Riens ne se peut comparer à Paris" – nothing compares with Paris, whether visited for the first or the hundredth time. The capital on the Seine is and will always be the city everyone dreams about, the highlight of any trip to France. Beautiful *Lutetia*, to what do you owe your fascination; what is the source of your legend, the secret of your spell?

Those who love Paris wax lyrical over the unique atmosphere of the city which for well over a century has set the tone in Europe: its magnificent sights and enthralling perspectives; its romantic squares and town houses, legacy of the Belle Epoque; its spacious boulevards and its charming walks through Montmartre and Saint-Germain-des-Prés; not to mention its incomparable restaurants and the endless opportunities for window shopping.

Dômes des Invalides

Magnificent burial place of Napoleon I

In spite of attempts at decentralisation, so much of importance in France continues to be concentrated in Paris, while the city itself is a melting pot of nations. La vie parisienne has a pulsating rhythm to it: cosmopolitan and colourful, hectic, a hint of seediness and corruption, a spiritedness, a nonchalance, and that melancholic magic immortalised in words and images by Jacques Prévert and Robert Doisneau. Paris, Ernest Hemingway wrote, is a movable feast, it stays with you for the rest of your life.

Each one of the French kings mounted his own display of grandeur in Paris, leaving behind a series of splendid urban monuments; the buildings of the Mitterrand era, such as the huge Grande Arche in La Défense and the Bibliothèque Nationale, opened in 1996, are no less magnificent. And where else do you find anything to compare with Paris's temples to the

Eiffel Tower

Undisputed symbol of Paris

Moulin Rouge

Its revue theatre is already a legend

the Seine

muses, especially the Louvre, unique treasure-house of art from all periods and every culture.

Parisian chic being synonymous with elegance, anyone wanting to know what the world will be wearing tomorrow need only visit the capital's internationally renowned fashion houses. Haute couture by Chanel, Dior and Gaultier is as much a feature of the city as the famous Eiffel Tower, the celebrated Champs-Elysées and the legendary bouquinistes. In Paris great theatre is produced, and a vibrant musical scene constantly attains new heights. No lover of ballet should miss the productions of the Opéra Garnier. Nocturnal revellers converge not just on the traditional haunts of Montmartre, Saint-Germain-des-Prés and Montparnasse, but also on what has become the latest scene in the area around the place de la Bastille, offering everything from old fashioned Revue to Top Disco.

The Forum des Halles
Site of the former market halls

And as is true throughout France, the food is always good, lacking nothing a gourmet might desire. "Très parisien" are the ever-busy bistros and cafés, stages for the people strolling by. The most delightful restaurants, with superb Art Nouveau decoration, date from the turn of the century; among them are the Deux Magots, Cafe de Flore and Le Dôme, once frequented by Jean-Paul Sartre and Simone de Beauvoir, Ernest Hemingway and Gertrude Stein. Such establishments are the very essence of "la vie parisienne", places where people come to celebrate flamboyance and a zest for life, to see and be seen, to converse, engage in heated debate and of course to flirt. For love in Paris and love of Paris seem inextricably linked, perhaps because each is so rich a source of happiness.

Very Parisian
The always popular cafés

The Louvre
The largest museum in the world

Nature, Culture, History

Facts and Figures

Coat of arms
of the
City of Paris

General

Cosmopolitan captial

Paris is the capital of the French Republic and the seat of the president, government, and National Assembly and Senate, the two houses of the French parliament. But Paris is much more than the political, economic and cultural capital of France; it is a truly cosmopolitan city, a cultural centre of great richness and diversity, a melting-pot of people from all over the world. In this pot-pourri of the exotic every nationality is represented, so are all the arts – the fine, the attention-grabbing, the culinary, Paris bewitches the senses, seducing with its inimitable elegance, its refreshing nonconformism and colourful eccentricity, its devotion to the art of living, its magic. Uniquely blending historicism with continual transformation, it is at once the centre of gravity of western Europe, the incarnation of the wider world, and France's stage.

Situation

Paris is situated in northern France, within the key-shaped cuesta landscape of the Paris Basin, the historic core of which is known as the Ile-de-France. This open region of plains and plateaux is watered by the Seine, the Marne and the Oise, which have throughout history and down to the present day played an important part as axes of human development. The fertile loess and clay soils of the Ile-de-France, long intensively cultivated, combined with the mild climate to make this area the granary of France, from which Paris profited as a trading centre.

Like the ship on the city's coat of arms, Paris stands firmly anchored in the Seine. The river, following a winding course, provides access to the sea. The historic nucleus of the city lies at altitudes between 27m/90ft and 127m/417ft, with Montmartre as its highest point. Major factors in determining the early settlement in this area were the two islands in the Seine, the Ile de la Cité and the Ile Saint-Louis, which offered an easy crossing of the river.

Also of importance was the fact that on the south bank of the Seine the land rose to the Montagne Sainte-Geneviève (the Quartier Latin), so that, like the north bank, it was safe from the danger of flooding. The heart of the Roman settlement thus lay on the south bank, while medieval Paris developed on the north bank. Paris was also well situated from the point of view of transport, lying as it did on the most important north-south route in early French history, from Flanders to the Mediterranean; and this fostered the development of the city.

◀ The Cathedral of Notre-Dame

Area and population

"Paris" can designate different areas, depending on the context. The historic heart of Paris – the Rive Droite (Right Bank) and Rive Gauche (Left Bank), from Notre-Dame to the Etoile and from Montmartre to Montparnasse – extends over an area of 20sq.km/7³/₄sq.miles and has a population of some 500,000. The extension of the city led to the establishment of a municipal area (the ville-département of Paris) of 105.4 sq.km/40³/₄sq.miles with a present population of 2,155,000. But the city continued to grow, and Greater Paris (the agglomération parisienne), including the suburbs and satellite towns, now covers an area of some 1800sq.km/695sq.miles with a population of just under 11 million, making it one of the most densely populated cities in the world.

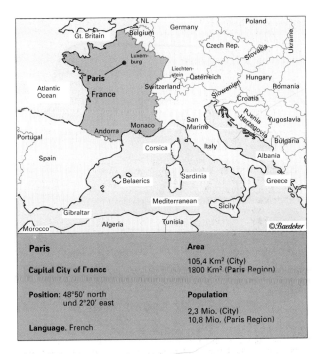

Paris	Area
Capital City of France	105,4 Km² (City)
	1800 Km² (Paris Region)
Position: 48°50' north und 2°20' east	Population
	2,3 Mio. (City)
	10,8 Mio. (Paris Region)
Language. French	

Administration

Paris together with the départements of Hauts-de-Seine, Seine-St-Denis, Val-de-Marne, Yvelines, Essonne and Val-d'Oise forms the administrative region of Ile-de-France. The city has been since 1977 both a commune and a département. The city administration is headed by an elected mayor (maire), the département by a Prefect (Préfet) appointed by the government and a Prefect of Police. The City Council (Conseil de Paris), with 109 members, is also the Conseil Général of the département.

The Prefect of Paris is also Prefect of the Ile-de-France region and in that capacity is chairman of the Conseil Régional, which determines the budget of the region.

Area and population

Arrondissements

Paris is divided into 20 *arrondissements* (wards or precincts), each of which is divided into four *quartiers* (quarters). The arrondissements are arranged in a spiral which starts at the Louvre (1st arrondissement) and circles twice round the historic core of the city, the Ile de la Cité, and ends at the Place de la Nation (20th arrondissement). When Jean Cocteau referred to Paris as a city made up of individual townships and villages he was thinking of the districts of the city which are also known as *quartiers* or *faubourgs*, with names which do not always coincide with their official designation. These *quartiers*, which have retained something of their individual stamp, take their names from old villages now incorporated in the city (Montmartre, Chaillot), churches (Saint-Germain-des-Prés), prominent buildings (Halles, Opéra) or some special historical characteristic (Quartier Latin). The *faubourgs* (literally "outside the town") are outlying districts, usually named after the nearest village: thus the Faubourg Montmartre was the district on the road to the village of Montmartre. The suburbs outside the present city boundary are known as the *banlieue*.

Paris
Arrondissements

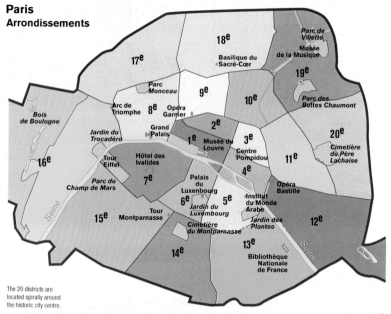

The 20 districts are located spirally around the historic city centre.

A colourful mix of races

France is concentrated in Paris. Here, on 2% of the country's total area, just under a fifth of its population live. The population of the city itself (the *ville-département*) is steadily falling because old buildings, mainly in the city centre, are being pulled down and replaced only by relatively few new apartments at high rents, while the population of the adjoining départements is increasing at an annual rate of 3–5%. Paris is not France, as it used to be claimed, but it is a magnet for workers from all over France, the French overseas départements and other countries. More than 60% of Parisians are incomers to the city, at least six out of ten of them from the French provinces. Every French region is represented in the population, and some of the outer districts have been almost taken over by immigrants from the south-

People of all nationalities can be found in the Champs-Elysées

west, Auvergne or eastern France, who celebrate their own festivals and almost always have a newspaper of their own.

Some 25% of the working population consists of foreigners; the largest group is Algerians, followed by Portuguese and Spaniards. In the Goutte d'Or, one of the redeveloped areas in eastern Paris, the population of around 35,000 belong to some 40 different nationalities, the largest number being North Africans.

Paris has long offered asylum to political refugees, most of whom nowadays come from South America and Indochina. The 13th arrondissement has become known as Chinatown, with many Asian inhabitants, mainly from Cambodia, Vietnam and Laos.

Paris is the seat of an archbishop and has 119 Catholic parishes. In addition there are 72 Protestant churches, 24 Greek and Russian Orthodox churches and seven synagogues with a membership totalling more than 220,000. The Muslim community, now the second most numerous, is served by three mosques.

Religion

Of the many international organisations which have their headquarters or a branch office in Paris the best known are UNESCO (which has had its headquarters in Paris since 1946), the Secretariat of the Organisation for Economic Cooperation and Development and the European office of Interpol.

International organisations

Urban development

Paris acquired its typical "classical" character in the time of Louis XIV (1638–1715). During his reign the 13th century town walls were pulled down and replaced by wide avenues, the "Grands Boulevards" – an

Development of the metropolis

Town Planner of the 19th century: Baron Georges Eugène Haussmann

This giant of a man, with his startling good looks, was born in Paris on March 27th 1809, the descendant of a German Protestant family from Cologne. After completing his studies Haussmann entered government service and soon drew attention to himself in public circles by his outstanding achievements. In 1853 he was appointed prefect of the département of Seine by Napoleon III and summoned to Paris, where the emperor presented him with his plans for the wide-ranging modernisation of the French capital – plans which he had drawn up during his imprisonment in the fortress of Harn. As a result, the historic appearance of the city was to undergo ambitious and far-reaching changes, with broad boulevards, radial roads, star-shaped intersections and extensive parks and gardens. These measures both served to create employment and also had the underlying aim of ensuring that the street barricades which went up during periods of civil unrest would be rendered ineffective.

At the time that Haussmann took on this task, the old centre of Paris mainly consisted of a web of narrow winding alleyways with large numbers of dilapidated houses dating from the 16th to 18th centuries. There was an urgent need for proper sanitation, most especially because the existing contamination of the water supply was constantly causing fresh outbreaks of disease. In order to create light and air in the overcrowded city environment Haussmann entrusted the landscape architect Alphand and the engineer Belgrand with the task of carrying out the modernisation measures he had planned and bringing his vision to fruition. The transformation of Paris was effected in three stages: first, two road axes were constructed which linked the north of the city with the south and the east with the west. A second stage of construction saw the opening up of the city with other boulevards and avenues, while a third involved the incorporation into the city of the area which lay between the customs wall and the defensive ramparts built in 1841. In order to see through his ambitious project Haussmann made sure that he had complete government support. Without it he would not have had the authority to carry on more or less unhindered with the essential measures of dispossessing the many small businesses in the affected areas and resettling whole working-class districts in the suburbs. It took almost 17 years for the construction work to be completed, leaving Paris with wide straight boulevards and magnificently conceived public squares which gave the city imposing perspectives in every direction and allowed the eye an unrestricted view of such historic buildings as Notre Dame, the Palais Royal and the Panthéon. The new thoroughfares were lit by some 3200 gas lamps and before long they were lined with luxurious palaces and town houses, followed by the first smart department stores, famous fashion houses, elegant restaurants and places of entertainment of every conceivable kind. All of these contribute to the unmistakable atmosphere which Paris still possesses today. In order to solve the acute problem of the drinking

water supply and sewage disposal, a cleverly thought-out system was installed of 800km/500 miles of water pipes and 600km/370 miles of sewers. In 1854 the architect Baltard started to build a complex of market halls right in the heart of the city, and these were still in use up to 1969. Public transport within the city was improved by the introduction of an "omnibus service" consisting of 570 horse-drawn carriages. By the end of 1860 the suburbs beyond the customs wall had been incorporated into the city proper and the resulting urban area of 7800 ha./30 sq.miles was divided up into 20 arrondissements. The high points of the second empire were the two world exhibitions of 1855 and 1867, organised by Haussmann, where crowned heads of state, diplomats, industrialists and renowned artists were able to come together and Haussmann himself was showered with countless decorations and honours.

The overthrow of his patron, Napoleon III, led to Haussmann's own tragic fall from grace: powerful criticism and intrigues ensured the dismissal of the prefect at the beginning of 1870. Haussmann then retired to the Castle of Cestas, which his wife had inherited, and remained there until he was called by Ismail Pascha to Constantinople, where an entire section of the city had been destroyed in a fire. Shortly after reconstruction work was completed there, Haussmann was entrusted with the task of modernising the Egyptian capital, Cairo. Energetic and enterprising to the last, Haussmann was still commuting at the age of eighty between Cestas and his apartment in Paris, where he died on January 12th 1891.

entirely new idea in 17th century Europe. The monarch thus demonstrated his absolute power and at the same time established the basis of the city's structure as we see it today. All Paris's later walls and fortifications, which in turn gave place to broad avenues, were laid out concentrically round the Sun King's ring of boulevards. The city planners of the 19th century likewise created circular and semicircular traffic arteries, and the modern ring road, the Boulevard Périphérique, follows the same concentric pattern. In the reign of Louis XIV, too, Paris became a major artistic centre whose influence extended throughout Europe. Many of the most celebrated artists of the period worked in Paris, including Jacques-François Blondel, Charles Le Brun, André Le Nôtre, François Mansart, Jules Hardouin-Mansart, Claude Perrault and Antoine Watteau.

From the mid 19th century, in the time of Napoleon III (1808–73) and his Prefect of Paris Baron Georges-Eugène Haussmann (1809–91), Paris underwent a further transformation which still marks the character of the city. Haussmann pulled down whole quarters of Paris; imposing new buildings, handsome squares, parks and broad avenues replaced the old slum areas; and the city's water supply and sewer systems were renewed. Although the replanning of Paris had active supporters it also attracted violent criticism as being insensitive to the historic and artistic character of the Paris townscape and as involving the demolition of much that was worth preserving. A sumptuous monument to the self-confident bourgeoisie of the 19th century and the crowning architectural achievement of the period was the Opéra designed by Charles Garnier (1825–98), which opened in 1875. The planning conception and the architectural style of Haussmann's Paris became models for the whole of Europe.

Paris has preserved much of its 19th century splendour, in spite of a series of controversial redevelopment proposals since the Second World War, such as the demolition of the old Halles in 1969. This ensemble of 12 market halls, designed by Victor Baltard and built between 1853 and 1858, was the first example of iron architecture on this scale in France. The climax of the Second Empire was marked by the world fairs organised in Paris between 1855 and 1867, followed by two other exhibitions in 1878 and 1889. The 1889 exhibition gave Paris one of its most famous landmarks, the Eiffel Tower.

The pompous style of the "Belle Epoque" (1890–1914) is reflected in the architecture of the period. Typical examples are the Grand and Petit Palais, the Gares de l'Est, du Nord and d'Orsay, the Bibliothèque Nationale, the glass dome of the Printemps department store and the Train Bleu restaurant in the Gare de Lyon (restored in 1993). Also characteristic of the Paris townscape is the Art Nouveau style which came into fashion around the turn of the century. It is found not only in architecture but also in the distinctive forms of everyday objects and jewellery, as well as in Hector Guimard's Métro entrances and tulip lamps. Many cafés and restaurants, pâtisseries and shops have preserved their old façades and authentic Art Nouveau interiors.

Redevelopment schemes

The 1960s saw a great wave of redevelopment in Paris, during which old buildings were pulled down, whether this was necessary or not, and replaced by new concrete office and apartment blocks. In many parts of the city areas which had grown up over the centuries were replaced by tracts of architectural monotony, involving major alterations in the population structure. Fortunately the historic centre was spared, but whole districts of the city were taken over by modern high-rise complexes, as in Montparnasse, La Défense and the 13th, 14th, 15th, 19th and 20th arrondissements. Since then, however, the policy of radical demolition has increasingly been called in question, and redevelopment is now seen as a policy of renewal, involving the preservation or restoration of older buildings. To what extent this approach will prove feasible when applied to the very latest redevelopment projects, such as in the Tolbiac quarter (13 arrondissement) around the Bibliothèque Nationale, remains to be seen (see Baedeker Special, pages 14–15).

The most ambitious redevelopment project, launched in 1985, concerns eastern Paris. Under the aegis of Mayor Jacques Chirac it is planned to improve the quality of life and stimulate economic activity in this hitherto neglected area – with a population of over a million – by specific structural measures, without destroying the character of the area. The object is to raise the standard of eastern Paris to that of the more privileged western districts. Old dwellings are to be restored and new ones built; more than 45ha/110 acres of parks and gardens will be laid out; and crèches and primary schools established. Office complexes and sites for commerce and industry are planned. The benefits as well as the negative effects of the redevelopment programme can be seen in such areas as the Bastille, Bercy, Belleville and Ménilmontant (see Paris from A to Z).

Eastern Paris

In order to check the uncontrollable growth of population in the Paris conurbation the government of Georges Pompidou launched in the mid sixties one of the largest town-building projects in Europe, involving the construction of five new towns round Paris. These towns were designed to provide new housing standards and quality of life for families flocking to Paris from the provinces, French settlers returning from the colonies and "guest workers" from southern Europe, and to afford also a wide range of employment opportunities and leisure facilities. Prominent international architects were given the task of transforming this ambitious plan for a carefully conceived and humanised process of urbanisation into reality. The new housing estates, each with its individual style, were to be designed on a

New towns

Marne-la-Vallé: Place Pablo-Picasso

A cosmopolition mix: they are all Parisians

human scale which should promote community life and communication. To the east of Paris was Marne-la-Vallée, to the south-east Melun-Sénart, to the south Evry, to the south-west Saint-Quentin-en-Yvelines and to the north-west Cergy-Pontoise. Whether judged successful, controversial or totally misconceived, the efforts of the town planners have resulted in the creation of five new towns, with a total population of one million, which have proved a magnet both for Parisians seeking relief from the high rents in the city and for incomers from less prosperous regions of France who hope for new jobs in the banlieue.

There has been much international interest in the architectural experiments in the new towns, whose outsize arcades, giant barrels and spectacular concrete blocks, by such architects as Manuel Nuñez-Yanowsky and Ricardo Bofill, will at once catch the visitor's eye. A notable example in Marne-la-Vallée, the oldest of the new towns, is Bofill's Mannerist Palacio d'Abraxas (1982), with its huge portal, one storey high, and its intimidating flights of steps. Opposite it is the Théâtre, a 19-storey tower block containing just under 600 apartments. That Nuñez shared his colleague's liking for huge buildings of surrealistic aspect is demonstrated by his Arènes de Picasso. Although it may still be possible to grasp the dimensions of the buildings, the area of the new towns is more difficult to encompass. Marne-la-Vallée alone covers an area of some 18,000 hectares/45,000 acres (compared with only 10,500 hectares/26,250 acres for Paris) and extends over 26 communes. This new town has become a counter-attraction to the western districts of Paris where in the past industry has been concentrated. The core of the new development is the commune of Noisy-le-Grand, whose Mont d'Est quarter (designed by Zubléna) has already been used as the setting of many futuristic films.

Cergy-Pontoise, situated in a bend on the Oise, is like an amphitheatre laid out above a number of artificial lakes, which in summer are the haunt of water sports enthusiasts. In the administrative and business quarter round the conical building occupied by the Prefecture an intricate system of bridges and underpasses provides for the segregation of pedestrian and vehicular traffic – a principle which was abandoned on grounds of cost in the later development of Cergy-Saint-Christophe. The Neo-Classical Belvédère de Saint-Christophe (1985) in Place des Colonnes again shows Bofill's leaning towards the monumental and towards classical forms.

Evry, now chief town of the département of Essonne, was for years a textbook example of a dormitory town, but now has the Agora, a cultural and business complex which provides employment for some 40,000 people. Mario Botta's massive new Cathedral is likely to prove a further attraction.

Melun-Sénart was designed as an extension to the existing small provincial town of Melun, with generous expanses of green and woodland and even of intensively cultivated arable land.

The only one of the new towns not to be developed out of an existing settlement was Saint-Quentin-en-Yvelines. Here, on a "green field" site, the architects (Ayguavives and Rodrigues) sought in the Trois Villages to re-create the character of an Ile-de-France village – though unfortunately even this new town was equipped with the inevitable monumental complexes favoured by such architects as Bofill.

The tentacles of Paris, however, continue to reach out beyond the territory we have been considering. Within its sphere of influence and strongly dependent on it is almost the whole of the Paris Basin, with the regions of Champagne-Ardenne and Burgundy to the east, the Centre region to the south, the Pays de la Loire to the south-west, Normandy to the north-west and Picardy to the north. The Ile-de-France, a centuries-old region though with repeatedly altered boundaries, is now shared between eight départements centred on the City of Paris (Ville de Paris, département No. 75). In the administrative reorganisation of the sixties and seventies three new départements were established – Hauts-de-Seine (No. 92), Seine-Saint-Denis (No. 93) and Val-de-Marne (No. 94), forming a ring round the city, the "petite couronne". Round this inner ring are the départements of Yvelines (No. 78), Val-d'Oise (No. 95), Essonne (No. 91) and Seine-et-Marne (No. 77). This administrative structure is overlaid by various functional divisions with different patterns of development and covering different areas. Thus according to INSEE (the government statistical office) the expanding Paris conurbation (*agglomération parisienne*) extends in a continuous built-up area well beyond the "petite couronne", taking in some 335 urban communes with a population of just under 9 million. Beyond this is a zone which is involved in a process of industrialisation and urbanisation but still preserves some rural features – the ZPIU (Zone de peuplement industriel et urbain) or Zone semi-rurale. The only area that can be regarded as truly rural (*"rural profond"*), with few traces of urbanisation, is the eastern part of the département of Seine-et-Marne.

Population trends in Paris, as in many other European cities, show a movement from the centre to the outskirts, although the decline in the population of the Ville de Paris has now slowed down markedly. Whereas in 1881 2.3 million out of the Ile-de-France's total population of 3.4 million lived in Paris, rather more than a hundred years later only 20% (2.1 million) of the region's population live in the city, while the outer districts, outskirts and suburbs of the city have experienced a continuing influx of population. Gigantic new housing complexes bear witness to the processes of restructuring and change which have been at work since the Second World War, beginning with Sarcelles to the north of Paris, the prototype scheme of low-cost housing (HLM, *habitations à loyer modéré*), built in 1954. Since then "sarcellisation" has

Paris and the
Ile-de-France in
the grip of
change

Conseil d'Etat: seat of the State Council

spread to almost the whole periphery of Paris. This has led to a particularly marked loss of population in the 1st to 10th arrondissements, while the larger and more densely populated 11th to 20th arrondissements have shown varying rates of population loss. Much the largest rates of increase are shown in the outer ring of départements, the "grande couronne". Almost the whole of the Ile-de-France's increase in population during the eighties was in this outer ring, a third of the increase being accounted for by the new towns.

Although there are still some large industrial establishments (such as the Renault automobile works in Boulogne-Billancourt, which closed down only in 1992) in Paris itself or in the "proche banlieue", the industry of the Paris region is increasingly moving to the periphery. In particular old-established small industrial firms and market installations in Paris (e.g. the Halles, La Villette and the Entrepôts de Bercy) have closed down or moved outside the city. As a result new industrial, residential, recreation and leisure zones, each devoted to its particular function, have been established in the outer-ring départements. An increasingly important aspect of this development is the number of workers (at present around a million) who commute daily between their home in the peripheral districts and their work in the city. And although current forecasts indicate that the rate of population growth is likely to slow down the process of structural change in the Paris region seems to be far from complete.

Economy

Economic
structure

Over 5 million people work in the Paris region: that is, a fifth of the whole employed population of France. More than a million workers commute daily from the suburbs. Since the Second World War employment opportunities have moved steadily from the city itself to the surrounding départements in the Ile-de-France: whereas in 1954 more than half of the employed population of the region worked in the city, by 1997 the proportion had fallen to barely a third. This fall is a result of the move of industry from the city itself to the outlying districts, its place being taken by the service trades. More than three quarters are now employed in the services sector.

Modern architecture reflects the increasing importance of the services sector. Examples of this are the Grand Ponant office complex (1989; architect Olivier Clément Cacoub), a massive structure of glass and metal built on the site of an old Citroën works; the Grande Arche (also completed in 1989, the bicentenary of the Revolution) in the expanding business district of La Défense; the monumental Ministry of Finance (architects Chemtov and Huidobro) in Bercy; and the Bibliothèque Nationale de France in the Tolbiac quarter, which with its hypermodern office and industrial complexes should add a new, futurist dimension to the Paris cityscape at the commencement of the 21st c.

Industries traditionally located in Paris are electronics, precision engineering, woodworking, textiles, pharmaceuticals, chemicals and the aircraft and automobile construction industries. Particularly affected by the move to the banlieue are the metalworking, engineering, textile and chemical industries, though the firms' head offices have frequently remained in Paris. The main reasons for the move away from the city have been the increased cost of land required for expansion, environmental protection costs and decentralisation measures. Those industries which have remained in Paris are mainly large groups and small and medium-sized firms, often midway between craft and industrial production, which still largely determine the

Industry and crafts

Sightseeing by boat: a bâteau-mouche on the Seine

Above & Below:
the Paris Métro

In the early summer of 1911 Franz Kafka noted in his travel diary: "The ease with which it can be understood means that the Métro is the best opportunity that an eager stranger has of acquiring the confidence to penetrate swiftly and unerringly, at the first attempt, right into the essence of Paris". Today that still is true for those who are attracted by the mysteries of large cities and "seek the true cultural heart of France", as the philosopher André Glucksmann once referred to the Paris underground system. Scarcely any other institution in the French capital offers such a broad palette of impressions as the city's fastest and most reliable method of public transport. The first métro line, which ran between Porte Maillot and Vincennes, was opened in time for the world exhibition of 1900 – its construction was the responsibility of the engineer Fulgence Bienvenue. Nine years later 70km/43 miles of track were in use; in 1934 the suburbs were linked up to the system, and at the beginning of the 1960s the RER express métro was added. Since 1998 the new Météore line has been in operation, creating even faster connections between the city centre and the east and south-east of Paris.

For just the cost of a single métro ticket the visitor can take a sightseeing tour of the city centre, using lines 2 and 6, and thereby sample a slice of everyday life in Paris. Make the starting point Barbès-Rochechouart Station – one of the few in Paris where passengers do not descend deep below pavement level, but instead have to climb steps. Here, both underneath and next to the grey iron struts supporting the métro line, can be found all the hustle and bustle of a Muslim souk, this area of the 18th arrondissement, known as the Goutte d'Or, being populated predominantly by Arabs, North Africans and black Africans. High above the boulevards métro line 2 clatters along over viaducts laden with ornamentation with fantastic views across the city. As far as Jaurès Station, the line keeps at the same level as the buildings, hurtling past

character of their particular quartier – the clothing trade mainly in the 2nd arrondissement, newspaper offices and printers in the 9th, publishers in the 6th, precision engineering in the 10th, 11th and 12th. Similarly for craftsmen's products: furniture workshops are traditionally to be found in the Faubourg Saint-Antoine (11th and 12th arrondissements), leather goods in the Marais (3rd) and jewellery in the Marais and the area between the Opéra-Garnier, rue Royale and place Vendôme. In the Faubourg Saint-Honoré and round place des Victoires are the renowned haute couture houses.

Service sector

More than 100 trade fairs and 1000 congresses are held in Paris every year. There are several centres for trade fairs and exhibitions, including the Palais des Congrès at Porte Maillot, the Parc des Expositions, CNIT at La Défense, the Parc des Expositions Paris-Nord and the Parc des Expositions at Le Bourget.

The large financial and insurance institutions are concentrated in the 2nd, 8th and 9th arrondissements and at La Défense, public offices and embassies mainly in the 7th, 8th and 16th. A new centre of the tertiary sector is developing in Tolbiac and Bercy.

With over 13 million visitors a year, tourism is a major element in the city's economy. The largest numbers of foreign visitors come from the United States, followed by Britain, Germany and Japan.

faded advertisement hoardings and flapping washing-lines. Just 10km/6 miles of the métro system run above ground, and almost all of that is on lines 2 and 6, which roughly follow the old city boundaries of 1789. And yet it is these sections of track, running high above the ground, which again and again have captured the imagination of writers, painters and filmmakers. This is where Marcel Carné shot his cult movie of 1946 "Les Portes de la Nuit", where the infamous Fantomas kidnapped an entire métro train, where Jean-Paul Belmondo, playing a policeman involved in a daredevil chase, jumped in spectacular fashion from one railway carriage to another – and it was the actor himself who shot the scene, not a stuntman. Just past Jaurès the trains caterpillar down into the bowels of the metropolis and do not see the light of day again until the other side of Bercy, where they emerge by the Babylonian towers of the new National Library, amid futuristic office buildings, while excavators clear yet more ground for fresh construction projects. On the Pont de Bercy there is time for a swift glance at the Ile Saint-Louis before the train switches to the left bank of the Seine. Now the track stays almost completely above ground, even if the route through the 13th and 14th arrondissements offers the sightseer little more than the view of functional-looking blocks of flats,

warehouses and *tabac-bistros*. From Pasteur Station onwards, the building façades reveal the increasing prosperity to be found around the boulevard Garibaldi and the rue de Grenelle, with the top of the Eiffel Tower appearing briefly above the roofs. The line now crosses the Seine again by the narrow bridge, the Pont de Bir-Hakeim, a technical tour de force, and this time follows the Rive Droite. Passy, on the right-hand bank of the Seine, is the gateway to the elegant 16th arrondissement, where the métro, however, immediately plunges down into a tunnel, only venturing above ground again at Anvers, not far from Pigalle, the heart of Paris's world of pleasure and entertainment, before finally coming to rest again at Barbès-Rochechouart.

Art lovers will always respond with enthusiasm to the elegant station entrances, created in the art nouveau style by Hector Guimard (1867–1942), which can be admired at Pigalle and Porte Dauphine on line 2, or right in the heart of the city at Cité Station, directly next to the Palais de Justice. At the same time the Louvre Station greets passengers with celebrated sculptures from the museum of art, Rodin's "Thinker" sits ruminating at Varenne Station, and at Belleville the "taggers", as the nocturnal graffiti desperados are known, tell of another way of life.

Transport

In spite of its situation on the western edge of the European mainland Paris is a hub of international communications. Thanks to the siting of its rail terminals and the construction of its underground system, the Métro (Chemin de Fer Métropolitain), Paris has been preserved from the fate of other large cities whose historical centres have been carved up by railway tracks.

Two large companies are responsible for carrying the more than 10 million people who travel every day by public transport to, from or through Paris. The State Railways (Société Nationale des Chemins de Fer, SNCF) convey annually over 85 million long-distance travellers and over 500 million making local journeys. The partly State-owned RATP (Régie Autonome des Transports Parisiens) carries over 1.9 billion people annually on the Métro and almost a billion on buses. A relatively new branch of the RATP, initiated in 1969, is the RER (Réseau Express Régional), which has four lines serving the outer suburbs and carries over 300 million passengers annually. The east-west and north-south axes of the RER intersect in the city centre in the vast Châtelet-Les Halles station. The average distance between stations is 543m/594yds, and the trains run at intervals of 90 seconds

Rail services, Métro, RER

at peak periods and between 2 and 7 minutes at other times. It is planned to improve services to the Paris suburbs by the opening of further RER lines and additional Métro stations by the year 2000.

Airports

The State airports corporation, Aéroports de Paris (ADP), runs Paris's three airports – Orly to the south of the city, Le Bourget and Roissy-Charles de Gaulle to the north. Together they handle over 35 million passengers and more than 900,000 tons of freight annually, giving them third place among European airports, after London and Frankfurt am Main.

After the opening of Roissy-Charles de Gaulle in 1974, Orly lost its leading place, with a sharp fall in passenger traffic. Charles de Gaulle has also become the largest handler of air freight, almost completely displacing Le Bourget in this field. A second *aérogare* was opened at Charles de Gaulle in 1989. Since 1995 Charles de Gaulle has been served by high-speed train (TGV). A third *aérogare* should be completed by the turn of the century. On the latest estimates passenger traffic is expected to rise to over 80 million a year by 2020.

Port

Although Paris's port on the Seine, the Port Autonome de Paris, is declining in importance as industry moves out of the city and freight has largely switched to road and rail, it is still France's major inland port. The main transhipment areas have long been outside the city, and the port installations on the Seine and the canals are now only of secondary importance.

Passenger traffic, now catering solely for the tourist trade, still has ports of call within the city, from which numerous bâteaux-mouches offer cruises on the Seine and its lateral canals.

Roads

Almost all the French motorways (tolls) radiate from Paris. The Autoroute du Nord (A 1/E 15) runs north to Lille, with A 2/E 19 branching off at Péronne towards Belgium (Charleroi, Liège). The Autoroute de l'Est (A 4/E 50) runs east to Reims, Metz and Strasbourg. Running south from Paris are the Autoroute du Sud (Autoroute du Soleil, A 6/E 15) to Lyons and southern France and the Autoroute Aquitaine (A 10/E 5) to south-western France via Orléans, Tours and Poitiers. To the west are the Autoroute Océane (A 11/E 50) to Chartres, Le Mans and Nantes, with an extension planned to Brest, and as A 81/E 50 from Le Mans to Rennes, and the Autoroute de l'Ouest (Autoroute de Normandie, A 13/E 5 and E 46) to Rouen and Caen.

All motorways are linked with the Boulevard Périphérique Extérieur, a ring motorway with between six and ten lanes which circles Paris.

In spite of its 33 bridges and 1300km/800 miles of streets, avenues and boulevards, Paris like other big cities has been faced for years with the problem of its steadily increasing traffic, with over 4 million vehicles now crowding through the city every day. In an attempt to reduce the growing congestion of traffic an expressway was constructed along the right bank of the Seine in 1967, and this was followed in 1973 by the Boulevard Périphérique and in 1990 by the introduction of the so-called *axes rouges*, imposing a total ban on stopping (except for deliveries between 8am and 1pm) on a number of strategic traffic arteries such as the Boulevard de Strasbourg, the rue de Rivoli, the boulevard Saint-Michel and the left bank of the Seine.

Art and Culture

Movements in 19th and 20th c. Art

A metropolis of the size of 19th century Paris was able to develop a rich and varied cultural life impossible for smaller towns. In spite of the conservative attitudes of the urban middle class the socio-cultural mix in Paris generated an atmosphere of liberality in which individualistic artistic movements, new ideas and delight in experiment were able to find expression.

Auguste Renoir: "Ball at the Moulin de la Galette"

The birth-date of Impressionism was April 15th 1874, when a group of painters opened an exhibition in the studio of the photographer Nadar which included a picture by the young painter Claude Monet entitled "Impression – Soleil Levant" ("Impression – Rising Sun") depicting the port of Le Havre in the morning mist. When a journalist discussing the exhibition took his cue from Monet's picture and referred to the painters mockingly as Impressionists he gave the new movement its name. At first used in a pejorative sense, the term later came to express an almost exorbitant admiration. The Impressionists, most of whom belonged to the upper middle classes, rejected the academic painting of the studios and saw their task as the representation of nature. Their last exhibition was held in 1886, after which the movement broke up; among those associated with it were Paul Cézanne, Edgar Degas, Edouard Manet, Claude Monet, Camille Pissarro, Auguste Renoir, Georges Seurat, Paul Signac and Alfred Sisley. Formerly displayed in the Jeu de Paume, the paintings of the

Impressionists are now to be seen in the Musée d'Orsay along with the works of other major 19th century artists. Among the best-known representatives of Impressionism in music are Claude Debussy (1862–1918), with his "Après-midi d'un Faune" and his opera "Pelléas et Mélisande", and Maurice Ravel (1875–1937).

Symbolism

After Impressionism a variety of other art movements came to the fore in Paris. In the closing years of the 19th century there was a reaction against Impressionism in the form of Symbolism. Among its leading representatives were Paul Gauguin, Odilon Redon and Gustave Moreau, whose house in Paris now contains a fascinating retrospective exhibition of his work. The intellectual and creative focal point of Symbolism became the Paris group known as the Nabis (in Hebrew, "Prophets"), consisting of Maurice Denis, Pierre Bonnard, Paul Sérusier, Edouard Vuillard and later Félix Vallotton and Aristide Maillol. In contrast to the naturalistic representation aimed at by the Impressionists the Nabis sought to achieve a synthetic and symbolic depiction of the world.

Fauvism

The first major artistic movement of the 20th century was Fauvism. In the Paris Salon d'Automne of 1905 a small group of like-minded painters showed their pictures for the first time, and the movement acquired its name when the critic Louis Vauxcelles described these paintings as the work of fauves (wild beasts). Among the leading representatives of the group were Henri Matisse, Maurice de Vlaminck and André Derain.

Cubism

Another movement of the early 20th century was Cubism, evolved by a small group of French, Spanish and Russian painters. Its forerunners were Georges Braque and Pablo Picasso, whose "Demoiselles

Fountain sculptures by Niki de St Phalle and Jean Tinguely in front of the Centre Pompidou

*Bronze group "The Captives" (1679) by Martin van den Bogaert in
the Cour Puget at the Louvre*

d'Avignon" (1907) is regarded as the first Cubist painting, marking
a fundamental turning-point in the artistic perceptions of the 20th
century.

The main centres of Expressionism and Futurism were in Germany
and Italy rather than in France, although Marinetti's "Futurist Manifesto" was published in the Paris newspaper "Le Figaro" on February
20th 1909.

Expressionism,
Futurism and
Surrealism

The development of Surrealism, on the other hand, was closely
associated with Paris. In 1924 André Breton wrote the "First Manifesto of Surrealism", and in the 1920s the German painter Max Ernst
joined the group of Surrealists in Paris, among whose other members
were Yves Tanguy, Joan Miró, Salvador Dalí, Hans Arp, André
Masson, Pablo Picasso, Man Ray, Marcel Duchamp and Francis
Picabia.

After the Second World War the Ecole de Paris again played a prominent part as the centre of a new artistic movement, Tachisme (from
tache, "blot, splotch of colour"), whose exponents included Georges
Mathieu, Jean Dubuffet, Jean Fautrier, Hans Hartung, Wols, Henri
Michaux and Alberto Giacometti. Central features of Tachisme were
the particular value attached to the observer's relationship to the
work and a new materiality implying a radical rejection of traditional
conceptions of the picture.

Tachisme

It was only in the mid sixties that Paris finally lost its predominant
position as an art centre to New York.

Paris nevertheless remains a leading centre of art. Evidence of this
is provided by museums, the numerous retrospective exhibitions of
work by major artists and the three great Salons held in spring (the

The art scene
today

Salon des Indépendants for painting, the Salon de Mai for sculpture) and autumn (Salon d'Automne for painting). In 1985 the New Paris Biennale succeeded its predecessor the Biennale of Young Art as a further forum for contemporary art.

There have also been a number of new foundations of cultural centres and museums which have contributed to Paris's reputation as a centre of art and culture. A landmark was the opening of the Pompidou Centre in 1977; altered and extended since then, it has retained its attraction and its influence. In 1984 Cartier founded in Jouy-en-Josas an "artists' park" as a centre of contemporary art for painters and sculptors. The same year saw the opening of the Zénith concert hall, the first part of the new cultural centre at La Villette, and this was followed in the later eighties by the huge Cité des Sciences et de l'Industrie and in 1996 by the Cité de la Musique. The Musée Picasso and Musée d'Orsay opened their doors at the end of 1986. In 1989 the glass pyramid in the Louvre and the new opera house in the place de la Bastille were inaugurated. In summer 1991 the reconstruction of the Jeu de Paume was completed, and it is now used for exhibitions of contemporary art. By 1999 the last of the work being carried out on the Louvre – the world's largest art gallery, and for every art lover the highlight of any visit to Paris – will be finished. There are also numerous galleries displaying work belonging to many different schools, concentrated mainly in the Saint-Germain-des-Prés, Faubourg Saint-Honoré and Beaubourg quarters and round the Opéra-Bastille.

Education, Literature and Theatre

Higher education

In addition to 13 universities (the Sorbonne having been divided into four universities in 1968) with some 380,000 students Paris has the elite *grandes écoles* such as the the Ecole Normale Supérieure (teachers' training), the Ecole Polytechnique (engineers), the Ecole des Hautes Etudes Commerciales (managers) and the Ecole Nationale d'Administration (civil servants). The *grandes écoles*, entry to which is by competitive examination, are the most renowned educational establishments in France, enjoying enormous prestige, and many of their graduates hold leading positions in public life.

Outstanding among France's many research institutes are those of the Centre National de la Recherche Scientifique (National Centre of Scientific Research) Although not an educational establishment, the historic Institut de France with its five academies, the best known of which is the Académie Française, enjoys great authority.

Prix Goncourt

Literature has long enjoyed a very special status in France. The most important French literary prize is the Prix Goncourt, which has been awarded by the Académie Goncourt annually since 1903. Edmond de Goncourt's idea in establishing the prize was to create a kind of dining club consisting of ten professional writers who meet every month in the Restaurant Drouant in Place Gaillon and once a year award the Prix Goncourt to the best novel published in the preceding twelve months. The prize is virtually guaranteed to make the recipient a best-seller. The Prix Renaudot, founded in 1926 and awarded by journalists, enjoys similar prestige.

Bookshops

Paris has an immense number of bookshops, including many excellent specialist shops. A whole series of renowned bookshops are strung along the boulevard Montparnasse. The old-established bookshop La Hune in the 6th arrondissement specialises in art; Joseph Gibert in the boulevard Saint-Michel sells remaindered books; Shakespeare and Co. in the Latin Quarter has an unbeatable range of foreign books, and also has periodic readings by authors. The Librairie des Femmes, which is associated with the publishing firm Editions des Femmes, offers an extensive range of women's literature and organises exhibitions on women; and in the 13th arrondissement is a feminist library, the Bibliothèque Féministe Marguérite Durand, named after the first woman editor of a daily newspaper.

The FNAC shops in the Forum des Halles and rue de Rennes are regular supermarkets for books and records, and also sell tickets for theatres.

Theatre

In and around Paris there are something like 150 theatres, most of them privately run: there are no municipally subsidised theatres in France. The private theatres, many of them small café and boulevard theatres, tend to go in for experimental productions; and during the two world wars and in the postwar years they put on the first performances of contemporary theatrical works. Nowadays they are in a rather precarious position; and although President Mitterrand introduced substantial state subsidies to support independent creative initiatives the competition of powerful property companies is increasingly compelling small theatres to close down.

In recent years some excellent theatres have opened in the outer banlieue, though many of them have no regular company. Particularly notable is the Théâtre du Soleil established by Ariane Mnouchkine in the Cartoucherie, a former gunpowder factory in the Bois de Vincennes. Well-known guest actors from all over Europe appear in Patrice Chéreau's Théâtre des Amandiers in Nanterre, which also features plays by the contemporary playwright Bernard-Marie Koltès and organises film and discussion evenings and readings by authors. Also very popular are Claude Fall's Théâtre Gérard-Philippe in Saint-Denis and Bernard Sobel's theatre in the working-class suburb of Gennevilliers, whose productions are directed largely to the social concerns of the suburbs. Among great French directors from outside Paris now working in the capital are Roger Planchon and George Lavaudant of the Théâtre Villeur-banne at Lyons. Claude Regy became known particularly for his productions of works by linguistic purists such as Marguerite Duras and Nathalie Sarraute. Since the 1970s increasing numbers of well-

The Théâtre Français, home of the Comédie Française

known foreign directors have worked in Paris, mostly in the 300-year-old Comédie Française. Particularly famous are the productions by Claus Peymann and Peter Stein and by Peter Brook in the Bouffes du Nord and the performances by visiting companies of plays in their original language in the Théâtre de l'Europe, now housed in the old classical-style Théâtre de l'Odéon.

Music

Classical music

For decades Parisian musical life was regarded as rather fuddy-duddy, but Rolf Liebermann, director of the Opéra from 1973 to 1980, gave it fresh life, and during the Presidency of François Mitterrand further important progress was made. First there was the establishment in the Centre Pompidou of IRCAM, the Institut de Recherche et Coordination Acoustique/Musique, headed by Pierre Boulez and from 1991 by Laurent Bayle; and in 1985 work began on the construction of a new opera-house in place de la Bastille, which opened on July 14th 1989, the bicentenary of the fall of the Bastille. With its larger auditorium, better visibility and acoustic equipment the new Opéra-Bastille is a considerable improvement on the old Opéra-Garnier, which had become too small for modern requirements. The new theatre will be devoted entirely to opera, while the Opéra-Garnier has become the home of ballet.

Paris has numerous large concert halls (Auditorium de Radio-France, Salle Gaveau, Palais des Congrès, Salle Pleyel, Théâtre des Champs-Elysées and the 1200 seat concert hall of the Cité de la Musique, which opened in 1996) providing a wide range of classical music performed by renowned orchestras (Orchestre National de France, Orchestre de Paris, Nouvel Orchestre Philharmonique de Radio-France). Modern works can be heard in the annual Festival d'Automne. The popular Sunday concerts given by the Orchestre des Concerts Lamoureux, the Concertes Colonne and the Orchestre Pasdeloup are permanent features of the Parisian musical scene.

There are excellent recitals and concerts of church music in many Paris churches, notably the Sunday evening concerts in Notre-Dame.

Ballet and
modern dance

For lovers of classical ballet there is the Opéra-Garnier, and in the east of the city, round the Bastille, in Ménilmontant and on the Buttes-Chaumont, there are a series of excellent establishments specialising in modern dance. Near the Bastille are the Café de la Danse and Sunset Studio; and the Studio des Pyrénées shows video clips with prominent pop stars. Nowadays dance is no longer merely the concern of choreographers: in many places it has developed into an inter-disciplinary exchange between artists, architects, fashion designers and film-makers housed in unconventional premises such as disused factories or old dance halls.

Music halls

Those interested in the traditional French chanson are catered for by numerous variety theatres and music-halls. Two of the most famous are Bobino (rue de la Gaîté) and Olympia (boulevard des Capucines). From such places as these international stars like Yves Montand, Edith Piaf, Ingrid Caven and Gilbert Bécaud set out on their dazzling careers. The Théâtre de la Ville and the Palais des Congrès also offer varied programmes of light music, while rock concerts are staged mainly in the Zénith theatre at La Villette.

Jazz, Afro, Latino

After a temporary decline in the seventies Parisian enthusiasm for jazz has recovered strongly in recent years. Much of the feeling of life in the early days of jazz is conveyed by Bertrand Tavernier in his film "Autour de Minuit", the story of an American jazz musician who came to Paris in the late fifties. Whereas in those days Paris's jazz spots were to be found exclusively on the Rive Gauche in the Saint-Germain-des-Prés quarter, there are now major venues on the right bank of the Seine, round the Centre Pompidou. Favourite haunts of jazz fans are the old-established Club Montana, Au Duc des Lombards and Le Petit Opportun, in the jazz "golden triangle" of Châtelet, and New Morning. The hottest Afro, Latino and Caribbean rhythms are to be heard in the Chapelle des Lombards, which for more than ten years has attracted numbers of fans with its low stage and crowded dance-floor.

The fame of Parisian night life seems to be immortal. Evening after evening visitors from abroad or from the remotest French provinces flock to the area round place Pigalle, at the foot of Montmartre, in quest of the city's legendary erotic delights. Great names in art and literature – Guillaume Apollinaire, Emile Zola, Hector Berlioz, Heinrich Heine, Henri Toulouse-Lautrec, Vincent van Gogh, Maurice Utrillo – have been associated with the picturesque and unconstrained life of the Butte Montmartre. Until the First World War the "Lapin Agile" cabaret (22 rue des Saules) and the "Bateau Lavoir" (5 rue Ravignan), a building housing artists' studios, were literary and artistic centres of the *vie de bohème*. In the studio shared by the Cubists Picasso painted the "Demoiselles d'Avignon". In the Moulin Rouge, established in 1889, the stars included Yvette Guilbert, Valentin le Désossé, Jane Avril and the can-can dancer La Goulue, while the Folies-Bergère saw the triumphs of Joséphine Baker.

Nowadays the *vie de bohème* has receded into the nostalgic past, and most night spots work on a shift system. There is a wide range of choice and a wide range of cost, from standard shows in "typical" settings aimed at tourists to champagne-style establishments cater-

Legendary night life

The "Balago" disco in the Bastille Quarter

Of Love and Sorrow

The "Sparrow of Paris", Edith Piaf

On July 16th 1857 a "chanson" was heard for the first time at a state funeral. It was *Les souvenirs du peuple*, a hymn to Napoleon I which had been whistled in every street and alley in France. The man who was being buried on this day, Pierre-Jean de Béranger, was the same man who had liberated song from the straitjacket of political propaganda in which it had existed since the days of the French Revolution. Just how passionate the Parisians' love affair with the chanson was, can be gauged from the pomp and extravagance which was lavished on this funeral. For the rulers of the Second Empire, while according the deceased poet the grandest of ceremonies, at the same time kept the population seeking to honour him in check with a contingent of 20,000 soldiers, for fear that a rebellion might break out.

Song and rebellion had always gone hand in hand together in France. As early as the middle of the 17th century the supporters of the rebellious faction in the Paris parliament, La Fronde, proclaimed their satirical verses from the Pont Neuf. The slogans of the French Revolution or the spirit of the Commune were transmitted most vividly through songs, of which admittedly only a small number have stood the test of time, though these include the *Marseillaise* and the *Internationale*. It was in fact the free spirit and popular poet Pierre-Jean de Béranger (1780–1857) who, with his five song collections, launched the popular chanson as we know it today. Ordinary people eagerly latched on to his popular songs and enjoyed singing them in their drinking haunts. All the important chansonniers of the 19th century were connected with the singing clubs belonging to the workers, artisans and lower middle classes of Paris and by 1848 there were some 500 of these clubs. No sooner had Louis Napoléon promoted himself to Emperor Napoleon III than he closed down almost all the sociétés chantantes in 1853, and the Parisians, avid for their chansons, looked for other ways of satisfying their craving, and so was born the era of "cafés-concerts". These provided singers with an audience in front of whom they could perform. Lyricists and composers as a result took a back seat, however, as songs were primarily sung for entertainment at the "caf'-conc", the artistic pretensions being of rather less importance. This situation changed when the cabaret *Le Chat Noir* opened in Montmartre in 1881. It was here that Aristide Bruant (1851–1925) sang of social evils and became the undisputed darling of the snobs and parvenus who treated his biting attacks as a joke and evinced nothing more than a pleasant frisson at his naturalistic depictions of low life. But Bruant's excesses belonged to the theatrical thunder of an older era – modern chanson came into its own with a contemporary of Bruart's, Yvette Guilbert (1867–1944). Guilbert, with her long black gloves, trod the boards for an hour each day at the *Concert Parisien* and entertained the ordinary people of Paris – it was only later that she performed at elegant salons. With her arrival the repertoire of the chansonniers began to include every nuance from speech to song in all kinds of registers, including "singing against the music".

Around the turn of the century the music scene in Montmartre began to change. The cabarets which had flourished since the opening of *Le Chat Noir* began to lose their importance, while "show business" along Anglo-American lines reached Paris with the advent of music-halls. In 1893 the *Olympia* opened, and has remained to this day the top place to see the "vedettes des chansons". At the same time the glamorous world of "revues" was brought to luxury theatres, with stars such as Mistinguett (1873–1956), Josephine Baker (1906–1975) and Maurice Chevalier (1888–1972). The last-named, who had known a childhood of absolute poverty in Paris at the beginning of the century, worked his way up through cafés to the largest Parisian stages, where he enjoyed an incredible following as an entertainer until well into the 1960s. His trademark was the clothes which he almost invariably wore: evening dress and a straw boater. But he was not the first entertainer to cultivate such an image – from very early on the chansonniers had had a taste for the extravagant – Bruart would appear in his black suit, high boots, wide protruding hat and red scarf, just as Toulouse-Lautrec painted him. Polin always wore a railwayman's uniform and waved an outsize brightly-coloured handkerchief, while Dranem wore checked trousers and paraded a funny little hat. Every era had its stars: the belle époque acclaimed Yvette Guilbert, the 1920s basked in the glorious revues of Mistinguett and the existentialists gathered round to hear Boris Vian in the clubs of St Germain-des-Prés.

But all these names have been eclipsed by the star of one incomparable artiste: Edith Piaf (1915–1963). From the humblest of beginnings as a street-singer among the Paris prostitutes, the "sparrow of Paris" rose to become the idol of French chanson and sang tirelessly of love in all its forms, scoring many of her greatest successes with the help of her lovers and friends. Fate, however, hardly treated her with kid gloves: her path through life was accompanied by a litany of disasters:

car accidents, illnesses, drug problems and the like, and, yet, through it all, she never lost the gift of holding the Parisian public in her thrall. In 1953 she appeared in Sacha Guitry's film *Si Versailles m'était conté* in which she sang her revolutionary song "Ça ira" to the Paris masses; in 1956 she aroused a storm of enthusiasm at the Carnegie Hall in New York and even in 1960 she appeared for several months on the stage of the Paris *Olympia* and sang her latest great success, her credo, *Je ne regrette rien*. When Edith Piaf died in 1963 aged only 47 she left behind her a void which could not easily be filled. And yet the world of chanson is still as alive as it ever was and the list of its stars is a long one: Georges Brassens (1921–1981); Juliette Gréco (b. 1927), who in the after-war years became famous throughout the world as the "Queen of the Existentialists" and the "black muse" of St Germain-des-Prés; "Monsieur 100,000 Volts" Gilbert Bécaud (b. 1927), whose magnificent stage show was booked to celebrate the reopening of the new *Olympia* in the Boulevard des Capucines; Barbara (b. 1930); the singing poet Jacques Brel (1929–1978); Yves Montand (1921–1991) and Patricia Kaas (b. 1966), the new queen of chanson.

ing for an affluent clientele, for example Régine's. These haunts of the rich and famous are open only to those who can produce suitable references. The traditional French can-can is still performed in the Moulin Rouge, while the celebrated Lido offers a super-show in the style of Las Vegas, with the Bluebell Girls, a waterfall, a skating rink and trained animals. The old Paradis Latin theatre in the Latin Quarter puts on a musical show, "Hello Paradis". The Crazy Horse Saloon offers strip-tease as an erotic artistic experience. Since 1993 the famous Folies-Bergère, Paris's oldest variety theatre, founded in 1867, has staged "Fous des Folies", a modern music hall-style revue produced by the avant-garde Argentinian director Alfredo Arias, a magical show, full of zip, with a wistful breath of nostalgia. The exotic, crazy and witty drag shows put on by Michou in the Alcazar and Chez Madame Arthur are popular with the French public as well as with visitors.

Dancing

Paris offers a wide range of exclusive discothèques and dance halls (boîtes), varying in popularity from time to time. Almost all the boîtes have doorkeepers who select the customers to be admitted in accordance with rules laid down by the establishment. Before midnight things are relatively quiet, and the real crowds come only from 2 o'clock onwards. One of the most famous Paris discothèques is the Palace, a technologically superbly equipped former theatre which can accommodate some 2000 visitors. The Tango is a popular night club and one of the oldest dance halls in Paris. The Trottoirs de Buenos Aires specialises in South American dance rhythms. Authentic local colour can be found in bals-musette such as the Boule Rouge, where on Sunday and Monday evenings elderly Parisians dance the old musette waltzes. Another old-established musette dance hall is Balajo in the Bastille quarter, with stucco decoration and murals by Henri Mahé, a friend of the writer Céline. Here tango music is played in the afternoon, while in the evening it becomes a disco frequented by a younger clientele.

Film

Rich cinematic tradition

Paris is indisputably a film metropolis of international standing. The intellectual milieu of the 1920s offered the right conditions for the production of a number of important films, among them Man Ray's "Retour à la Raison", Fernand Léger's "Ballet Méchanique", Luis Buñuel and Salvador Dalí's "Chien Andalou". After Hitler came to power in Germany many leading film-makers working in the Berlin studios – Fritz Lang, Billy Wilder, Max Ophüls, etc. – went into exile by way of Paris. From there they carried the atmosphere of René Clair's poetic images of Paris ("Le Quatorze Juillet", "Sous les Toits de Paris") to Hollywood, which then produced amusing films set in Paris, such as Vincente Minnelli's "An American in Paris".

Many cult films are set in Paris, from early works like Marcel Carné's "Les Enfants du Paradis" from the book by Jacques Prevert to more recent films like Bernardo Bertolucci's controversial "Last Tango in Paris", an Italian-French co-production, and Mehdi Charef's "Tea in Archimedes' Harem", which depicts the problems of suburban youth and Woody Allen's comedy "Everyone Says I Love You" – Paris, after all, is the city of lovers. The leading organ for a whole generation of young film critics was the "Cahiers du Cinéma", published in Paris from 1951 onwards. Paris was also both the source of inspiration and the studio for the best known French film directors, among them Claude Chabrol, Jean-Luc Godard, Jacques Rivette, Eric Rohmer and François Truffaut (see Famous People).

In 1942 Marcel Carné's cult film "Children of Olympus" made the great mime and theatre master Jean-Louis Barrault the "pierrot" for all time

Paris, including the suburbs, has around 500 cinemas. The pro-   Cinema city
gramme always changes on Wednesdays, when frequent French or
even world premières are staged. The cinemas all show both new and
many older films, with foreign films shown in the original version.
The larger houses are in the Champs-Elysées quarter, Montparnasse,
round Saint-Germain-des-Prés and on the main boulevards. The
smaller cinemas, which tend to specialise in classic and cult films, are
to be found in the Quartier Latin, round the Sorbonne Place Saint-
Michel.

Some cinemas are worth a visit for the sake of their interior architecture alone. One such is Le Rex – originally a theatre, with a pseudo-
Baroque interior in which the annual presentation of "Césars" (the
French equivalent of Hollywood's Oscars) takes place. For an exotic
atmosphere there is the Pagode, a Japanese pagoda which was
shipped to Paris in sections at the turn of the century and was originally the Chinese Embassy, before being converted in 1931 into the
present popular two-house cinema.

Two examples of modern high technology are the Géode at La
Villette, a gigantic spherical cinema 36m/118ft in diameter, and the
IMAX panoramic cinema, also spherical, at La Défense. The new
cinema centre place d'Italie is unique in Europe; its central feature is
a cinema for an audience of 800 with a huge screen measuring 20 by
10 metres (66 by 33 feet).

The Vidéothèque in the Forum des Halles shows non-stop films on
life in Paris. In the Palais de Chaillot is the Musée du Cinéma, with a
wide range of exhibits, film sets and costumes illustrating the technical and artistic aspects of the history of cinema. Paris also has two
Cinémathèques, in the Palais de Chaillot and the Centre Pompidou,
which put on retrospective shows devoted to particular directors
or actors. In the Palais de Tokyo, immediately adjoining the new

The Géode (a gigantic spherical cinema) at La Villette

National Photographic Centre, is the Fondation Européen des Métiers de l'Image et du Son (FEMIS). The Fâte du Cinéma is celebrated on June 30th, when anyone with a cinema ticket can see as many films as they want in Paris cinemas of their choice.

Famous People

Listed alphabetically below are prominent figures who were born, lived, worked or died in Paris and whose reputations reach beyond the frontiers of France.

Honoré de Balzac is regarded as the founder of "sociological realism" in literature. In contrast to the Romantic style of his period, he depicts his characters in realistic detail, set in a brilliantly exact representation of their setting, portraying an enormous range of figures caught up in the interplay of social forces and human passions.

Honoré de Balzac (1799–1850)

His principal work is the "Comédie Humaine", a panorama, in more than forty volumes, of French society from the Revolution through the Napoleonic period to the Restoration. Among the most important novels in the series are "La Peau de Chagrin" (1831), "Le Colonel Chabert" (1832), "La Femme de Trente Ans" (1831–44), "Eugénie Grandet" (1833), "Le Père Goriot" (1834–35), "Le Curé de Village" (1838–39), "Les Illusions Perdues" (1837–39, 1843), "Splendeurs et Misères des Courtisanes" (1839–47), "La Cousine Bette" (1846) and "Le Cousin Pons" (1847). In all Balzac was the author of 90 novels and novellas, 30 short stories and five plays the latter of which were poorly received.

His mother's family, being prosperous cloth merchants in the Marais quarter, Balzac grew up in a world which considered money important. Driven by business failures, risky speculation and a luxurious life-style to produce this enormous literary output, he ruined his health. Night after night, hour upon hour, he worked at his writing, ever hopeful of reducing his mountainous debts. Inspired by his love for the Polish Countess Evelina Hanska-Rzewuska and by an extraordinary optimism, he soon again fell into debt, purchasing a splendid house in a street off the Champs-Elysées, which he furnished lavishly — on credit, of course. By then a dying man, he moved in shortly after his marriage to Madame Hanská. Three months later he died, worn-out, at the age of only 51. His final resting place was the Père-Lachaise Cemetery, on raised ground with the whole of Paris spread out below.

The life of the writer Simone de Beauvoir was decisively marked by her meeting with Jean-Paul Sartre, whose student and later life companion she was. Born in Paris, she studied philosophy and became a teacher in Marseilles, Rouen and Paris before retiring in 1943 to devote herself to writing. In 1954 she won the Prix Goncourt for her much discussed *roman à clef* "Les Mandarins" on the circle of left-wing intellectuals round Sartre, in which she challenged the conformist morality of the bourgeoisie. She combined her philosophical theses on individual freedom and responsibility in the spirit of Sartre's existentialism with a strong social and political commitment. With the publication of her novel "Le Deuxième Sexe" (2 vols, 1949), which was banned by the Catholic Church, she became one of the leading theorists of the feminist movement, which saw the passive role of women on the sexual, social and intellectual planes as the

Simone de Beauvoir (1908–86)

Illustrious life-long companions: Jean-Paul Sartre and Simone de Beauvoir

product of a patriarchal society and called for it to be changed with the emancipatory aim of women's self-realisation.

Among her best known works in addition to those mentioned are the novels "L'Invitée" (1943), "Le Sang des Autres" (1945), "Tous les Hommes sont Mortels" (1946) and "Les Belles Images" (1966), the short story "La Femme Rompue" (1967), the autobiographical writings "Mémoires d'une Jeune Fille Rangée" (1958), "La Force de l'Âge" (1960), "La Force des Choses" (1963), "Une Mort très Douce", "Tout Compte Fait" (1972) and "La Cérémonie des Adieux" (1981) and two accounts of travels in North America, "L'Amérique au Jour le Jour" (1948), and China, "La Longue Marche" (1957).

Antoine-Henri Becquerel
(1852–1908)

Antoine-Henri Becquerel, a native of Paris, became a professor in the Musée d'Histoire Naturelle in 1892 and moved to the Ecole Polytechnique in 1895. He is regarded as the real discoverer of radioactivity, having found in 1896 that uranium salts emit a special type of rays resembling X-rays. Three years later he was able to demonstrate photographically the deflection of part of these rays, the beta particles, in electrical fields. For this discovery of spontaneous radioactivity he won the Nobel Prize for Physics in 1903 jointly with Pierre and Marie Curie, who on the basis of Becquerel's work had succeeded in isolating radium from uranium ore.

The unit of radioactivity (becquerel, bq) is named after him.

Jean Cocteau
(1889–1963)

Jean Cocteau was an artist who combined and gave expression to a variety of talents. He was not only a successful novelist ("Le Grand Ecart", "Les Enfants Terribles"), lyric poet, film director ("La Belle et la Bête", "L'Eternel Retour"), screenplay writer ("Les Enfants du Paradis"), dramatist ("Orphée") painter, choreographer and librettist (his librettos for operas and ballets were set to music by Arthur

Honegger, Igor Stravinsky, Darius Milhaud and other composers). Cocteau sympathised with the intellectual and literary trends of the day, gave decisive impulses to all avant-garde movements and was for decades one of the most interesting personalities on the French literary scene. His work included experiments in Futurism and Dadaism but over all is best seen as late Surrealism.

Cocteau became a member of the Académie Française in 1955.

Henri IV, the "bon roi Henri", became king of Navarre in 1562 and leader of the Huguenots in 1581. Through his marriage with Marguerite de Valois, sister of Charles IX of France, he sought to achieve a reconciliation with the Catholic party. This aim was frustrated by the Massacre of St Bartholomew (August 24th 1572), when the leaders of the Huguenot nobility who had come to Paris for the wedding were murdered along with thousands of fellow Protestants on the orders of Catherine de Médici, the Queen Mother. Henri was able to save himself only by abjuring his faith, and was held prisoner at the court until he fled in 1576.

Henri IV
(1553–1610)

After the death of Henri III in 1589 Henri laid claim to the throne, but it was only in 1594, after long and bitter conflict and after his conversion to Catholicism ("Paris is well worth a mass") that he was crowned as the first king of the House of Bourbon.

As king Henri sought to overcome the consequences of the religious wars and reconcile the Catholic and Protestant faiths by granting religious freedom and equality of rights (Edict of Nantes, 1598), reorganising the state's finances and opening up the country by the building of roads. As legend has it, he wanted every peasant in France to have a chicken in the pot on Sundays.

The colonisation of Canada began during his reign, Quebec being founded in 1668. At the same time his restoration of centralised authority set France on the road to absolutism. Henri was assassinated in 1610.

Victor Hugo, the son of one of Napoleon's generals, was a leading figure and pioneer of the French Romantic movement as a dramatist, a novelist and a poet. He set out the programme of the Romantic movement in the preface to his play "Cromwell" (1827) and founded and edited the "Muse Française", which became the organ of the Romantic school. After the success of his early poems ("Odes et Ballades", 1826) and his play "Hernani" (1830) his novel "Notre-Dame de Paris" (1831) brought him a further triumph, and its lively and colourful portrayal of life in medieval Paris inspired a sympathetic reappraisal of Gothic architecture (see Saint-Denis). In 1841 he became a member of the Académie Française.

Victor Hugo
(1802–85)

After his daughter's suicide in 1843 Hugo for a time lost his creative powers. He turned to politics, became a member of the Constituent and Legislative Assemblies and was a candidate for the Presidency in 1848. At first a supporter of Louis-Napoléon, he became a bitter enemy after Louis seized power in 1851 and in the following year had himself proclaimed Emperor of the French as Napoleon III. Hugo then went into exile in Brussels and later in Jersey and Guernsey, and became the idol of the left-wing opposition.

After his return to France in 1870 he completed the cycle of poems entitled "La Légende des Siècles" (1859–83), in which he interwove legends from East and West in a powerful literary tapestry. Among the best known of his other works are the plays "Le Roi s'amuse" (1832) and "Lucrèce Borgia" (1833), the collections of poems "Les Chants du Crépuscule" (1835) and "Les Voix Intérieures" (1837), and the historic novel "Les Misérables" (1862), This latter has given rise to several films as well as a successful musical.

Hugo was given a national funeral in 1885, when his remains were conveyed from the Arc de Triomphe and laid to rest in the Panthéon.

A Poet of the Camera –
Robert Doisneau

A black and white photograph: people streaming past the Hôtel de Ville in Paris; in the foreground, half out of the picture, a man sitting at a bistro table. In the centre of the picture stand the young couple, caught in a seemingly casual, yet passionate kiss. A simple snapshot, yet perhaps one of the most famous photographs of all time, and for many the quintessence of the Parisian way of life, and the city's special associations with love and romance. *The Kiss*, by Robert Doisneau, is a picture of which millions of copies have circulated around the world, either as postcards or posters. To capture such moments the photographer Doisneau would often wait for hours, incognito, hidden among the crowds of people and out of sight of the "actors" in his countless scenes of Parisian life. A lovable voyeur, an angler after that chance moment of happiness, that instant of revelation – those are the words which Doisneau happily used to describe himself. But he also admitted that countless pictures of his had already been taken in his head long before he ever pressed the shutter release on his camera. And sometimes he was not above giving his pictures a helping hand: *The Kiss* is actually a staged scene, but the fact that we are aware of that and Doisneau never tried to make a secret of it takes nothing away from the picture's charm. Waiting for just the right moment does allow time for thought and besides his work Doisneau developed a mini-philosophy for his time. He called his camera his "time editing machine" and he referred to

photography as a "movement of the hand, by which one seizes from the fugitive passage of time a picture which one can hold up as proof of the existence of one's own individual world."

His own world and life-span began in the shabby Parisian suburb of Gentilly in 1912 and basically Doisneau always remained true to this milieu of the ordinary working man. He was never attracted by the career of a glossy high-profile photographer which beckoned him after the war; his interest lay in the inhabitants of the Parisian suburbs which he knew so well and in the daily life of the streets of Paris. He laid bare the quirks and weaknesses of the middle classes but he never sought to expose or show up the people of Paris, his "accomplices". It was with an affectionate and yet, at the same time, meditative gaze that he looked through his viewfinder, and this kind of visual reflection won him friends among intellectuals. Blaise Cendrars and Jacques Prévert stood by his side and accompanied him when his books were published. After the Second World War, fame, success and recognition came Doisneau's way. In 1949 he caused a furore with his book "La Banlieue de Paris"; in 1951 the Museum of Modern Art in New York staged the first large international exhibition of his work and soon his books and prints were gaining enormous sales. When Doisneau died in 1994 he left behind a hoard of 325,000 negatives which in their entirety constitute his own personal chronicle of

Francois
Mitterrand
(1916–96)

In the country which "invented" both absolutism and revolution, something of the old aristocrat still lives on in the office of the head state, political persuasion being of secondary importance. François Mitterrand, the Fifth Republic's first and so far only socialist president, conducted business in the grand manner, embellished Paris with large and magnificent buildings, and manoeuvred his way through numerous crises with more noblesse than was possessed by many a Bourbon, he surrounded himself, too, with an aura of inscrutability, His talents and personality shone brightly, showing many facets: he wrote eighteen books, oversaw the abolition of the death penalty, yet was responsible for the attack on the Greenpeace ship "Rainbow

Doisneau's photograph captures a moment in time

his city – a humorous and poetic vision of half a century of Parisian life. He documented the life and work of Les Halles shortly before the buildings were demolished, he portrayed the gloom and depression of the satellite towns, and he captured those tiny gestures which tell so much: for instance, the cabaret scene in the picture *Le petit balcon* (1953) where an exhausted dancer is sitting on the floor of a smoky cabaret, her weary arm resting on the thigh of an elderly gentleman. At times his photographs oscillate between the world of everyday and that of dreams: there is something surreal in the picture *Waltz for the 14th July* (1949), in which the brightly depicted couple dance elatedly all on their own in the street, surrounded by the dark gloomy outlines of the Parisian shops. With a little patience it is possible even today to come across similar scenes in the back streets which line the banks of the River Seine. And then one can almost hear Doisneau saying: "Paris is a theatre where anyone prepared to while away their time gets a ticket to see the show".

Warrior". A nature lover and poet, he was at the same time a cunning strategist, as Jacques Chirac discovered when working closely with him during the years of *cohabitation* (1986–88).

The son of a station-master from western France, Mitterrand had a thorough grounding in politics, his life-long profession. Born in Jarnac (Département Charente) in 1916, by the age of 25 he was already a politician of some standing and authority. The award of the *Francisque*, a Vichy decoration conferred by Marshal Pétain, head of the collaborationist régime, became a source of considerable controversy later in his career: but the young Mitterrand's response to the events of the war years was in fact to join the Résistance, reflect-

ing the strong nationalistic bent in this patriotic son of lower middle-class Catholic backgound.

It was while working with de Gaulle in opposition that Mitterrand committed himself to the Socialists, thereby distancing himself from the unpopular General. After 1945 Mitterrand occupied numerous positions of power at the centre of French left-wing politics, holding ministerial posts in eleven cabinets during the Fourth Republic. He was a co-founder of the UDSR (Union démocratique et socialiste de la Résistance), leader from 1965 to 1968 of the FGDS (Fédération de la gauche démocrate et socialiste, an alliance of the socialist SFIO, the Parti radical and left-wing political clubs of the Convention des institutions républicaines), and in 1971 was elected First Secretary of the newly formed Socialist Party of France (PS). He was twice defeated in presidential elections before, in May 1981, gaining a decisive majority over the incumbent President Giscard d'Estaing.

Following the parliamentary election held soon after he took office, the new government, a Socialist and Communist coalition, introduced a comprehensive programme of reform, but were unable to solve the country's economic problems. When the Socialists fared badly in the European elections of June 1984, Mitterrand adopted a less radical, more pragmatic course, a result of which the Communists left the government. The Socialist president thus found himself following in the footsteps of de Gaulle, to whom he had been diametrically opposed. He was soon called upon to demonstrate his great capacity for reconciliation. When the 1986 parliamentary election was won by an alliance of the Guallists and solidly middle-class UDF, Mitterrand threw himself into sharing power with the new Conservative government, so averting the risk of polarisation in French politics. The France emerging from the 1980s and 1990s bears the unmistakable stamp of the man who, in one of his last interviews, remarked: Yes, I do like history, and I like to leave my mark on history".

Yves Montand
(1921–91)

Yves Montand was born as Ivo Livi in Monsummano Terme, a small village in Tuscany. When the Fascists came to power in Italy his father planned to emigrate to North America but, unable to raise the money for the sea passage, the family got no farther than Marseilles, where from 1923 onwards, they remained and where Ivo grew up. After his father's broom factory failed he worked from the age of 13 as a waiter, a barman and a barber's assistant. He did not earn much, but it was enough to enable him to take lessons in dancing and singing and to buy all the records of Maurice Chevalier and Charles Trenet; for he had made up his mind that he wanted to sing – not as a concert or operatic tenor but for the ordinary people in the street to whom he belonged. He began by singing in the city's suburban bars, and enjoyed his first success in the Alcazar in Marseilles. All that was wrong was his name, and, remembering the phrase with which his mother used to call him in from playing in the street, "Ivo, monta!" (Ivo, come up!), he took the professional name of Yves Montand.

In 1944 he went to Paris, where Edith Piaf was conquering France with her powerful voice. She took him in hand, correcting the nasal sounds and rolling r's of his Marseilles accent, and helped him to promote his career, having convinced herself of his masculinity and resolved to make him king of the French chanson. He gained that title, cultivating the *chant populaire* with such songs as "Les Feuilles

Mortes", "Luna Park" and "La Vie en Rose", which hit exactly the right note for the 1950s, the generation devoted to the existentialism of Sartre and Camus in Montparnasse.

The cinema gave Montand an opportunity to show his talent as an actor. He made more than 70 films, including such international successes as "Le Salaire de la Peur" (1952), "Let's Make Love" (1960, with Marilyn Monroe), "César et Rosalie" (1972, with Romy Schneider) and "Manon des Sources" (1986 "Manons Rache"), partnering such stars as Romy Schneider, Catherine Deneuve and Simone Signoret, who was his lifetime companion until her death in 1985.

Montand repeatedly drew attention to himself by his political commitment. Originally an active member of the French Communist Party, he broke with the party in 1982 over events in Poland and thereafter was a vehement supporter of Solidarnosàcà.

From 1988 Montand lived with his wife Carole Amiel on an estate in Normandy. He died in Paris in 1991, mourned by the nation as few before him.

Napoleon Bonaparte, scion of a patrician family in Corsica, won rapid promotion in the French revolutionary army. A brigadier-general at the age of 24, he became commander-in-chief in France and in the French campaigns in Italy and Egypt, achieving a position of power which enabled him to overthrow the Directoire (after Robespierre's reign of terror the supreme governing body in France) and seize power as First Consul. After winning a nation-wide plebiscite he made himself Consul for life in 1802 and first Emperor of the French as Napoleon I in 1804. The traditional enmity with Britain led him into wars with the Grand Alliance, the coalition headed by Britain, in which he defeated Austria and Prussia. Next he occupied Portugal and Spain in order to bring Britain to its knees by a continental blockade – the earliest example of out-and-out economic warfare in history – and then set his sights on the conquest of Russia (which opposed the continental blockade) as a means of gaining mastery over the whole of Europe.

Napoleon I
(1769–1821)

The failure of his Russian campaign, defeat in the Battle of the Nations at Leipzig in 1813 and the Allied occupation of Paris compelled Napoleon to abdicate in 1814, and he was exiled to the island of Elba. In 1815, in the famous "hundred days", he tried to win back power but was finally defeated at Waterloo. He was then banished to the British island of St Helena in the South Atlantic, where he died in 1821. In 1840 his remains were brought back from St Helena to Paris, with great pomp and ceremony, and buried in the Invalides.

Unlike his nephew Louis-Napoleon Bonaparte (Napoleon III), Napoleon has lived on in the hearts of the French. His image as the saviour of the Revolution was glorified by the Romantic movement, and in particular by Victor Hugo. There is a monument to him in every small town in France, and in Paris he stands on a column in Place Vendôme in the garb of a Roman emperor. And the Code Civil which he promulgated in 1804 – France's first code of civil law – did indeed enshrine the provisions relating to property and economic relationships which were the fundamental achievements of the French Revolution.

The writer and philosopher Jean-Paul Sartre was the son of middle-class parents in Paris, where he went to school and university. In the thirties he taught philosophy in Le Havre and Berlin; then during the

Jean-Paul
Sartre
(1905–80)

Second World War, after a period as a prisoner of war (1940–41), he became an active member of the Resistance. In 1945 he abandoned his teaching career and founded a literary and political review, "Les Temps Modernes". In 1973 he was one of the founders of the newspaper "Libération". He became a member of the French Communist Party, but left it in 1956 after severely criticising the Soviet intervention in Hungary. His political commitment grew stronger in the late sixties and early seventies, when he attacked the Warsaw Pact intervention in Czechoslovakia, presided over the Vietnam Tribunal initiated by Bertrand Russell and defended various left-wing organisations.

In 1943 Sartre published "L'tre et le Néant", which ranks as the fundamental work of French existentialism. Starting from Kierkegaard, Husserl, Heidegger, Hegel and Jaspers, he developed the atheistic basic idea – which negates all absolute transcendental conceptions – that existence precedes essence. On this theory man exists in a meaningless world in which his spirit strives after the essence which is lacking in him. He is thus himself fully responsible for developing his freedom, his existential behaviour in a particular situation. The quest for an illusionless humanism manifests itself in conscious action which carries mere existence ad absurdum, defined by Sartre as "committed freedom" for a particular objective. In his second major political work, the "Critique de la Raison Dialectique" (1960), Sartre enlarged individual human freedom through collective consciousness and political commitment, based on a corrected and expanded Marxist dialectic.

The concern with existentialist problems, in particular the problem of freedom, also characterises his littérature engagée. Among his best known plays are "Les Mouches" (1943), "Huis Clos" (1944), "Le Diable et le Bon Dieu" (1951), "Les Séquestrés d'Altona" (1960), "Les Troyennes" (1965) and "Bariona et le Fils du Tonnerre" (1970); his most significant novels are "La Nausée" (1938) and "Les Chemins de la Liberté" (1945–49); and his most notable screenplays are "Les Jeux sont Faits" (1947) and "L'Engrenage" (1948). As a literary critic Sartre tried in his monumental biography of Flaubert ("L'Idiot de la Famille: Gustave Flaubert de 1821 à 1857", 1971–73) to combine psychoanalytical, phenomenological and Marxist approaches.

François Truffaut
(1932–84)

François Truffaut, as director, screenplay writer, actor and film critic, devoted his life to the cinema. The son of a Paris architect, he enjoyed little of the security of family life. A truant from school, a vagabond and a shoplifter from an early age, he left the Lycée Rolin at 14 and spent some time in a reformatory, which offered him a means of escape. While still at school he was interested only in the cinema. A fateful event in his life was his meeting with André Bazin, editor of the Paris film review, "Les Cahiers du Cinéma" and the grand old man of modern French film criticism. Bazin and his wife took an interest in the film-struck youth, became surrogate parents and encouraged him to work as a journalist for the film pages of the review "Travail et Culture" and later as film critic with the "Cahiers du Cinéma". Now with an established reputation in the film world, Truffaut called for "authors' films" in which the director should be free to work in his own personal fashion, in place of the traditional system which had come to a dead end. His models were such directors as Renoir, Ophüls, Lang, Rossellini and

Hitchcock. His marathon 50-hour interview with Hitchcock in 1967, "Le Cinéma selon Hitchcock", is one of the major documents on the history of cinema.

Truffaut's first feature film, "Les Quatre Cents Coups", made in 1959 with the support of his then father-in-law the director Ignace Morgenstern, won the director's prize at Cannes. This biographical film, based on his experiences in his own "difficult" youth, was one of the principal works of the Nouvelle Vague (New Wave) cinema. There-after film followed film, including films in the Hitchcock manner such as "Tirez sur le Pianiste" ("Shoot the Pianist", 1960) and the poetic "Jules et Jim" (1962), after a novel by Henri Roché about a pure love affair *á trois*. In "L'Enfant Sauvage" (1970) and "La Nuit Américaine" (1973), which won an Oscar in 1974, and in which Truffaut also appeared as an actor. "Le Dernier Métro" (1981) a tragicomic story of theatre life in occupied Paris in 1942, with Catherine Deneuve, Heinz Bennent and Gérard Depardieu, won ten Césars (the French equiva-lent of Oscars). With his companion of his final years, the equally good looking actress Fanny Ardent he made two unforgettable films, "La Femme d'à-côté" (1981) and "Vivement le Dimanche" (1983).

Truffaut was also strongly committed in matters of cinema politics. Thus in 1968 he supported Henri Langlois, founder of the renowned Paris Film Museum, against de Gaulle's government and succeeded in preserving the museum from closure by arguing the case on a lec-ture tour.

Truffaut died in Neuilly, a district of Paris, at the age of 52.

History of the City

Prehistory and Roman period

Recent archaeological excavations in the Bercy quarter unearthing jewellery and everyday items from neolithic times, show that man settles the Ile-de-France region of the Seine valley no later than the 4th millenium B.C. In the 3rd c. B.C. a Celtic tribe, the Parisii, settle on the island in the Seine known today as the Ile de la Cité, at which point a land route crosses the river. Here the Gauls establish their capital Lucotesia or "louk-teih" ("marshy place"). The Celts sustain themselves mainly by fishing but are already also trading extensively – as is shown by the wide dispersal of coins of this period).

52 B.C. Beginning of Roman rule

In 58 B.C. the Romans led by Julius Caesar march into Gaul; in 52 B.C. they reach the capital, which the inhabitants destroy before fleeing. The Gauls quickly end their resistance against the more powerful Romans and reach a peaceful accommodation with their conquerors. The Pax Romana, the Eternal Roman Peace, allows Roman culture and infrastructure to develop without a repressive military presence. Lutetia, the Roman town, extends along the left bank of the Seine, where remains of thermae (near the Hôtel Cluny) and an amphitheatre, the Arènes de Lutèce (east of the Panthéon) have been preserved. As early as A.D. 250 the Benedictine monk Dionysius, known as the "Apostle of Gaul", introduces Christianity. The celebrated abbey of Saint-Denis to the north of Paris, for centuries the burial place of the French kings and a national shrine, is dedicated to him. In the 4th c. Julian the Apostate, one of the later Roman emperors, halts at the Seine to repel repeated Frankish incursions. At this time the city takes the name of the original Celtic tribe: Civitat Parisiorum.

Middle Ages Merovingians

The close and peaceful relations between Gauls and Romans survive until the 5th c., when the Merovingians under Clovis drive the Romans back and establish the first great Frankish empire. In 508 they make Paris their capital and the palace on the Cité from which the Romans have governed becomes a Merovingian imperial palace. Under the Carolingians the centre of political power shifts eastwards to the Rhine. Despite losing its former status, Paris grows in importance on account of its trade. Already by about 800 the city boasts a population of over 20,000.

Capetians (987–1328)

Under Hugo Capet, the first Capetian on the French throne (987–96), Paris is once again a royal city. In subsequent centuries it outgrows the island, expanding onto the river banks either side. Towards the end of almost 400 years of Capetian rule, the population has risen to some 100,000 and Paris is one of the largest and most influential cities in western and northern Europe. Trade flourishes due to the vitality of its river port, which expands rapidly after 1141 when Louis VII allows the Paris watermen – already with a monopoly over shipping on the whole of the River Seine – to take over the Place de Grève, an ideal commercial landing place. During the reign of Philippe II (Philippe Auguste, 1180–1223), urban development accelerates. The king commissions the building of covered markets and new fountains, has the streets paved and erects the first stone bridges. He also orders the construction, between 1190 and 1204, of a new ring of fortifications to protect the city, with a stronghold on the north side, the Louvre. The town within the walls now has three clearly defined districts:
- La Cité, the central island in the Seine, site of the royal palace, the bishop's palace and, since 1163, the soaring spire of the cathedral of Notre-Dame.

- La Ville, the burgher district and commercial centre on the north bank of the Seine where the rue St-Denis becomes the city's main commercial thoroughfare.
- L'Université on the south bank or Rive Gauche, to which masters and pupils of the cathedral school of Notre-Dame move at the start of the 12th c.; around 1210 the individual colleges merge to form a "universitas", precursor of the medieval university.

In the High Middle Ages Paris enters its most glorious period with the accession of Louis IX (1226–70). An effective administration is introduced, a judicial supreme court, the Parlement, is established, and the burghers of Paris are granted the right to form their own police force in place of the royal guard. The fervently religious Louis, afterwards canonised, amasses a collection of reliquaries, to house which he builds on the Ile de la Cité the royal chapels of Sainte Chapelle, together with a very large and costly shrine. In 1257 Canon Robert de Sorbon founds a college for poor students, later to become the Sorbonne; by the end of the 13th c. it has about 20,000 students.

With the demise of the Capetian dynasty the English king Edward III lays claim to the French throne. The resulting war between France and England lasts over a hundred years, from 1339 to 1453. Paris suffers the effects of war. There are epidemics and famine and for a time the English occupy the city, being finally driven out only in 1436. Added to this there is internal upheaval. In 1358, while John the Good is temporarily imprisoned by the English, Etienne Marcel, who as "Prévôt des Marchands" represents the most influential guilds, seizes the moment to appoint himself regent. When the king regains his freedom later the same year, this first burgher revolt is bloodily suppressed. The corporative struggle for power and ensuing friction between middle classes and king, causes Charles V, on acceding to the throne in 1364, to move his residence from the Palais on the Cité to the Louvre Fortress, which has been extended for use by the court.

Hundred Years' War (1339–1453)

Life in Paris is slow to return to normality following the years of war. With the king opting for the security of a court removed a safe distance from Paris, the stimulus for urban development is also lacking.

In 1527 François I makes Paris the royal seat once more. The Hôtel de Ville is rebuilt and the city's first banks and bourse constructed, all in the Renaissance style. François also begins the rebuilding of the Louvre and in 1530 founds the Collège de France, which is independent of the Church. Although he and his court reside mainly at the palace of Fontainebleau, to which he attracts artists such as Andrea del Sarto, Benvenuto Cellini and Leonardo da Vinci, henceforth Paris is the centre vital of France. During the 16th c. the Marais east of the Louvre becomes the district favoured by the nobility. In 1564 the Tuileries Palace is built to the west of the Louvre by Henri II's widow Catherine de Médici as her residence in retirement. Until 1574 she acts as Regent of France during the minority of Charles IX. A puppet in the hands of powerful aristocratic families, she is unable to avert the religious wars in the second half of the 16th c. In the St Bartholomew's Day Massacre on August 23rd/24th 1572, the leaders of the Protestant Huguenots and thousands of their followers are slaughtered in Paris.

Renaissance and Absolutism

Reign of François I (1515–47)

Persecution of the Huguenots only ceases with the accession of the Bourbon king Henri IV, himself a Huguenot. By converting to Catholicism while guaranteeing a limited measure of religious freedom to Protestants under the Edict of Nantes (1598), Henri restores peace to his country. Meanwhile he embarks on a radical reconstruction of the city, the population of which is now 400,000. He has roads straightened and squares laid out, all part of a comprehensive plan, and prescribes a unity of style in building. He commissions the first

Reign of Henri IV (1589–1610)

bridge not lined with houses, the Pont Neuf, and conceives the idea for the place des Vosges (then called place Royale), a harmonious architectural ensemble which quickly becomes the centre of aristocratic life and a model for other similar squares.

Cardinal Richelieu (1585–1642)

The early years of the 17th c. are dominated by Louis XIII's chief minister, Cardinal Richelieu, who on the eve of the period of absolutism stamps his imprint on Paris. He founds the Académie Française in 1635, creates a strong ministerial administration independent of the nobility, and turns Paris into a centre of the Counter Reformation. After 1622 when the city becomes an archbishopric – having for centuries been part of the diocese of Sens – numerous Catholic churches and monasteries are built under Richelieu's patronage.

Reign of Louis XIV the Sun King (1643–1715)

With the death in 1661 of Richelieu's successor, Cardinal Mazarin, Louis XIV, having reached his majority, rules alone. Backed by what for the time is a huge army, he keeps the aristocracy in check, perfects government by centralised bureaucracy and acts out the doctrine of the divine right of kings. In 1682 he transfers his court to magnificent Versailles, while not neglecting to immortalise himself in buildings in Paris. The city walls are demolished and replaced by tree-lined boulevards; where formerly the city gates stood, there are now huge triumphal arches (1672 Porte St-Denis, 1674 Porte St-Martin). The Louvre is enlarged and the Tuilerie Gardens laid out. Louis also commissions Hardouin-Mansart to build the Place Louis-le-Grand, the present Place Vendôme. When he dies in 1715, the Sun King leaves the state perilously weakened financially. In subsequent years the authority of the state is increasingly subverted by the arbitrary rule of Louis XV. Critical Enlightenment voices are raised in the salons and on the streets discontent grows.

The French Revolution

On July 14th 1789 the Paris mob storm the Bastille, the state prison which has become the symbol of absolutist repression. In its early stages the French Revolution is orchestrated by liberal forces from all levels of society. The National Assembly establishes a constitutional monarchy and promulgates the Declaration of the Rights of Man and

The Storming of the Bastille on July 14th 1789 (coloured lithograph ca. 1840)

of the Citizen. Louis XVI is forced to leave Versailles, becoming de facto a prisoner of the Revolution in the Tuileries. In 1792 the bourgoisie-dominated National Convention declares a Republic. The following January the king dies on the guillotine, which for the next two years is put to almost continuous use on the Place de la Révolution (from 1795 Place de la Concorde). The ever more violent excesses of the masses, the Reign of Terror instigated by the Committee of Public Safety, and the growing threat from the royalist alliance abroad, throw France into political turmoil. In Paris the lower orders in particular suffer hunger and poverty.

In 1799, following a coup d'état, Napoleon Bonaparte, who has risen to prominence as commander of the French army during the Revolutionary Wars, is installed as head of state. He upholds the interests of the real beneficiaries of 1789, the upper middle classes, while also consolidating the principal achievements of the Revolution. At the same time he introduces a form of police state administered by a servile bureaucracy, and wages war, at great cost in lives, throughout almost the whole of Europe, Russia and several colonial regions. Crowned emperor in 1804, Napoleon I embellishes Paris with the Arc de Triomphe, a new and architecturally homogeneous rue de Rivoli, and an enlarged Louvre, which since 1793 has been a public museum and which he fills with the spoils of war.

Napoleon I
(1799–1815)

In the period following the Congress of Vienna of 1814/15 which saw monarchy restored, the upper middle class re-emerge as a political force. The "Citizen King" Louis Philippe (1830–48) is at pains to encourage capitalism. In 1837 France's first railway line opens between Paris and Saint-Germain-en-Laye. And gas lamps light up the city's boulevards, asphalted three years earlier. As industrialisation accelerates, class conflict increases. The centre and west of the city are gradually transformed into a splendid bourgeois metropolis, while the outer districts degenerate into working class slums. In 1831 a cholera epidemic sweeps the confined and overpopulated quarters of the old city, claiming 20,000 lives. In February 1848 tension erupts into street fighting. Within a few months however the bourgoisie suppress the revolt by the Paris proletariat and the Second Republic is established.

**The Revolution
of 1848 and the
Second Republic**

In December 1851 the acting president, Louis Napoleon Bonaparte, nephew of Napoleon I, mounts a coup against the Republic and has himself elected emperor of the Second Empire. Over the next 20 years the population of the capital doubles to two million and Paris undergoes rapid, large-scale redevelopment, the inspiration for which comes chiefly from the préfet, Baron Georges Haussmann. Huge swathes are cut through the medieval town to create splendid new thoroughfares. The great pattern of streets, the twelve avenues around the place de l'Etoile, and the boulevards on the visual axes, give the city a new, sophisticated face. At the same time they allow shows of military strength and make surveillance of the population easier. Napoleon III turns large areas of green into public parks (Bois de Boulogne, Bois de Vincennes), installs what is then the world's most advanced urban sewerage system, and fosters the development of transport. Fine monumental buildings like Charles Garnier's new opera house, and numerous ironwork arcades are built. Paris becomes the most modern city of the age, the "Capital of the 19th c." as Walter Benjamin so aptly describes it.

**Napoleon III and
Haussmann**

Defeat at Sedan in 1870 spells the end of the Second Empire. A provisional government proclaims the Third French Republic but is unable to prevent the siege and capture of Paris. Spurred by shortages in occupied Paris and by the humiliating peace terms imposed by

**Franco-Prussian
War and the
Commune**

Germany, a socialist workers front, the so-called Paris Commune, rises against the ruling bourgeois-monarchist National Assembly. Government troops mercilessly suppress this first workers' uprising in a matter of weeks.

Third Republic (1870–1914):
Belle Epoque

Whilst France is forced to cede the political leadership of mainland Europe to Germany, Paris continues to glitter with the undiminished brilliance of the "Belle Epoque". With its series of world exhibitions marked by spectacular feats of construction (1889: the Eiffel Tower; 1900: the Grand Palais, Petit Palais, Pont Alexandre III and the first Métro line), its opulent department stores and magnificent palaces of commerce (banks, insurance offices, hotels), Paris is unique among capitals. Long after this period has ended, the city remains the international playground and art centre of the world.

Between the two world wars

Despite having its status as a great power restored under the 1919 Treaty of Versailles, France does not escape the worldwide economic crisis of the early 1930s. In Paris, where the population peaks at 3 million in 1921, the economy stagnates. Even so there is great cultural vitality: in addition to Bohemian artists and writers, the leaders of the Surrealist movement gather in the orbit of the Gare Montparnasse. When in 1932/33, in France as elsewhere, the party political structure is polarised by the emergence of radical groups, dissatisfaction with the government once again gives rise to demonstrations, strikes and fighting in the streets. Between 1936 and 1938 the Popular Front, an alliance of Socialists and Communists, briefly wins support for a comprehensive package of social reform.

Vichy Regime and Résistance

On June 14th 1940 German troops occupy Paris. The Nazis attempt to preserve the outward appearance of a cultural metropolis open to the world; but for the people of Paris the reality is different. The Gestapo respond to any show of resistance, active or passive, with severe retaliation. The government of unoccupied France, led by Marshal Pétain, establishes itself in Vichy on the northern edge of the Central Massif. The French nation faces the acid test of division, between occupied and unoccupied France, resistance and collaboration. The Résistance is led by General Charles de Gaulle, at first from London and later from Algiers. In Paris in the summer of 1944, with the Allies having reached the Seine on both sides of the city, resistance turns to open rebellion. The German commandant Choltitz rejects Hitler's order to destroy the city and on August 26th 1944 de Gaulle and his troops enter Paris.

Post-war years
Fourth Republic (1946–58)

The immediate post-war years bring the country a precarious Fourth Republic. The years up to 1958 are characterised by numerous internal crises as well as conflict with liberation movements in the colonies.

Algerian crisis

In particular the war against Algerian rebels threatens France's financial and economic stability. The internal tensions erupt in strikes, bombings, arbitrary military action and countless provisions made by ever-changing governments. On May 13th 1958 the French army in Algeria is involved in a coup; the unrest spreads to the mother country and a few days later a state of emergency is declared.

The de Gaulle era
(1958–69)

Charles de Gaulle, who withdrew from politics after 1953, retains in the eyes of the majority of the French people, the charisma and reconciliatory powers needed to resolve the national crisis. He is appointed head of state with sweeping authority. The adoption in September 1958 of a new constitution

Fifth Republic
(from 1958)

incorporating wide-ranging presidential powers marks the inauguration of the Fifth Republic. In 1962 the crisis in Algeria is brought to a successful conclusion, with the country being granted independence (this despite the fact that in Paris in October 1961 several hundred demonstrating Algerians are gunned down by the police). The conservative politics of the de Gaulle government enable France to make the transition to a modern industrial society. From the mid 1960s onwards La Défense, the architecturally ambitious west Paris business quarter, symbolises France's economic strength. As dwellings make way for offices and rents rise, the less privileged in Paris society migrate to satellite towns; the city's population falls progressively to around its present two million mark. In 1962 the scholar and author André Malraux, Minister of Culture, introduces legislation for the protection and renovation of historic buildings. Thanks to the "Loi Malraux", Paris's monuments regain their splendour and the Marais quarter is restored.

The deepening division in French society into rich and poor leads in May 1968 to violent disturbances. This time the rebels are students from the city's universities and institutes of higher education, protesting against the cultural and social policies of de Gaulle. Workers throughout the country support the demonstrations through wild-cat strikes bringing public life to a standstill. Paris is in chaos; once again barricades are set up and hundreds of thousands take to the streets. De Gaulle manouvres cleverly through the crisis. Carefully timed elections leave the Gaullists firmly in power.

1968: Student protests

De Gaulle's immediate successor, Georges Pompidou, president from 1969 to 1974, sets the presidential fashion for architectural *beaux gestes* with the demolition in 1969 of Paris's old covered markets, Les Halles, designed by Baltard. They are replaced with the Forum des Halles above a vast and labyrinthine Métro station. The Pompidou Centre close by, a massive complex housing the Centre National d'Art et de Culture, finally opens in 1977 after being eight years under construction. In the same year Paris elects its first mayor, the city having previously been administered by a government-appointed préfet.

De Gaulle's successors

Following the presidency of Valéry Giscard d'Estaing, whose energies were concentrated more on Europe than the French capital, the presidential election of 1981 returns a Socialist head of state for the first time – François Mitterrand. He holds office for two full terms, until 1995. When it comes to embellishing Paris with fine buildings, where Pompidou had favoured large-scale technocratic projects, Mitterrand's preference is for culture. In 1986 the new and imaginatively presented museum of science and technology, the Cité des Sciences et de l'Industrie, opens in the Parc de la Villette; also in 1986 the Gare d'Orsay is transformed into an impressive museum of the Belle Epoque. The predilection among politicians for grandiose projects reflects an element of cultural elitism. In December 1986 students protest violently against changes to higher education (limits on student numbers, competition between individual universities); the legislation is withdrawn. Mid 1988 sees the opening of the Institut du Monde Arabe, an Islamic cultural centre and forum for reconciliation and understanding, intended to lay the ghosts of the colonial past. But also in the 1980s, many of the less privileged on low incomes are forced to move to the suburbs, where rents are affordable but where the rate of increase in crime reaches double figures.

The Mitterrand era

The bicentenary of the French Revolution in 1989 is marked by further architectural and cultural projects. They include the opening of the glass pyramid in the great courtyard of the Louvre, signalling the start of a comprehensive programme of modernisation. Four years later, on the 200th anniversary of the opening of the museum, the remodelled Richelieu Wing is inaugurated. Work on the Louvre should be completed by 1999. Among Mitterrand's other *grands travaux* are the new people's opera in the Place de la Bastille, completed in 1989; the Grande Arche in La Défense, intended as a counterpart to Napoleon's Arc de Triomphe; and, finished in the same year, the gigantic new Ministry of Finance in the Bercy quarter.

In late autumn 1990, as so often in the city's history, the streets become a stage for political demonstrations. This time thousands of schoolboys and girls protest against conditions in Paris schools. In stark contrast, in November a historic meeting of the Conference on European Security and Co-operation (CSCE) takes place behind closed doors; the "Paris Charter", to which 34 states are signatories, announces the end of the decades-long division of Europe.

The rash of building and changes wrought to the face of Paris and the surrounding countryside ends as the turn of the century approaches. In April 1992 Euro Disney opens at Chessy, 32km/20 miles east of Paris; in February 1995 the Cité de la Musique, a large study and performance centre for music and dance, designed by Christian de Portzamparc and situated on the edge of the Parc de la Villette in northern Paris, is completed. In the same year Mitterrand inaugurates the last of his great architectural monuments, the huge new building in the Tolbiac quarter housing the Bibliothèque Nationale, fully operational only in 1997.

1995–99

Mitterrand, who dies the following year, is not a candidate in the presidential election of 1995. On May 7th 1995, for the first time in 21 years, France once again has a Gaullist president, the veteran mayor of Paris Jacques Chirac. He faces, however, another period of so-called *cohabitation*, this time with the Socialist prime minister Lionel Jospin.

By the end of 1999, after almost two decades, the massive transformation of the Louvre into the world's largest museum of art, will finally be completed.

Quotations

The following quotations are arranged in chronological order.

The motto, under a ship in full sail, is "Fluctuat nec mergitur" ("It tosses on the water but does not sink"). The ship is a symbol of the city, or more precisely of its first nucleus on the Ile de la Cité, and also alludes to Paris's original source of wealth, the shipping traffic on the Seine.

Motto in the city's coat of arms

In this great city, where near a million of persons are collected, with very little knowledge of each other, every one fixes in the spot most suitable to his fortune, or most favourable for his pleasures. The majority of the population of each quarter is composed of a particular sort of inhabitants, with peculiar habits and manners, and the active and polished Parisian, in the environs of the Louvre, or the Chaussée d'Antin, is certainly very different from the pensive inhabitants of the Marais, and still more from the laborious, but coarse, natives of the faubourgs.

Galignani's Paris Guide, 1821

   The constitution of the Parisians, in general, is good and sound, their complexion tolerably fair, particularly in the women, who possess those lively charms and graces which many think superior to beauty. The Parisian is industrious and inventive, polite, and gentle, curious, enthusiastic, and inconstant, endowed with wit and taste, but satirical; frivolous, a slave to fashion, fond of luxury and eager for pleasure . . . The conversation of the highest classes is delicate and polished, and the learned are easy of access and communicative. The middling and lower classes are certainly good, kind and virtuous; though it cannot be doubted that the disorders of the revolution have had an unfortunate influence on their habits and morals . . .

   The inhabitants of the Marais are annuitants or persons of small fortune. Lodgings are spacious and very cheap, and the manners of the people there are like those of the inhabitants of a provincial town. In the tranquil and airy faubourg Saint Germain many persons, and chiefly the old nobility, live in a handsome style. The quartier of Saint Jacques, commonly called the Pays Latin, is peopled by young men, different in every respect from those of the Chaussée d'Antin. Professors, men of letters, students of law and medicine, have always been the inhabitants of this learned seat of the Muses. In the neighbourhood of the Palais de Justice reside a great many lawyers, attorneys, and notaries; and, as we approach the faubourgs, we find the laborious classes, and the weavers and cotton spinners collected in the vast buildings of the ancient monasteries. On the borders of the river of the Gobelins are tanners, dyers, brewers, houses for spinning wool and cotton, and manufactories of pottery and blankets. The extremities of the faubourgs are occupied by waste grounds or gardens full of early flowers, vegetables and shrubs necessary for the wants and luxury of the metropolis.

In twenty minutes I was in Paris, entering it through the triumphal arch of the Boulevard Saint-Denis, which was originally built in honour of Louis XIV but now served to glorify my entry to Paris. I was truly astonished by the crowds of well-scrubbed people, very smartly dressed, like illustrations in a fashion magazine. Then, too, I was impressed by the fact that they all spoke French: with us that is a characteristic of the genteel world, so here everybody is as genteel as the nobility in our country. The men were all so polite and the beautiful women all so smiling. If someone bumped into me by accident without at once begging my pardon I could be sure that he was a

Heinrich Heine German poet (1797–1856)

countryman of mine; and if any fair one had a rather sour air I knew that she had eaten sauerkraut or that she could read Klopstock in the original. I found everything so amusing, and the sky was so blue and the air so agreeable, so generous, and there was still, here and there, a flicker of the July sun; the cheeks of the fair Lutetia were still red from the flaming kisses of that sun, and the bridal bouquet on her bosom was not yet completely withered. At street corners, it is true, "Liberté, égalité, fraternité" had already been obliterated . . .

From "Travel Sketches", 1826

Frédéric Chopin
Polish composer
(1810–49)

Here you find, side by side, the greatest luxury and the greatest inde-
cencies, the greatest virtues and the greatest vices, noise, shouting,
banging and filth – more than you can imagine. In this paradise people disappear, and that is all right, for no one is interested in the lives
of other people. Paris is whatever you want it to be. You can amuse
yourself in this city, you can be bored, you can laugh or weep or do
anything you like, and no one will take any notice; for there are thousands of people doing the same as you, each one as he pleases.

From a letter to Tytus Woyciechowski, December 12th 1831

Mark Twain
American writer
(1835–1910)

Versailles! It is wonderfully beautiful. You gaze, and stare, and try
to understand that it is real, that it is on the earth, that it is not the
Garden of Eden – but your brain grows giddy, stupefied by the world
of beauty around you, and you half believe that you are the dupe of an
exquisite dream. The scene thrills one like military music! A noble
palace, stretching its ornamented front block upon block away, till it
seemed that it would never end; a grand promenade before it,
whereon the armies of an empire might parade; all about it rainbows
of flowers, and colossal statues that were almost numberless, and yet
seemed only scattered over the ample space; broad flights of stone
steps leading down from the promenade to lower grounds of the park
– stairways that whole regiments might stand to arms upon and have
room to spare; vast fountains whose great bronze effigies discharged
rivers of sparkling water into the air mingled a hundred curving jets
together in forms of matchless beauty; wide grass-carpeted avenues
that branched hither and thither in every direction and wandered so
seemingly interminable distances, walled all the way on either side
with compact ranks of leafy trees whose branches met above and
formed arches as faultless and as symmetrical as ever were carved in
stone; and here and there were glimpses of sylvan lakes with miniature ships glassed in their surfaces. And everywhere – on the palace
steps, and the great promenade, around the fountains, among the
trees, and far under the arches of the endless avenues, hundreds and
hundreds of people in gay costumes walked or ran or danced, and
gave to the fairy picture the life and animation which was all of perfection it could have lacked.

From "The Innocents Abroad", 1869

Baedeker's
"Paris"
(1884)

The general appearance of Paris is more uniform than that of most
other towns of its size, partly owing to the mixture of classes resulting
from the Great Revolution, but principally on account of the vast
schemes of improvement carried out in our own days.
   The stranger is almost invariably struck by the imposing effect
produced by the city as a whole, and by the width, straightness, and
admirable condition of the principal streets. Picturesqueness has
doubtless been greatly sacrificed in the wholesale removal of the older
buildings, but the superior convenience and utility of those spacious
thoroughfares is easily appreciated; and the amount of traffic in them
proves that their construction was a matter of almost absolute neces-
sity. Most of them, built at the same period and often as a mere

building speculation, exhibit an almost wearying uniformity of style, but in those at a distance from the central quarters considerable variety of taste is often shown.

The central quarters of the city are remarkably bustling and animated, but owing to the ample breadth of the new streets and boulevards and the fact that many of them are paved with asphalte, Paris is a far less noisy place than many other large cities. Its comparative tranquillity, however, is often rudely interrupted by the discordant cries of the itinerant hawkers of wares of every kind who thrust themselves on our attention. Among these are the "old clothes" men, the vendors of various kinds of comestibles, the crockery-menders, the "fontaniers" (who clean and repair filters, etc.), the dog-barbers, and the sellers of special editions of the newspapers. As a rule, however, they are clean and tidy in their dress, polite in manner, self-respecting, and devoid of the squalor and ruffianism which too often characterise their class . . . Another characteristic, though modern, feature in the street-noises of Paris consists of the coarse blasts of the horns of the tramway-cars.

As a rule the Parisian may be said to invite and deserve the confidence of travellers. Accustomed by long usage to their presence, he is skilful in catering for their wants, and recommends himself to them by his politeness and complaisance.

From the 8th edition of Baedeker's "Paris, Handbook for Travellers", 1884

Paris Exhibition 1889

The Exhibition is the triumph of iron, not only in regard to the machinery but also from the point of view of architecture. And yet architecture is still only at the beginning, for it lacks an artistic décor appropriate to this material. Why were soft materials like clay used alongside this rough, harsh metal? Why is there alongside these geometric lines with their modern character this whole range of old ornament polished up by Naturalism? The engineer-architect ought to have a new decorative art, perhaps bolts and screws as ornament, projecting edges of iron, as it were a Gothic tracery of iron. We find something of this in the Eiffel Tower.

Le Moderniste Illustré (1989)

From an article on the Exhibition in "Le Moderniste Illustré", July 1889

I have left Paris, and indeed, France because in the course of time the Eiffel Tower got too much on my nerves.

It was not only that you could see it from every direction: you found it everywhere, modelled in every conceivable material, displayed in every shop window, an inescapable and tormenting nightmare.

I wonder what they will think of our generation unless this tall, gaunt pyramid of metal ladders is torn down in some popular rising – this giant skeleton, totally lacking in grace, with a base which seems made to bear some magnificent cyclopean monument but instead dwindles into a ridiculous and insignificant factory chimney.

Guy de Maupassant French writer (1850–93)

From "Travel Sketches", 1890

Confined to the island of La Cité in its early existence, Paris has gone on spreading through centuries, swallowing up fields, forests, villages. The history of its gradual increase is written in the names of its streets. One may almost trace the limits of the boundary of Paris under Philippe-Auguste or Charles V in following the Rues des Fossés-S.-Bernard, des Fossés-S.-Victor, des Fossés-S.-Marcel, de la Contrescarpe-S.-Marcel, des Fossés-S.-Jacques, des Fossés-Monsieur-le-Prince, de la Contrescarpe-Dauphine, des Fossés-S.-Germain-l'Auxerrois, des Fossés-Montmartre, des Fossés-du-Temple, du Rempart, &c.

"Paris" (1900)

Quotations

Of other streets, many take their names from churches and chapels; some (as des Grands Augustins, des Blancs Manteaux, des Mathurins, Petits-Pères, Récollets, &c.) from convents; some (as Filles-du-Calvaire, Filles S.-Thomas, Nonnains-d'Yères, Ursulines) from monasteries; the streets of S. Anne, Bellefond and Roche-chouart from three Abbesses of Montmartre. A number of streets are named from hotels of nobles, as d'Antin, de Duras, Garancière, Lesdiguières, de Rohan, du Roi de Sicile; others from nobles themselves, as Ventadour, de Choiseul, de Grammont, &c. In the Marais many of the streets are named from the palace of the Hotel de S. Paul and its surroundings, as the Rue du Figuier-S.-Paul, from its fig-garden; Beautreillis, from its berceau of vines; Cerisaie, from its cherry-orchard; Lions-S.-Paul, from its menagerie. A vast number of streets are named from bourgeois inhabitants, as Coquillière, Geoffroy-Lasnier, Gît-le-Coeur (Gilles le Queux), Simon-le-Franc (Franque); others from tradesmen, as Aubry-le-Boucher, Tiquetonne, &c.; others from municipal officers, as Mercier, Thévenot, &c.; others from officers of Parliament, as Bailleul, Mesley, Popincourt, &c. Still greater in number are the streets named from the signboards which formerly hung over the shops, as de l'Arbalète, de l'Arbre Sec, du Chaudron, du Coq-Héron, du Coq.-S.-Jean, des Deux-Ecus, de l'Hirondelle, des Ciseaux, du Sacot, du Cherche-Midi, &c. Many streets take their name from history or legends, as the Rue Pierre-Levée, where a menhir is believed to have stood; the Rue des Martyrs, by which SS. Denis, Rusticus, and Eleutherius are supposed to have gone to their death at Montmartre; the Rue des Frondeurs, where the barricades of the Fronde were begun; the Rue des Francs-Bourgeois, of which the inhabitants were free from taxation. The Rue de l'Enfer, formerly Rue Inférieure, had its name corrupted in the reign of S. Louis, when the devil was supposed to haunt the Château de Vauvert. The evil character of their inhabitants gave a name to such streets as the Rue Mauvais-Garçons, Mauconseil, Vide-Gousset, &c. In the more modern Paris a vast number of streets are named from eminent men, as Bossuet, Corneille, Casimir-Delavigne, d'Aguesseau, Richelieu, Montaigne, &c.; and some from victories, as Rivoli, des Pyramides, Castiglione, d'Alger, &c.

From "Paris", 1900

Friedrich Sieburg
German writer
(1893–1964)

Montmartre is one of the quietest villages in France and at the same time the noisiest and most vicious place in the world. Narrow streets like staircases climb up obliquely towards the heavens, affording a glimpse of little dilapidated houses with cats sunning themselves on their cracked doorsteps, and finally leading to grassy squares adorned with a rectangle of little trees. In several of the peasant-like cottages the cooking-pot still hangs by a chain over the open fire, and there is a wooden pen at the side through whose moss-grown boards a goat thrusts its pink muzzle. The old roofs slope away gradually, as a sleeping beggar's cap slips down over his face, and the attics and chimneys combine to form a strange medley of lines. Into this idyllic little spot the pale countenance of Paris thrusts itself in the shape of barrack-like dwelling-houses with drab, yellow, washed-out fronts, which try in vain to protest against the grubby, jolly village-life on the top of Montmartre.

From "Is God a Frenchman?", 1931

Ernest
Hemingway
American
novelist
(1899–1961)

If you are lucky enough to have lived in Paris as a young man, then wherever you go for the rest of your life, it stays with you, for Paris is a moveable feast.

Letter to a friend, 1950

A sight and an object, the Eiffel Tower is also – and in this is perhaps its most intensive life – a symbol; and in this role it has undergone an unexpected development. Certainly it was intended from the beginning to symbolise the Revolution (the centenary of which was then being celebrated) and industry (a great exhibition of which was then being held); but these significations have not really survived, and others have taken their place. In social terms its symbolic significance was not Democracy but the City of Paris. It is astonishing that Paris had to wait so long for a symbol.

From "Tour Eiffel", 1970

Roland Barthes
French literary
critic and essayist
(1915–80)

What will the Paris of tomorrow be like? I was thinking about this as I contemplated the delicate splendour of the buds which covered the trees in a light veil on the mist-shrouded banks of the Seine. Paris is of such beauty that I am sometimes worried, because I feel how fragile and how threatened that beauty is. Threatened mainly by our town-planners. Which young architect will at last give us the city of the future, a beautiful city which will be just as seductive for the generations of the future as the Paris which has taken shape through the centuries has enchanted us? Is it too much to dream of a visionary who should be a poet of space and not one of those organisers of "life in ugliness", as Baudelaire would say, one of those fanatics for the maximum use of space who hunt down every unbuilt-on patch of land and erect their modern buildings everywhere, graceless lumps of steel and concroto full of the noise and clamour of television and the next-door house's drains . . . Some destructions are unavoidable, and we cannot eternally moan about what once was. But experience should have taught us not to be so foolish as to protect precisely those things that were not intended to last, like all the houses with a life of at most a hundred years which have been built in odd corners of the Marais and in the Faubourg Saint-Antoine and which people are now trying to patch up as best they can.

On the threshold of the 21st century we are still living with the most outdated ideas, particularly in the matter of town-planning. There can of course be no question of getting rid of the past. We should use it as a source of memory; and the stock of buildings available to the future should in the first place include whatever of beauty has been presented to us by earlier generations since man cut the first block of stone.

From "Paris", 1983

Julien Green
French writer
(b. 1900)

If we follow Walter Benjamin's argument, Paris was the capital of the 19th century. It may not, in Benjamin's view, be the capital of the 20th century, but it still remains the centre of France and the gravitational centre of western Europe. That is of course true also of foreign images of France. Paris is the stage on which we play out our fantasies about France.

We are thus almost inevitably referred back to Paris when we try to understand in a spatial dimension the social and symbolic differences within present-day France . . .

No part of Paris stands completely outside the permanent process of transformation to which the city is exposed, but in some areas it goes ahead particularly fast and particularly visibly. On the Champs-Elysées, for example, "the world's finest street", as it is often called. In the past this was the meeting-place of the great world. Smart idlers valued the streets as a worthy setting for their elegance; elegant parfumeries, fashion houses and cafés valued the smart idlers as worthy clients; foreign visitors valued the worthy hotels and the parfumeries, fashion houses and cafés as the incarnation of the great

Karl Heinz Götze
German
journalist
(b. 1947)

world, in the exclusiveness of which they could share, disturbed only occasionally by a state visit, a 14th July parade or the final stage of the Tour de France, and once in a generation by a revolt. The names of the buildings are legend: the Lido, Guerlain, Vuitton, Claridge's, La Païva's mansion . . .

Nowadays the Champs-Elysées is one of the most inhospitable places in Paris, sticky with the ketchup of the fast food establishments and the sugar-water of the lemonade sellers who clutter up the pavement . . .

To the east, round the Bastille, the transformation process is going on at the fastest pace. This slum district of small craftsmen, where during the last two centuries most of the major revolutions in our world started, is becoming a new "in" quarter. Not even Haussmann was able to bring order into this district – narrow, cramped, crooked, irregular – where the first shots of the 1789 Revolution were fired, where in June 1848 the highest barricade (immortalised by Victor Hugo in "Les Misérables") was erected, where the musette waltz was invented, later danced in the "Balayo" by Céline, Arletty and Edith Piaf. Now the craftsmen's workshops are being converted into smart flats, the coal depots into restaurants and the whole district to an entertainment quarter.

This continuing transformation of Paris is taking place also in parts of the city to which tourists never penetrate. In Billancourt, for example, on the Ile Séguin. Here there was the most famous industrial plant in France, the main Renault works. Up to 40,000 workers were employed here, and though the numbers later fell as subsidiary plants were established elsewhere Billancourt remained the symbol of large-scale French industry. And also the symbol of the labour movement . . . Now Billancourt is no more. On March 31st 1992, after the last shift, the last workers quietly left the factory. 31 hectares of land in western Paris, conveniently situated, now await investors.

What are we to make of this? Is Paris a ready-made open-air museum of past history or a place where reality is continually being transformed? Perhaps it is both – not in the ordinary sense in which everything has something to be said for it, but in a precisely determinable sense. Perhaps it is Paris's particular mix of historicity and transformation that makes it possible to experience both with particular intensity.

From "French Affairs", 1993

**Paris from
A to Z**

Sightseeing in Paris

These suggested itineraries are intended to help first-time visitors to Paris make the most of a relatively short stay. Place-names in **bold** type indicate a corresponding entry in the A to Z section of this guide.

Flying visits

Visitors with only an hour or two for sightseeing in the capital should opt for one of the organised bus tours or guided walks (see Practical Information, Sightseeing).

Suggested Walks

Métro

Weather permitting the city centre can easily be explored on foot. For sightseeing further afield it is best to make use of the very efficient Métro system (plan on pages 286–287).

Walk 1

Start at the Ile de la **Cité**, the historic as well as geographic centre of Paris, and one time power base of the French kings. Not to be missed are the Gothic cathedral of ★★ **Notre-Dame**, the two-storeyed ★ **Sainte-Chapelle**, and the **Conciergerie** where, during the Revolution, Marie-Antoinette, Danton and Robespierre were held while awaiting sentence. Crossing to the Left Bank, the **boulevard Saint-Michel** leads straight into the lively ★ **Quartier Latin** and ★★ **Saint-Germain-des-Prés**, notorious stamping ground of existentialist Bohemia and still one of the most charming districts of Paris. Pause here to enjoy a coffee in one of those cultural hotbeds known elsewhere as cafés, where Jean-Paul Sartre, Ernest Hemingway and Picasso were once among the regulars; rummage about in the antique shops and avant-garde boutiques, or stroll around the colourful market in the little rue de Buci. Now cross the river to the Right Bank for the undisputed highlight of any trip to Paris, a visit to the ★★ **Louvre**, the ultimate in museums and a real treasure house of art of all ages and cultures. You cannot hope to do justice to it in an afternoon, indeed a week would hardly suffice; so decide on your priorities at the start. Afterwards, if the weather is fine, take a walk through the Jardins des ★ **Tuileries** to the ★★ **place de la Concorde** at the southern end of the famous ★★ **Champs-Elysées**. Later, having started the evening in one of the city's many excellent restaurants (see Practical Information, Restaurants), the pulsating night-life of ★ **Montparnasse** or ★★ **Saint-Germain-des-Prés** beckons. Paris, like New York, is "a city, which never sleeps".

Walk 2

Starting point for the second walk is the ★★ **Musée d'Orsay** with its celebrated collection of Impressionist paintings. Proceed next to the ★★ **Musée Rodin**, not far from the monumental Cathédrale des ★ **Invalides**, the church in which Napoleon lies buried. Then cross the park-like **Champs-de-Mars** to the ★★ **Tour Eiffel**, technological marvel of the 1889 World Exhibition and still Paris's number one landmark. From the top there is a wonderful view over the roofs of the capital.

For the best view of Gustave Eiffel's masterpiece, cross the river to the ★ **Palais de Chaillot**, the twin wings of which house four museums – on French architecture, the history of cinema, ethnology, and French naval and merchant naval history. From the palace the wide avenue Kléber runs northwards to the busy ★ **place Charles de Gaulle**, its centrepiece the huge ★ **Arc de Triomphe de l'Etoile** dedicated to the

◀ *The Basilica of the Sacré-Cœur, one of the great Paris landmarks*

victorious French armies of the Revolution and First Empire. Time now for a stroll down the "most beautiful avenue in the world", the celebrated ★★**Champs-Elysées**. In the ★avenue Montaigne, which branches off the Champs-Elysées at the Rond Point, the tone is set by the fashion houses of top designers such as Dior, Ungaro and Jean-Louis Scherrer – with window displays out of this world and prices to match. Soon the Champs-Elysées opens into the magnificent ★★**place de la Concorde** at the north-west end of the Jardins des ★**Tuileries**. Devotees of fashion should turn left up the ★**rue Royale** in the direction of the Madeleine to the ★**rue Faubourg Saint-Honoré**, here to pay homage to the crème of French couturiers, Lanvin, Hermés, Christian Lacroix and others, in the city's "golden triangle". The elegant ★★**place Vendôme** just off to the north of the rue Saint-Honoré is one of the finest examples of harmony in urban architecture in Europe.

Skirting the north wing of the ★★**Louvre**, the Napoleonic section of the ★**rue de Rivoli** with its little boutiques and colourful souvenir shops offers a further opportunity for window-shopping. And what more appropriate climax to this feast of fashion than a visit to the ★Musée de la Mode et du Textile, re-opened in 1997 in the Rohan Wing of the Louvre. Every constraint of form coupled with grace of movement is illustrated here, from the fish-bone corset to Christian Dior's New Look.

◄ Bronze statue in front of the Palais de Chaillot

If no table has been reserved at one of the superlative gourmet restaurants, all of which stay open late into the evening, there is a choice of delightful Belle Epoque brasseries instead. This will leave plenty of time for a visit to one of the "in" places of the moment in ★★**Saint-Germain-des-Prés**, the ★★**Marais** or the Quartier ★**Bastille**. (The monthlies "Nova" and "Paris Capitale" have all the latest on the Paris scene; see also Practical Information, Night Life.)

The third walk starts east of the ★★**Centre Pompidou** in one of the most select districts of the Old City, the ★★**Marais**. At its heart lies the unique ★★**place des Vosges** with its stuccoed Renaissance façades from the time of Henry IV; an idyllic spot for picnicking on the grass. Within a short distance are three first-class museums: a collection of 18th c. paintings bequeathed to the city by department store-founder Ernest Cognacq-Jay and housed today in the Hôtel de Donon; the ★**Musée Carnavalet** which traces the city's history from Roman Lutetia to the reign of Louis XVI; and, in the elegant surroundings of the Hôtel Salé, the ★★**Musée Picasso**, established by André Malraux. For friends of the hunt there is also the neighbouring Musée de la Chasse et de la Nature, with a collection of trophies and animal studies. The rue des Rosiers is the hub of Jewish life in Paris, the best kosher restaurants being found on the south side.

Walk 3

Now cross to the ★**Ile Saint-Louis** with its cosy bistros and idyllic embankments, just the place for romance to flourish, then over onto the Left Bank and uphill through the student quarter with the **Sorbonne** and élite *grandes écoles*, to the ★**Panthéon**, last resting place of the nation's great and good. A little to the east, in the rue de Navarre, remains of the **Arènes de Lutèce**, a 2nd century amphitheatre, bear witness to the city's Roman beginnings. In the ★**Jardin des Plantes** in 1795 Parisians were treated to their first sight of real live elephants; 100 years later the Muséum National d'Histoire Naturelle was opened here. Today its ★Grande Gallerie is devoted to a fascinating exhibition on the history of evolution.

Now return towards the start of the walk. Situated on the Seine embankment near the Pont de Sully is the ★ **Institut du Monde Arabe,** designed by Jean Nouvel and a celebration of the art and culture of the Islamic world. From the bridge the boulevard Henri-IV runs east to the Place de la ★ **Bastille,** where the huge, coolly functional building of the Opéra-Bastille occupies a site of almost 15ha/37 acres. The acoustics are first-class and seats very sought-after, so early booking is essential. The narrow streets of the adjacent "Bastoche", Paris's latest in-vogue district, present a mixture of the off-beat and the chic; little rear courtyards, small art shops and today's name in fashion design, not to mention dance halls, discos and jazz bars for those wanting to live it up at night (see Practical Information, Night Life).

Suggestions for a longer stay

There is so much to see and experience in Paris – the treasures in its museums, its picturesque quarters, its magnificent avenues, boulevards and palaces, its landmarks and viewpoints, fashion, shopping, cuisine and festivals – that three short walks scarcely begin to do justice to it. Those with more time at their disposal should certainly not miss ★ **Montmartre** and the **Sacre-Cœur,** the ★★ **Centre Pompidou,** and the evocative turn-of-the-century shopping arcades or take a stroll in the ★ **Bois de Boulogne** or the enchanting ★ **Parc des Buttes-Chaumont,** and see at least one of Paris's ★ cemeteries with graves of prominent figures. Then there is the Parc de ★★ **La Villette,** one of the major attractions for children, with its Cité des Sciences et de l'Industrie, Cité de la Musique and huge spherical cinema. Also very popular with young and old alike are the ★ **Vincennes** zoo, the

The Louvre: its art treasures must be seen by every visitor to Paris

All types of nightlife can be enjoyed in Paris

spectacular ★Grande Galerie at the **Muséum National d'Histoire Naturelle**, and the ★Musée Grevin (waxworks) in the boulevard Montmartre. The ★★**Musée de Cluny** has a collection of furniture, jewellery and medieval weaponry. And for a comprehensive survey of modern architectural history where better than ★La Défense, the booming business quarter with its huge ★Grande Arche, a contemporary restatement of the ideals of *liberté, égalité et fraternité*.

With yet more time available there are many things to see in the environs of Paris (see Practical Information, Excursions). They include the famous palaces at ★★**Versailles**, ★★**Fontainebleau** and ★**Rambouillet**, and the basilica of ★★**Saint-Denis**, for more than twelve hundred years the burial place of all but one or two of the French kings. Children will want to make a beeline for ★★**Euro Disney**, at Chessy, 30km/18 miles outside Paris. The ★Parc Astérix, a theme park dedicated to Gaul's favourite hero and his friend Obelix, is an excellent value for money alternative. ★Le Pays France Miniature at Elancourt, about 10km/6 miles south-west of Versailles, features scaled-down models of old French farmhouses, cathedrals and the châteaux of the Loire.

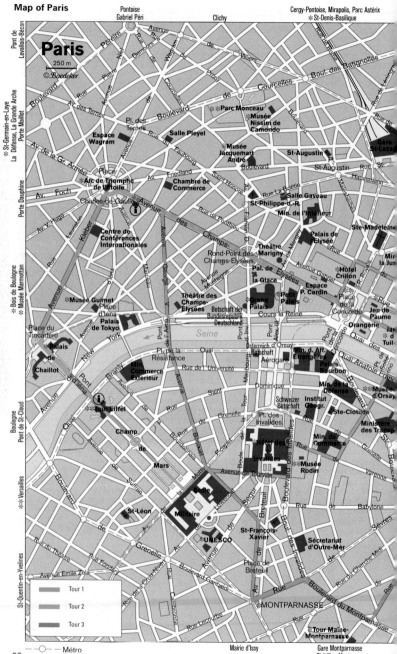

Map of Paris

Pontoise
Gabriel Péri
Clichy

Cergy-Pontoise, Mirapolis, Parc Astérix
✳ St-Denis-Basilique

Paris
250 m
©Baedeker

Pont de Levallois-Bécon

✳ St-Germain-en-Laye
La Défense, La Grande Arche
Porte Maillot

Porte Dauphine

Bois de Boulogne
✳ Musée Marmottan

Boulogne
Pont de St-Cloud

✳ Versailles

St-Quentin-en-Yvelines

Avenue
Rue
Pereire
de
Demours
Rue
Pierre
Avenue
Wagram
de
Villiers
Courcelles
Boul. des Batignolles

Boulevard
Av. des Ternes
Pl. des Ternes
✳✳ Parc Monceau
Musée Nissim de Camondo

Espace Wagram
Salle Pleyel
Rue du Faubourg
✳ Musée Jacquemart André
St-Augustin
Gare St-Lazare
Pl. St-Augustin
Rue Haussmann

Av. de la Gr. Armée
Place
✳ Arc de Triomphe de l'Etoile
Av. Friedland
Chambre de Commerce
Av. Franklin
Rue La Boëtie
Salle Gaveau
St-Philippe-d.-R.
Min. de l'Intérieur

Av. Foch
Charles de Gaulle
Avenue des Champs
Rue de Ponthieu
Palais de l'Elysée
Ste-Madeleine

Av. V. Hugo
Kléber
Centre de Conférences Internationales
Av. Marceau
Rond-Point des Champs-Elysées
Théâtre Marigny
Pal. de l'Elysées
Hôtel Crillon
Mi la Jus

Rue
Avenue Montaigne
Pal. de la Glace
Espace P. Cardin
Place de la Concorde
Jeu de Paume

✳ Musée Guimet
Place d'Iéna
Théâtre des Champs-Elysées
Grand Palais
Petit Palais
Orangerie
Jar d Tuil

Palais de Tokyo
Botschaft der Bundesrepublik Deutschland
Cours la Reine
Quai des

Place du Trocadéro
Palais de Chaillot
New
York
Pont de l'Alma
Seine
Österreich d'Orsay Botschaft
Aérogare
Min. d. Aff. Etrangères
Quai Anatole France
✳✳ Musée d'Orsay

Pl. de la Résistance
Quai
Rue de l'Université
Palais Bourbon

Min. Commerce Extérieur
Av.
Branly
Dominique
Schweizer Botschaft
Institut Géogr.
Min. de la Défense
Ste-Clotilde

✳✳ Tour Eiffel
Champ
Rue
de
Grenelle
Pl. des Invalides
Ministère des Transp

de
Mars
Av.
Bourdonnais
Pigot
Av.
Hôtel des Invalides
Min. du Commerce

Suffren
Boulevard
Avenue de Tourville
✳ Musée Rodin

St-Léon
Ecole
Militaire
Ségur
Babylone

✳ UNESCO
St-François-Xavier
Rue
Secrétariat d'Outre-Mer

Avenue Emile Zola
Grenelle
Place de Breteuil
Sèvres

Tour 1
Tour 2
Tour 3

— ○ — Métro

Boulevard du Montparnasse

✳ MONTPARNASSE

✳✳ Tour Maine-Montparnasse

Mairie d'Issy
Gare Montparnasse
Châtillon-Montrouge

Map of Paris

67

Sights from A to Z

Académie Française

See Institut de France

★★Arc de Triomphe   E 4

Location
Place Charles-de-
Gaulle (16th arr.)

Métro station
Charles de
Gaulle-Etoile

RER station
Charles de
Gaulle-Etoile

Buses
22, 30, 31, 52, 73

Opening times
Oct. 1–Mar. 31,
10am–5pm;
Apr. 1–Sep. 30,
10am–5.30pm.
(exc. pub. hols.)

**Admission
charge**

The Arc de Triomphe de l'Etoile is dedicated to the glory of the victorious French armies of the Revolution and the First Empire. Napoleon
ordered the building of this mighty structure in 1806 but did not live
to see its completion in 1836. It was designed by J.-F. Chalgrin (1739–
1811) and completely restored in 1988–89.

On the east and west fronts of the arch, which is 50m/164ft high
and 45m/148ft wide, are four reliefs with over-lifesize figures depicting the departure, the victories and the glorious return of the French
armies. Particularly notable is the relief by François Rude (1784–
1855) on the Champs-Elysées front, "Departure of the Volunteers of
1792", also known as "The Marseillaise", which depicts the troops
setting out, led by the winged spirit of Liberty. On the inner surface
of the arch are the names of over 660 generals and more than a
hundred battles.

From the viewing platform (reached in a lift by way of an intermedi-
ate level) are panoramic views, among the most striking in Paris,
along the twelve avenues which radiate from the Place de l'Etoile
(see entry; now officially Place Charles-de-Gaulle): the straight line
running from the Champs-Elysées to Place de la Concorde and the
Louvre; in the opposite direction the Grande Arche in the heart of La
Défense; to the north-east Montmartre, with the Sacré-Coeur; and to
the south the Eiffel Tower, the Dôme des Invalides and the Tour
Montparnasse.

A small museum below the platform contains an exhibition illustrating the history of the Arc de Triomphe, mementoes of Napoleon and
relics of the First World War.

At the foot of the Arc de Triomphe is the Tomb of the Unknown
Soldier, dedicated in 1921 as a memorial to the dead of the First World
War. Every evening at 6.30pm a small delegation of old soldiers
rekindle the flame at the tomb, and every year on November 11th,
the anniversary of the Armistice of 1918, there are ceremonies
commemorating the dead of both world wars.

★Place de l'Etoile – Place Charles de Gaulle

The famous Place de l'Etoile (*étoile* – "star"), in the centre of which
stands the Arc de Triomphe, has officially been called Place Charles
de Gaulle since 1970, but to most Parisians it is still Place de l'Etoile.
Here twelve avenues converge in the form of a star on a circular
place is surrounded by architecture of the time of Haussman. The
twelve imposing buildings around the square were designed by
Hittorff. The names of the streets recall figures of the Empire. From
the platform on top of the Arc de Triomphe there are wide views
over Paris and also a bird's eye view of the traffic eternally circling
the square below.

In the centre of a "star", where twelve avenues converge, stands Napoleon's triumphal arch

Arènes de Lutèce   J 6

The remains of the Roman amphitheatre of Paris, discovered in 1869, give some idea of the huge size of the original structure. The elliptical arena, 56m/184ft long by 48m/157ft across, is roughly the same size as the interior of the Colosseum in Rome. Gladiator and animal fights were staged here.

Location
Rue de Navarre
49 rue Monge
(5th arr.)

Métro station
Monge

The amphitheatre was built in the Roman city of Lutetia about a.d. 200, but later in the same century, during a barbarian incursion in 205, it was used as a quarry of stone for building defensive walls. Although it had only 36 tiers of seating it could accommodate an audience of 17,000 – almost the whole population of the city. Today it is once again the stage for occasional festival events.

Assemblée Nationale

See Palais-Bourbon

Bastille (Place de la Bastille)   K 5

Now only the name of the spacious square, Place de la Bastille, is a reminder that the notorious state prison known as the Bastille, the much hated symbol of absolutist power, once stood here. Nothing is left of the building except a few foundations in the Métro, for after the storming of the Bastille on July 14th 1789 it was completely

Location
East central Paris
(3rd arr.)

Métro station
Bastille

Bastille

Buses
20, 29, 65, 69, 76,
86, 87, 91

demolished within a few months. Stones from the Bastille were used in the construction of the bridge over the Seine at Place de la Concorde.

In the Bastille Métro station is a huge mosaic (by Odile Jacquot, 1988), a free interpretation of the Revolutionary flag in the national colours of blue, white and red. There is a model of the Bastille as it was before its demolition in the Musée Carnavalet (see entry).

History

The Bastille ("small bastion") was begun in 1370, in the reign of Charles V, in order to reinforce the newly built town wall at this point, at the end of Rue Saint-Antoine. His successor enlarged the bastion, which by 1382 had become a massive ring fort with eight towers over 20m/65ft high. Even so it provided rather ineffective protection, for out of six occasions on which it was besieged during the civil wars it was taken six times. It became a state prison in the time of Cardinal Richelieu, Louis XIII's minister. The number of prisoners, however, was never very great: in the reign of Louis XIV there were only some 40, and in that of Louis XVI no more than 19. Most of them were persons of rank and standing, few of whom had committed any crime. The majority were grumblers, free thinkers or liberals who were frequently confined on the strength of a royal order (lettre de cachet), without any judicial process. Conditions in the prison were not always disagreeable. Some of the prisoners had their own servants and could receive visitors: Cardinal de Rohan, while in the Bastille, gave a dinner for twenty guests. Among those confined here was Voltaire, who had expressed himself indiscreetly in "Candide" and wrote his "Œdipe" while a prisoner, Mirabeau, Fouquet and the Marquis de Sade, who in the end was transferred to an asylum. On July 14th 1789, when the mob stormed the Bastille, they found only seven prisoners to liberate – petty criminals, including, it is said, two who were insane. They celebrated their triumph none the less.

Storming of the Bastille

The French writer and diplomat François-René de Chateaubriand describes the taking of the Bastille in his "Mémoires d'Outre-Tombe": "On July 14th the Bastille was taken by storm. I was a witness of this assault directed against a couple of old soldiers and a faint-hearted governor. If the gates had been closed the people would never have made their way into the fortress. I saw two or three cannon-shots fired, not by the old soldiers but by the Gardes Françaises, who had already occupied the towers. De Launay, the Governor, was fetched from his hiding-place and after much manhandling was slaughtered on the steps of the Town Hall. Flesselles, leader of the merchants, had his skull shattered by a pistol-shot – a spectacle much enjoyed by the heartless lookers-on.

"As in the street fighting in Rome in the time of Otho and Vitellius, the mob indulged in unbridled orgies in the midst of the slaughter. The victors of the Bastille, drunk with success and hailed as conquerors in the taverns, were driven round the town in carriages, accompanied by prostitutes and sansculottes who joined in the triumph.

"Passers-by, with respect inspired by fear, took off their hats to these heroes, some of whom died of exhaustion at the height of their triumph. The number of keys of the Bastille kept increasing, and they were sent to highly placed boobies far and wide . . . The experts proceeded to conduct post-mortems on the Bastille. Makeshift cafés were established under canvas, and people thronged to them as to a fair. Innumerable carriages drove past or stopped at the foot of the towers, the stones of which were being pulled down amid great clouds of dust . . . It was a rallying-point for the most famous orators, the best known writers, leading actors and actresses, the most popular dancers, the most distinguished foreigners, the great lords of the court and envoys from all over Europe. The old France had come to take farewell for ever, the new France to make its debut."

The anniversary of the fall of the Bastille is France's National Day (July 14th), which is celebrated all over the country with dances, street festivals, military parades, firework displays and other special events.

National Day
July 14th

In the centre of Place de la Bastille is the 51m/167ft high Colonne de Juillet, topped by a graceful figure of Liberty (by Dumont), which was regilded in 1989. It commemorates not the fall of the Bastille but the Republicans killed during the July Revolution of 1830 which overthrew Charles X and brought Louis-Philippe to power. Four Gallic cocks and a lion relief on the base of the column symbolise the free people of France. A spiral staircase (283 steps) inside the column leads to a viewing platform from which there is an impressive view of the new Opéra-Bastille.

Colonne de
Juillet

★Opéra de la Bastille

The site of the Bastille is now occupied by the new Opera House designed by the Uruguay-born Canadian architect Carlos Ott and officially opened by President Mitterrand on July 13th 1989. The first performance, after the final completion of construction work, was of Berlioz's "Trojans" on March 17th 1990.

Information
11 bis avenue
Daumesnil
(12th arr.)
Tel. 01 40 01 17 89

Ticket office
Tel. 01 40 01 19 70
Fax. 01 40 01 20 82

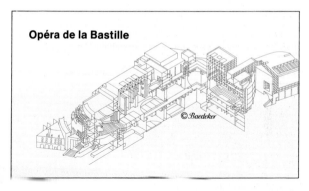

Opéra de la Bastille

© Baedeker

This prestigious building, a combination of rectangles and curves, covers an area of some 15 hectares/37 acres. The stepped lattice-work glass façade has a cool and functional appearance. The bright foyer forms a kind of semicircle round the auditorium, whose tent-like glass ceiling harmonises well with the steeply raked rows of white seats below. At the entrance is a colourful statue of the Genius of Femininity by Niki de Saint-Phalle. The gigantic stage of the main house, which has seating for 2700, is surrounded by five subsidiary stages of similar dimensions beside it and behind it. The view of the stage from the auditorium and the acoustics are both excellent. The complex also includes an amphitheatre with seating for 600, a theatre which can be arranged to seat audiences of varying size between 600 and 1300, a studio with seating for 280, rehearsal stages, a library and a vidéothèque.

Adjoining the Opera is the Grandes Marches restaurant, demolished and rebuilt as a historical replica.

Les Grandes
Marches

★Bastille quarter

The building of the new Opera was the first stage in the transformation of the area round Place de la Bastille. Like the Marais (see entry) some years ago, the Bastille quarter (the Bastoche) is being steadily upgraded into a quartier branché, a smart and sought-after part of the city. In Rue du Faubourg-Saint-Antoine and the adjoining streets, whose narrow houses with their labyrinth of little courtyards and passages were formerly occupied by carpenters and furniture-makers, the old craftsmen's workshops are increasingly being converted into studios, designer boutiques, "in" bars and galleries. Since the mid eighties such well-known gallery proprietors as Leif Stähle, President of the Swedish Art Fair, and André Lavignes, who shows work by Andy Warhol and Mimmo Rotella among other contemporary artists, have been established in Rue de Charonne. Close by is the À Jean-Pierre café, with a charming Art Nouveau façade. In Rue de la Roquette, opposite the avantgarde Théâtre de la Bastille, is the gallery of the Donguy brothers, showing experimental art and photography. In Rue de Lappe, once occupied by coal-merchants' establishments and bals-musette, are galleries of abstract art, chic cafés and antique dealers. The Balajo, frequented in the thirties by such stars as Arletty and Edith Piaf, is still a fashionable resort. In the cosy inner courtyards of the Cour du Bel Air in Rue du Faubourg-Saint-Antoine (No. 56) a gallery of contemporary photography rubs shoulders with an old-established tapestry works, while at No. 30 is a Jean-Paul Gautier fashion house.

The Bastille quarter has long been the home of a mixed population of immigrants to Paris. The Auvergnats were followed by the Bretons and later by Italians, Spaniards, Russians, Jews, Arabs and people from the former French colonies. Each population group brought its

The Opéra de la Bastille, all glass and bluish-grey granite

own culture, which left its mark on the local bars, dance halls and shops. The bustling market in Place d'Aligre, with its 19th century market hall, now protected as a national monument, is very typical of the varied and colourful life of the quartier. This trendy new district of the nineties is a fascinating mixture of the chic and the seamy. Side by side in the narrow streets can be seen designer-styled establishments, quaint old shops and quiet courtyards presided over by a concierge. In the Balajo slow waltzes and tangos are still danced into the small hours, but the unstoppable process of modernisation can be seen everywhere at work.

Beaubourg

See Centre Pompidou

Belleville and Ménilmontant

L/M 4/5

The most celebrated inhabitant of Belleville, the chanteuse Edith Piaf, is said to have been born on the steps of the dilapidated house at 72 rue de Belleville. Whether that is true or not, the "grande dame de chanson" certainly grew up in this district and sang in the streets when only a child. The small museum at No. 5 rue Crespin du Gast displays photographs, letters, drawings and other memorabilia covering the varied life led by the celebrated singer (open: Mon.–Thur. 1–6pm by arrangement, tel./fax 43 55 52 72 see also Baedeker Special p.32–33).The special atmosphere of eastern Paris, personified by the "sparrow of Paris" and Maurice Chevalier in the thirties, has long since gone, and the Belleville, Ménilmontant and Barbès quarters, like much else in Paris, are in process of change.

Belleville, like the neighbouring districts of Charonne, Ménilmontant and Barbès, was originally a small village which began to be industrialised in the early 19th century. Between 1820 and 1860 the population of Belleville rose from 8000 to 60,000. Around the turn of the century it was incorporated in Paris as the 20th arrondissement, which became the home of numbers of refugees, including many Jews from Central and East Europe. They have left their mark on the quarter, still visible in the area round Rues Ramponeau, Dénoyer and Lacroix, in which is the Synagogue. When in the 20th century many industrial undertakings moved to the outskirts of Paris on cost grounds the occupants of the old houses changed. Today the quarter is multicultural, and around the Couronnes, Belleville and Goncourt metro stations Europeans, black Africans and Asiatic immigrants, Jews, Christians, Muslims and Buddhists all live together relatively peacefully. As elsewhere in Europe, the "beurs", the second generation which has grown up in France, remains torn between assimilating the customs of the country while retaining old family traditions – even though personalities such as the beautiful actress Isabelle Adjani, the Tunisian fashion guru Azzedine Alaia or tennis star Yannick Noah have long been regarded as French.

Location
20th arr.

Métro stations
Belleville,
Couronnes,
Ménilmontant

Buses
26, 46, 96

The city has launched a large-scale programme for the rehabilitation and redevelopment of Belleville, Ménilmontant and Barbès. Many old houses have been pulled down and replaced by blocks of modern flats. An example of successful renovation, with the preservation of historic old buildings, is the area round the church of Saint-Germain-de-Charonne. In Rue Saint-Blaise old houses rub shoulders with new buildings designed to fit in with their environment, and only a stone's throw away are ugly apartment blocks of the sixties. The difficulty

Rehabilitation
programme

73

about the renovation programme, as always, is the unavoidable increase in rents which hitherto have been relatively low. It is only a question of time, therefore, before this working-class area becomes an expensive middle-class quarter. The present tenants will then be forced to move out into one of the dormitory suburbs in the banlieue, often in unattractive living conditions, which were so sharply delineated in the film by the Algerian director Mehdi Charef, "Tea in Archimedes' Harem"; and local civic initiatives and the efforts of the people themselves are likely to make little difference. So far, however, the district has managed to preserve its village-like charm and the atmosphere of the colourful weekly markets, the Norman cheese shops, the Breton fish-sellers and the Provençal vegetable dealers, with the addition of the exotic shops and restaurants of incomers from the French West Indies, black Africans and Arabs, the little theatres, the dance halls and the artists' studios. There is a lively market held here every Tuesday and Friday. On the side of the street with odd numbers will be found one Arabian restaurant after another, offering couscous, taijnes and other delicacies

Bercy   L 7

Location
12th arr.

Métro station
Bercy

In the late seventies, under the large-scale programme for the rehabilitation of eastern Paris, work started on the redevelopment of the area between the Gare de Lyon and the Porte de Bercy; and now the Bercy quarter, like La Défense (see entry) at the other end of Paris, has become another business district, and the old dock installations in this area, formerly highly industrialised, have given place to numerous futuristic office blocks.

The new Ministry of Finance on the banks of the Seine

This "palace of all sports" at 8 Boulevard de Bercy (Michel Andrault and Pierre Parat, 1984) was built on the site of an old wine warehouse. This truncated pyramid, covered with grass, has glass façades on a steel framework and contains three halls capable of being adapted for events of all kinds and equipped with the most modern technology. There are facilities for every kind of indoor sport, and for opera evenings and rock concerts up to 17,000 spectators can be accommodated. Thanks to computer-controlled technology and ultra-modern recording studios concerts and circus performances become an unforgettable experience.

Palais Omnisport de Bercy

The adjoining Parc de Bercy on the banks of the Seine is still in process of being laid out.

In order to increase the exhibition space in the Musée du Louvre, the Ministry of Finance, which for over 100 years, since the time of the Duc de Morny, Napoleon III's minister, had occupied the north wing of the Louvre (see entry), was compelled to move to new offices 3km/2 miles upstream.

Ministère des Finances

Here, on a site 5 hectares/12 acres in extent, some 216,000 sq.m/2,325,000 sq.ft of office and residential accommodation for 6000 officials were provided between 1983 and 1989. The architects of this gigantic complex, 360m/395yds long, were designer Paul Chemetov, who had also worked on the Halles project (see entry), and Borjo Huidobro. As if passing through a gateway into eastern Paris, the Seine expressway runs under the south wing of this huge building, which is apt to arouse a mixture of astonishment and shock in the beholder and has been the subject of much controversy. A series of bridges and passages leads between plain grey walls into the interior of the massive complex. The concrete tower is topped by a helicopter landing pad.

Bibliothèque Nationale de France Bibliotheque François Mitterrand L 7

The new National Library in the Tolbiac quarter in the east of Paris was dedicated in 1995. Following the extension to the Louvre (see entry), the Grande Arche in La Défense (see entry), the Ministère des Finances in Bercy (see entry) and the Opéra de la Bastille (see Bastille), this was the last of the extravagant projects by means of which François Mitterrand (see Famous People) hoped to leave his mark on the history of France.

Location
11 quai François Mauriac (13th arr.)

Métro station
Quai de la Gare

This spectacular library, covering an area of 7.5ha/18½ acres, was designed by the architect Dominique Perrault. Four 78m/256ft high glass towers, each shaped like an open book, stand at the corners of an inner courtyard 1200sq.m/1435sq.yds in area and planted with Normandy pines; the reading rooms are arranged around it on two floors in cloister-like fashion.

Information
Tel. 53 79 59 59

Opening times
Reading room:
Tue.–Sat.
10am–6pm,
Sun. noon–6pm

Officially opened in December 1996, it is anticipated that by the end of the millenium its 430 kilometres/270 miles of shelves will accommodate some 11 million books, mainly removed from the old city library in rue Richelieu; the latter will in future be used to house manuscripts, maps and coin collections. With 3600 seats for students – 2000 in the research department on the ground floor and a further 1600 for the general public on the first floor – the National Library boasts dimensions far in excess of comparable institutions in the USA and Great Britain. Valuable items are stored in concrete capsules to avoid damage from climatic changes, those in the towers are kept at a constant temperature and humidity level in multi-glazed containers – the high cost of air-conditioning has already become a political issue. An internal rail system can transport books from the stores to the reading areas within a quarter of an hour.

The New Paris –
Changes in the 13th Arrondissement

Town planners are inclined to carry out major surgery on whole areas of a city if allowed to. In Hamburg, at the end of the 19th century, they did away with a merchants' area, which had evolved over many generations, in order to build the present "warehouse city", and in London during the last fifteen years the Tory government's architects were also given their head in the Docklands. Paris can without doubt look back on the longest tradition of radical town-planning measures. Haussmann's opening up of the city in the last century, the building of La Défense in the 1960s and Les Halles in the 1970s are just the most striking examples of the untrammelled mania for construction projects associated with successive Paris city administrations. By now there is no free space left in the city centre for any architectural surprise coups – everything now has its well-defined place there and is brilliantly conserved for the tourists and the picture postcards.

In the south-east of the city, however, on the edge of the suburbs, there was an area which until recently had lain unnoticed and forgotten, but which now has been taken under the wing of the technocrats of the Conseil de Paris. This district, called **Tolbiac**, had hitherto probably only been known to a small minority: for example, those French schoolchildren who found the location of the decisive battle of Chlodwigs, fought against the Alemannen, in their history books, and of course the readers of the detective novels of Georges Simenon and Léo Malet. Both authors liked to make their murders happen in the 13th arrondissement, a district of run-down charm and a chaotic central point, the place d'Italie. In the time of Pompidou large numbers of unattractive high-rise blocks of flats were built and now, in their shadow, can be found the exotically coloured lights of Chinatown. But that is not the whole of Tolbiac: there is also the **Salpêtrière**, built in 1634 by the royal government as a saltpetre factory, later a hospice for the needy and a women's

prison, and finally at the end of the 19th century under the direction of Jean Martin Charcot a trailblazing psychiatric clinic. Here, in close proximity to the large goods station, the flour for Paris's baguettes was milled in the **Grands Moulins de Paris** right up until the beginning of 1997. This is also where Panhard, one of the oldest makes of car in the world, had its factory and where in 1933 Le Corbusier had the opportunity to build his first "dwelling machine". The Cité du Refuge, reception centre of the Salvation Army, a building composed of concrete cubes, was a prototype of those vast urban developments which were later put up almost overnight in so many districts of Paris. Tolbiac itself was spared such large-scale building projects – until now. For recently cranes and excavators have moved into the area along the bank of the Seine to the south-east of the Pont d'Austerlitz. One of the latest *Grands Travaux* is beginning to emerge, stretching for 3km/nearly 2 miles: the project known as the **Seine Rive Gauche**. Once again the planners have not gone for half measures: the hall of the Gare d'Austerlitz, an impressive cast-iron structure dating from the last third of the 19th c., is to be bisected by a road. On a level with the **rue de Tolbiac** a three-storey underground station, Masséna-Tolbiac, will have been completed by 1998, with the tracks remaining above ground being covered over by the largest cast concrete slab yet to have been seen in Paris. On top of it, occupying an area of 130ha/½ sq.mile, three new building complexes are planned.

However, the impetus for yet more new buildings is being curbed by the surplus of expensive office space in the centre of Paris. And on the other side of the Seine, Bercy has in recent years has seen a new shopping centre shoot up, along with a redesigned park and the monumental bastion of the finance ministry. The gigantic office block Bercy Expo, however, was still standing absolutely empty a year after its completion. In addition a growing resistance to so much

Gigantic glass towers of the new Paris Bibliothèque Nationale

new building started to be registered in the district. After a judicial clash between residents of the **rue du Chevalier** and the city government the Seine Rive Gauche plan had to be revised. Jean-Pierre Le Dantec, director of a Parisian school of architects, sees a radical reorientation in this: "The Rive Gauche project is both the apotheosis and the apocalypse of Neo-Haussmannism. In future Paris will be renovated and redeveloped in small manageable homeopathic doses." The more leisurely pace of change opens up various alternatives: business premises are being converted into university buildings, cycle paths and green spaces are also being incorporated into new planning blueprints. A former cold-storage depot, **Le Frigo**, is being preserved for the colourful band of people who live there, including artists, jazz musicians, puppeteers and the homeless, while the old flour mills are soon to house a "Cité des Arts". In the meantime, what stands out from all this

chaos is the new symbol for the Rive Gauche, the Bibliothèque Nationale, with its almost 80m/260ft high storage towers. The metaphor that is apposite is of something speaking volumes, in fact library volumes. The intention was that these books would gradually and visibly from the outside, fill the complex's four glass corner buildings themselves representing open books. Conservative voices of caution in the end spoke out against so much transparent glass, so now the books are to be stored in climatized rooms, the light glass façade being now merely a screen. The complex, with its monumental towers, the barrier-like base to the staircase and the inaccessible inner courtyard, makes a rather cold impression and it remains to be seen how it will fit in with the surrounding district. Inside, however, the picture changes completely. Here, a perfect and harmoniously proportioned reading environment has been created.

★Bois de Boulogne   A–D 3–6

Location
Western outskirts
of city (16th arr.)

Métro stations
Sablons,
Porte Maillot,
Porte Dauphine,
Porte d'Auteuil

Buses
32, 43, 52, 63, 73,
244, PC

This 865 hectare/2135 acre park, criss-crossed by footpaths and bridle-paths but also traversed by broad motor roads, lies on the western boundary of Paris, between the Boulevard Périphérique on the east and the Seine on the west. It takes its name from the old pilgrimage church of Notre-Dame de Boulogne-le-Petit, built in the 14th century by pilgrims returning from a pilgrimage to Notre-Dame de Boulogne-sur-Mer. In the 15th century a small settlement called Boulogne grew up on the site, and the name was subsequently applied also to the wood of holm oaks which surrounded it. For long a royal hunting ground and also the haunt of bandits and other undesirables, it surrounded in the 16th century, in the reign of Henri II, by a wall with eight gates. Louis XIV's minister Colbert, on the king's orders, laid it out as a park with paths converging in the form of a star and threw it open to the public. During the Regency (early 18th century) and again from the mid 19th century onwards the park became the resort of the fashionable world – in the latter case mainly because of the opening of racecourses at Longchamp and Auteuil and the new landscaping of the park by Baron Haussmann, Prefect of the Seine, after Napoleon III presented it to the city.

Nowadays the Bois de Boulogne is a popular recreation area, drawing large numbers of people to walk in the park, picnic on the grass, row on the lake or simply do nothing. During the day the park is frequented by joggers, cyclists, riders, dog-owners and the indefatigable boule players. After dark there is a different public with different interests, and prostitution is well established here.

Visitors who are short of time should at least drive through the park. The following are the main things to see.

★Bagatelle   B 4

Location
Route de Sèvres
à Neuilly
(16th arr.)

Métro station
Pont de Neuilly
Buses
43, 244

Opening times
Park: in summer
daily 9am–8pm,
in winter daily
9am–5.30pm:
Château:
Apr. 1st–Oct. 31st
Sat., Sun.
3–4pm

**Admission
charge**

In the north-western part of the Bois de Boulogne, set in beautiful gardens, stands a charming little chateau in the style of the late 18th century, when the nobility met here for hunting or merry parties. Bagatelle is the only one of the four chateaux in the Bois de Boulogne which was not destroyed during the Revolution. It got its name in 1720, when the Duchesse d'Estrées built a little country house here. After several changes of ownership the chateau fell into ruin. It was acquired in 1772 by the young Comte d'Artois (later Charles X); then, when his sister-in-law Marie-Antoinette wagered 100,000 livres that he would not be able to restore the elegant little chateau within two months, he engaged 900 workmen, who managed to complete a picturesque "folly" (as little country houses used purely for entertainment were known), designed by François-Alexandre Belanger, within the time allowed. The château was restored in 1987 on the basis of the original plans.

Particularly attractive features of this enchanted park include Lord Seymour's Blue Gate (mid 19th century), the orangery with its evergreen plants, a Japanese water garden and the most northerly of the four ponds with its display of water-lilies. The site of the old manège is now occupied by a marvellous rose-garden laid out by Jean-Claude Forrestier in 1906. An international competition for new varieties of roses is held annually in June. Finally there is a beautiful English-style garden with pleasant quiet footpaths, designed by the Scottish gardener Thomas Blaikie.

Grande Cascade

An artificial waterfall 10m/35ft high at the Carrefour de Longchamp.

Pré Catelan

In the Pré Catelan (named after a troubadour, Armand Catelan, who was murdered here around 1300), a small enclosed garden in the centre of the Bois de Boulogne, are two small châteaux and a majestic 200-year-old copper beech. The Jardin Shakespeare, laid out in 1953, contains specimens of all the plants mentioned in Shakespeare's plays (conducted visits at 11am and 1, 3 and 4.30pm).

The Lac Inférieur (Lower Lake) is over 1000m/1100yds long and 1.5m/ 5ft deep. Visitors who are not content merely to walk round the lake can take a ferry from the west side to the two islands, on one of which is a café-restaurant, or can hire a rowing boat at the north end of the lake. There is also a footpath round the Lac Supérieur (Upper Lake), which is 400m/440yds long and, like the Lower Lake, is man-made.

Lac Inférieur
Lac Supérieur

On the west side of the Lac Supérieur is the Auteuil racecourse, opened in 1850. The main stand is on the side of a low hill, the Butte Mortemart, formed from soil excavated from the two lakes. Steeplechasing only (mid February to end of April, end of May to mid July, mid October to mid December).

Hippodrome d'Auteuil

Longchamp racecourse, opened in 1857, is one of the largest of the kind in the world, with room for 10,000 spectators (May and September–October).

Hippodrome de Longchamp

The Jardin d'Acclimatation, now a children's amusement park, was originally a zoo (in which some episodes of Proust's "À la Recherche du Temps Perdu" are set). Among the attractions for young visitors are animal enclosures, donkey rides, a miniature railway, a traffic training circuit, a karting track, a skateboarding rink, fair booths, a children's museum and a theatre (open: daily 10am–6pm).

Jardin d'Acclimatation

At 6 Avenue du Mahatma-Gandhi is the Musée National des Arts et Traditions Populaires (Folk Museum; open: daily except Tue. 10am–5.15pm).

Musée National des Arts et Traditions Populaires

Bois de Vincennes

See Vincennes

Boulevards

The word boulevard, which is cognate with the English "bulwark", is applied to a street or avenue laid out on the line of old fortifications which have been demolished. It can be seen from a plan of the city how Paris has grown outwards from its original nucleus on the Ile de la Cité in a series of ever wider rings.

The first ring, on the line of the 14th century town walls, is formed by the Boulevards Beaumarchais and du Temple, the "Grand Boulevards" Saint-Martin, Saint-Denis, Bonne-Nouvelle, Poissonnière, Montmartre, des Italiens, des Capucines, de la Madeleine and – linked by Rue Royale, Place de la Concorde (see entries) and the Pont de la Concorde – the Boulevard Saint-Germain on the left bank of the Seine.

The principal streets in the second ring are the Boulevards Rochechouart and de Clichy to the north, de Courcelles to the west, de Grenelle and du Montparnasse to the south and Picpus and de Charonne to the east.

The third ring is the Boulevard Périphérique Intérieur, all the streets in which are named after generals and marshals, and the fourth is the Boulevard Périphérique Extérieur, the ring motorway which marks the present boundary of the city.

The town-planning programme carried through by Baron Haussmann between 1853 and 1870 completely transformed the city, with the construction of the boulevards, railway stations, the first market halls and department stores, five new bridges and extensive new parks. Haussmann's plan, which involved the demolition of almost 30,000 houses and the rehousing of 300,000 people, had several objects in view. In addition to the embellishment of the city by the construction of imposing new buildings he had in mind mainly economic necessities. The new traffic arteries made possible the rapid transport and faster circulation of goods and people between different parts of the city, and between railway stations, market halls and department stores in particular. And finally the broad boulevards had advantages from the point of view of military strategy, making for faster movement and better control if it became necessary to deploy troops.

From the beginning the Grands Boulevards became popular places of promenade, where people went to see and be seen, to visit a restaurant or go to the theatre. The terms boulevard theatre and boulevard paper came to reflect the things that attracted people on the boulevards – noise, sensation, spectacle. In our own day these attractions are provided by cinemas, gaming saloons and discothèques.

The western end of the Grands Boulevards, round the Opéra-Garnier, is a fashionable area, with expensive boutiques and restaurants. In and around the Faubourgs Montmartre, Saint-Denis and Saint-Martin in the eastern part of the city visitors will get a better impression of ordinary everyday life in a big city.

Grands Boulevards

Boulevard Saint-Michel   H 5–7

The Boulevard Saint-Michel (Boul' Mich' for short), on the boundary between the 5th and 6th arrondissements, runs south from the Seine, crosses the Boulevard Saint-Germain and continues past Place de la Sorbonne on the left and the Jardin du Luxembourg (see entry) on the right to the Port-Royal RER station, where it meets the Boulevard du Montparnasse and the Boulevard de Port-Royal.

The Saint-Michel Métro station is a popular meeting-place; and whether the rendezvous is in front of the Fontaine Saint-Michel or in one of the numerous cafés round the square this is a good starting-point for walks along the Quais flanking the Seine, to the Cité, in the Quartier Latin, to Saint-Germain-des-Prés or up the boulevard to the Jardin du Luxembourg (see entries).

If you are looking for shoes or the latest style in jeans or some little bit of nonsense or other, the shops along the Boul' Mich' offer a wide choice, as do the street traders with their various displays of Indian shawls, leather goods, Far Eastern perfumes and jewellery.

During the school and university year (October to June) the boulevard is busy with schoolchildren and students from all over the world. In the summer months the crowds consist mainly of tourists, who are sometimes disappointed to meet only their own kind. It is more interesting to explore the little side streets of the Quartier Latin to left and right of the boulevard with their numerous restaurants and cafés.

Location
Centre, on left bank of Seine
(5th and 6th arr.)

Métro stations
Saint-Michel, Cluny-La Sorbonne

RER stations
Luxembourg, Port-Royal

Buses
21, 27, 38, 85

◀ *The Café Flore – today the meeting place of the younger generation of writers*

Bourse (des Valeurs) H 4

Location
Place de la
Bourse
(2nd arr.)

Métro station
Bourse

Buses
20, 29, 39, 48, 74,

Like other buildings dating from the time of Napoleon, such as the Arc de Triomphe and the Madeleine, the Stock Exchange (by A.-T. Brongniart, 1808–27) is neo-classical in style. The original plan was in the form of a Greek temple; the side wings, giving it a cruciform ground-plan, date only from 1902–03.

Trading in the Exchange reaches its peak around midday. From the gallery (reached by stairs in the vestibule on the left) visitors can watch the hectic activity of the brokers and speculators. Most of them will understand little of what is going on, and will welcome the audio-visual aids which give an introduction to the work of the Exchange; for information, apply in the gallery (open: Mon.–Fri. 1.30 – 4pm).

Catacombs H 7

Location
Place Denfert-
Rochereau
(14th arr.)

Métro station
Denfert-
Rochereau

Buses
38, 68

Opening times
Tue.–Fri.
2–4pm;
Sat. and Sun.
9–11am and 2–
4pm

**Admission
charge**

Under Paris, extending over something like a third of its area, is a network of quarries and shafts which from the 11th to the 19th century supplied building material to meet the ever-growing needs of the city. Most of them are under the three hills of Montparnasse, Montrouge and Montsouris. Here medieval stonemasons quarried the limestone blocks for Notre-Dame, and from here too came the masses of stone required for Haussmann's 19th century transformation of Paris. Particularly sought-after was the gypsum of Montmartre, which was exported as far afield as America; the last shafts were closed down only in 1860. Also within Paris's underground labyrinth are huge caverns dating from Roman times, road tunnels, underground car parks and Métro lines; there is even an underground canal, the Canal Saint-Martin, carrying a traffic of barges between Bastille and Place de la République.

This mysterious underground world has fascinated many writers. Thus a skeleton found at the turn of the century during the construction of a reservoir of water for firefighting under the Opéra-Garnier inspired Gaston Leroux's "Phantom of the Opera" (1910), which in turn has been filmed and presented on the stage, most recently in Andrew Lloyd Webber's successful musical.

The existence of these workings under the city has frequently given rise to problems. In 1774 a cavity 30m/100ft deep opened up in Rue d'Enfer (now Rue Denfert-Rochereau); in 1880 a 20m/65ft stretch of the Boulevard Saint-Michel collapsed; and in 1961 an area of 6 hectares/15 acres subsided. From time immemorial, too, this system of underground passages and chambers served as a refuge for thieves and smugglers. During the Second World War they housed the headquarters of the Resistance.

Although entry to the catacombs is now prohibited, they still tempt many caving enthusiasts to explore them, and necrophiliacs have sometimes excavated for human remains. On security grounds many of the entrances are now blocked up.

The only official entrance to the catacombs is at the Barrière d'Enfer, the old customs checkpoint in Place Denfert-Rochereau (Entrance No. 1). From 1786 until the mid 19th century the abandoned quarries were used to store human remains from the many graveyards in Paris which were cleared to make way for new districts of the city. On the model of the catacombs of Rome and Naples, the remains, arranged according to the graveyards from which they came, were stacked high against the walls of the winding passages. For a visit to this hidden underworld it is advisable to take a pocket torch.

Egouts de Paris   See entry

Cemeteries

The cemeteries described below are open at the following times: March 16th to November 5th 7.30am–6pm, November 6th to March 15th 8.30am–5pm; Sundays from 9am.

Opening times

Main entrance: Rue Rachel, under the bridge (18th arr.).
Métro station: Place de Clichy; buses: 30, 54, 68, 74, 80, 81, 95.
This cemetery, the third largest in Paris, was opened in 1795. It contains the graves of Heinrich Heine, Jean-Honoré Fragonard and Hector Berlioz (Avenue Hector Berlioz), Théophile Gautier (Avenue Cordier), Edgar Degas (Avenue de Montebello), Jacques Offenbach (Avenue des Anglais), Stendhal (Avenue de la Croix), Emile Zola (Carrefour de la Croix), François Truffaut, Samuel Beckett and many other notable figures.

Cimetière de Montmartre G/H 2

Main entrance: Boulevard Edgar-Quinet (14th arr.).
Métro stations: Edgar Quinet, Raspail.
This is Paris's second largest cemetery, opened in 1824. It contains the graves of Charles Baudelaire, Ossip Zadkine and Tristan Tzara (Avenue de l'Ouest), César Franck and Guy de Maupassant (Avenue du Boulevard), André Citroân (Avenue Thierry), Camille Saint-Saâns and Vincent d'Indy (Avenue du Nord) and the double grave of Jean-Paul Sartre and Simone de Beauvoir (section 20, to right of entrance).

Cimetière du Montparnasse G 7

Main entrance: Boulevard de Ménilmontant (20th arr.).
Métro stations: Père Lachaise, Philippe Auguste; Buses: 61, 69.
Paris's largest (44 hectares/100 acres) and most beautiful cemetery, named after Louis XIV's confessor, Père La Chaise, was laid out in 1804 on land belonging to the Jesuits. It contains the grave of the last Communards, who were shot here against the Mur des Fédérés in

★Cimetière du Père-Lachaise M 5

Montparnasse Cemetery: Double grave of Jean-Paul Sartre and Simone de Beauvoir

1871, and a memorial to those who died in Nazi concentration camps. Among the many famous people buried here are Molière (Jean-Baptiste Poquelin), Jean de La Fontaine, Honoré Balzac, Marcel Proust, Gérard de Nerval, Eugène Delacroix, Frédéric Chopin, Oscar Wilde, Guillaume Apollinaire, Alfred de Musset, Jean-Louis David, Dr Guillotin (inventor of the guillotine), Edith Piaf, Colette, Gertrude Stein, Max Ernst, Paul Eluard, Modigliani, Maria Callas, Jim Morrison, Serge Gainsbourg, Simone Signoret and Yves Montand. To the east of the Avenue Principale is the old Jewish part of the cemetery, with the graves of Camille Pissaro, Rothschild and Singer. A plan with a list of the graves can be obtained at the entrance.

Cimetière de Passy
D 5

Entrance: 2 Avenue Paul-Doumer (16th arr.).
Métro station: Trocadéro.
This cemetery contains the graves of prominent people who have died since 1870, including Edouard Manet, Jean Giraudoux, Gabriel Fauré, Claude Debussy, Tristan Bernard and Fernandel.

★★Centre Pompidou/Beaubourg   J 5

Location
Rue Rambuteau/
Rue Saint-Martin
(4th arr.)

Métro stations
Rambuteau,
Hôtel de Ville,
Châtelet-Les
Halles

Address
F-75191 Paris
Cedex 04

RER station
Châtelet-
Les Halles

Buses
21, 29, 38, 47, 58,
67, 70, 72, 74, 75,
76, 81, 85, 96

Between the Halles district and the Marais (see entries) is the Centre Pompidou (Centre National d'Art et de Culture Georges Pompidou), which since it was opened in 1977 had become one of Paris's major attractions, corner with over seven million visitors a year. This house of culture with the character of a workshop covers a wide range of activities. It was designed as a centre for creative work and the exchange of information, presenting art, architecture, design, literature and music in a setting in which they could interact and supplement one another. The Centre Pompidou houses the National Museum of Modern Art (Musée National d'Art Moderne, MNAM), the Centre of Industrial Design (Centre de Création Industrielle, CCI), an institute of contemporary music (IRCAM), a library (Bibliothèque Publique d'Information, BPI), a graphics room, the Brancusi studio and the Centre Wallonie-Bruxelles. On its six floors there are concerts, modern operas and experimental ballets, and outside, on the forecourt, there is a lively mix of entertainers, buskers and fire-eaters.

An architectural competition for the building of the Centre Pompidou which attracted almost 700 entries from 50 different countries was won by a young architectural team, the British architect Richard Rogers and the Italian Renzo Piano, who were also responsible for the extension of IRCAM. Under their direction there took shape, over a period of five years and at a cost of almost a billion francs, a building which immediately sparked off a lively controversy. Its opponents see it as a "monstrosity", a "Utopian oil refinery"; its supporters see in the Centre Beaubourg (Beaubourg is the name of the district) a contribution towards making Paris on the threshold of the 21st century what it was from the end of the 19th century to the Second World War, the art capital of the world.

This structure of steel and glass, 166m/545ft long, 60m/197ft wide and 42m/138ft high, does indeed resemble a refinery. All the services (electricity, etc.) are in brightly coloured ducts on the outside of the east front, and on the other side are lifts and a "glass caterpillar" containing escalators. In one respect, however, the Centre Beaubourg can be compared with a very different Paris monument, the Cathedral of Notre-Dame (see entry). With its complex structure fully exposed to view, it shares with Notre-Dame a fundamental architectural principle: all the load-bearing elements of the structure are on the outside of the building, and as a result the internal space (150m/490ft by 50m/165ft) on the ground floor and five upper floors is free of all bearing elements and can thus be arranged in any way desired – a great advantage for temporary exhibitions.

House of Culture with the character of a workshop – the Centre Pompidou

The main objective of the Centre Beaubourg was not to assemble documentation and display museum collections but to foster creativity and artistic production. Although less emphasis is now laid on the original idea of a close relationship between conservators, artists and the public and the artists now tend to exhibit their works in the centre rather than create them there, while the public go rather to see than to participate, the Centre Pompidou still tries to remain true to the basic idea of a contemporary cultural centre. It is in line with the government's new cultural policy, too, that the French regions are represented in exhibitions and events in the Centre and that exhibitions organised by the Centre are shown in provincial museums.

In 1991, in order to solve serious functional problems which had emerged in recent years and to improve co-ordination between different departments of the Centre the Minister of Culture, Jack Lang, invited the new director of the Centre, Dominique Bozo (who died in 1993) to reorganise the Centre. Thereupon MNAM and CCI were combined in a single department and a new department for research and the teaching of art was established.

In 1996 the architects Rogers and Piano were asked to re-design the Brancusi Studio, which re-opened in 1997. In the tent on the forecourt visitors can obtain information about progress in the re-organisation of the Culture Centre; work is expected to last until the end of 1999. Details are also available in the information tent regarding current events (Mon., Wed.–Fri., Sun. 12.30–6pm, Sat. 2–6pm).

Re-organisation work in progress until 1999
Information
tel. 01 44 78 12 33

An escalator runs up through the "glass caterpillar" to the Bibliothèque Publique d'Information, which from 1999 will be housed in the Galerie Nord (1st and 2nd floors). Visitors can consult some half a million books free of charge. There are also collections of slides, videos and microfilms available for consultation, and a "médiathèque" with

Bibliothèque Publique d'Information (BP)

learning programmes in 95 languages. Until re-organisation is completed in 1999 the library is housed at 11 rue Brantome; for information tel. 01 44 78 12 75.

Musée National d'Art Moderne (MNAM)

On the third and fourth floors is the Museum of Modern Art, a large collection beginning with the Fauves (Matisse and Bonnard), continuing with Cubism (Picasso, Braque, Léger) and Surrealism (Dali, Ernst, Magritte), Abstract Expressionism (de Staâl and Poliakoff, and Pop Art (Warhol, Oldenburg). There is also an outstanding collection of modern sculpture (Arp, Moore, Giacometti, Calder, Laurens and Duchamp-Villon).

Centre de Création Industrielle (CCI)

The Centre of Industrial Design, on the mezzanine floor, houses a collection of plans, models and industrial objects which are displayed in rotation.

Galerie d'Exposition, restaurant

The fifth floor is reserved for temporary exhibitions of modern art and biographies of artists. From the café-restaurant there is an extensive view over the roofs of Paris.

IRCAM

Considerably extended in 1996, the adjoining Institut de Recherche et de Coordination Acoustique/Musique is devoted to research and development in the field of contemporary music. The present director, appointed in 1991, is Laurent Bayle, who is concerned to promote closer co-operation with the other elements of the Centre. The building is open to the public only for concerts (for information tel. 01 44 78 49 43).

Atelier Brancusi

On the forecourt on rue Rambuteau a small two-part building – now re-opened after extensive restoration work – houses the studio of the Romanian sculptor Constantin Brancusi (1876–1957) with a lovingly

The IRCAM devoted to the development of contemporary music

assembled collection of his work (open: Mon., Wed.–Fri. noon–10pm, Sat., Sun. 10am–10pm).

The Atelier des Enfants, which caters for children between the ages of 5 and 13, puts on periodic special exhibitions and has a workshop equipped with toys; for information tel. 01 44 78 47 06.

Atelier des Enfants

Events held in the Centre Wallonie-Bruxelles on rue Saint-Martin (entrance at 46 rue Quincampoix) include concerts, literary readings and films in memory of the famous director; for information tel. 01 44 78 44 22.

Centre Wallonie-Bruxelles

The south side of the Centre on rue Saint-Meri is adorned with sixteen colourful fountain sculptures by the Parisian sculptress Niki de Saint Phalle and her partner of many years, the Swiss sculptor Jean Tinguely. The rotating fountain is named after the ballet of the same name by the Russian composer Ivor Stravinsky; the square itself is similarly named.

★Fontaine Le Sacre du Printemps

Centre National de la Photographie

See Palais de Tokyo

Champ-de-Mars   E/F 5

The Champ-de-Mars (Field of Mars), originally (1765) a military training ground, is now a large park-like area between the Eiffel Tower (see Tour Eiffel) and the Ecole Militaire (see entry).
   In 1780 Paris's first horse race, between a British and a French rider, was held here. In 1783 and 1784 the Champ-de-Mars was the scene of two spectacular (unmanned) balloon flights. During the French Revolution the Festival of Federation was celebrated here on July 14th 1790, when Louis XVI and representatives of all the French provinces swore to uphold the new constitution, which established a constitutional monarchy on the British model; and it was here too, after the royal family's unsuccessful attempt to flee from Paris, that the Paris mob called for their death.
   In 1794 the painter Jacques-Louis David organised a festival in honour of the "Supreme Being" (Être Suprème) who was to be worshipped in the new state religion proclaimed by Robespierre. This was the climax of Robespierre's reign of terror: four months later he too lost his head on the guillotine. In 1867, 1878, 1899, 1900 and 1937 a series of international exhibitions were held on the Champ-de-Mars, extending in each case along the banks of the Seine.

Location
Western Paris (7th arr.)

Métro stations
Ecole Militaire, Bir Hakeim

Buses
28, 42, 49, 69, 80, 82, 87, 92

★★Champs-Elysées   E–G 4

The Avenue des Champs-Elysées, the most famous and most splendid of Paris's broad avenues, just under 2km/1¼ miles long, is divided into two parts by the Rond-Point des Champs-Elysées, its largest intersection. The upper part, extending to the Arc de Triomphe (see entry), is lined by luxury shops and hotels, innumerable restaurants and pavement

Location
Between Arc de Triomphe and Place de la Concorde (8th arr.)

The Champs-Elysées is lined with elegant shopping arcades and friendly pavement cafés

Métro stations
George V, Franklin D. Roosevelt, Champs-Elysées-Clemenceau

Buses
28, 32, 42, 49, 73, 80, 83, 93

cafés, cinemas and theatres, the offices of the big banks and international airlines – and now increasingly by fast food outlets and souvenir stalls. This is the meeting-place of all the world, in a confusion of many tongues. The lower part of the Champs-Elysées, towards Place de la Concorde, is flanked by gardens in which are museums, theatres and a number of restaurants.

Until the end of the 16th century this area consisted of fields and marshland. At the beginning of the 17th century the first road in the area, the Cours de la Reine, was built along the Seine from the Tuileries palace. After the completion of the Tuileries the landscape gardener Le Nôtre laid out a broad, shady avenue running from there up the hill which is now topped by the Arc de Triomphe. In the early 18th century this avenue was named the Champs-Elysées (Elysian Fields), but was not further improved until it became the property of the city on 1828. The Champs-Elysées as a whole now form part of the *voie triomphale* (triumphal way) which was completed in the reign of Napoleon III, running from the Arc de Triomphe de l'Etoile by way of Place de la Concorde to the Arc de Triomphe du Carrousel. This magnificent main axis of Paris now extends from the Pyramid in the Louvre to the Grande Arche at La Défense (see entries).

The renovation of the Champs-Elysées which was begun by Jacques Chirac in 1991 and completed in 1995 is designed to restore the avenue's legendary charm by restructuring and redesigning the terraces flanking the street. The parking places have been beautifully repaved and are now reserved for pedestrians, gaps in the lines of plane trees have been filled and sick trees replaced, and historic buildings have been restored in the original style. In addition the George V Metro station has been enlarged and a large underground car park with room for 850 cars has been constructed at the corner of Rue de Washington and Rue La Boétie.

Between Place de la Concorde and the Champs-Elysées are the "Horses of Marly", two fine Baroque sculptures by Guillaume Coustou which were set up here in 1796.

In the lower part of the Champs-Elysées are bronze sculptures of corpulent figures by the Colombian sculptor Botero, presented to the city by Mayor Jacques Chirac at the beginning of the nineties.

Horses of Marly

One of the most renowned fashion streets in Paris, Avenue Montaigne, branches off the Champs-Elysées at the Rond-Point and runs, straight as a die, to Place de l'Alma on the banks of the Seine. The old mansions in this street are now occupied by the great *haute couture* houses – Christian Dior, Celine, Ungaro, Hanae Mort, Jean-Louis Scherrer, Valentino, Nino Ricci – whose fashion shows attract wealthy Parisiennes.

Avenue Montaigne

Chantilly

The little town of Chantilly (pop. 12,500), famed for its racecourse and black pillow lace, lies on N 16, a little way west of Senlis. The château and its park are a popular destination for excursions from Paris.

Chantilly takes its name from a Roman named Cantilius who built a villa on the island here. In the Middle Ages the site of the villa was occupied by a castle which passed by marriage into the hands of the Montmorency family. At the beginning of the 16th century the castle was rebuilt by Pierre Chambiges in Renaissance style. During the 17th and 18th centuries Chantilly was the residence of the Condé family, a collateral branch of the royal House of Bourbon. Here the famous chef Vatel served Louis XIV for the first time with whipped cream, thereafter known as crème Chantilly.

During the French Revolution the Grand Château was almost completely destroyed, but the Petit Château survived almost unscathed. The Grand Château was rebuilt in Renaissance style by Daumet in 1875–81 for the Duc d'Aumale, fifth son of King Louis-Philippe. Dying without heirs in 1897, he bequeathed the property, with its art treasures and valuable library, to the Institut de France (see entry).

Location
40km/25 miles N of Paris (N 16)

Rail service
Departure: Gare du Nord

Opening times
Châteaux:
Daily except Tues.
Mar.–Oct.
10am–6pm
Nov.–Feb.
10.30am–12.45pm, 2–5pm

The Grand Château now houses the Musée Condé. The Picture Gallery contains works by Italian, Flemish, French and British masters from the Renaissance to the 19th century, including Raphael, the Carracci, Van Dyck, Watteau, Delacroix, Ingres, Reynolds and 40 miniatures from a Renaissance prayer-book.

The finest item of the Cabinet des Gemmes is the valuable pink diamond known as the Grand Condé after its owner.

Grand Château
★Musée Condé

The 16th century Petit Château is also open to the public. The most notable features are the sumptuously appointed rooms, the chapel with its magnificent high altar and above all the valuable library in the Galerie des Livres (Book Gallery), with almost 13,000 rare books and 1500 manuscripts. Its principal treasure is the Duc de Berry's prayer-book, "Les Très Riches Heures du Duc de Berry", with illuminations by the Limburg brothers (early 15th century).

Petit Château
★Galerie des Livres

The enchanting park round the châteaux was laid out in 1663 by the royal gardener André Le Nôtre, who equipped it, on the model of Versailles, with a large canal, an antique temple and a romantic Island of Love. Other attractive features of the park are a little hunting lodge, the 17th century Maison de Sylvie, a tennis court (Jeu de Paume) of 1756 and the 18th century Hameau, a reconstruction of a little village which served as a setting for the pastoral plays then in vogue.

Park

Grandes Ecuries
Musée Vivant du
Cheval

To the west of the château are the Grandes Ecuries (Great Stables) and the world-famous Chantilly racecourse, laid out in 1834. The palatial stables, just under 190m/210yds long, were built in 1791 by Louis-Henri of Bourbon, 7th Count of Condé (who was persuaded that he would be reborn as a horse) and at one time accommodated up to 240 horses and over 500 dogs.

The stables are now occupied by the Musée Vivant du Cheval (Living Museum of the Horse), where visitors can see a large collection of exhibits illustrating the history of the horse as well as about 30 living horses. There are also daily riding displays by riders in historic costume, to the accompaniment of music, singing and dancing. Open: Apr.–Oct.: Mon., Wed.–Fri. 10.30am–5.30pm, Sat., Sun., 10.30am–6.30pm: Nov.–Mar., Mon., Wed.–Fri., 2pm–5pm, Sat., Sun.: 10.30–5.30pm: tel 03 44 57 40 40.

Châtelet   J 5

Location
Place du Châtelet
(4th arr.)

Métro station
Châtelet-les
Halles

Buses
21, 38, 47, 58, 67,
69, 72, 74, 75, 76,
81, 85, 96

Théâtre Musical
de Paris

Théâtre de la Ville

Place du Châtelet and the large Châtelet Métro station are named after the Grand Châtelet, a 12th century fortress built to protect the Ile de la Cité (see entry). It was later used as a prison, and thereafter was the seat of the Provost of Paris (Prévot des Marchands; see Hôtel de Ville).

In 1802 Napoleon had the fortress pulled down, and during the Second Empire two theatres were built on its site: on the west side of the square the Théâtre du Châtelet, with a façade in Italian Renaissance style, and on the east side the Théâtre Sarah Bernhardt. For many years the Théâtre du Châtelet specialised in operetta and ballet, until in 1980, after extensive renovation, it became a National Theatre and was renamed the Théâtre Musical de Paris. Its programme now includes operas, musicals and concerts. The gallery (modernised in 1989) is decorated with a work by Garouste. The theatre on the opposite side of the square, now known as the Théâtre de la Ville, was acquired in 1899 by the famous actress Sarah Bernhardt, who enjoyed great triumphs here with her interpretations of "La Dame aux Camélias" and "Tosca". The theatre's programme ranges from classic modern plays to performances by visiting ballet companies with renowned choreographers.

Tour
Saint-Jacques

Between Place du Châtelet and Rue de Rivoli is the Tour Saint-Jacques, the Late Gothic tower of the old parish church of Saint-Jacques-de-la- Boucherie (patron saint of butchers), which was built by Jean de Félin between 1508 and 1522.

In the Middle Ages this church was the assembly point for pilgrims setting out on the pilgrimage to Santiago de Compostela in northwestern Spain, the legendary burial-place of the Apostle James (in Spanish Santiago) and one of the three great places of pilgrimage of medieval Christendom (the others being Jerusalem and Rome). The pilgrims, coming from the north along Rue Saint-Martin, continued on their way south along Rue Saint-Jacques.

On the tower (52m/170ft high) is a statue of St James.

The emblem of the pilgrims was a scallop-shell, the coquille Saint-Jacques which has long been famed as a culinary delicacy.

★Cité   H/J 5/6

Location
Centre
(1st and 4th arr.)

The Ile de la Cité is the historical and geographical centre of Paris. Here, on the little island protected by two arms of the Seine, a Celtic tribe, the Parisii, established a settlement in the 3rd century B.C. Here

A wrought-iron gate from the time of Louis XVI marks the entrance to the Law Courts

too the Romans built the Gallo-Roman city of Lutetia, and here the inhabitants of the city sought refuge during raids by Germanic tribes, Norsemen and Huns. It was only in the High Middle Ages that the city was able to establish a durable presence on the two banks of the Seine and a centre of power and authority. From the 6th to the 14th century the kings of France resided on the island, on which were the secular palace (see Palais de Justice) and its religious counterpart, Notre-Dame, the "Cathedral of France". When the royal residence was transferred elsewhere the aspect of the Ile de la Cité changed, since it was no longer necessary to have spacious streets and squares for the festivities of the court. There now grew up a dense huddle of narrow lanes and closely packed houses in the shadow of the Gothic towers of Notre-Dame. In the 19th century the aspect of the Cité was again radically altered by Baron Haussmann. In a massive campaign of clearance and redevelopment which involved the rehousing of more than 25,000 people space was cleared for the broad avenues running north-south through Paris, the Préfecture de Police, the Tribunal de Commerce, the extension to the Palais de Justice and the rebuilding of the Hôtel-Dieu, and an unobstructed view of Notre-Dame was opened up on all sides. With only a few exceptions the historic core of the city was transformed, so that the Cité is no longer the "old town" of Paris in the sense in which that term is usually employed.

A walk round the Ile de la Cité offers a series of fine views of the Seine with its bridges and the panorama of Paris on both banks of the river. The main sights on the island itself are Notre-Dame, the Sainte-Chapelle, the Conciergerie and the Palais de Justice (see entries). Other features of interest include the following:

Métro station
Cité

RER station
St-Michel-Notre-Dame

Buses
21, 24, 27, 38, 47, 81, 85, 96

Tour

Cité

Square du Vert-Galant

The little garden at the north-western tip of the island commemorates Henri IV, who was known as the Vert Galant ("Lusty Gallant"). There is an equestrian statue of the king on the terrace above the garden, a place frequented by lovers and street entertainers.

Place Dauphine

South-east of the Square du Vert-Galant, beyond the Pont Neuf, is Place Dauphine, which dates from the time of Henri IV – one of the finest architectural ensembles of that period in Paris. In 1607 the wealthy Président (Chief Justice) Achille de Harlay was given the site by the king with instructions to build a complex of houses with uniform façades. He built 65 terraced houses of light-coloured stone and red brick, with two storeys over an arcaded ground floor. The square, named after the Dauphin, the future Louis XIII, soon became the resort of actors, quack doctors, strollers and the merely curious. In 1872 the whole of the east side of the square, on Rue de Harlay, was pulled down and replaced by houses in neo-classical style. The only houses which survive from the original square are Nos. 14 and 26.

Hôtel-Dieu

The barrack-like Hôtel-Dieu, a hospital, was built in 1868–78 on the site of a 7th century convent whose nuns were dedicated to the care of the sick and the needy. The Hôtel-Dieu can thus claim to be one of the oldest hospitals in Europe.

Rue des Ursins

The little streets to the north of Notre-Dame have retained some flavour of the past. Among them is Rue des Ursins, which was largely spared by Haussmann's transformation of Paris. From the Quai aux Fleurs, where the flower market is held, there is a view of the ivy-clad front of No. 21 (La Colombe restaurant), with a small plate giving the original name of the street, Rue d'Enfer (Hell Street) – so called because of the tunnel-like character of the narrow little street. The adjoining building (No. 19) is all that is left of the Romanesque chapel

Gothic figures on the west front of Notre-Dame

of Saint-Aignan, which along with Notre-Dame and the Sainte-Chapelle is one of the last three of the 23 churches which once stood on the island.

At the south-east corner of the square in front of Notre-Dame, at the end of the Pont au Double, is the little Square Charlemagne, with a statue of Charlemagne.

Square Charlemagne

This monument, at the south-eastern tip of the island, commemorates those who were deported to German concentration camps during the Second World War.

Mémorial de la Déportation

Collège de France   J 6

The Collège de France, originally known as the Collège des Trois Langues, is one of the most celebrated academic centres of teaching and research in France. The original building, with three wings round an arcaded courtyard (designed by Chalgrin, 1778), was considerably extended in the 19th century and again in 1930.

Location
Rue des Ecoles/
rue St-Jacques
(5th arr.)

The Collège des Trois Langues (College of the Three Languages), also known as the Collège des Lecteurs Royaux (College of the Royal Lecturers), was founded in 1530 by François I, who thus established his reputation as "father and restorer of learning". An admirer of the Italian Renaissance, he desired to create a centre of learning independent of the Church in which the three languages of antiquity – Hebrew, Greek and Latin – would be studied, as in Italy, on the basis of the original texts. The lecturers were paid by the king himself and not, as was the normal practice, by the students.

Métro stations
Cluny-La
Sorbonne,
Maubert
Mutualité,
Saint-Michel

Buses
47, 63, 86, 87

The freedom of the teaching staff from any academic constraints and the students' freedom of access to lectures without payment of any fee have been maintained down to the present day. The Collège de France, however, differs from the Sorbonne in granting no degrees, diplomas or titles. Its teaching programme now extends to almost all the humanities and the natural sciences.

Opening times
Seen by
appointment:
apply at entrance

Among the best known professors who have taught at the Collège de France are the physicist André Ampère, the historian Jules Michelet, the writer and poet Paul Valéry, the philosopher Henri Bergson, the ethnologist Claude Lévi-Strauss, the philosopher Michel Foucault and the literary critic Roland Barthes.

Comédie Française

See Théâtre Français

Conciergerie   H/J 5

The Conciergerie, originally part of the medieval palace of the Capetian kings (see Cité) and later a prison which achieved a melancholy fame during the French Revolution, is now a museum and also a popular venue for concerts. Part of the building is used as a remand prison attached to the adjoining Palais de Justice (see entry).

Location
1 quai de
l'Horloge
(1st arr.)

The three High Gothic halls of the Conciergerie were built around 1300, in the reign of Philippe le Bel, and these are the only parts of the original palace that survive. In those days the castellan of the palace and the head of the royal household was known as the Concierge (a term which has come down in the world to mean the caretaker of a

Métro stations
Cité, Châtelet

Buses
21, 24, 27, 38, 81,
85, 96

► The Grande Arche at La Défense: a 110m-high triumphal arch of white Carrara marble

Opening times
Apr. 1 to Sept. 30, daily 9.30am–6.30pm;
Oct. 1 to Mar. 31, daily 10am–5pm

Admission charge

Conducted tour

block of flats). Presumably he also had some kind of judicial authority, since the building soon became the palace prison and later a state prison. Among those confined here were the murderers of Henri IV and the Duc de Berry, Charlotte Corday (who killed Marat), Marie-Antoinette, Danton and Robespierre.

From the Quai de la Mégisserie on the opposite side of the Seine there is a good view of the Conciergerie, with its 19th century neo-Gothic façade, its three round towers and the Tour de l'Horloge (Clock Tower), in which Paris's first public clock was installed around 1370 (destroyed in 1793 and restored in the 19th century). The entrance to the Conciergerie is on the Quai de l'Horloge, to the right.

Visitors first enter the 14th century Salle des Gardes (Guard Room), with heavy vaulting borne on massive piers, the capitals of which are richly decorated (animal fights, etc.). The adjoining Salle des Gens d'Armes (Hall of the Men-at-Arms), the dining room of the palace's armed guard, is a jewel of Gothic secular architecture (by Philippe de Bels, 1285–1314). Measuring 70 by 30 metres (230 by 100 feet), it has ribbed vaulting supported on three rows of pillars.

The kitchens, dating from around 1350, were equipped to cater for banquets with two or three thousand guests and drew their supplies directly from boats on the Seine, since in those days there was no quay. The open fireplaces were large enough to roast oxen whole.

The Rue de Paris, a passage separated from the Salle des Gens d'Armes by a grating, was so called after the executioner, known as Monsieur de Paris, to whom the condemned prisoners were handed over here. The Salle des Girondins, originally the palace chapel, was used during the Revolution as a special prison for supporters of the Girondist party (opponents of the Jacobin dictatorship). In this room are displayed a variety of relics of the bloody days of the Terror, include a guillotine blade, prison regulations and a facsimile of Marie-Antoinette's last letter. The Rue de Paris continues to the prisons, including the cell in which Marie-Antoinette was confined after an unsuccessful attempt to rescue her. Here, after a trial lasting 20 hours, she awaited execution, like thousands of other prisoners of the Revolution. Visitors are also shown the cell in which Danton and later Robespierre were imprisoned before going to the guillotine.

★La Défense   A/B 2

In the west of the city, at the end of Avenue Charles-de-Gaulle, which continues the main east-west axis of Paris (Champs-Elysées-Arc de Triomphe-Avenue de la Grande-Armée), is La Défense, a complex of high-rise blocks developed since the mid sixties. The name La Défense recalls the bitter resistance by French forces in this area

Location
Western outskirts

La Défense

Métro station
Esplanade de
la Défense

RER station
Grande Arche de
la Défense

during the Franco- Prussian War of 1870–71. Nowadays it is seen as heralding Paris's entry into the 21st century.

The layout of this new business district of futuristic aspect gives effect to the two principles of urban planning, functionality and the separation of vehicular and pedestrian traffic, laid down by Le Corbusier in the thirties. Motor traffic is confined to a ring road round the outside of the district and the Métro and RER run underground, there are expanses of open space and gardens between the skyscrapers, and the area round the Esplanade de la Défense is diversified by the multiple jets of the Agam Fountain and works of sculpture such as the "Grand Toscano" (by Igor Mitoraj, 1983) on the Plan de la Coupole. The high-rise office blocks are occupied mainly by large French and international financial, computer and oil companies – EDF, ELF, CGE, Total, Saint-Gobain, IBM, Mobil, Unilever, Hitachi, etc. – employing over 100,000 people. Thus La Défense is mainly a business district, though it also has housing for over 20,000 people, with a large shopping centre (4 Temps) and numerous restaurants, cafés, cinemas, sports clubs and other leisure facilities. Cultural needs are catered for by concerts and exhibitions, including an annual Musical Festival and a national jazz competition.

Architecture

In the almost 40 years since it was established La Défense has become a show-place of contemporary architecture, with the more recent tower blocks showing greater freedom of form than the less imaginative buildings of the sixties. Between the CNIT building of 1958 and the Grande Arche lie three generations of high-rise blocks. The first generation ranged up to a height of 100m/330ft (e.g. Roussel-Hoechst Aurora and Europe); from 1970 office blocks, on the American model, reached heights of up to 200m/660ft (GAN, Fiat, Assur, Générale, etc.); while in the eighties the emphasis was on small offices with ample daylight, energy-saving building methods and new technologies (e.g. Elysée-La Défense, Les Miroirs, ELF, Descartes). Whereas the original development plan provided for some 300,000sq.m/360,000sq.yds of office space, the present figure is already over 2.3 million sq.m/2.7 million sq.yds; and it is expected that by 2005 this area will have been doubled and that the east-west axis will have been extended by another 3.3km/2 miles. In order to strengthen the residential function of the La Défense district, however, the plan for the area to the west of the Grande Arche provides for a maximum of 600,000sq.m/720,000sq.yds of office space but twice that amount of housing accommodation. It is also planned to replace the ESSO building by 190,000sq.m/227,000sq.yds of new office space in separate groups of buildings (architects Viguier and Jodry).

CNIT

The great glory of the early years of La Défense was the huge CNIT building (Centre National des Industries et Techniques) on the Espace Benjamin-Franklin. This great vaulted structure (area 90,000sq.m/ 108,000sq.yds) in the form of an upturned shell borne on only three supports houses a large conference and business centre, the World Trade Center, a market for information technology (Informait) and a centre of business communications (IT-Com), together with shops, restaurants and a hotel.

Dôme IMAX,
Musée de
l'Automobile

Beside the spherical Dôme IMAX cinema is the Musée de l'Automobile, which illustrates the history of the automobile from its beginnings down to the present. Among the exhibits are a Hippomobile of around 1890, a Ford model T, a Rolls-Royce Phantom III dating from the 1930s and a Ferrari Dino 156 (open: daily 10am–7pm).

★Grande Arche

The Grande Arche, a huge rectangular triumphal arch 110m/360ft high faced with white Carrara marble, was inaugurated in 1989 on the bicentenary of the French Revolution: a contemporary "window on the world" and a symbol of fraternity. The architect was a Dane, Johan Otto von Spreckelsen. Among the organisations housed in the Grande Arche are an international society concerned with human rights and the action group "Future", formed by the author Martin Gray for the youth of the world. Lifts bring visitors to the viewing platform measuring 1ha/2.5 acres on the roof where temporary exhibitions are regularly held (open: daily 10am – 7pm: information tel. 01 49 07 27 27).

Beside the CNIT building another futuristic complex, the Tour sans Fin, is under construction. This 400m/1300ft high "tower without an end", designed by Jean-Marc Ibos, will provide additional office accommodation for various service industries.

Tour sans Fin

★★Disneyland · Paris

Disneyland Paris, a theme park covering an area of almost 2000 hectares/5000 acres, a gigantic fairyland of fantasy and adventure with over 50 rides in five magic lands and a variety of shows, parades and other events, was opened in April 1992. Like the whole of the French tourist trade, Disneyland was hit by the economic recession, and the further development that was planned has been postponed.

Admission tickets ("passports") for 1, 2 or 3 days (not necessarily consecutive) and annual season tickets can be bought at the main entrance to the park. Information about conducted visits, particular shows and special events can be obtained from the Guest Relations office or in City Hall on Town Square (tel. 01 64 74 30 00).
Internet: http://www.disneylandparis.com.
Advance reservations: Disneyland Paris S.C.A. BP 104 77777 Marne-la-Vallée Cedex 4 fan 01 00 30 60 65 Disneyland Paris is open April to September daily 9am–11pm, October to March, Mon.–Fri. 10am–6pm, Sat., Sun. 9am–8pm

The seven theme hotels (see Practical Information, Hotels) are within a few minutes' walk of the park. There is a bus serv-

Location
Marne-la-Vallée
32km/20 miles
E of Paris

RER station
Marne-la-Vallée-Chessy
(Line A)

Bus and rail services
Direct buses from Orly and Roissy airports
TGV station

Admission charge

With Peter Pan in Never Never Land: Captain Hook's three-masted pirate ship

ice to the Davy Crockett camping site. Other amenities for visitors are swimming pools, bicycle hire, pony rides, tennis courts and a golf course. Facilities for refreshment range from the exclusive Victorian-style Walt's Restaurant by way of a variety of specialist eateries scattered about the park to the snack wagons selling hot popcorn, hot dogs, bagels and other American-style delicacies.

Walt Disney – Creator of Dreams

Probably nobody has had a more lasting influence on the world of children in this century than Walt Elias Disney, who was born in Chicago in 1901. He may not have discovered the ideal world, but he certainly filled it with immortal figures. The "baddies" are immediately recognisable from their stubbly beards or hook-like hands, while the "goodies" are not only attractive to look at but always win in the end. There are no bloody wars, the worst afflictions being tummy-aches and sniffly colds – the greatest sins greed, envy and not keeping your room tidy. The world appears to be so wonderfully simple, as children always know it is, unlike adults.

Blessed with a bubbly passion for fantasy, Disney spent his childhood in a small town in Missouri, the Main Street of which provided the model for Main Street USA in his theme parks. From an early age he showed a remarkable talent for drawing, and in 1919–21, while working in a small advertising studio, he took classes in drawing at Kansa City Art Institute. However, he himself never actually put any of his illustrious characters down on paper as a drawing pure and simple; he inspired and motivated his colleagues to do that for him. Mickey Mouse, for example, came from the pen of Ub lwerks in 1928, and Donald Duck was the inspiration of Art Babbitt and Dick Huemer in 1934. In 1922, with his head full of ideas and 40 dollars in his pocket, Disney went to Hollywood, and in the following year, along with his brother Roy, founded the Disney Brothers Studio. He produced his first film, a five-minute short entitled "Little Red Riding Hood", in his uncle's garage in California with 300 dollars of starting capital.

On November 18th 1928 Mickey Mouse made his first appearance and Disney achieved his international breakthrough with "Steamboat Willie", the first cartoon film with synchronised sound. During the 1930s there followed a string of ninety films featuring Mickey Mouse, who became ever more popular and brought Disney world fame. In 1932 Disney successfully began producing films based on well-known fairy-tales. December 1937 saw the premiere of "Snow White and the Seven Dwarfs", the world's first full-length and completely animated cartoon film – during the three years it took to produce some 750 artists were employed in drawing nearly one million pictures by hand. One of the reasons for his success was Disney's insistence on perfection. For "Bambi" (1942), for example, he had his artists observing deer in the studio for months on end. By the middle of the thirties Mickey Mouse and company had been joined by Donald Duck and his family. Then in the late 1940s Disney produced the first of his much-praised nature and adventure films such as "The Desert Lives" or "20,000 Miles Under the Sea".

In 1955 the first Disneyland theme park was opened at Anaheim near Los Angeles. This was the realisation of a childhood dream in which Disney invested some 50 million dollars. At an admission charge of one dollar per person during its first ten years, the investment paid off. Disney did not live to see the opening of the second park in Florida – he died on December 15th 1966 during the filming of "Jungle Book" (1967). His legacy – a multi-billion dollar empire and a life's work that was to be continued to this day in the true Disney tradition – the creation of a magical fantasy world in which dreams of harmony, friendliness and peace become reality. In 1991 "Beauty and the Beast" was the first computerised animation – this romantic cartoon also received an Oscar as the best film of the year. Thanks to modern techniques the pictures in "The Hunchback of Notre-Dame" (1996) appear perfectly three-dimensional. The latest cult films "King of the Lions" (1994), "Pocahontas" (1995) and "Hercules" (1997) have also broken box-office records. And Disney's success story will surely continue for a long time yet.

Disneyland Paris

In Disneyland's busy Victorian-style Main Street USA visitors can take
a ride in a veteran automobile or a horse-tram of turn-of-the-century
vintage; in Liberty Court they can be present at the inauguration of the
Statue of Liberty in 1886; they can learn about the great inventions of
the Industrial Revolution in Discovery Arcade; they can be shaved in
the Harmony Barber Shop as in the good old days; and they may be
tempted by the nostalgic general stores with their giant lollipops,
brightly coloured ices or other delicacies.

Main Street

The best way of getting a general impression of the wonders of
Disneyland is to take a trip on the Disneyland Railroad. The train,
drawn by a steam engine, runs by way of the Grand Canyon Diorama
to Frontierland and Fantasyland Station before returning via
Discoveryland to Main Street.

Disneyland
Railroad

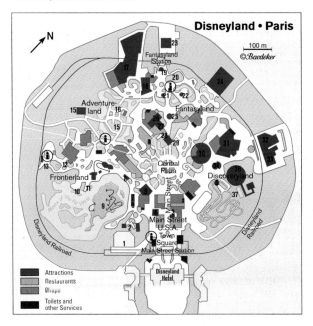

Disneyland · Paris

100 m
©*Baedeker*

- Attractions
- Restaurants
- Shops
- Toilets and
  other Services

1 Grand Canyon Diorama	14 La Cabane des Robinson	27 Blanche-Neige et les
2 Phantom Manor	15 Indiana Jones et le	Sept Nains
3 Main Street Motors	Temple du Peril	28 La Tanière
4 Liberty Court	16 Adventure Isle	du Dragon
5 Lucky Nugget Saloon	17 Pirates of the Caribbean	29 Le Château de la Belle
6 MT et MB	18 Peter Pan's Flight	au Bois Dormant
7 Riverboat Landing	19 Fantasy Festival Stage	30 Le Visionarium
8 Rustler Roundup Shootin'	20 Alice's Curious Labyrinth	31 Videopolis
Gallery	21 Dumbo the Flying Elephant	32 Star Tours
9 Big Thunder Mountain	22 Mad Hatter's Tea Cups	33 CinéMagique
10 Indian Canoes	23 Le Petit Train du Cirque	34 Orbitron
11 River Rogue Keelboats	24 It's a Small World	35 Autopia
12 Cottenwood Creek Ranch	25 Le Carrousel de Lancelot	36 Space Mountain
13 Frontierland Depot	26 Les Voyages de Pinocchio	37 Nautilus

Frontierland

In eerie Phantom Manor the cadaverous master of the house waits impatiently to show his visitors round. After this you can take a trip on the Rivers of the Far West, either in a sternwheeler which would have been familiar to Mark Twain, an Indian canoe or a shallow keelboat reminiscent of the tales of Davy Crockett. Cottonwood Creek Ranch recalls the days of the Wild West, and the adjoining Bonanza Shop sells jeans, cowboy hats and Indian jewellery and ornaments. Then visitors can have a dizzy-making ride through the narrow gorges of Big Thunder Mountain; and thereafter hungry gold-diggers can restore their energies with a substantial American meal in the Lucky Nugget Saloon.

Adventureland

Among the adventures offered in Adventureland are the log cabin of the Swiss Family Robinson, an underground ride through the lair of Caribbean pirates, precarious suspension bridges over tumbling waterfalls, Captain Hook's Pirate Ship and a loop-the-loop through 360 degrees. For those in need of refreshment there is a choice between Oriental markets, African meals and Caribbean seafood, all served in appropriate settings.

Fantasyland

The Castle of the Sleeping Beauty

The main attraction in Fantasyland is the Château de la Belle au Bois Dormant (Sleeping Beauty's Castle). On the first floor of the castle the story of the Sleeping Beauty is depicted in stained glass and tapestries, while the vaulted cellars are occupied by a fire-breathing dragon. After this visitors can pay a call on Snow White and the Seven Dwarfs (Blanche-Neige et les Sept Nains), accompany Pinocchio on his daring journey, fly with Peter Pan over night-time London to Never Never Land, wander through Alice's Curious Labyrinth, soar in the air with Dumbo the flying elephant, travel through Fairyland or take a musical cruise through "It's a Small World". For refreshment there are a princely restaurant, British sandwiches or Vienna strudel.

Discoveryland

In the futuristic world of Discoveryland the inventions of famous European visionaries such as Leonardo da Vinci, Jules Verne and H. G. Wells are displayed. In the Visionarium visitors can enter various marvellous flying machines or the Time Machine; In Cinémagique Michael Jackson as Captain EO is involved in a 3–D inter-galactic adventure; Vidéopolis presents the latest video clips; Star Tours offers a breathtaking flight through the fourth dimension; and in Autopia visitors can head for the future in racing cars.

Opposite the theme park, by Lake Buena Vista, are the glittering towers of Festival Disney – "America live" for nightbirds, with non-stop action into the early hours. Among the attractions are the planet Hollywood Restaurant with its cinematic decor, Hurricanes disco-thèque, a children's theatre on Peter Pan's island in Never Never Land and the new Gaumont cinema complex with eight screens and roller-skating waitresses, who carry out their duties, as in the 1950s, to the accompaniment of Elvis Presley's and Chuck Berry's songs.

Disney Village

Buffalo Bill's Wild West Show (performances at 6.30pm and 9.30pm) is a colourful spectacle, with intrepid cowboys, sharp-shooting Annie Oakley, the Sioux chief Sitting Bill, buffaloes and wild longhorn steers. It is modelled on the original show with which Buffalo Bill toured Europe and North America at the end of the 19th century.

Buffalo Bill's Wild West Show

Dôme des Invalides

See Invalides

Ecole Militaire   F 5/6

The Ecole Militaire (Military Academy; originally the school for train-ing officers of the royal army) stands at the opposite end of the Champ-de-Mars (see entry) from the Eiffel Tower (see Tour Eiffel). The building was designed by Jacques-Ange Gabriel and built in two stages between 1759 and 1782. With its clear and uncluttered archi-tectural forms it is a fine example of early neo-classicism.
   In 1785 a young officer graduated from the officers' training school established by Louis XV with a report from his superiors that "in certain circumstances he might go far". The young officer took advantages of the circumstances of his time and went a long way as Napoleon I, first Emperor of the French.

Location
Avenue de la Motte-Piquet (7th arr.)

Métro station
Ecole Militaire

Buses
28, 49, 80, 82, 87, 92

Behind the north front of the main building on Place Joffre (statue of Marshal Joffre) is the Grand Courtyard (Cour d'Honneur), along the sides of which are Doric colonnades. The Chapelle St-Louis, in Louis XVI style, is one of Jacques-Ange Gabriel's masterpieces. The white walls of the interior are decorated with reliefs by Pajou and pictures (by Vien, van Loo, Durameau, Lagrenée the Elder and Beaufort) depicting scenes from the life of St Louis.
   Visits only on written application to the General Commandant d'Armes, Ecole Militaire, 1 Place Joffre, 75007 Paris.

Cour d'Honneur

Chapelle Saint-Louis

Egouts de Paris (Sewers of Paris)   E 5

To get some impression of the scale and complexity of Paris's sewage system those interested can visit an exhibition on the city's sewers in (or rather under) Place de la Résistance (entrance opposite 93 Quai d'Orsay). Here are several galleries containing plans and documents and an audio-visual show illustrating the development of Paris's water supply and sewage systems from Roman times by way of the large reservoir (the Grand Siphon de l'Alma) constructed by an engineer named Belgrand in the reign of Napoleon III to present-day Paris (open: Sat. to Wed. 11am–4 or 5pm; admission charge).

Location
Quai d'Orsay

Métro station
Alma Marceau

RER station
Pont de l'Alma

Buses
42, 63, 80, 92

Eiffel Tower

See Tour Eiffel

Etoile

See Arc de Triomphe

Faubourg Saint-Germain   G 5

Location
7th arr.

Métro stations
Bac, Solférino,
Varenne

RER station
Musée d'Orsay

Buses
28, 49, 63, 69, 83,
84, 94

The Faubourg Saint-Germain extends from Saint-Germain-des-Prés to the Invalides (see entries). A select aristocratic district in the 18th century, it now contains the residence of the Prime Minister, various ministries and foreign embassies and, in the eastern part of the faubourg, high-class antique shops and art galleries.

Towards the end of the 17th century the Marais (see entry) fell out of favour and the aristocracy and new-rich nobility moved to this area and to the Faubourg Saint-Honoré (see entry). The court's return to Paris speeded up the process, and numerous hotels (town mansions) were built here. Since then the Faubourg Saint-Germain has remained the favoured residential district of the upper ranks of Paris society. Some streets in the area still give an impression of the homogeneous urban architecture of those earlier days. In Rue de Varenne, for example, are the Hôtel de Gallifet (No. 50), the Hôtel Matignon (No. 57), residence of the Prime Minister, and the Hôtel Biron, now occupied by the Musée Rodin (see entry). In Rue de Grenelle are the Hôtel d'Avaray (No. 79), the Hôtel de Bauffremont (No. 87) and the Hôtel de Maillebois (No. 102), as well as the Fontaine des Quatre-Saisons (1739–46), a masterpiece by Edmond Bouchardon, one of the most fashionable sculptors of the time of Louis XV.

★Faubourg Saint-Honoré   E–G 3/4

Location
8th arr.

Métro stations
St-Philippe-du-
Roule, Madeleine

Buses
24, 28, 38, 42, 49,

Bounded by rue Royale (see entry), the boulevards Malesherbes and Haussmann and the Champs-Elysées (see entry) is the Faubourg Saint-Honoré, the name of both a district and a street, which calls up a variety of images – haute couture, the residence of the President of the Republic, the embassy quarter. The most interesting section of the faubourg extends between rue La-Boétie and rue Royale.

At Nos. 55–57 is the President's residence, the Palais de l'Elysée; built at the beginning of the 18th century, it belonged at one time to Louis XV's favourite, Madame de Pompadour. Diagonally opposite, on place Beauvau, is the Ministry of the Interior. At No. 39 is the former Hôtel de Charost (1723), which since 1814 has been the British Embassy.

The great attraction of the Faubourg Saint-Honoré, however, lies in its luxurious shops and famous fashion houses. In rue du Faubourg-Saint-Honoré are the establishments of Hervé Leger (No. 29), Chloé (nos. 54/56) Lanvin (No. 22), Hermès (No. 24), Christian Lacroix (No. 73), Fendi (No. 74), Louis Féraud (No. 88), Liliane Romi (No. 90), Zilli and Versace. There are also renowned art galleries, such as those of Hervé Odermatt (No. 85; modern art) and Pacitti (No. 174; 19th and 20th century art), and numerous jewellers.

The Elysée Palace –
the President holds court

For centuries the Elysian Fields were a place of supreme happiness on the edge of the world which people would dream of with longing. That might still have been true of the Parisian Champs Elysées in the 18th century; today, however, the avenue is a brightly-lit tourist promenade with Paris traffic thundering down the centre. But just behind the park gates beyond the Grand Palais lies a tiny microcosm, shielded from the city's hustle and bustle, which registers merely as a soft hum behind thick walls. This secret world is the Palais de l'Elysée, address: 55 rue du Faubourg-Saint-Honoré – quiet enough on the surface, but with its own buzz of activity. Since 1873 this has been the residence of the President of the Republic and in recent years the office has required a household of over 900 civil servants. In fact it is rather like being at a court. Every morning at eight o'clock the changing of the guard takes place, just like at Buckingham Palace in London; the president's study is resplendent in lavish gold from the 18th c. and when the head of state's television addresses, which are recorded in a special studio on the premises, come to an end, the floodlit façade of the Palais is shown on the television screens, in just the same way that the French love to see their national monuments transmuted by son et lumière. That may explain why the Parisians refer to the official residence of their president with a twinkle in their eye as *Le Château*.

The country seat built in 1718 outside the city gates by the wealthy Comte d'Evreux had already acquired an eventful history, when in 1959 the President of the Fifth Republic, Charles de Gaulle, took up residence. Before that the standing of the republican occupants of the palace had had a whiff of operetta, whereas de Gaulle, besides the power entrusted to him, also brought dignity and discipline to the Elysée Palace – and not before time. Previously government bulletins had hardly existed and, instead,

gossip and tittle-tattle were the main things to be purveyed to the world outside the palace. Even its second occupant, the Marquise de Pompadour, mistress of Louis XV and a grande dame of the Rococo, became the talk of Paris society. Later rumours circulated of an aristocratic brothel being housed there, on another occasion details of spiritualist séances were bruited. By contrast, there were also times when the building was merely used as a dance-hall. And yet the atmosphere associated with the palace has never been completely lost – only recently it was the subject of a detective novel : "Death at Elysée". But in the midst of so much anecdotage and romancing we should not forget that important history has been, and is being, written here. It was at the palace that Napoleon I signed his abdication in 1814, while his nephew Napoleon III installed the military headquarters of the Second Empire here. Today the cellar contains the "Jupiter" bunker, which will be used by the president as a command centre in a nuclear emergency. A few flight of steps further up is the Salon Murat where the council of state meets every Wednesday. Its sessions are kept so secret that even the notes made by the participants are burnt afterwards. Apart from that the palace is used for the everyday business of the president: studying briefs and documents, meetings, official and social functions Eighteen cooks are employed in the kitchens, 13,000 pieces of silverware have to be kept polished, while the fleet of 49 cars is maintained by some of the 300 guardsmen. Once a year, on July 14th, the complete machinery runs at full steam and 5000 invited guests enjoy the annual garden party which celebrates the national holiday. A more gracious and respectable occasion could scarcely be imagined, and when the 1500 bottles of champagne have been consumed, the guests feel that much closer to Elysium, while the pleasant hum of their conversation drowns the noise of the city outside.

Rue du Faubourg-Saint-Honoré, a centre of high fashion

★★Fontainebleau

Location
60km/37 miles
SE of Paris
(A 6, N 6, N 7)

Rail service
from Gare de
Lyon

The little town of Fontainebleau (pop. 20,000) in the département of Seine-et-Marne lies south-east of Paris in the beautiful Forest of Fontainebleau, the largest state forest in France, covering an area of almost 20,000 hecttares/50,000 acres, which is a favourite weekend resort of the citizens of Paris. The principal attraction is the historic and beautiful old Château, which Stendhal called a "dictionary of architecture". For some 800 years the château was the favourite country residence of French kings and emperors: monarchs from Louis VII to Napoleon III lived here, building, rebuilding and altering it down the centuries.

★★Château de Fontainebleau

Opening times
Daily except Tue.
Oct.–May
9.30am–12.30pm,
2–5pm
June–Sept.
9.30am–5pm
July–Aug.
9.30am–6pm

**Admission
charge**

Napoleon's reference to Fontainebleau as "the work of centuries, the home of kings" expresses the intimate relationship which the French monarchs had with their summer palace and hunting lodge.

The present extensive complex of the château with its beautiful French-style and English-style gardens dates back to a small 12th century hunting lodge. This was replaced in 1528 by a château in Renaissance style built for François I by Gilles Le Breton, Pierre Chambiges and Philibert Delorme which was subsequently enlarged by Henri II, Henri IV and Louis XV.

Napoleon, who was particularly fond of Fontainebleau, signed his first abdication here on April 6th 1814 and then took leave of his army on the entrance courtyard, now known as the Cour des Adieux. The courtyard is also called the Cour du Cheval Blanc, after a white equestrian statue of the Emperor Marcus Aurelius (a replica of the original on the Capitol in Rome).

The present main front (the entrance front) of the Château, which is built of sandstone, is dominated by the double horseshoe-shaped staircase (by Jacques Androuet, 1634), which with its strong lines reflects the transition to Baroque and seems massive against the more delicately articulated central section of the façade, which is older (1615). The lateral sections of the main front date from the time of François I and were built by Primaticcio, the Bolognese architect who worked at Fontainebleau from 1532 onwards. Exterior

The wing on the left of the Cour des Adieux is one of the oldest surviving parts of the château, built about 1540 for officials of François I's court. The wing on the right, built by Jacques-Ange Gabriel in the 18th century, contained lodgings for the royal household.

The passage under the arcades to the right of the horseshoe staircase leads into the Cour de la Fontaine, which opens on to the large Carp Pond on the right. To the left is the François I Gallery (first floor), beyond which is the Garden of Diana (Jardin de Diane).

A feature of the interior is the successful combination of stucco ornament with the carved wood panelling on the walls, which creates an impression of warmth. The principal sights are the François I Gallery, the Chapel and the Ballroom, all on the first floor and reached by way of the horseshoe staircase. Interior

The François I Gallery (1534–37) was used only as a passage linking the royal apartments with the chapel, in which tradesmen offered various fashion accessories for sale. The sumptuous appointments of the gallery, therefore, are a little surprising. Here a group of renowned Italian painters, sculptors and stucco-workers, headed by Francesco Primaticcio (1507–70), Niccolò dell'Abbate (c. 1512–71) and Rosso François I Gallery

Cour des Adieux at Fontainebleau where Napoleon took leave of his army on April 6th 1814

Fiorentino (1494–1540), worked together to produce a total effect in Mannerist style (the transitional stage between Renaissance and Baroque). They founded what later became known as the "school of Fontainebleau", of which the François I Gallery is the supreme achievement. The finely contrived blending of architecture, painting and stucco decoration, the delicate use of colour and the profusion of allegorical themes together create a complex work of art. There are numerous cross-references, in both composition and significance, between the twelve large mural frescoes, the smaller paintings, the forms of the frames and the stucco ornament which we can hardly now hope to decipher.

Among the artists who came to François I's court and has a lasting influence on the whole of the 16th century was a painter who enjoyed the king's particular patronage: Leonardo da Vinci, whose "Mona Lisa" found its way into the royal collections and remained there for many years before passing to the Louvre (see entry).

Ballroom

The Ballroom, begun in 1547, during the reign of François I, was continued in 1552–56 by Henri II, who was also a keen patron of art. The massive pilasters in this richly gilded room show that it was originally to have had a medieval-style vaulted ceiling, but instead it was given a "modern" flat ceiling, spanning an area 30 by 10 metres (100 by 33 feet). The numerous mythological scenes are by Niccolò dell'Abbate after sketches by Primaticcio. The scenes depicting Diana, goddess of hunting, are also to be understood as a tribute to Diane de Poitiers, François I's last favourite. After his death she became the mistress of his son Henri II, who was almost thirty years younger than she. Their initials, D and H, appear frequently in the decoration of the room.

Chapel

The Chapelle de la Sainte-Trinité (entrance on 1st floor) is two storeys in height. It was built by François I, continued by Philibert Delorme for Henri II and decorated with a ceiling painting by Frémiet in the reign of Henri IV.

Royal Apartments

Also on the first floor are the royal apartments. They consist of six rooms overlooking the Cour Ovale, including François I's apartments, later altered by Louis XIV (with the room in which Louis XIII was born, the Salon de Louis XIII), and eleven rooms looking on to the Jardin de Diane. Among these are the Appartements de Marie-Antoinette, the Salle du Trône (Throne Room) and the Salle du Conseil (Council Chamber).

Petits Appartements de l'Empereur

Napoleon's apartments are in Empire style. In the Salon Rouge is a small round table on which Napoleon signed his abdication in 1814. Also very fine are Napoleon's private apartments (Petits Appartements de l'Empereur), formerly Louis XIV's apartments, on the ground floor, looking on to the Jardin de Diane. They were furnished by Napoleon in Empire style from 1806 onwards.

Petits Appartements de l'Impératrice

Marie-Antoinette's private apartments were later occupied by Napoleon's wife Joséphine (Petits Appartements de l'Impératrice) and were altered from 1806 onwards.

Galerie de Diane

The Galerie de Diane, another side wing of the château, was built in the reign of Henri III. It now serves as a library and picture gallery.

★Gardens

The gardens of the château are not to be missed. To the west of the Carp Pond is the Jardin Anglais, laid out in the reign of Napoleon. To the east is the Parterre, designed by the famous landscape gardener

Le Nôtre, with delightful pools and garden figures. North-east of this, beyond the canal constructed in the reign of Henri IV, extends the park, in which are a maze and the Treille du Roi (King's Arbour), with trellised vines. From the Trois Pignons, three sandstone crags to the south-west, there are fine panoramic views.

★Forêt de Fontainebleau

The Forest of Fontainebleau, which covers an area of 25,000 hectares/ 62,000 acres bounded on the north-east by the windings of the Seine, is a popular resort of Parisians at the weekend. The terrain is hilly, consisting mainly of sand and sandstone, with magnificent old trees and deep gorges. Particularly impressive are the wild Gorges de Franchard, in which rock-climbers learn their skills. The fantastic landscapes of the forest have attracted many painters, including particularly the Barbizon school. For walkers there are numerous waymarked hiking trails and footpaths.

Grand Palais   F 4

The Grand Palais – now rivalled by the Centre Pompidou (see entry) – is the setting of Paris's most important art exhibitions, devoted either to the work of individual artists (e.g. Monet, Matisse, Chagall, Miró, Picasso, Gauguin, Renoir) or to particular periods (e.g. Impressionism, Symbolism) or countries. Other regular shows held here are the Salon d'Automne, FIAC (the Foire Internationale d'Art Contemporain) and the Salon des Antiques (Antiques Fair). (Open: Mon. and Thu.–Sun. 10am–8pm, Wed. 10am–10pm).

The Grand Palais was built for the 1900 International Exhibition. It has an Art Nouveau interior, with a structure of iron and steel; the exterior is predominantly neo-Baroque. The mighty glass dome is 43m/141ft high.

Location
31 Avenue du Général Eisenhower (8th arr.)

Métro station
Champs-Elysées-Clemenceau

Buses
28, 42, 49, 72, 73, 83, 93

Admission charge

★Palais de la Découverte

The Palais de la Découverte (Palace of Discovery) has been housed in the west wing of the Grand Palais sine 1937. It seeks to present in a practical way the history of the natural sciences and their results and applications. There are separate rooms devoted to astronomy, physics, chemistry, biology and medicine in which visitors can carry out experiments for themselves. Notable features include the large hall devoted to our solar system and the Planetarium (presentations at 2, 3.15 and 4.30pm: additional presentations and film lectures at 2.30 and 4pm: conducted tours in French only).

Les Halles   J 5

Since the controversial demolition of the old Halles (Market Halls) and the transfer of the markets to Rungis in the late sixties the Halles quarter has been completely remodelled. It is now an extensive pedestrian area, crowded throughout the day, mainly by young people.

From medieval times onwards the markets were the focal point of the Rive Droite. The first covered market halls were built in 1183, in the reign of Philippe Auguste, and seven centuries later, under Napoleon III, Victor Baltard (1805–75) constructed the huge functional iron halls which soon became one of the city's landmarks and a popu-

Location
Centre (1st arr.)

Métro station
Les Halles

RER station
Châtelet-Les Halles

Les Halles

Buses
21, 29, 38, 47, 67,
74, 85

lar haunt of revellers after a night on the town. After the demolition of the Halles – the "belly of Paris", as described in Zola's novel "Le Ventre de Paris" – the site lay empty for years, with a huge hole in the ground which became known as the Trou des Halles. Finally the hole was filled with an equally huge architectural ensemble, designed by Claude Vasoni and Georges Pencreach, and developed into one of the largest underground traffic hubs in Paris: two RER lines intersect a Métro line here, and there is a connection to the Châtelet station, the junction of four Métro lines. Above the RER and Métro tunnels and underground car parks but still below ground level is the huge funnel-shaped complex of the Forum des Halles, opened in 1979. Here, on four glassed-in levels surrounding a courtyard, nearly 300 shops and boutiques, cinemas, theatres, restaurants and cafés, with the Pavillon des Arts (exhibitions). The book and photographic chain FNAC has

Pygmalion sculpture

its largest Paris store here.The marble figure of Pygmalion is by the Argentinian sculptor Julio Silva.

Grévin Forum

On Level 1/Grand Balcon on rue Pierre Lescot in the Palais des Mirages (built for the 1901 World Exhibition) is a branch of the popular Musée Grévin, with wax figures depicting the Paris of the *belle époque*, with a *son et lumière* show, "Promenade 1900". Open: Mon.–Fri. 10.30am–6.45pm; Sun. 1–7.00pm.

Vidéothèque de Paris

The Vidéothèque de Paris, opened in 1988, houses within its area of 4000sq.m/43,000sq.ft the most modern audiovisual archives in the country, with a great range of cinema and television films; the collection is expected to reach a total of 20,000 cassettes within the foreseeable future. Thanks to the Magnus computer system (named after Gaston Leroux's legendary three-armed character) visitors have access to 50 television screens on which they can select the films they

The funnel-shaped complex of the Forum des Halles, opened in 1979

want to see. There are also three rooms in which films can be shown to audiences of up to 300 people. Open: Tue.–Sun. 2.30–11pm.

After the redevelopment of the Halles quarter the Fontaine des Innocents (1549) was returned to its original position in the Square des Innocents, between Rue Saint-Denis and Rue Berger. This was the site until 1786 of the church and churchyard of the Innocents. The architect of the fountain, which was remodelled in the form of a temple in the 18th century, was Pierre Lescot, who was also responsible for the Lescot front in the Cour Carrée of the Louvre (see entry). The reliefs on the three older sides of the fountain, the originals of which are now in the Louvre, were the work of the great French Renaissance sculptor Jean Goujon. On the fourth side are figures of nymphs by Augustin Pajou (1788).

Fontaine des Innocents

Hôtel de Ville J 5

Paris, for long "a capital without a head", has since 1977 again been headed by a Mayor. His official residence is the Hôtel de Ville (Town Hall), to which the mayors' offices (mairies annexes) of the 20 arrondissements are answerable. (On the administrative structure of Paris and the surrounding area see Facts and Figures, General, Administration.)

In the Middle Ages the city's chief administrator was the provost of the merchants (prévot des marchands), head of Paris's corporation of merchant shippers, the Marchands de l'Eau, which belonged to the Hanseatic League. The provost, who was directly responsible to the king, was a man of great influence: in 1358, for example, the provost of the merchants, Etienne Marcel, led the first (unsuccessful) revolt of the burghers against feudalism and the monarchy. In 1789 the last provost – who as a royal official represented the monarchy – was executed by the revolutionary mob.

After the French Revolution Paris had its own Mayor for only brief periods (1789–94, 1848, 1970–71). For the rest of the time, until 1977, it was ruled by government officials, the Prefect of the Seine and the Prefect of Police.

The first Town Hall, built in the 14th century, was replaced by a new building in 1533. In the early 19th century this Renaissance building was extended in a faithful reproduction of the original style. In 1871 the Town Hall was burned down during the repression of the Commune, which had established its headquarters in the building, but was subsequently completely restored.

The present building, in neo-Renaissance style, dates largely from the time of the Third Republic. On the richly decorated façades are 136 statues and medallions of famous French artists, writers and thinkers, and on the clock tower is the city's patron goddess.

There are guided tours of the sumptuously appointed but somewhat over-ornate state apartments, which contain many historical relics and mementoes. Notable among the works of art are Rodin's bronze bust of the Republic and the murals by Puvis de Chavannes. For information apply to the reception office in the Town Hall (tel. 01 42 76 59 27). On the third Sunday in June each year the "waiter race" takes place on the Place de l' Hôtel de Ville: competitors have to race around the 8km/5 mile course while balancing a tray containing a bottle of beer and three glasses.

Location
Place de l'Hôtel-de-Ville (4th arr.)

Métro station
Hôtel de Ville

Buses
38, 47, 58, 67, 69, 70, 72, 74, 75, 76, 96

Ile de la Cité

See Cité

★Ile Saint-Louis J/K 5/6

Location
Centre (4th arr.)

Métro station
Pont Marie

Bus
67

The Ile Saint-Louis was formed in 1609 out of two smaller islands, the Ile aux Vaches and the Ile Notre-Dame. Under a project initiated by Cardinal Richelieu and carried out by three contractors, Marie, Poulletier and Le Regrattier, the two little islands were joined, connected with the right bank of the Seine by two bridges and laid out on a rectangular grid with houses in uniform style. By 1664 the work was completed and the first craftsmen and merchants had moved in; and soon afterwards they were followed by the aristocracy, who built their elegant mansions along the quais. In addition to the noble families illustrious writers such as Charles Baudelaire, Théophile Gautier, Camille Claudel and Emile Zola came to live on the island, and other residents have included Voltaire, Rousseau and such famous statesmen as Léon Blum and Georges Pompidou. And the 6000 inhabitants of the island still include well-to-do writers and artists.

Much of the 17th century architecture has preserved its character and its dignity. The harmony of the close-packed lines of houses, the little cafés where a *petit noir* can be enjoyed at leisure, the quiet quais and the aura of the past which pervades the island give it a particular charm. Along the island's main street, Rue Saint-Louis-en-l'Ile, are numbers of little shops, cosy crêperies and smart restaurants, often in vaulted cellars, which form an attractive setting for an elegant meal. A stroll along the quais or a picnic on the banks of the Seine offers views of the Hôtel de Ville on the right bank of the Seine, the Quartier Latin and the Panthéon on the left bank and, to the west, the Ile de la Cité and Notre-Dame.

Imposing buildings along the river frontage of the Ile Saint-Louis give the island a special charm

A popular rendezvous: pavement cafés on the banks of the Seine

The church of Saint-Louis-en-l'Ile was begun in 1664 by Louis Le Vau (1612–70) and completed in 1726 by Jacques Doucet. In the Baroque interior are pictures by Charles Coypel (1694–1752; "The Disciples at Emmaus"), Pierre Mignard (1612–95; "Rest on the Flight to Egypt") and Francesco Vecellio, Titian's brother (16th c.; "Entombment"). In summer there are concerts of church music almost every evening.

St-Louis-en-l'Ile
Rue St-Louis-en-l'Ile

The Hôtel Lauzun (1657) is also attributed to Louis Le Vau, Louis XIV's court architect. It now belongs to the city, which uses it as an official guest-house. In the mid 19th century it was the home of Baudelaire, Gautier and the painter Beauvoir, all members of the legendary Club des Hachichins. The house is sumptuously decorated with frescoes, stucco-work and sculpture. It can be visited only by prior arrangement with the Caisse Nationale des Monuments Historiques (tel. 01 48 87 24 14).

Hôtel Lauzun
17 quai d'Anjou

The Hôtel Lambert (1640), also built by Le Vau, belongs to the Rothschild family and is not open to the public. With its semicircular courtyard and open staircase hall, oval vestibule, Galerie d'Hercule (with scenes from the legend of Hercules by Le Brun and Eustache Le Sueur), it is a consummate example of the art and culture of its period.

Hôtel Lambert
2 rue St-Louis-en-l'Ile

Institut de France   H 5

The Académie Française, founded by Cardinal Richelieu in 1635 to foster the French language, is the oldest of the five learned academies of the Institut de France which have their headquarters in the Palais de l'Institut de France. The members of the Academy, the "quarante Immortels", who are appointed for life, decide whether a word should

Location
23 quai de Conti
(6th arr.)

Métro station
Pont Neuf

Buses
24, 27, 58, 70

Opening times
Conducted tours
by appointment:
apply to
Secrétariat de
l'Institut,
23 quai de Conti,
75006 Paris

be admitted into their authoritative Dictionnaire de la Langue Française and thus officially recognised as a French word.

On the 350th anniversary of the Academy's foundation President Mitterrand was presented with one of the first copies of the 9th edition of the Dictionary, which contains 45,000 words (the 8th ediion of 1935 had only 35,000).

The other academies carry out and promote research in the fields of classical history and archaeology (Académie des Inscriptions et Belles Lettres, founded 1664), the natural sciences (Académie des Sciences, 1666), the humanities, law and the social sciences (Académie des Sciences Morales et Politiques, 1832) and art (Académie des Beaux-Arts, 1816).

Origins

Cardinal Mazarin, dying in 1661, bequeathed money for the foundation of a college to take 15 young nobles from France's new provinces of Artois, Alsace, Piedmont and Roussillon. This Collège des Quatre-Nations, which continued in existence until 1790, was housed in 1691 in a new building, with a chapel and a library, designed by Louis Le Vau. In 1805 Napoleon transferred the five academies, which since 1795 had been brought together in the Institut de France, from the Louvre to the College.

The Palais de l'Institut de France was designed as a counterpart on the left bank of the Seine to the Cour Carrée of the Louvre (see entry) on the right bank. This accounts for its unexpected size (for only 60 students) and its imposing architecture, which shows the characteristic features of classical French Baroque – the emphasis given to the ends of the main front by the two pavilions (projecting blocks with high-pitched roofs), the alignment of the façade and the drum supporting the dome and the closely set columns. A particular feature is the semicircular façade, with a six-column portico behind which is the dome of what was originally the chapel.

The chapel was converted into the large council chamber in which the academies and the Institute as a whole meet in plenary session. Here too the academies elect new members to fill vacancies caused by death and formally admit the new members.

Membership

In spite of assertions to the contrary by critics of the institution, membership of one of the academies still ranks as the climax of any career. Although the membership of the Académie Française has included many internationally renowned figures (Victor Hugo, Prosper Mérimée, Jean Cocteau, René Clair and Eugène Ionesco among them), it is also true that many great philosophers and writers, including Pascal, Mollère, Rousseau, Diderot, Balzac, Zola and Proust, have failed to secure admittance to the select company sous la Coupole (under the Dome). In 1980, for the first time in the history of the academies, a woman (Marguerite Yourcenar) was admitted to the Académie Française, followed by the admission of Yvonne Choquet-Bruhat to the Académie des Sciences.

The main feature of interest in the interior of the Institut de France is the Council Chamber under the dome, in which is the tomb of Cardinal Mazarin (by Antoine Coysevox, based on a design by Jules Hardouin-Mansart).

Bibliothèque
Mazarine

Cardinal Mazarin's private library, the Bibliothèque Mazarine, in the east wing of the Palais, contains more than 450,000 volumes, manuscripts and valuable incunabula (open: Mon.–Fri. 10am–6pm).

★Institut du Monde Arabe   K b

On the banks of the Seine opposite the Pont de Sully is the Institut du Monde Arabe, a tall rectangular building (completed 1988) with a façade which has the effect of filigree work. This cultural centre, established to promote relations between East and West, was designed by Jean Nouvel in a style with reminiscences of Arab architecture. It consists of two slender parallel slabs, nine storeys high, housing a library, lecture rooms, a museum and a documentation centre.

A feature of the building is the fenestration of the south front: square windows reaching the full height of the storey with ornamental metal openwork screens filtering light into the rooms. The Museum and Documentation Centre, extending over seven storeys, give a comprehensive view of the art and culture of the Islamic world, with displays of calligraphy, printed books, coins and astrolabes, valuable carpets, textiles and other everyday objects, including contemporary work. From the restaurant on the roof terrace there are superb views over the Cité to the Arc de Triomphe and on clear days as far as La Défense (see entries).

Location
23 quai St-Bernard
(5th arr.)

Métro station
Jussieu

Opening times
Tue.–Sun. 10am–6pm

Admission charge

★Invalides (Hôtel des Invalides)

F 5

The Hôtel des Invalides was founded as a home for disabled soldiers. At one time it had 7000 places, but there are now only a few pension-

Location
Avenue de Tourville (7th arr.)

Eglise Saint-Louis-des-Invalides

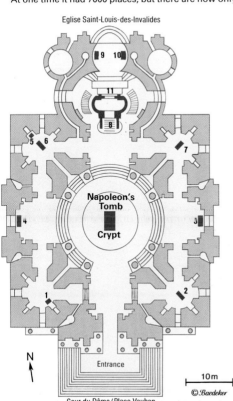

Eglise du Dôme des Invalides

1 Tomb of Napoleon's brother Jérôme Bonaparte (d. 1860) in Chapelle St-Jérôme

2 Tomb of Napoleon's brother Joseph (d. 1844)

3 Tomb of the great military engineer Vauban (d. 1707), with his heart

4 Tomb of Marshal Henri de La Tour d'Auvergne, Vicomte de Turenne (d. 1675)

5 Heart of General Théophile de La Tour d'Auvergne (d. 1800)

6 Tomb of Marshal Lyautey (d. 1934)

7 Tomb of Marshal Foch (d. 1929)

8 Altar with twisted columns and baldachin

9 Tomb of General Henri Bertrand (d. 1844)

10 Tomb of General Duroc (d. 1813)

11 Access to Crypt: at entrance two large bronze statues; in interior, round Napoleon's tomb, twelve colossal figures symbolising his victories; to rear the tomb of Napoleon's son François-Charles-Joseph Bonaparte (d. 1832)

N

Entrance

10m

© Baedeker

Cour du Dôme / Place Vauban

ers living in what is the finest complex of 17th century buildings in Paris, still completely preserved. Most of the rooms are now occupied by museums and by the military authorities. For those interested in military matters there are two important museums, the Musée de l'Armée (see entry) and the associated Musée des Plans-Reliefs.

Before the time of Louis XIV disabled soldiers received medical care, if at all, in hospitals or monasteries, but were usually reduced to begging. With the Hôtel des Invalides the "Sun King" founded the first home for men disabled while serving in his armies. At that time it lay outside the city and was surrounded by moats and bastions. It was built in 1671–76 under the direction of the architect Libéral Bruant, centred on the church of Saint-Louis-des-Invalides. The nave of the church (in which excellent organ recitals are given from time to time) is festooned with flags and standards won by Napoleon's victorious armies. Since the church was too plain for the king's taste he commissioned Jules Hardouin-Mansart to build another, the Eglise Royale (completed 1706), which later became known as the Eglise du Dôme des Invalides.

During the main season there are evening concerts and son et lumière shows (historical presentations, mainly of Napoleon's career, with light effects) in the main courtyard (Cour d'Honneur) of the Hôtel des Invalides. Under the central arcade of the south pavilion is a bronze statue of Napoleon as the "Little Corporal" in contemporary costume, and at the entrance to the gardens on the north front are captured German tanks. The Esplanade des Invalides, the spacious forecourt which extends from here to the banks of the Seine, was laid out by Robert de Cotte in 1704–20.

The Eglise du Dôme des Invalides, built between 1675 and 1706, contains Napoleon's tomb, installed here in 1840. Designed by the great architect Jules Hardouin-Mansart, it is the outstanding ecclesiastical building of the French classical period, fit counterpart to Hardouin-Mansart's secular master-work, the Palace of Versailles (see entry). The mighty dome, over 100m/330ft high, from which the church takes its name harmonises perfectly with the Doric and Corinthian columns on the façade. In the richly decorated area under the dome, with paintings by Charles de la Fosse, is a circular opening exposing the crypt, which has the same diameter (11m/36ft) as the dome.

In the centre of the crypt, on a base of green granite, is Napoleon's red porphyry sarcophagus. It is surrounded by twelve figures (by James Pradier) of victory goddesses, symbolising Napoleon's twelve victorious campaigns between 1797 and 1815.

In a small chapel opening off the crypt is the tomb of Napoleon's only legitimate son, who bore the titles of Napoleon II, Roi de Rome and Duc de Reichstadt but died in Vienna in 1832 at the age of 21.

In other side chapels are the tombs of famous figures in French history, including Joseph Bonaparte (1768–1844; Napoleon's eldest brother, King of Spain), Jérome Bonaparte (1784–1860; Napoleon's youngest brother, King of Westphalia), Marshal Turenne (1611–75), General Théophile de la Tour d'Auvergne (1743–1800), Marshal Lyautey (1854–1934), General Bertrand (1773–1844; Napoleon's major-domo on St Helena), General Duroc (1772–1813), Marshal Foch (1851–1929) and Marshal Vauban (1633–1707), Louis XIV's great military engineer.

Métro stations
Latour
Maubourg,
St-François-
Xavier, Invalides

Buses
28, 49, 63, 69, 82,
83, 92

Opening times
Oct. 1–Mar. 31,
daily 10am–5pm;
Apr. 1–Sept. 30,
10am–6pm

Admission charge

Cour d'Honneur

Dôme des Invalides

Napoleon's sarcophagus

Tombs in the side chapels

◀ An outstanding building of the French classical period –
the Dôme des Invalides

Jardin des Plantes   J/K 6

Location
57 rue Cuvier
(5th arr.)

Métro stations
Jussieu,
Austerlitz

RER station
Gare d'Austerlitz

Buses
24, 57, 61, 63, 65,
67, 89, 91

The Jardin des Plantes (Musée National d'Histoire Naturelle; area 235,000sq.m/281,000sq.yds) offers visitors a comprehensive view of the various fields of natural history – botany (the School of Botany has a collection of over 10,000 plant species), mineralogy (particularly notable are the giant crystals), zoology, ecology and palaeontology. It is also a place of work and study for students of the nearby University Paris VII (Jussieu).

At the beginning of the 17th century Louis XIII's doctors laid out a herb garden here, and this soon grew into a large plant collection. A school of botany and pharmacy was established, and in 1650 the garden was thrown open to the public. The aristocrat and naturalist George-Louis Leclerc de Buffon (1707–88) extended the garden into a park, laid out partly in the English style and partly in rigorously geometric style. The 19th century saw the erection of the iron and glass galleries of palaeontology, botany and mineralogy, with glasshouses, an aviary and exhibition buildings (to left of main entrance). The acacia between the galleries of botany and mineralogy, planted in 1636, is believed to be the oldest tree in Paris.

In the part of the park farthest from the Seine is a low hill with a small maze and a handsome bronze temple – a favourite retreat for romantics both past and present.

★Grande Galerie

During the French Revolution the people of Paris had their first sight of wild animals when they were transferred from the royal menagerie at Versailles to the English park of the Jardin des Plantes. In 1795 they could wonder at the first elephant, in 1826 at the first giraffe. Napoleon established a bear-pit. In 1994 the Grande Galerie de l'Evolution at rue Geoffroy-Saint-Hilaire, designed in 1889 by Jules André, was re-opened after extensive restoration, it now displays fascinating exhibitions on the story of evolution.

Opening times

For the Natural History Museums, which opens every day except Tuesday (admission charge), the opening times are as follows: Grande Gallerie: Wed.–Mon., 10am–6pm, Thur., 10pm: Galleries of Mineralogy, Palaeobotany and Palaeontology: Mon., Wed.–Sun., 10am–5pm, Sat., Sun., in summer 11am–6pm: Galerie d'Entomologie (insect collection): Mon., Wed.–Fri. 9am–1pm, Sat., Sun., 10am–5pm in winter, 11am–6pm in summer.

Jeu de Paume (Galerie Nationale du Jeu de Paume)   G 4

Location
Jardin des
Tuileries,
Place de la
Concorde (1st
arr.)

Métro station
Concorde

Buses
24, 42, 52, 72, 73,
84, 94

At the north-east corner of the Tuileries Gardens, to the left of the Place de la Concorde entrance, is the Jeu de Paume, originally a court for a game similar to tennis known as the *jeu de paume* (from *paume*, "palm", with which the ball was struck). The Jeu de Paume was built in 1851, under the Second Empire, but was considerably altered in 1931.

Until 1986 the Jeu de Paume housed the Louvre's world-famous collection of Impressionists, now displayed in the Musée d'Orsay (see entry). After being remodelled by Antoine Stinco the Galerie National du Jeu de Paume reopened in June 1991. Its 2000sq.m/21,500sq.ft of exhibition space, on two floors, now house periodic special exhibitions of contemporary art (open: Tue. noon–9.30pm, Wed.–Sun. noon–7pm; admission charge).

★★Louvre   H 5

The long and complex history of the Louvre extends over eight centuries of planning, building, destruction and reconstruction. Successive kings of France, from François I to Louis XIV, enlarged the medieval fortified castle into a sumptuous palace, until the establishment of absolutist rule led to the sudden transfer of the court to Versailles. The Louvre was then abandoned, half completed. Thereafter it provided homes and studios for such renowned painters as Fragonard and Chardin; Louis XVI returned briefly to his city palace; and finally in 1793 the Louvre became the prototype of the modern art museum.

The latest plan for the development of the Louvre, the "Grand Louvre" project, was launched in 1981 and is due to be completed by the end of the millennium. France's largest museum will then be the crowning feature in the government's programme of *grands projets* for the closing years of the 20th century.

In November 1993, on the 200th anniversary of the Louvre as a museum, the second and most important part of the Grand Louvre project was completed. It had begun in 1989 with the departure of the Ministry of Finance from the northern (Richelieu) wing of the palace, which it had occupied for over a hundred years, since the time of the Duc de Morny, Napoleon III's minister, to new premises at Bercy (see entry). As the opening of the new entrance to the museum under I. M. Pei's glass pyramid had signalled the completion of the first phase of the project, so the opening of the north wing (also designed by Pei) on November 18th 1993 marked the successful completion of the second. In the next phase, which was completed in 1997, the rooms in the Denon and Sully wings were re-arranged, providing a further

Location
34–36 quai du
Louvre (1st arr.)
Tel. 01 40 20 50 50

Métro stations
Louvre, Palais-
Royal-Musée du
Louvre

Buses
21, 24, 27, 39, 48,
68, 69, 72, 81

Grand Louvre

Arc de Triomphe du Carrousel: originally the grand entrance to the Tuileries Palace

10,000sq.,/107,000sq.ft of exhibition space. By 1999 a further 5000sq.m/54,000 sq. ft should have been added. After 15 years of rebuilding work the total exhibition space available to the museum will have almost doubled to 61,300sq.m/660,00sq.ft. At the same time the construction of the Carrousel du Louvre, the underground facilities to be provided under the courtyard round the Arc de Triomphe du Carrousel (an underground car park with over 700 places, a service centre with shops, restaurants and function rooms, all privately run), linked with the museum's reception area, has been completed. In addition the façades of the palace have been restored and the Jardin du Carrousel replanted. Finally, the palace façades have been carefully restored and the Tuileries gardens (see entry) to the west revamped.

With the reopening of the remodelled rooms on the first floor of the Sully wing round the Cour Carrée in December 1992 the planned rearrangement of the Louvre's picture collections began. In future they are to be displayed in national schools, since French painting accounts for more than half the museum's holdings. The schools of northern Europe will be shown in the north (Richelieu) wing; the southern schools, as hitherto, will be in the south (Denon) wing; and French painting will be mainly in the Sully wing round the Cour Carrée. The present division into seven departments – Oriental (including Islamic) art, Egyptian (including Coptic) art, Greek, Etruscan and Roman art, sculpture, painting, applied and decorative art and graphic art – will be retained, though the separation of genres will not be absolutely rigid. Sculpture will be displayed mainly on the ground floor of the Denon and Richelieu wings, and painting and graphic art will be brought closer together.

Building history

The Palais du Louvre stands on the site of the medieval stronghold built on the right bank of the Seine by Philippe II (Philippe Auguste) about the year 1200. This side of the river was then known as Lupara, which later became Louvre. Remains of Philippe Auguste's fortress can be seen on the mezzanine level below the Cour Carrée. Louis IX (St Louis) added a large hall and extended the crypt (excavation finds on mezzanine level); then in the reign of Louis V Raymond du Temple enlarged the castle still further, and in 1360 the king moved into it, although the palace on the Ile de la Cité (see entry) remained his official residence. Until the reign of Henri II the French kings lived only sporadically in their town palace. Detailed evidence on the history of the building in the time of Charles V is provided by the "Très Riches Heures du Duc de Berry", the prayer-book illuminated by the Limburg brothers. In the 15th century the Louvre served mainly as an arsenal for the storage of weapons, since the kings preferred to live in their châteaux on the Loire. Then in the first half of the 16th century François I, the "Renaissance king", took an interest in the palace. He

Grand Louvre: Cross-section

had the keep pulled down and commissioned the architect Pierre Lescot and the sculptor Jean Goujon, following Italian models, to build the halves of the west and south wings of the Old Louvre which meet at a right angle round the present Cour Carrée. After François' death these parts were completed by Lescot and Goujon, and in 1566 they were extended by the Petite Galerie (at right angles to Lescot's south wing). At almost the same time (1564 onwards), after the death of Henri II, the Tuileries Palace was built as a residence for his widow Catherine de Médicis only 500m/550yds west of the Old Louvre (along the present Avenue du Général-Lemonnier). In the reign of Henri IV this palace was linked by the long south wing along the Seine, the Galerie du Bord de l'Eau, with the Petite Galerie. After the murder of Henri IV his widow moved to the Palais du Luxembourg (see entry). Their son Louis XIII completed the Cour Carrée and the Pavillon Sully. Louis XIV commissioned Le Brun and Le Vau to remodel the Petite Galerie and Claude Perrault to build a monumental façade on the east wing, now known as the Colonnade. Both the Louvre and the Tuileries were occupied only for short periods, and after Louis XIV moved his residence to Versailles they fell into such a state of dilapidation that in the mid 17th century consideration was given to their possible demolition. Louis XV, however, began the process of renovation. At this time the idea first emerged of bringing together in the Louvre the royal collections of masterpieces of art. In 1776 the Grande Galerie was declared a museum. After the Revolution, on August 10th 1793, the people were able for the first time to see the royal apartments. Napoleon enlarged the courtyard in front of the Tuileries (now the Jardin du Louvre and Place and Square du Carrousel) and set up in its centre the Arc de Triomphe du Carrousel, and also began the construction of the north wing along Rue de Rivoli. In the reign of Napoleon III the Louvre and the Tuileries were joined up, and Baron Haussmann laid out the Jardin du Louvre and Place and Square du Carrousel in their present form. Only a few years later, however, on May 23rd 1871, the Tuileries Palace was burned down by the Commune. Fortunately the fire was extinguished before it reached the Louvre, but the Tuileries was completely destroyed and was not rebuilt. Finally in autumn 1981 President Mitterand initiated the ambitious project to make the Louvre the biggest museum in the world, the Grand Louvre, which was to be a temple of culture worthy of the historic site on which it stood.

The buildings round the square Cour Carrée belong to the Old Louvre (Vieux Louvre), the Palais du Louvre proper, now known as the Sully wing. It occupies the site of Philippe Auguste's original stronghold. The Lescot façade was begun in the reign of Henri II, the other wings in the time of Louis XIII and XIV, but they were completed only by

Vieux Louvre (Old Sully)

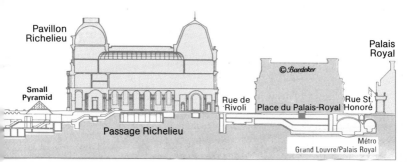

Harmony of traditional and modern: the historic Pavillon Richelieu and the Glass Pyramid

Napoleon. The Pavillon de l'Horloge (Clock Pavilion), better known as the Pavillon Sully, is designed to match the style of the Lescot façade; it was built in the 17th century by Jacques Lemercier, who also added the northern part of the west wing in a quasi-Renaissance style.

Lescot façade

The southern half of the west wing of the Cour Carrée, built between 1559 and 1574 by the architect Pierre Lescot (1510–78) and the sculptor Jean Goujon (1510–68) is a masterpiece of Renaissance architecture. In its conspicuous harmony it illustrates how the men of the Renaissance sought to achieve the regularity of their antique models in a clear and modest form but not necessarily without ornament – a style very different from the monumental classicism of the late 18th century, as seen, for example, in the Madeleine and the Panthéon (see entries). Both horizontally, in the alternation of the doorway and pediment levels with the window level, and vertically (if the low upper storey is seen as a unit with the roof) there is a clear division into three; and the relationship between the door and window sections and between the height of the storeys and the projecting moulding that marks them off also shows a ratio of 3 to 1. The round-headed windows on the ground floor give it the effect of an arcade. On the middle floor every two windows with triangular pediments alternate with a window with a semicircular pediment (again showing the rhythm in threes). The top floor is famed for Jean Goujon's marvellous relief decoration in the semicircular pediments, between which is a richly ornamented balustrade. The reliefs in the pediments are allegorical, representing nature (left; Ceres for agriculture, Neptune for seafaring, genius with cornucopia), war (centre; the war god Neptune, the war goddess Bellona, prisoners) and learning (right; Archimedes for astronomy, Euclid for geometry, genius of learning).

In 1665 Ludwig XIV sought by holding an architectural competition to secure the best architects of the day to design a suitably imposing east front for the Old Louvre. Among those who entered the competition were the French architects Jean Marot and Jacques Lemercier and the Italian Lorenzo Bernini, architect of St Peter's Square in Rome. The winning design was the joint work of Claude Perrault, Louis Le Vau and Charles Lebrun. Their Colonnade, which can now be seen in its full height, represents a compromise between French Baroque and Italian neo-classical models. The twin columns and flat roof are characteristic of the Italian neo-classical style, while the emphasis given to the central section with its triangular pediment and to the ends of the façade is typically French.

East front
Colonnades

Now that the basement structure has been exposed the colonnade with its 18 Corinthian columns is given the height and the distance which the architects intended. The classical severity of the façade was designed to be relieved by a series of statues along the roof balustrade, but this part of the project was not carried out. After the court departed for Versailles building work stopped and was resumed only in the time of Napoleon. From that period date the sculpture in the pediment (Minerva, 1811) and the relief over the arch of the doorway (the goddess of Victory in a four-horse chariot); higher up, to right and left, are medallions with the initials of Louis XIV.

The Pavillon de Flore and the Pavillon de Marsan were linked until 1871 by the Tuileries Palace. The Pavillon de Flore takes its name from the relief of the "Triumph of Flora" (by Jean-Baptiste Carpeaux, 1866) on the side facing the Seine.

Pavillon de Flore

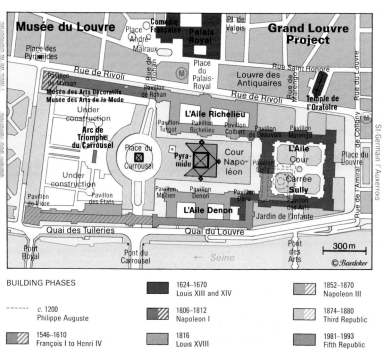

BUILDING PHASES

------ *c.* 1200
Philippe Auguste

1546–1610
François I to Henri IV

1624–1670
Louis XIII and XIV

1806–1812
Napoleon I

1816
Louis XVIII

1852–1870
Napoleon III

1874–1880
Third Republic

1981–1993
Fifth Republic

Louvre

Carrousel du Louvre

Between the Place du Carrousel and the Tuileries Gardens a large underground complex was constructed between 1989 and 1993. As well as a large car park it includes a shopping arcade with high-class boutiques, restaurants, galleries and a complex of four halls in which are held trade exhibitions and concerts as well as fashion shows by famous couturiers. During the excavation work a 16th c. town wall 130m/430ft long was discovered, and the architects Ming Pei and Michel Macary skilfully oncorporated this into their elegant new building of light-coloured stone and concrete. A surmounting pyramid provides the entrance hall with light – Pei's counterpart to his glass pyramid which forms the entrance to the Louvre Museum.

Arc de Triomphe du Carrousel

The carefuly restored Arc de Triomphe du Carrousel, originally the grand entrance to the courtyard of the Tuileries Palace, is a reproduction of the Arch of Septimius Severus in Rome. It was built in 1806–08 (architects Percier and Fontaine) to commemorate Napoleon's victories. The imposing chariot which crowns the arch was the work of F.-J. Bosio (1828). With the destruction of the Tuileries the arch lost its function as the entrance to the palace, and it now looks rather isolated. "Carrousel" was the name of the equestrian games in a medieval tournament, and the square is named after the carrousel held during the celebrations in honour of the birth of the Dauphin, Louis XIV's son, in 1662.

Opening times
Conducted visits, information

Admission charge

★★Musée du Louvre

The main entrance to the Louvre Museum is the glass pyramid in the Cour Napoléon; a second entrance from the Carrousel du Louvre; and there is a third entrance, the Passage Richelieu between Place du Palais-Royal and the Cour Carrée, for Friends of the Louvre (Amis du Louvre), groups and visitors to the auditorium and restaurant only. A further entrance, the Porte des Lions is to be opened in 1998.

The Museum is open Mon. and Wed.–Sun. 9am–6pm; on Mondays the three wings are open in rotation until 9.45pm, on Wednesdays the whole museum. The rooms begin to close at 5.30–9.30pm respectively. The special exhibitions, rooms on the history of the Louvre, the exhibition on the medieval Louvre, the museum bookshop, the Restaurant Grand Louvre and the Café du Louvre, all on the mezzanine level, are open daily until 10pm. During construction work on the Grand Louvre some rooms are temporarily closed; information on the present position can be obtained at the information desk or from the electronic indicators in the reception area under the pyramid. General information: tel. 01 40 20 51 51 (answerphone in five languages); 01 40 20 53 17 (reception) Internet address: http:/www.Louvre.

Cassette guides in six languages are available; for conducted visits and workshops tel. 01 40 20 52 09 (individual visitors), 01 40 20 51 77 (groups); fax 01 40 20 58 24: information on events in the auditoria, tel. 01 40 20 52 99; Amis du Louvre, tel. 01 40 20 53 34. Those wishing to avoid long queues can obtain tickets in advance from FNAC (tel. 01 49 87 54 54), valid until Jan. 31st of the following year.

The "Victory of Samothrace" (end of 3rd c. B.C.)

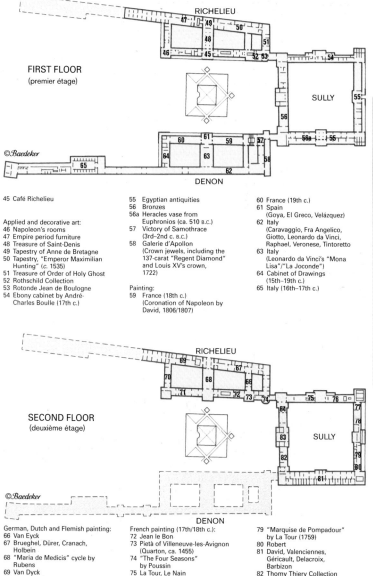

FIRST FLOOR
(premier étage)

RICHELIEU

SULLY

DENON

©Baedeker

45 Café Richelieu

Applied and decorative art:
46 Napoleon's rooms
47 Empire period furniture
48 Treasure of Saint-Denis
49 Tapestry of Anne de Bretagne
50 Tapestry, "Emperor Maximilian Hunting" (c. 1535)
51 Treasure of Order of Holy Ghost
52 Rothschild Collection
53 Rotonde Jean de Boulogne
54 Ebony cabinet by André-Charles Boulle (17th c.)

55 Egyptian antiquities
56 Bronzes
56a Heracles vase from Euphronios (ca. 510 B.C.)
57 Victory of Samothrace (3rd–2nd c. B.C.)
58 Galerie d'Apollon (Crown jewels, including the 137-carat "Regent Diamond" and Louis XV's crown, 1722)

Painting:
59 France (18th c.) (Coronation of Napoleon by David, 1806/1807)

60 France (19th c.)
61 Spain (Goya, El Greco, Velázquez)
62 Italy (Caravaggio, Fra Angelico, Giotto, Leonardo da Vinci, Raphael, Veronese, Tintoretto
63 Italy (Leonardo da Vinci's "Mona Lisa"/"La Joconde")
64 Cabinet of Drawings (15th–19th c.)
65 Italy (16th–17th c.)

SECOND FLOOR
(deuxième étage)

RICHELIEU

SULLY

DENON

©Baedeker

German, Dutch and Flemish painting:
66 Van Eyck
67 Brueghel, Dürer, Cranach, Holbein
68 "Maria de Medicis" cycle by Rubens
69 Van Dyck
70 Rembrandt
71 Vermeer, Ruisdael

French painting (17th/18th c.):
72 Jean le Bon
73 Pietà of Villeneuve-les-Avignon (Quarton, ca. 1455)
74 "The Four Seasons" by Poussin
75 La Tour, Le Nain
76 Le Brun, Jouvenet
77 Watteau
78 Chardin

79 "Marquise de Pompadour" by La Tour (1759)
80 Robert
81 David, Valenciennes, Géricault, Delacroix, Barbizon
82 Thomy Thiery Collection Corot, Moreau Nelaton Collection
83 De Croy Lyon and Beistegui Collections
84 French Drawings

Louvre
Musée du Louvre

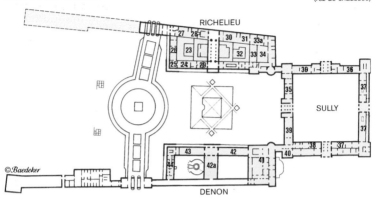

Sculpture:
23 Cour Marly ("Marly Horses" by Guillaume Coustou, 18th c.)
24 Romanesque and Gothic art
25 Madonnas (14th c.)
26 Tomb of Philippe Pot (d. 1493)
27 Statue of Diana (16th c.) from Château d'Anet
28 Sculpture by Sarazin (18th c.)
29 Café Marly
30 "Les Grands Hommes" Gallery (Portrait bust by Pigalle, Houdon and Rude, 18th–19th c.)
31 Animal bronzes by Barye
32 Cour Puget (Milon de Crotone, 1682)

Oriental antiquities:
33 Statues of Gudea;
33a Hammurabi's Code of Laws (ca. 1790–1770 B.C.)
34 Cour Khorsabad (Throne room from Khorsabad, 8th c. B.C.)
35 Syrian, Mycenaean, Cypriot and Phoenician art
36 Oriental antiquities
37 Egyptian antiquities

Greek, Etruscan and Roman antiquities:
38 Venus de Milo (B.C.)
39 Room of Caryatids ca. 100 (Roman sculpture, copies of 4th c. B.C Greek works)
40 Panathenaic frieze from Parthenon (5th c. B.C.)
41 Sarcophagus from Cerveteri (6th c. B.C.)
42 Galerie Daru
42a Salle du Manège (copies of ancient busts)

43 Italian sculpture (Canova's "Cupid and Psyche"; Michelangelo's "Slaves" ca. 1513)

44 German, Dutch and Flemish sculpture

▶
"Cupid and Psyche" – neo-classical marble sculpture by Antonio Canova

Musée du Louvre

Project Grand Louvre

HALL NAPOLEON
Niveau Accueil (-2)

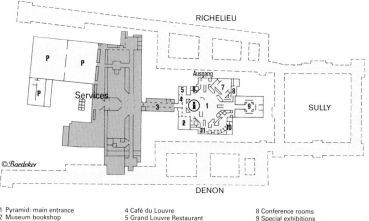

1 Pyramid: main entrance
2 Museum bookshop
3 Post office/exchange office;
  Friends of Louvre; Print Cabinet

4 Café du Louvre
5 Grand Louvre Restaurant
6 Audiovisual rooms
7 Auditorium

8 Conference rooms
9 Special exhibitions
10 Conducted tours
11 Cloakroom

HALL NAPOLEON

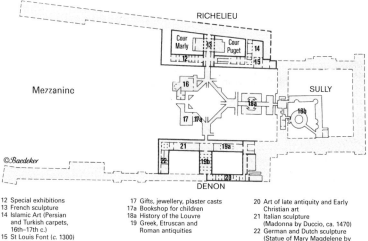

12 Special exhibitions
13 French sculpture
14 Islamic Art (Persian
   and Turkish carpets,
   16th–17th c.)
15 St Louis Font (c. 1300)
16 Cafeteria

17 Gifts, jewellery, plaster casts
17a Bookshop for children
18a History of the Louvre
19 Greek, Etruscan and
   Roman antiquities

20 Art of late antiquity and Early
   Christian art
21 Italian sculpture
   (Madonna by Duccio, ca. 1470)
22 German and Dutch sculpture
   (Statue of Mary Magdelene by
   G. Erhart, ca. 1540)

Louvre

★Glass Pyramid, Hall Napoléon (Niveau Accueil)

The main entrance, in the centre of the Cour Napoléon, is the glass pyramid (22m/72ft high; 675 panes of glass) designed by the Chinese American architect Ieoh Ming Pei (b. 1917) and opened in 1989. This gives access to the underground Hall Napoléon, in which are information desks, the ticket office, the bookshop, café and restaurant, auditoria, the Print Cabinet and rooms for special exhibitions. From here corridors and escalators take visitors to the various departments.

Mezzanine level

Before construction work on the Louvre began archaeologists carried out excavations in the Cour Carrée and Cour Napoléon and brought to light the remains of Philippe Auguste's fortress of c. 1200, with its keep, and Charles V's 14th century palace. An exhibition in two parts recounts the history of the Louvre, and visitors can see the remains of the medieval crypt.

Aile Richelieu

On the lower floor (basement level) of the Richelieu Wing, opened in November 1993, are contemporary exhibitions, French sculpture and Islamic art; on the ground floor, round two covered inner courtyards, the Cour Marly and the Cour Puget, are French sculpture and Oriental antiquities; on the first floor is applied and decorative art and on the second floor German, Flemish, French and Dutch painting.

Aile Sully

On the lower floor of the Sully Wing (the east wing round the Cour Carrée) are the new department on the history of the Louvre and the excavations of the medieval crypt; on the ground floor are Oriental and Egyptian antiquities, Coptic art, Greek, Etruscan and Roman work, including the famous Venus de Milo; on the first floor are applied and decorative art, Egyptian, Greek, Etruscan and Roman antiquities (Victory of Samothrace) and 18th century French painting; and on the second floor are the 17th and 19th century French schools and graphic art.

Aile Denon

On the lower floor of the Denon Wing (south side of the Cour Napoléon) are Greek, Etruscan and Roman antiquities, the art of late antiquity and Italian, German and Dutch sculpture; the ground floor also displays Greek, Etruscan and Roman antiquities, together with Italian, German, Flemish and Dutch sculpture; and on the first floor are the Galerie d'Apollon (treasures from the royal collections), large-scale 19th c. French paintings, such as David's "Coronation of Napoleon", Spanish and British masters as well as Italian paintings and graphic art from the 11th to the 18th c., including Leonardo da Vinci's "Mona Lisa" and works by Raphael, Veronese and Tintoretto.

The Collections

Origins

The first royal collector was François I, who brought together in his palace of Fontainebleau (see entry) paintings, sculpture and reproductions in the Italian style, including the enigmatically smiling "Mona Lisa". Another king interested in art was Louis XIV, who acquired the collections of Cardinal Mazarin and a celebrated financier and art-lover, Jabach, which included Titian's "Entombment". In 1683 the royal collection contained over 2000 pictures. On August 10th 1792 the Royal Museum was established, and from 1794 onwards this was enriched by thousands of works of art brought back as booty by the French armies. Deprived after the fall of the Empire of all these stolen treasures with the exception of a few works such as Veronese's "Marriage in Cana", the Louvre continued to make fresh acquisitions. In the course of the 19th century the departments of Egyptian and Oriental antiquities were established, and later successive architects tried to bring order into the museum's maze of rooms. Since then the seven departments of the museum have grown steadily through new acquisitions and gifts from over 2700 donors.

The Museum now possesses over 30,000 works of art. It is possible, therefore, to give only a general account of the scope and variety of the collections and a selection of the most famous works on view.

Each of these three sections is displayed separately. The history of ancient art from the beginnings of Greek art to the last days of the Roman Empire is illustrated by a magnificent collection of marble and bronze sculpture, frescoes, mosaics, gold, ivory and glass. Among particular treasures are the Etruscan sarcophagus from Cerveteri (6th c. B.C.); fragments of Phidias's Parthenon frieze (447–438 B.C.); metopes from the Temple of Zeus at Olympia (5th c. B.C.), presented by Greece in gratitude for French support during its war of independence (1829); the famous Venus de Milo (illustration, p. 104) from the collection of the Marquis de Rivière, a statue of the 2nd c. B.C. based on a 4th century original which was found off the island of Melos in 1820, one of the most perfect representations of the Greek ideal of beauty; the Doric "Lady of Auxerre" (c. 630 B.C.), one of the oldest examples of Greek statuary; the Ionic "Hera of Samos" (c. 560 B.C.), whose cylindrical form points to Mesopotamian influences; the beautiful "Rampin Head" (c. 550 B.C.), from an equestrian figure whose torso is in the Acropolis Museum in Athens; the "Apollo Sauroktonos" and "Cnidian Aphrodite", 4th century copies of originals by Praxiteles; the "Victory of Samothrace" (Hellenistic, late 3rd or early 2nd c. B.C.; illustration, p. 122); the "Borghese Wrestler" (1st c. B.C.); the bust of Agrippa (1st c. A.D.), son-in-law and counsellor of the Emperor Augustus; the head of a young prince of the Antonine dynasty (2nd c. A.D.); the altar of Domitius Ahenobarbus (1st c. B.C.) from the Temple of Neptune in Rome; the "Birth of the Tiber" (1st c. B.C.); fragments of the Ara Pacis, Augustus's Temple of Peace in Rome; antique bronzes, including the "Apollo of Piombino" (c. 500 B.C.), and everyday objects, such as an Etruscan mirror with incised ornament (3rd c. B.C.); a collection of Roman sarcophagi of the 2nd and 3rd centuries A.D.; Greek and Roman frescoes and mosaics, including the "Judgment of Paris" (a mosaic from Antioch, 2nd c. A.D.); and Greek vases from the Geometric (9th–8th c. B.C.) to the Hellenistic period (2nd c. B.C.)

Antiquity
Greek, Etruscan and Roman antiquities

◄

The famous "Venus de Milo" (2nd c. B.C.)

Napoleon's Egyptian campaigns aroused interest in antiquity and the East. Further material came from excavations, sometimes carried out by the Louvre itself, new acquisitions and gifts, and from the collections of the National Library transferred to the Louvre. Among the most important works in the department covering ancient Mesopotamia, Sumer and Akkad are the Stele of Naram-Sin, king of Akkad *c.* 2270 B.C., commemorating his victory over the barbarians in the Zagros Mountains; various statues of Gudea, the Sumerian ruler of Lagash in the 3rd millennium B.C.; and decorative elements from the palaces of Nimrud, Nineveh and especially Khorsabad, the residence of King Sargon II (721–705 B.C.), including 4m/13ft high winged animals which give some idea of the scale of the palace. The principal treasure of this department, however, is the Stele of Hammurabi

Oriental antiquities

Two basalt sarcophagi from the Egyptian collection (2nd. c. B.C.)

(1792–1750 B.C.), king of the first Babylonian kingdom, a conical basalt cylinder 2.25m/7ft 5in. high inscribed with Hammurabi's code of laws written in Akkadian in cuneiform script.

Egyptian antiquities

The Egyptian department, founded in 1826 by Jean-François Champollion, who deciphered the Egyptian hieroglyphics, covers the art and culture of Egypt from the Old, Middle and New Kingdoms down to the Christian era. Notable items in the extensive collections are King Wadji's majestic stele, the Stele of the Snake Goddess Zet, of the Thinite period (c. 3100 B.C.); the Stele of Antef, a high official in the reign of Tuthmosis III (c. 1490–1439 B.C.); an ivory-handled dagger of the early dynastic period (c. 3300 B.C.) from Djebel el-Arak; a triangular harp of the Saite period (7th–6th c. B.C.); the head of King Didufri, successor to Cheops in the Old Kingdom (c. 2250 B.C.); the "Squatting Scribe", a painted sandstone figure found in a 5th Dynasty tomb at Saqqara (c. 2500 B.C.); the fine wooden figures of an official of Memphis and his wife (c. 2350 B.C.); a sandstone statue of the High Prophet Amenemhatankh (c. 1850 B.C.); a bust of King Amenophis IV/ Akhenaton (c. 1365–1349 B.C.); the sarcophagus of Chancellor Imeneminet (8th c. B.C.); and Coptic reliefs in stone and wood, tapestries and bronze liturgical utensils of the 5th–7th centuries.

Sculpture

The Musée des Monuments Français, which was closed down under the Restoration, provided the nucleus of the Louvre's collection of sculpture, which has since been steadily expanded. Among the numerous works of the 12th to 19th centuries the most notable are a representation of Daniel in the lions' den on a Romanesque capital from the old Paris church of Sainte-Geneviève; the 12th century "Auvergne Madonna"; the masterly Gothic figure of the "Queen of Sheba" (c. 1180); the Norman "Madonna of Maisoncelles" (14th c.); the figure of King Charles V (c. 1390); the tomb of Philippe Pot, Grand

Seneschal of Burgundy (d. 1493); the Gothic St George's Altar by Michel Colombe (early 16th c.); a bas-relief by Jean Goujon from the Fontaine des Innocents (1547–49); Germain Pilon's group of the Three Graces, bearing an urn with the heart of Henri II (c. 1560); a bronze figure of Anne of Austria (Louis XIII's wife) by Simon Guillan (1642); Puget's "Milo of Crotone" (1862) from the park of the Château de Versailles; the "Marly Horses" by Guillaume Coustou (1739–45); Houdon's graceful "Diana the Huntress" (1790); Canova's neo-classical "Cupid and Psyche" (1793); Pigalle's "Mercury attaching his wings to his heels" (1744); vigorous animal studies by Bayre and Rude's "Neapolitan Fisherman" (1833); James Pradier's "Satyr and Bacchante" (1834); and Michelangelo's magnificent "Dying Slave" and "Rebel Slave" (1513–15), originally intended for the tomb of Pope Julius II as a secular counterpart to the "Apotheosis" of the Holy Father.

Painting

Few museums in the world possess such a variety of paintings of different schools and in different formats as the Louvre. Originating as François I's picture gallery, greatly enriched in the reign of Louis XIV and later by spectacular new acquisitions, the Louvre collections offer a wide-ranging survey of the development of European painting. Almost two-thirds of the exhibits are of the French school, ranging in date from the Middle Ages to the 19th century.

French school

The principal works of the late Middle Ages are the "Pietà of Villeneuve-lès-Avignon" (15th c.), a work of tragic nobility, probably by Enguerrand Quarton; the portrait of King Jean le Bon by an unknown artist (c. 1360), the earliest known French panel painting; and Jean Fouquet's portrait of Charles VII (c. 1445). Characteristic of the 16th century Fontainebleau school are the masterly portraits of court dignitaries by the Clouet family. Antoine Caron's "Massacre of the Triumvirs" (1566) alludes allegorically to the horrors of the religious wars. In the early 17th century new artistic impulses came from Italy. During this period Georges de La Tour painted his candle-lit scenes – "Magdalene with Night-Light", "The Card-sharper", "St Joseph in the Carpenter's Shop", c. 1630–40; Louis Le Nain produced his realistic genre studies ("Peasant Family", c. 1643); the great age of classicism began with the mythological and lyrical pictures of Nicolas Poussin ("The Inspiration of Poets", c. 1630) and Claude Gellée, called Le Nain ("Cleopatra's Arrival in Tarsus", 1642–43); and historical painting enjoyed a heyday, with Charles Le Brun's vivid portraits ("Chancellor Séguin at Louis XIV's Entry into Paris", c. 1655) and the ceremonial portraits of Hyacinthe Rigaud ("Louis XIV", 1701).
   In the 18th century fresh possibilities were opened up by Antoine

◄
"Louis" XIV by Rigaud (1701)

Detail from "The Cheat" by Georges de La Tour (1630)

Watteau, a colourist who found inspiration in the Italian commedia dell'arte ("Pierrot", 1718). Scenes of a more relaxed morality, sometimes degenerating into libertinage, were depicted by Boucher ("Diana resting after her bathe", *c.* 1750) and Fragonard ("Women Bathing", *c.* 1770). Louis David's "Oath of the Horatii" (1784) was the manifesto of neo-classicism; his masterpiece, however, was his "Coronation of Napoleon in Notre-Dame" (1805–07). Among the leading representatives of Romanticism was Géricault, with the dramatic "Raft of the 'Méduse'" (1819). Eugène Delacroix' "Liberty Guiding the People" (1830) represented a revolution of passionate feeling, colour and movement; his oil painting "Dante and Virgil" caused something of a scandal; but his portrait of Chopin (1838) was more romantic in effect. Camille Corot, with his poetic freshness and preference for an unconventional play of light ("Souvenir de Mortefontaine", 1864), can be seen as a forerunner of the Impressionists. Other landscape painters such as Théodore Rousseau in his "Edge of the Forest, Fontainebleau" also use a varying intensity of light. Jean-Dominique Ingres' "Bathers, Valpinçon" (1808) and "Turkish Bath" (1862) reflect his admiration of the harmonious compositions of the Venetian and Florentine masters.

Italian school

The second largest body of painting in the Louvre is formed by Italian work from the second half of the 13th century to the end of the 18th. The early period of the Florentine school is represented by Cimabue's "Madonna with Angels" (c. 1270) from the church of San Francesco in Pisa. Giotto's "St Francis Preaching to the Birds" (c. 1300), from the predella of the altar of San Francesco in Assisi, already shows a concern with three-dimensionality. The beginning of the Renaissance in the Quattrocento is marked by Fra Angelico's "Coronation of the Virgin" (1434–35) from the church of San Domenico in Fiesole, with its use of perspective and freedom from Byzantine rigidity, and his "Martyrdom of St Cosmas and St Damian" (1440). Andrea Mantegna achieves a geometric depth ("Calvary", 1459), while delicate curving lines and translucent colours characterise the transfigured faces in the allegorical frescoes (c. 1483) of Sandro Botticelli. The heyday of the Italian Renaissance, from the end of the 15th century to the first half of the 16th, is represented by the Louvre's fine collection of the work of Leonardo da Vinci, including the "Annunciation" (1475), "Virgin and Child with St Anne" (c. 1506) and the smiling "Mona Lisa" or "La Gioconda" (in French La Joconde) of 1503–05. The sitter, famed for her enigmatic smile, is believed to have been Monna Lisa

The enigmatic Mona Lisa

Gherardini, wife of the Florentine patrician Francesco di Zanobi del Giocondo. The fine modelling of the face in the changing play of light cannot unfortunately be fully appreciated because of the protective screen of bullet-proof glass. Other 16th century treasures are Raphael's "Holy Family" (better known as "La Belle Jardinière"), painted in Florence in 1507, and his "Portrait of Baldassare Castiglione" (1516), Titian's tender and melancholy "Entombment" (c. 1525) and Paolo Veronese's huge "Wedding Feast at Cana" (1563). Caravaggio's "Death of the Virgin" (c. 1605) caused a scandal because of his realistic depiction of the scene, while Guido Reni's elegant and theatrical "Rape of Helen" (1631) was one of the most admired paintings of its day. Outstanding 18th century works are Francesco Guardi's series of paintings (c. 1770) depicting the festivities on the occasion of the enthronement of Doge Alvise Mocenigo IV in Venice.

The masterpieces of German, Flemish and Dutch painting in the Louvre range from Late Gothic by way of the Renaissance to the 17th century. Among the principal Flemish works are Jan van Eyck's "Madonna of Autun" (c. 1435), Hans Memling's "Portrait of an Old Woman" (c. 1470), Quentin Metsys' genre scene "The Moneylender and his Wife" (1514) and Peter Breughel the Elder's "Beggars" 1568), which alludes to the revolt of the Geusen ("Beggars") against Philip II of Spain. Peter Paul Rubens, who had an enduring influence on the 17th century Flemish school, has a room to himself for the hagiographical cycle of 21 paintings commissioned by Marie de Médicis for the Palais du Luxembourg (1622–25). In the unfinished study "Hélène Fourment and two of her Children" (c. 1636) Rubens gives expression to his tender feelings for his young family. Other important Flemish works are van Dyck's imposing portrait of Charles I (c. 1635) and Jacob Jordaens's "Four Apostles", from his early period (1617–31).

German, Flemish and Dutch schools

Among the Dutch painters all the great names are represented – Hieronymus Bosch with his almost surrealist "Ship of Fools" (c. 1490), Frans Hals with his bold character study of "The Gipsy Girl" (1628–30), Jan Vermeer van Delft with his poetic "Lacemaker" (1664) and his "Astronomer" (1668), Jakob van Ruisdael with "The Sunbeam" (c. 1670) and above all Rembrandt with his self-portraits, the moving "Disciples at Emmaus" (1648), the gripping portrait of Hendrickje Stoffels, companion of his last years, and the nude "Bathsheba Bathing", holding in her hand David's letter declaring his love (1654).

Although the collection of German paintings is smaller it contains some notable works, among them the elegant self-portrait of the 22-year-old Albrecht Dürer (1493), Lucas Cranach the Elder's "Venus" (1529) and Hans Holbein the Younger's "Anne of Cleves" (1539) and "Erasmus of Rotterdam", painted in Basle in 1523.

British school

British art of the 18th and 19th century is represented by portraits by Gainsborough ("Conversation in the Park") and his rival Reynolds ("Master Hare", 1788–89), Raeburn, Lawrence, Constable ("Weymouth Bay", 1824), Turner ("Landscape", c. 1830) and Burne-Jones ("The King's Daughter", 1865–66).

Spanish school

Among the masterpieces of Spanish art of the 14th to 18th centuries are El Greco's "Christ on the Cross, with Two Donors" (c. 1585), José Ribera's "Man with a Club Foot" (1642), Francisco de Zurbarán's "Burial of St Bonaventure" (c. 1630), Murillo's "Young Beggar" (1650), with a typically Sevillian use of colour, a portrait (c. 1654) of the Infanta Margarita, Philip IV's daughter, which is attributed to Velázquez and a marvellous series of portraits by Goya, including "Don Evariste Perez de Castro" (1805), the doctor and member of parliament "Fernando Guillemardet" (1798) and the proud Marquesa de la Solana (c. 1810).

Applied and decorative art

The department of applied and decorative art possesses many treasures from the monastery of Saint-Denis, confiscated in 1793, the royal furniture stores and rich private collections. Among the finest items are medieval stained glass, liturgical utensils and bronzes, including an equestrian statue of Charlemagne (9th c.), Byzantine ivories (Hrabaville Triptych, mid 10th c.), a 5th century diptych, the Suger Eagle (porphyry vase with gold ornament, 12th c.), pottery and majolica of the school of Palissy, figures of Henri IV and Marie de Médicis (c. 1610), the crown jewels (in the Galerie d'Apollon), with the crown made for the Empress Eugénie by Gabriel Lemonnier (1855), the crown used at Louis XV's coronation and the 137 carat Regent's Diamond (found in India in 1698 and acquired by Philippe d'Orléans in 1717), silver by Thomas Germain, a cabinet by Molitor, goldsmith's work by Froment-Meurice, a Chinese tea service which belonged to Queen Marie-Amélie, superb tapestries, including "Maximilian Hunting" (Brussels, c. 1530), and furniture and bronzes of the 17th and 18th centuries from the royal palaces of Saint-Cloud and the Tuileries.

Graphic art

The Louvre possesses over 120,000 drawings, including work by the court painters Lo Brun, Pierre Mignard and Antoine Coypel, 4500 engravings by Rembrandt and drawings by Leonardo da Vinci ("Isabella d'Este", c. 1490), Pisanello, Jacopo Bellini, Veronese, Raphael, Füssli (Fuseli), Goya, Dürer, Corot, Delacroix and the Impressionists.

★Luxembourg   H 6

★Jardin du Luxembourg

Location
Boulevard St-Michel (6th arr.)
Main entrance:
place Edmond-Rostand

Children and students from the nearby Quartier Latin (see entry) are the most regular visitors to the Luxembourg Gardens, Paris's best known park after the Tuileries. They were laid out in the 17th century when the Palais du Luxembourg was built, and were given their present form in the 19th century by the architect J.-F. Chalgrin (1739–1811).

Métro station
Odéon

The large octagonal pond with a fountain is flanked by two terraces. This part of the park is laid out in the French classical style, symmetrically, with straight lines, while the outer parts with their winding paths and quiet corners between irregularly grouped clumps of trees are in the less formal English style. Along the terraces and paths are statues of prominent men and women from the worlds of art and politics. A popular meeting-point is the picturesque Fontaine de Médicis, hidden under trees opposite the east front of the palace. The fountain basin, with a Renaissance monument on the pediment of which are the river gods of the Rhône and the Seine, dates from around 1620 and is a reminder of the Luxembourg's former owner Marie de Médicis. The large pond is usually surrounded by children sailing their boats (and boats can be hired at a kiosk by the pond), while younger children enjoy the Grand Guignol (the equivalent of a Punch and Judy show) in the south-west of the park near the tennis courts.

Until a few years ago elderly women used to patrol the park collecting charges for the use of seats; nowadays, however, all the seats and benches are free of charge. At dusk the park-keeper's whistle is the signal that the gates are about to be closed for the night.

RER station
Luxembourg

Buses
21, 27, 38, 82, 84, 86, 89

Opening times
Daily 9am to dusk

Palais du Luxembourg (Musée du Luxembourg)   H 6

The Palais du Luxembourg is the seat of the Senate, the second chamber of the French Parliament, the other house of which is the Assemblée Nationale (see Palais-Bourbon). Apart from the Museum only parts of the palace are open to the public, and only on Sundays.

Marie de Médicis, Henri IV's widow, acquired the property from Duke Francis of Luxembourg in 1612 as the site of a dower house. She wanted it to be in the Florentine style of her homeland, but the palace erected between 1615 and 1631 to the design of Salomon de Brosse is very much in line with French architectural tradition. The main wing and the side wings, flanked by pavilions (domed structures with high-pitched roofs) surround a grand courtyard, the Cour d'Honneur; the residential apartments, in the classic sequence of garderobe, cabinet, antechamber and bedroom, form separate units; and there are two long galleries intended for the display of cycles of paintings. Marie de Médicis never lived in the palace, however, for soon after its completion she had to flee the country, having lost the game of political intrigue with her opponent Cardinal Richelieu, and she died in exile in Cologne in 1642. After several changes of ownership the palace was selected by Napoleon as the seat of the Senate and reconstructed for its new function by J.-F. Chalgrin.

The famous cycle of pictures by Rubens depicting the life of Marie de Médicis is now in the Louvre; a planned cycle of paintings devoted to Henri IV was never realised.

The library, which has fine murals by Eugène Delacroix (1845–47), is not open to the public.

Location
19 rue de Vaugirard (6th arr.)

Métro stations
Odéon, Luxembourg

RER station
Luxembourg

Buses
58, 83, 84, 85

Opening times
Museum:
Tue., Wed., Fri.–Sun.
1–7pm
Thur. 12.30–9pm

Admission charge

★Madeleine   G 4

The church of St Mary Magdalene (Sainte-Marie-Madeleine), generally known simply as the Madeleine, is in the form of a Greek temple of considerable size (108m/354ft long by 43m/141ft wide) surrounded by 54 Corinthian columns 15m/49ft high.

The story of the building of the Madeleine reflects the vicissitudes of French history from the closing years of the Ancien Régime to the bourgeois monarchy of 1830–48. The foundation-stone of a domed cruciform Baroque church was laid in 1763, in the reign of Louis XV. In the reign of Louis XVI it was decided to alter the plan to a neo-classical church on the model of the Panthéon (see entry), which was then under construction, but to give more prominence to the dome. After

Location
Place de la Madeleine (8th arr.)

Métro station
Madeleine

Buses
24, 42, 52, 84, 94

The Madeleine, neo-classical in style, surrounded by Corinthian columns

the Revolution work on the building came to a standstill, and various plans for converting it for use as a stock exchange, parliament building or bank were considered and rejected. In 1806 Napoleon resolved to build a Hall of Fame for the army in the style of the Parthenon in Athens; then, shortly before his abdication, reverted to the idea of a church. After the Restoration Louis XVIII wanted to make it a church of atonement for the Revolution. Finally, in the reign of Louis-Philippe, the church was at last completed in its present form and consecrated in 1842.

Pediment sculpture

In the pediment on the main front is a representation of the Last Judgment (by Philippe-Henri Lemaire, 1833; restored 1991–93). On the bronze door are reliefs related to the Ten Commandments.

Interior

The vestibule, the nave and the semicircular choir receive light through three large domes, with fine 19th century sculpture, including François Rude's "Baptism of Christ". In the spandrels are reliefs of the twelve Apostles, and on the high altar is a marble group (1837) representing the assumption of Mary Magdalene into heaven. Over the altar is a gigantic fresco depicting Constantine the Great, Frederick Barbarossa, Joan of Arc, St Louis, Michelangelo, Raphael, Dante, Cardinal Richelieu, Napoleon and other leading figures in western history. There is a famous Cavaillé-Coll organ on which there are periodic recitals.

★Rue Royale

The rue Royale, between place de la Concorde (see entry) and the Madeleine and laid out in the 18th c. is one of the most elegant streets in Paris. Many of the 18th c. buildings are now protected as national

"Florès" provides a quiet haven for refreshment in the Village Royale arcade

monuments. Elegance and high prices are traditional characteristics of the luxury shops in rue Royale. Among them are Villeroy et Boch (porcelain), several renowned jewellers, Christofle (tableware), Fauchon (fine foods) and Verutti (gentlemen's outfitter). At No. 3 is the world-famous Maxim's Restaurant, with its Art Nouveau decor a reminder of Paris's *belle époque*.

Also of interest is the Village Royale shopping arcade (entrance at 25 rue Royale), with sixteen high-class boutiques selling Limoges porcelain, the latest designer fashions and elegant shoes by Jean Louis Scherrer – all at a price? Florè's tea shop is the lunch-time rendezvous of the local world of fashion: in fine weather visitors can enjoy the fine cuisine on the terrace.

★Village Royale

Maisons-Laffitte

The impressive Château de Maisons was built by François Mansart in 1642–51) for René de Longueil, President of the Parlement de Paris, the supreme French court of justice. It is the finest example of the early classical château of the 17th century. Here for the first time Mansart used the high-pitched roof with tall windows which became known as mansards.

The château's present name comes from its owner in the reign of Louis-Philippe, Jacques Laffitte, banker and prime minister.

The whole of the interior dates from the 17th/18th century. Notable features are the numerous twin pilasters with their fine detail and the royal apartments on the first floor, including the beautiful Cabinet aux Miroirs.

Location
20km/12¹/₂ miles
NW of Paris
(N 308)

RER station
Maisons-Laffitte

Opening times
daily 10am–noon,
1.30pm–5pm: 6pm
in summer

Admission charge

135

★Malmaison

Location
Rueil-Malmaison
16km/10 miles
W of Paris
(N 13)

RER station
Rueil-Malmaison

Bus
258A (from La
Défense)

Opening times
Mon. and Wed.–
Sun.
10am–1pm, 1.30–
5pm;
closed Tue. and
pub. hols.

Conducted visits

The château of Malmaison, in the western suburb of Rueil-Malmaison, contains many mementoes of Napoleon and the Empress Joséphine. Since 1906 it has been a national museum, the Musée National du Château de Malmaison.

The château, in Early Baroque style, was built in 1620 and was acquired in 1799 by Joséphine de Beauharnais, Napoleon's first wife. After being divorced by Napoleon she lived here retired and alone. She died in Malmaison in 1814, ten months before Napoleon, after the failure of his "hundred days", came here to take farewell of his family and his country before going into exile on St Helena. Napoleon III bought the property in memory of his grandmother and had it restored. A later owner presented it to the state in 1904.

The interior is in Empire style. Most of the furnishings belong to the château, but some came from the palaces of Saint-Cloud, Fontainebleau (see entry) and the Tuileries. On the ground floor are the Billiard Room, the Gold Saloon (Salon Doré), with valuable Sèvres porcelain, the Music Saloon (with its original furnishings of 1812, including Joséphine's harp and her daughter Hortense's piano), the Dining Room (with a gilt table service which was a coronation gift from the city of Paris in 1804), the Council Chamber (with furniture from Saint-Cloud and Compiègne) and the Library, which has been preserved in its original state. On the first floor are the private apartments of the Emperor and Empress, including the Marengo Saloon, with a mural (by Louis David, 1801) depicting Napoleon's victory at Marengo.

★★Marais   J/K 5/6

Location
4th arr.

Métro stations
Saint-Paul,
Rambuteau

Buses
20, 29, 67, 69, 75,
76, 70, 96

The Marais quarter corresponds broadly to the 4th arrondissement. During the last forty years a costly restoration programme has saved a whole chapter in the history of Paris.

The Marais, with the Place des Vosges (see entry) as its finest example of urban planning, was the birthplace of the *hôtel*, the magnificent town mansion of a family of the country nobility. The heyday of these aristocratic palaces (though under the Ancien Régime the term "palace" was applied only to a royal residence) was in the 16th and 17th centuries, when Paris had become the brilliant metropolis of Europe and fashionable society met in the mansions of the Marais. The hôtels of this period typically have a courtyard (the *cour d'honneur*) opening on to the street, the main range of buildings flanked by side wings, and a terrace and garden to the rear. Towards the end of the 17th century the quarter lost its attraction for the aristocracy and well-to-do middle classes, who followed the court to Versailles or moved to the Faubourg Saint-Germain. Then craftsmen and small traders moved into the quarter. The Revolution left terrible scars on the Marais, the mansions fell into ruin or were pulled down to make way for new housing, and the occasional attempts at restoration in the 19th century made little difference.

Restoration

It was only in 1962 that the Ministry of Culture, then headed by André Malraux, began to tackle the urgent task of conserving this historic quarter, rediscovering in the process the almost forgotten *hôtels*. Although the restoration and redevelopment of the Marais may have brought in the speculators, the traditional atmosphere of the Marais has been preserved. It has now become an "in" part of the city in which modern boutiques rub shoulders with old craftsmen's workshops and chic designer shops, temples of gastronomy, luxury hotels

Bagels, blinis and gefüllte fish can all be found in the rue des Rosiers, the centre of the Jewish Quarter

and small art galleries have been established. In a stroll through the narrow streets you will sense the "discreet charm of the bourgeoisie" and be struck by the successful combination of a medieval setting and a modern way of life.

Today the centre of the Jewish community lies around the lively rue de Rosiers, a colourful mix of small fashion shops, snack bars with the best *falafel* ("mushy peas") and kosher food shops, such as Fenkelsztajn's (27 rue de Rosiers and 24 ruw des Ecouffes), where tarama, pickled herring, blinis, borsch and pastry confections have been produced since 1946. Oriental Jewish delicacies can be enjoyed at the wooden tables in "Chez Marianne" (2 rue des Hospitalières-St-Gervais), while the "Jo Goldenberg" (7 rue des Rosiers) is both a speciality restaurant and a delicatessen – it gained unfortunate notoriety in 1982 when six men were killed there during a terrorist attack. Brides seeking their wedding dress will find some wonderful creations at Lolita Lempicka's (3 rue des Rosiers).

★**Jewish quarter**

Since 1998 the new Jewish Museum house in the Hôtel St-Aignan (built 1644–47) has displayed medieval gravestones. Torah scrolls and documents relating to the culture and history of the Jewish community in France – with over 700,000 members, one of the largest in Europe.

★**Musee d'Art et d'Histoire du Judaisme**

Among the most notable of the *hôtels* are the following:

1 rue du Figuier, tel. 01 42 78 14 60; Métro: Saint-Paul.
The Hôtel de Sens, built between 1475 and 1607 by the archbishops of Sens, is one of the oldest houses in Paris. It now houses the Forney Library, which contains important material on art and industrial technology (open: Tue.–Fri. 1.30–8pm, Sat. 10am–8pm).

Hôtel de Sens
Bibliothèque
Forney

► *In the Marais quarter: the Place des Voges with its elegant 17th c. town mansions*

Hôtel d'Aumont
Tribunal Administratif de Paris

7 rue de Jouy; Métro: Saint-Paul.
The classically elegant Hôtel d'Aumont, built between 1630 and 1650 by Louis Le Vau and altered in 1656 by François Mansart, is now occupied by the Paris Administrative Tribunal (visits by written request).

Hôtel de Beauvais

68 rue François-Miron, Métro: Saint-Paul.
The Hôtel de Beauvais was built by Antoine Lepautre in 1658–60. The young Mozart stayed here during his visit to Paris in 1763.

Hôtel d'Hallwyll

28 rue Michel-le-Comte; Métro: Rambuteau
The Hôtel d'Hallwyll, built in 1765 by Claude-Nicolas Ledoux, was the residence of Louis XVI's minister Jacques Necker and his daughter Madame de Staâl.

Hôtel Amelot de Bisseuil
Dutch Embassy

47 rue Vieille-du-Temple; Métro: Rambuteau.
The Hôtel Amelot de Bisseuil (by Antoine Lepautre, 1657–60) is now the Dutch Embassy (Hotel des Ambassadeurs de Hollande). It was here that Beaumarchais wrote his satrical comedy "The Marriage of Figaro" in 1784.

Archives Nationales

28 rue des Francs-Bourgeois; Métro: Rambuteau, Saint-Paul.
The French National Archives, founded at the beginning of the 19th century and housed in the Hôtel de Rohan-Soubise, are one of the largest archive collections in the world. Much needed additional accommodation has recently been provided in the modern CARAN building (Centre d'Accueil et de Recherche des Archives Nationales), 11 rue des Quatre-Fils, 75003 Paris, tel. 01 40 27 64 18.

The Hôtel de Rohan-Soubise, with a colonnaded courtyard, was built by Pierre-Alexis Delamair in 1704–12 for the Princesse de Soubise and was converted to its present purpose in 1808. It contains, in the Musée de l'Histoire de France (open: weekdays except Tue. noon–5.45pm, Sat., Sun. 1.45–5.45pm) on the first floor, several million documents on the history of France from the 7th century to the Second World War. Among them are a papyrus scroll of 629 signed by King Dagobert, letters of Joan of Arc, Napoleon's will and reports by the French Resistance hero Jean Moulin.

Of the state apartments the most notable are the Rococo rooms, in particular the fanciful Salon Ovale (1708), a masterpiece of decoration by Germain Boffrand and the painters Natoire, Boucher and van Loo.

87 rue Vieille-du-Temple; Métro: Rambuteau, Saint-Paul.
The Hôtel de Rohan-Strasbourg, also designed by Delamair, contains notarial records. The only rooms open to the public are those in which the Archives put on special exhibitions.

In the second courtyard is a lively high-relief by Robert Le Lorrain (18th century), "Apollo's Horses of the Sun".

1 rue de la Perle; Métro: Saint-Paul, Chemin-Vert.
The Hôtel Libéral Bruant was built by the architect of that name in 1685 for his own occupation. It is now occupied by the Musée Bricard, which contains an extensive collection of material on the locksmith's craft from Roman times to the present day (open: Tue.–Sat. 2–5pm; closed Aug.).

Hôtel de Rohan-Soubise
Musée de l'Histoire de France

Hôtel de Rohan-Strasbourg

Hôtel Libéral Bruant
Musée Bricard

Hôtel Guénégaud ★Musée de la Chasse et de la Nature	60 rue des Archives; Métro: Rambuteau. The Hôtel Guénégaud, built by François Mansart in 1651 for the royal treasurer François de Guénégaud, is now occupied by the Museum of Hunting and Nature. The nucleus of the museum was the collection assembled by the industrialist François Sommer, a keen sportsman. The exhibits include old guns, hunting knives, trophies, animal studies by François Desportes (1661–1743) and hunting scenes by Lucas Cranach, Pieter Breughel the Elder, Rubens, Chardin and Oudry (open: Mon. and Wed.–Sun. 10am–12.30pm and 1.30–5.30pm).
Hôtel Lamoignon Bibliothèque Historique de la Ville de Paris	24 rue Pavée; Métro: Saint-Paul. The Hôtel Lamoignon (by Jean-Baptiste Androuet du Cerceau, 1584) now houses the Library on the History of Paris (regular special exhibitions; open: Mon.–Sat. 9.30am–6pm).
Hôtel Carnavalet	See Musée Carnavalet
Hôtel Salé	See Musée Picasso
Place des Vosges	See entry
Hôtel de Béthune- Sully	62 rue Saint-Antoine; Métro: Saint-Paul. This sumptuous mansion (by Jean Androuet du Cerceau, 1624) was the town house of Henri IV's minister Maximilien de Béthune. The courtyard and the sculptural decoration on the garden front are particularly fine. It is now occupied by the Caisse Nationale des Monuments Historiques et des Sites, the body concerned with the protection of historic monuments and sites.
Hôtel de Donon ★Musée Cognacq-Jay	8 rue Elézvir; Métro: Saint-Paul. The Hôtel de Donon, built for Médéric de Donon in the 16th century, was completely renovated in 1991 and now accommodates the Musée Cognacq-Jay, which until 1989 was on the Boulevard des Capucines. The valuable Cognac-Jay collection, assembled by the businessman Ernest Cognacq and his wife Louise Jay and bequeathed to the city in 1928, displays artistic masterpieces of the siècle des lumières (18th century), including works by Fragonard, Boucher and Watteau (open: Tue.–Sun., 10am–5.40pm).

Marché aux Puces (Flea Market)   H 1

Location N boundary of 18th arr. **Métro station** Porte de Clignancourt **Buses** 56, 85, PC **Opening times** Sat.–Mon. 7.30am–7pm	Paris's flea market, the kingdom of bric-a-brac, lies between the Porte de Clignancourt and the Porte de Saint-Ouen, outside the ring motorway marking the northern boundary of the city. Approaching the market from the Porte de Clignancourt Métro station, you may at first be disappointed by the rows of stalls selling jeans, leather goods and cheap clothing which line the pavements. The real flea market, however, begins beyond the motorway underpass. Here too the wares on offer are very mixed – clothing straight from the factory, worthless junk and (possibly) genuine antiques, pictures, furniture, books and crockery. Purchasers need to know what they are after. If you are not looking for anything particular you can browse happily amid the welter of valuable antiques, skilful imitations and mere rubbish. Some sections of the flea market specialise in particular types of article and have their own names – Malik (clothing, spectacles, records, CDs), Jules-Vallès (rustic furniture), Paul-Bert (crockery, dolls), Serpette (1930s furniture), Cambo (household utensils, pictures), Biron (valuable antiques), Vernaison (period furniture, knick-knacks). There is also the legendary Restaurant Louisette, famed for its chansonniers.

Monnaie (Mint)   H 5

The Mint (Monnaie de Paris, Hôtel de la Monnaie), built between 1771 and 1777, is one of the few buildings in Paris in early Louis XVI style. Begun at the end of Louis XV's reign to the design of Jacques-Denis Antoine, it is notable in lacking the elaborate decoration of Baroque and Rococo. The doorway in the 117m/384ft long façade has allegorical representations of Trade and Agriculture.

Since 1973 French coins have been minted at Pessac (Gironde). The workshops on the Quai de Conti, which are open to the public (Tue. and Fri. 2.15–2.45pm), still mint special silver and gold coins. The Museum illustrates the history of coinage from the Renaissance to the present day (open: Tue.–Fri.: 11am–5.30pm, Sat., Sun. noon–5.30pm).

Location
11 quai de Conti
(6th arr.)

Métro stations
Pont Neuf,
Odéon

Buses
24, 27, 58, 78

★Montmartre   G/H 3

There are two common explanations for the name Montmartre. One is that it comes from Mons Mercurii (Mercury's Mount), after a temple of Mercury which is said to have stood here. The other is that the name is a corruption of Mont des Martyrs, since legend has it that St Dionysius (Denis), first bishop of Paris, was executed here along with his companions Rusticus and Eleutherius (see Saint-Denis).

Nowadays there are three Montmartres: the Butte Montmartre, the hill (129m/423ft) on which are the Sacré-Cœur (see entry), the Place du Tertre and various little theatres and revues like Michou's crazy drag show in Rue des Martyrs; the residential quarter of Montmartre; and the entertainment quarter on the Boulevard de Clichy with its numerous erotic establishments, which are also to be found round the legendary Moulin Rouge and in the adjoining side streets.

Location
Northern Paris
(18th arr.)

Métro stations
Place Clichy,
Blanche, Pigalle,
Anvers, Abbesses

Buses
30, 31, 60, 80, 85,
Montmartrobus
(54, 55), 95

The Butte Montmartre is a place of legend and of history. From the 12th century this was the site of a large convent of Benedictine nuns, Saint-Pierre-de-Montmartre, which was razed to the ground in 1794: only the name of Place des Abbesses is a reminder that it once stood here. For a time during the Revolution the hill was renamed Mont Marat, after the revolutionary killed by Charlotte Corday. In 1871 it was the scene of the bloody beginning and the still bloodier end of the Commune, whose defenders made their last stand here and on the Buttes Chaumont. The old wine-growing village, which was incorporated in Paris only in 1860, owed its international fame to the artists' colony which grew up on the Butte towards the end of the 19th century and attracted chansonniers, writers and painters from far and wide, among them Manet, Van Gogh, Toulouse-Lautrec, Utrillo, Guillaume Apollinaire, Max Jacob, Picasso, Braque, Vlaminck, Emile Bernard, Courteline and Pierre MacOrlan. Picasso's studio, the "Bateau-Lavoir", became the centre of the Cubist movement, while the "Lapin Agile" with its chansonniers was the rendezvous of bohemian Paris. After the First World War, however, the artistic and intellectual hub of Paris moved steadily to the Montparnasse quarter (see entry).

But the charm of Montmartre lies not only in its memories. Although art and commerce have become one and the same thing in the Place du Tertre and people may argue about the "wedding-cake" architecture of the Sacré-Cœur, it is still true that if you take time to stroll about in the narrow streets and the steep flights of steps of Montmartre and enjoy the many, often quite unexpected, views of Paris it will be borne in on you very strongly what Paris has to offer – an infinite variety of impressions.

Butte Montmartre

Montmartre

Place du Tertre: a stage for lightening portrait painters surrounded by cafés and souvenir shops

Funicular

Montmartre, Paris's highest hill, has its only funicular, running between Place Saint-Pierre and the Sacré-Cœur (daily 6.45am to 45 minutes after midnight).

Place du Tertre

The Place du Tertre, the old village square, surrounded by cafés and restaurants, is, after the Sacré-Cœur (see entry), one of Paris's most popular sights. Painters, portraitists and caricaturists of all nationalities display their wares and offer their services – though their work has usually less to do with art than with the souvenir trade.

The low 18th century houses round the square, including the old mairie of 1790 at No. 3, form a picturesque backdrop to the hustle and bustle of tourists which carries on throughout the year.

Sacré-Coeur

See entry

Saint-Pierre-de-Montmartre

The church of Saint-Pierre in Rue du Mont-Cenis is a relic of the 12th century Benedictine convent whose last abbess died on the guillotine in 1794. Four black marble columns in the choir and at the west end of the nave have survived from the original Merovingian church built in the 7th century on the site of a Roman temple of Mercury. The present church is mainly Early Gothic; the choir was consecrated in 1147 in presence of the great Catholic reformer Bernard of Clairvaux.

Moulin de la Galette

The last but one of the several windmills which once stood on the hill on Montmartre is, unfortunately, no longer open to visitors. The neighbouring Moulin Radet (83 rue Lepic) makes use of the illustrious past in the form of the Moulin de la Galette restaurant which offers Italian cuisine (tel. 01 46 06 84 77).

★Musée du Vieux Montmartre

This little museum in Rue Cortot (No. 12) offers a nostalgic view of earlier days in Montmartre. It occupies a picturesque 17th century building which became the home of many artists who gained an international reputation. Auguste Renoir had his studio here in 1876, and he was followed later by Susanne Valadon and her son Maurice Utrillo, Emile Bernard, Maximilian Luce and Maurice Delcourt.

Among the exhibits displayed in the museum are the original sign of the "Lapin Agile", sketches of posters by Théophile Steinlen (mainly advertising the popular "Chat Noir" cabaret) and humorous studies of the Montmartre milieu by Francisque Poulbot (open: Tue.–Sun. 11am–6pm).

In the triangular Place des Abbesses is one of the handsomest of Paris's Métro stations, with an Art Nouveau entrance by Victor Guimard. Opposite it is the church of Saint-Jean-l'Evangéliste (by Anatole de Baudot, 1904), a concrete structure faced with red brick notable for its simplicity and clarity of form. At weekends many of the shops and stalls in rue des Abesses close, and the locals enjoy a coffee and snack in the Sancerre" (No. 35) or the neighbouring "Le Vrai Paris") (No. 33).

Place des Abbesses

In Place Emile-Goudeau, a little tree-planted square, is an unremarkable, rather irregular house at No. 13 (originally, before the square had a name of its own, 13 rue Ravignan) which was the birthplace of Cubism. A long series of famous painters had their studio in this house, the Bâteau-Lavoir, lived here or came as visitors, including Paul Gauguin, Juan Gris, Otto Freundlich, Max Jacob, André Salmon, Brancusüi, Modigliani and Picasso, who moved in here in 1904 and a year or two later painted his "Demoiselles d'Avignon", the first Cubist picture. In those days the house had neither heating, running water or electricity. It was burned down in 1970 but was later rebuilt by the city in its original form, with modern artists' studios.

Place Emile-Goudeau Bâteau-Lavoir

Round the corner in the steep Rue des Saules (No. 22) is another turn-of-the-century relic, the "Lapin Agile" ("Agile Rabbit"). This famous cabaret takes its name from the sign painted by André Gill showing a rabbit jumping out of a cooking-pot. Celebrated artistes performed here, including the chansonnier Aristide Bruant immortalised by Toulouse-Lautrec and his friend Frédéric Gérard, known as Père Frédé, who entertained their mostly middle-class audiences with witty and disrespectful songs. The "Lapin Agile" still has talented chansonniers who appeal to a wide public – though nowadays everything is rather dearer than it used to be (see Baedeker Special, pp.32–33).

Lapin Agile

This museum in Rue Chaptal (No. 16) displays numerous mementoes of the artistic and literary figures who frequented the salon of the Dutch painter Ary Scheffer (1795–1858) in this elegant villa of the Restoration period, among them George Sand and Chopin, Delacroix, Liszt, Ingres, Lamartine and Turgenev (open: Tue.–Sun. 10am–5.40pm).

Musée de la Vie Romantique

On the south-western fringe of the Butte Montmartre, between Place de Clichy and Place Pigalle, lies one of the main centres of Paris night life, with the legendary Moulin Rouge (illustration, p. 144). On the Boulevard de Clichy and in the side streets running towards Place Pigalle, Place Blanche and Place de Clichy is everything that commercialised sex can offer – sex shops, porno shows, striptease joints, uninhibited cabarets and revues, bars and prostitution.

Between Place de Clichy and Place Pigalle

For over a hundred years the Moulin Rouge has been synonymous with the art of veiled erotica, the birthplace of the can-can and frivolous revues and all that represents the *belle époque*, and intimately linked with such names as Edith Piaf, Josphine Baker and Yves Montand. Feathers, tulle, sequins, paint and leather also form a part

Moulin Rouge

Birthplace of the French can-can: the legendary Moulin Rouge

of the present "Formidable Show", which juggles with a mixture of Parisian myth, exotic scenes and beautiful birds of paradise.

Cimetière de Montmartre

See cemeteries

Montparnasse   G 6

Location
On boundary between 6th and 14th arr.

Métro stations
Vavin, Edgar Quinet, Montparnasse Bienvenue

Buses
28, 48, 58, 68, 82,

The Montparnasse quarter is now almost more celebrated for the 59-storey Tour Maine-Montparnasse than for the old artists' colonies whose last remnants have survived in the southern part of the 14th arrondissement. While between the turn of the century and the First World War Montmartre (see entry) and in the decade following the Second World War Saint-Germain-des-Prés (see entry) were the haunt of artists and intellectuals, this role fell during the twenties and thirties to Montparnasse. Among the habitués of the cafés, bars and restaurants at the intersection of Boulevard du Montparnasse and Boulevard Raspail – the Dôme, the Coupole, the Select, the Rotonde – were Simone de Beauvoir and Jean-Paul Sartre, Ernest Hemingway, Henry Miller and James Joyce. Here too were the studios of Matisse, Kandinsky, Modigliani and Chagall. The café-restaurant Closerie des Lilas was the domain of the poets Paul Fort and Guillaume Apollinaire, and Jean-Paul Sartre was a regular customer. Near the Vavin junction, where a bust of Balzac by Rodin has stood since 1939, was once the scene of the weekly model market, where Kiki, the "muse of Montparnasse" was said to have been discovered. Numerous shops specialising in artists' materials bear witness to the fact that there are still a lot of painters and sculptors working in Montparnasse. Its many cinemas and excellent restaurants make the district very popular in the evenings.

The whole district is now dominated by the 209m/685ft high Tour Maine-Montparnasse at 33 Avenue du Maine. Designed by Beaudoin, Cassan, de Marien and Saubot, it was built between 1969 and 1972. From the panoramic restaurant on the 56th floor and the open terrace on the 59th there are extensive views over Paris reaching for up to 40km/25 miles, fully comparable with those from the Eiffel Tower; there are telescopes to bring the views even closer. A 20-minute film show by Albert Lamorisse, "Paris jamais vu" ("Paris as you never saw it before") presents fascinating views of Paris from the air, and there are changing exhibitions on the history of the city.

Tour Maine-Montparnasse
Opening times
summer, daily 9.30am–11.30pm; winter daily 9.30am–10.30pm
Admission charge

★Panoramic views

Adjoining the tower is the new Montparnasse Station (trains to western France), built in the early seventies. At the Pont des Cinq-Martyrs-du-Lycée-Buffon is the Gare de Vaugirard (opened 1991) from which the high-speed TGV trains run to the Atlantic coast. The railway lines are roofed over and covered by the "Jardin de l'Atlantique", which forms a link between the Vaugirard and Plaisance districts.

Gare de Montparnasse

On Allée de la 2e DB there is a small museum in memory of the resistance fighter Jean Moulin and the French resistance movement (open: Tue.–Sun. 10am–5.40pm).

Musée Jean Moulin

Since the 1960s the city has been carrying out beyond Montparnasse Station one of the largest and most radical redevelopment programmes in Paris. The area between Rue Vercingétorix and Rue Commandant-René-Mouchette, once favoured by artists such as the naïve painter Henri Rousseau, had become increasingly dilapidated, until finally an almost complete clearance of an area of 80 hectares/200 acres was carried out. The functional concrete structures in a kind of neo-Classical style, often with something of the appearance of stage-settings, which took the place of the old buildings continue to be the subject of controversy.

Renovation and redevelopment

The Tour Maine-Montparnasse dominates the surrounding area

"Paris – A Movable Feast"

For seven months it remained on the American best seller list, and for 19 weeks in first place: **Ernest Hemingway's** last book "Paris – A Movable Feast". Between 1957 and his death in 1961 Hemingway had worked on this autobiographical memoir of his time in Paris, those celebrated years of the 1920s when he achieved his literary breakthrough and at the same time the Hemingway myth of bullfighting, alcohol and women was conceived. In 1921, at the age of only 22 the ambitious young foreign correspondent for two Canadian newspapers travelled to Paris. After the First World War the French capital was an ideal destination for Americans, large numbers of whom flocked there, largely on account of the favourable exchange rate for the dollar. Their favourite area was the left bank of the Seine. While prim, old-fashioned opinions were being preached in America, Paris was a ferment of avant-garde currents, and while America was under the grip of the prohibition laws, champagne in Paris flowed like water. "Anyone who has the good fortune to live in Paris as a young man," wrote Hemingway, "will always retain that experience, whatever happens to him in later years, for Paris is a movable feast."

Anyone who walks an imaginary triangle between Montparnasse Station, Port Royal and Saint Germain, can, in a manner of speaking, uncover the artistic and cultural history of the first 40 years of this century and to some extent even experience it themselves. Among the most famous cafés on the boulevard du Montparnasse is **La Coupole**, where in the days before the revolution Lenin and Trotsky discussed issues of socialism. Their compatriot, the composer Igor Stravinsky, found life at Montparnasse so attractive that he became a naturalized French citizen. Picasso and his friends, the painters

Max Jacob and Modigliani, used to meet in the **Rotonde**, while not far away, in the **Closerie des Lilas**, the writers André Gide, Apollinaire and John dos Passos were frequent guests and Hemingway wrote a large part of his first novel "Fiesta". His name is commemorated by a brass plate at the bar of the present-day restaurant, while their highly popular peppered steak also bears the writer's name. In the Closerie – earlier also a favourite café of the symbolists and Dadaists – Hemingway would follow a burst of writing with a cognac or a whisky and soda, would then go to the museum, play tennis or look through the latest new literary issues in Sylvia Beach's bookshop **Shakespeare and Company**. Another of the most popular meeting places of American painters and writers on the boulevard du Montparnasse was the **Dôme** – these days a top recommendation for fish gourmets. Not far away at rue Delambre 10 in the **Dingo Bar** Ernest Hemingway met his almost equally successful fellow-writer Scott Fitzgerald ("The Great Gatsby") for the first time. And when Jimmy, the universally popular bartender at the Dingo, opened the **Café Falstaff** in 1925, his literary clientele moved there with him.

Later on Hemingway used to like to style himself as a poor devil down on his luck, who had a hard time keeping his head above water financially during his Paris years 1921–1926. The fact is that he could not make ends meet from his work as a foreign correspondent, but his wife on the other hand had the use of a substantial private income which she had acquired from an inheritance. Anyone looking for Hemingway's home at rue Notre-Dame-des-Champs 113, where he lived with his first wife Hadley, will look in vain – it has long ago been replaced by prosperous-looking apartment blocks. The same is true of

In the "golden 20s" night after night in the cafés of Montparnasse and Saint-Germain-des-Prés discussions took place on contemporary art

the former home of the poet, Ezra Pound, who lived rather modestly at no. 70 in the same street. By contrast, the well-to-do writer and patroness of the arts, Gertrude Stein, was able to afford an elegant studio at rue de Fleurus 27, where she kept her large collection of pictures by Picasso, Matisse, Renoir, Gauguin and Manet.

The café which Hemingway preferred above all others in Saint Germain des Prés was situated at the corner of rue des St Pères and rue Jacob and was called *Michaud* - James Joyce is said to have eaten there regularly with his family. Today the brasserie *Escorailles* is to be found here, although its menu no longer boasts the legendary cherry tart which Hemingway used to enjoy so much. The other cafés in the Bohemian district mentioned by name in "Paris – A Movable Feast" also include **Les Deux Magots**, still famous today, with its

inviting terrace, situated opposite the mediaeval church of Saint Germain des Prés. At the nearby **Café de Flore** France's most important post-war dramatist and existentialist, Jean-Paul Sartre, was a regular for a number of years when he was living a few steps away in the rue Bonaparte. Sartre's partner Simone de Beauvoir is supposed to have written a large part of her much discussed cult novel "The Second Sex" in *Flore*. Publication of this book led to her becoming one of the most important theorists of the feminist movement. One of Hemingway's other favourite establishments was the **Brasserie Lipp**, famous for its beer, sausage and sauerkraut, which had been founded after the 1870/1871 war by an Alsatian. François Mitterrand was also a regular here, although he would have had to pay twice what Hemingway paid for a litre of beer!

Echelles du Baroque, Amphithéâtre

The most recent example of the new style, built in 1986, is the huge office and apartment complex called the Echelles du Baroque in Place de Séoul. This elliptical structure faced with blue glass and the associated Amphithéâtre contain a total of 270 apartments. The architect was Ricardo Bofill, the Catalan who is also known for his monumental complexes at Marne-la-Vallée and Saint-Quentin-en-Yvelines (see Facts and Figures, General, New Towns).

In 1994 the Fondation Cartier took over a new museum for temporary exhibitions of contemporary art at 261 Boulevard Raspail, a few yards from Rodin's bust of Balzac. Jean Nouvel designed the glass and aluminium complex, while Lothar Baumgartem created the gardens which were opened in 1995 (open: Tue.–Sun., noon–8pm, Thur., 10pm).

Cimetière du Montparnasse

See Cemeteries

Mosquée de Paris   J 6

Location
39 rue Geoffroy-St-Hilaire (5th arr.)

Métro stations
Monge, Censier Daubenton

The Paris Mosque, with a 33m/110ft high minaret, was built in 1922–26. The building also houses the Islamic Institute of Religious Studies. The prayer hall may be entered every day but Friday; shoes must be taken off before entering.

Within the complex are a Turkish bath (hammam) and a small Arab restaurant.

★Musée Carnavalet   K 5

Location
23–29 rue de Sévigné (3rd arr.)

Métro stations
Saint-Paul, Chemin Vert

Buses
29, 69, 76, 96

Opening times
Tue.–Sun.
10am–5.40pm,

Admission charge

Carnavalet is a garbled form of the name of the former owner of the house, the widow of the Sire de Kernevenoy, a Breton. The house was built in the 16th century, probably by Pierre Lescot, the architect responsible for the Renaissance façade of the Louvre (see entry). The main doorway, with carvings of lions by Jean Goujon, and the range of buildings facing the entrance date from the 16th century. The other wings round the courtyard, in the centre of which is a fine statue of Louis XIV (by Antoine Coysevox, 1698), were remodelled by François Mansart in

The Pharmacie Lescot – part of the Musuem of the History of Paris

the 17th century. The Hôtel de Carnavalet was occupied from 1677 to 1696 by Madame de Sévigné, whose letters to her daughter, over 1500 in number, describing life in Paris and at the court in Versailles are valuable documents on the age of the Sun King.

The Museum of the History of Paris has been housed here since 1880. The accommodation available to the Museum was considerably extended around the turn of the century, and it was further enlarged in 1989 by the incorporation of the adjoining Hôtel Le Peletier de Saint-Fargeau. The sober style of this mansion, built in 1686–90 by Pierre Bullet, shows the influence of François Blondel.

The Museum of the History of Paris displays in a series of finely contrived rooms a comprehensive collection of pictures, sculpture, engravings, ceramics, furniture and everyday objects of the most varied kinds which gives a vivid picture of the history of Paris from its Gallo-Roman beginnings to the time of Louis XVI, while the four new rooms in the Hôtel Le Peletier de Saint-Fargeau carry on the story from the French Revolution to the present day. Among the most notable features are the Galerie Sévigné, the Bouvier collection, the workshop of the jeweller Fouquet (by Alfons Mucha, 1900) and the ballroom designed by José Maria Sert for Mme de Wendel (1924).

Musée de l'Histoire de Paris

Musée Condé

See Chantilly, Grand Château

Musée d'Art Moderne de la Ville de Paris

See Palais de Tokyo

★★Musée de Cluny (Hôtel de Cluny)   H 6

The former Hôtel de Cluny, now a museum of medieval art and culture, stands on the site of Roman baths, the remains of which can be seen at the corner of the Boulevard Saint Michel (see entry) and Boulevard Saint-Germain.

At the beginning of the 14th century the Benedictine abbey of Cluny in Burgundy acquired the site in order to build a town house for its abbots. The Hôtel de Cluny was then built between 1485 and 1510 under the direction of Abbot Jacques d'Amboise. This house, in the Flamboyant style of the Late Gothic period, and the Hôtel de Sens in the Marais (see entry) are the only late medieval aristocratic mansions surviving in Paris. After frequent changes of ownership from the medieval period onwards it fell into disrepair after the French Revolution. It was acquired in 1833 by the art collector and antiquary Alexandre du Sommerard and in 1842 by the State. It has been a museum since 1844.

The Musée de Cluny has a magnificent collection of medieval art, the nucleus of which was Alexandre du Sommerard's private collection. In the Cour d'Honneur (courtyard) the charm of this building, reflecting the period of transition from Late Gothic to Renaissance style, is revealed in all its splendour. The beautiful fountain dates from the 15th century.

Location
6 place Paul-Painlevé (5th arr.)

Métro stations
Cluny-La
Sorbonne,
St-Michel, Odéon

Buses
21, 24, 27, 38, 63,
85, 86, 87, 96

Opening times
Daily except Tue.
and pub. hols.
9.15am–5,45pm

Guided tours
Wed, 3.30pm
Sat., Sun. 11am
and 3.30pm

Admission charge

Musée de l'Armée

Ground floor	The museum's medieval tapestries are among the finest in France. On the ground floor is the oldest of the tapestries, the "Offrande du Coeur", a delicate declaration of love (Flemish, 15th c.). Other treasures displayed here are Romanesque and Gothic sculpture, including four statues of Apostles (1245–48) from the Sainte-Chapelle and 21 heads of kings (1210–30) from the west front of Notre-Dame, lost during the French Revolution and rediscovered only in 1977 (Room IX), and a 7th century stone sarcophagus (Room X).
	Room XII, with its massive vaulting, is part of the Roman baths (see below). The best preserved part of the baths is the frigidarium (cold room), which is 20m/65ft long, 12m/40ft wide and 16m/53ft high. The capitals of the pillars supporting the vaulting on the north side are in the form of ships' prows, which suggests that the baths were built at the expense of the nautae, the wealthy corporation of Paris boatmen. The remains of the temple of Jupiter on the Ile de la Cité which were excavated under the choir of Notre-Dame and are displayed in the frigidarium bear a dedication by the nautae. Known as the Autel des Nautes (Altar of the Nautae), they have carvings of Roman and Gallic deities which are the oldest pieces of sculpture found in Paris (1st c. A.D.).
First floor	On the first floor are enamels and goldsmiths' work of the 7th to 13th centuries, including nine of the twenty Visigothic votive crowns which were discovered near Toledo in the mid 19th century (Room XIII). Also on this floor are medieval stained glass (Room XVI) and French, Italian and Spanish ceramics (Room XVII). Among the most valuable items is a gilded altar frontal (11th c.) presented to Basle Cathedral by the Emperor Henry II (Room XIX).
	The greatest treasure in the collection of tapestries is the famous "Lady with the Unicorn" (Dame à la Licorne) series (15th c.), probably made in Brussels, which is displayed in a circular room of its own. The six scenes in the series are thought to be an allegory of the five senses and the joys of the senses.
	On the walls of the Late Gothic chapel which was the abbot's oratory (Room XX) is another series of fine 15th century tapestries from Auxerre with 23 scenes from the legend of St Stephen (Etienne).
Thermes de Cluny	The impressive remains of the huge Roman bath complex, built about A.D. 200 and destroyed in 380, are in the gardens of the Musée de Cluny. They are not open to the public but can be seen from the street outside. It is planned to construct a protective roof over the remains.
	Only the large frigidarium has been preserved by being incorporated in the Hôtel de Cluny (see Room XII). The other rooms are a caldarium (hot bath), tepidarium (warm bath), two gymnasia and a 10m/33ft long swimming pool.

Musée de la Marine

See Palais de Chaillot

★Musée de l'Armée   F 5

Location Hôtel des Invalides (7th arr.) **RER station** Invalides	The Army Museum, founded in 1794 as the Artillery Museum, occupies the wings round the courtyard of the Invalides (see entry). It has a large collection of military equipment and uniforms, weapons, prints and curiosities of many periods and from many countries. There are mementoes and relics of Napoleon and well-known generals, and plans of French campaigns. Of particular interest are a number of exhibits

dating from the Late Gothic and Renaissance periods. There are also displays of relief models of fortified towns, forts and port installations.

The entrances to the Museum (open: Oct. 1st to Mar. 31st, daily 10am–5pm; Apr. 1st to Sept. 30th, 10am–6pm) are in the middle of the side wings flanking the courtyard. On the ground floor documentary films on the two world wars are shown, starting at 2pm.

Métro stations
Latour Maubourg,
St-François-
Xavier, Invalides
Buses
28, 49, 63, 69, 82,92
Admission charge

Musée de l'Homme

See Palais de Chaillot

Musée des Monuments Français

See Palais de Chaillot

★★Musée d'Orsay   G 5

Built for the Paris Exhibition of 1900 (architect Victor Laloux) on the banks of the Seine opposite the Tuileries, the Gare d'Orsay, the former railway station which now houses the Musée d'Orsay, is a huge glass and iron construction topped by a glass dome and surrounded on three sides by the palatial façades of the Hôtel d'Orsay. Passengers entering the spacious entrance hall could not see the platforms from which trains left for south-western France, for the railway

Location
62 rue de Lille
(7th arr.)
Main entrance;
1 rue de
Bellechasse

Sculpture in the central hall of the Musée d'Orsay

Musée d'Orsay

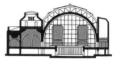

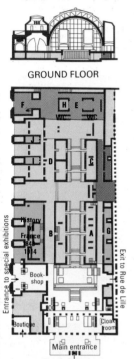

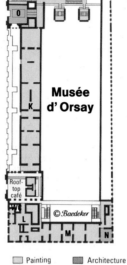

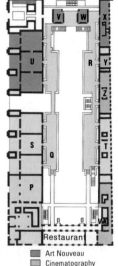

GROUND FLOOR · UPPER LEVEL · MIDDLE LEVEL

Painting · Sculpture · Architecture · Applied art

Art Nouveau · Cinematography · Special exhibitions

A Ingres and Ingrisme, Delacroix, Chassériau, historical and portrait painting 1850–80

B Daumier, Chauchard Collection, Millet, E. Rousseau, Corot, Realism, Courbet

C Puvis de Chavannes, Gustave Moreau, Degas before 1870

D Manet, Monet, Bazille and Renoir before 1870, Fantin-Latour, Plein Air painting, Personnaz and Eduardo-Mollard Collections, Realism, Orientalism

E Opera Hall

F Upper Pavilion: architecture 1850–1900, Viollet-le-Duc, Pugin, Morris, Webb, Mackmurdo, Jekyll, Godwin, Sullivan

G Dossier 1

H Dossier 2

I Dossier 3

J Photography and the graphic arts

K Impressionism: Moreau-Nélaton Collection, Whistler, Manet, Degas, Monet, Renoir, Pissarro, Sisley, Cézanne, Degas (pastels)

L Van Gogh, Gachet Collection, Redon (pastels)

M Douanier Rousseau Pont-Aven school: Gauguin, E. Bernard, Sérusier Neo-Impressionism: Seurat, Signac, Cross, Luce

N Toulouse-Lautrec, small pictures

O Dossier 4 (on three floors) Down to middle level: Dossier 5 Press Corner Kaganovitch Collection Tables of dates

P Art and interior decoration of Third Republic

Q Barrias, Coutan, Frémiet, Gérôme, Rodin

R Desbois, Rosso, Bartholomé, Bourdelle, Maillol, J. Barnard

S Salon painting 1880–1900, Naturalism, foreign schools, Symbolism

T Painting after 1900: Bonnard, Denis, Vallotton, Vuillard, Roussel; transition to 20th century

U Art Nouveau in France and Belgium: Guimard Nancy school: Gallé, Carabin, Charpentier, Dampt

V Guimard

W International Art Nouveau

X Vienna, Glasgow, Chicago

Y Dossier 6

Z Dossier 7

152

tracks were several metres lower. As engines became more powerful, however, and were able to pull more coaches the platforms of the Gare d'Orsay proved to be too short. In 1939 the station ceased to handle long-distance traffic and was confined to local trains, and finally it lost even this function to the RER. In 1973 the station and the hotel were scheduled as national monuments, and plans were developed for converting them to a museum. The reconstruction was carried out under the direction of Pierre Colboc, Renaud Bardon and Jean-Paul Philippon; Gae Aulenti was responsible for the interior.

The Musée d'Orsay opened its doors in 1986, with 17,200sq.m/180,000sq.ft of display space for the art of the period from 1848 to 1916. The exhibits are arranged chronologically according to broad themes and artistic techniques (including music and literature). Within the various schools the works of particular artists are so far as possible displayed together: for example there are rooms for Daumier, Courbet and Van Gogh, a courtyard for Carpeaux, a terrace for Rodin. Only in the former ballroom are the sculpture and pictures selected for their appropriateness to the turn-of-the-century Rococo decor.

Contemporary events and intellectual movements forming the background to the works displayed are documented in separate rooms (French history, the press, tables of dates). On Tuesdays and Saturdays there are guided tours in French and other languages, taking as their theme "discovering the Musée d'Orsay"

The entrance to the former Hôtel d'Orsay, on the west side of the building, leads into the reception area, with bookshops and a Boutique (open: Tue.–Sun., 9.30–6.30pm, Thur. to 9.30pm). The area formerly occupied by platforms, on a lower level, is now a sculpture gallery, on either side of which, at ground floor level, are rooms devoted to painting, photography and architecture.

Métro station
Solférino

RER station
Musée d'Orsay

Buses
24, 63, 68, 69, 73, 83, 84, 94

Information:
Tel, 45 49 49 49
40 49 48 48

Opening times
Tue., Wed., Fri., Sat.
10am–6pm,
Sun. 9am–6pm,
Thu. 10am–9.45pm;
June 20 to Sept. 20
open from 9am

Admission charge

Edgar Degas: "Foyer of the Danse à l'Opera" (ca. 1872)

Musée d'Orsay

The glass dome of the station is still visible above the central hall (138m/150yds long, 40m/44yds wide, 32m/105ft high; illustration, above), but the various floors of the hotel and the station concourse have been converted into exhibition rooms.

Ground floor
Second Republic and Second Empire

In the mid-19th c. balance and purity of line characterised the neo-Classical work of Ingres ("The Spring", 1820–57) and bold brushstrokes and wild use of colour ("The Lion Hunt", 1854) that of the Romantic Delacroix. In 1832 Honoré Daumier painted uncompromising caricatures of the National Assembly, the landscapes of Jean-François Millet realistically depicted the hard lives led by the peasants, while the blunt ugliness with which Gustave Courbet portrayed the bourgeoisie in his "Funeral in Omans" (1849) led to quite a scandal. The pictures by the open-air artist Camille Corot reflect a poetic concept of nature, the pre-Impressionist Eugène Boudin gives priority to atmospheric moods and the vibration of light. Without doubt the two major artists of the second half of the 19th c. are Edgar Degas ("The Bellelli Family", ca. 1858) and Edouard Manet ("Olympia", 1863), both of whom in their early works combined the style of the old masters with new, bold painting techniques. Admirers of the Second Empire will find on the ground floor sculptures by the "Florentines", for example, Ernest Christophe's "Comédie Humaine", which inspired Baudelaire's poem "Le Masque" in the "Fleurs du Mal". The fashion for polychrome sculpture and the taste for Orientalism prevalent in Europe during this period are reflected, for example, in Charles Cordier's "Nègre du Soudan". An example of Empirical splendour is found in the model of the Opéra Garnier (see entry) which made use of various styles, while sheer joy of living and excitement is epitomised in Carpeaux's "Allegory of the Dance" (1869), which was intended for the façade of the opera house.

Upper floor
★Impressionists

When the Musée d'Orsay was opened the celebrated collection of Impressionist works formerly in the Jeu de Paume (see entry) was transferred here. All the great masters of the Impressionist movement, which marked the emergence of the modern school in painting between 1870 and 1900, are represented in the upper gallery. Rapid brushstrokes and richly contrasting colours for an effective use of light and shade are seen in Edouard Manet's famous "Déjeuner sur l'Herbe" (1863), while the American-born James Abbott McNeil Whistler made sparse use of line combined with realistic forms in his well-known portrait of his mother (1871). Auguste Renoir immortalised himself in Montmartre in 1876 with

Van Gogh's "Church at Auvers-sur-Oise"

his vibrantly coloured painting of the Moulin Rouge. Fascinated by the world of opera and ballet, Degas shows in his paintings life behind the curtain and dancers training, and with the use of intensive pastel shades he emphasised the shimmering effect of artificial lighting. Post-Impressionists include Vincent van Gogh ("Church at Auvers-sur-Oise" and "Self Portrait", 1889), Rousseau ("The Snake-charmer", 1907), Paul Gauguin ("Arearea", "The Grey Horse", ca. 1898), and Paul Cézanne ("Woman with Coffee-pot", 1890), the Pointillistes George Seurat ("The Circus", 1891), Henri Matisse ("Luxury, Peace and Bliss", ca. 1904) and Paul Signac, together with the unclassifiable work of Toulouse-Lautrec.

Naturalistic painting is displayed on the middle level (including Cormon's "Cain", 1880), together with the Symbolists such as Sir Edward Burne-Jones and Winslow Horner ("Summer Night", 1890). After the sculpture of Maillot, Camille Claudel ("Ripe Old Age", 1899 to 1903) and Auguste Rodin ("Gateway to Hell", ca. 1880), the works of Nabis Viullard and Bonnard together with the section devoted to the international Art Nouveau school (including furniture by Hector Guimard and Henry van der Velde and glass and enamel work by Emile Gallé), the visit ends with the section on "Sources of the 20th Century" and the beginnings of film. The photographic collection contains some 10,000 items, from daguerreotype (1839) to the end of the First World War, including examples of work by Félix Nadar, Clarence White and Gustave Le Gray.

Mezzanine
Naturalism, Symbolism, Art Nouveau

Musée du Louvre

See Louvre

★Musée Guimet   E 5

The Musée National Guimet has the most important collection of Indian, Indonesian, Japanese, Nepalese and Tibetan art in France. The foundation of the museum was laid at the end of the 19th century, when the Lyons industrialist and traveller Emile Guimet (1836–1918) bequeathed his collection to the city of Paris. Since then the collection has been continuously enlarged in co-operation with the associated Institute for Research into East Asian Culture.

Particularly notable items on the ground floor are the Khmer sculptures from Cambodia (6th–13th c.), bronzes from Java and Lamaist jewellery, paintings and religious objects from Nepal and Tibet, among them a fine gilt bronze figure of a Dakini dancing.

The first floor presents a survey of Indian art from the 3rd millennium B.C. to the 20th century, with valuable Buddhist reliefs of the school of Amaravati (1st–3rd c.), sculpture from Gandhara (1st–6th c.) and the cosmic dance of Shiva. Also on this floor are Chinese lacquered furniture, jade, bronzes and vases (including an elephant vase of the 10th c. B.C.)

The ceramic collection on the second floor offers a comprehensive view of Chinese ceramics, including valuable porcelain ranging in date from the Tang period to the Compagnie des Indes. On this floor, too, Korea is represented by small bronzes and Japan by theatre masks, jewellery and painting (notably a 16th century screen depicting the arrival of the Portuguese in Japan).

In the Hôtel Heidenbach (19 Avenue d'Iéna), where the museum exhibits are on display until 1999 during renovation work, is an

Location
6 place d'Iéna (16th arr.)

Métro stations
Iéna, Trocadéro

Buses
32, 63, 82

Closed for renovation until 1999
(Information tel: 01 45 05 00 98)

Hôtel Heidenbach

annexe to the Musée Guimet, with the Galeries du Panthéon Bouddhique du Japon et de la Chine, installed here in 1991. They contain some 300 Asian works of art, 250 of them from Japan alone (including figures of Buddha of the 6th–15th centuries and 23 copies of statues in the Toji Temple, Kyoto).

★Musée Marmottan   E 5

Location
2 rue Louis-Boilly
(16th arr.)

Métro station
La Muette

Buses
32, 63, PC

Opening times
Tue.–Sun.
10am–5.30pm

Admission

The Musée Marmottan, situated close to the Bois de Boulogne (see entry), is a Mecca for lovers of the Impressionists. The nucleus of the museum was the collection assembled in the latter part of the 19th century by the industrialist Jules Marmottan and his son Paul. In 1934 they bequeathed their villa and art collection to the Institut de France. The value of the collection was later greatly enhanced by donations from Donop de Monchy in 1948 and Monet's son Michel in 1966.

Among the museum's principal treasures are a number of masterpieces by Monet, including the famous "Impression, Soleil Levant" (1872) which gave Impressionism its name, "Train dans la Neige" (1875), "Pont de l'Europe" (1877), "Parlement" (1905) and studies for his "Nymphéas" ("Water-lilies"). There are also pictures by Renoir, Sisley and Pissarro which belonged to Monet. Other notable items are Italian panel paintings (14th–15th c.), tapestries from Burgundy (16th c.), Late Gothic sculpture from Germany, wood figures from Mechlin (15th–16th c.) and rooms in Empire style with gouaches by Carmontelle, busts by Bosio and views of châteaux by Carle Vernet.

Musée National d'Art Moderne

See Centre Pompidou

★Musée National des Arts Africains et Océanians   N 7

Location
293 avenue
Daumesnil
(12th arr.)

Métro station
Porte Dorée

Buses
46, PC

Opening times
Mon. and Wed.–
Fri.
10am–noon and
1.30–5.30pm,
Sat. and Sun.
12.30–6pm

Conducted tours
Wed., Fri. and
Sat
3.30pm

**Admission
charge**

The Museum of African and Oceanian Art, at the west entrance to the Bois de Vincennes (see entry), was built by Albert Laprade on the occasion of the Colonial Exhibition of 1931, "La France d'Outre-mer", on the initiative of Marshal Lyautey, the great French colonial administrator. The golden figure of Minerva (symbolising France in its civilising role) which stood at the entrance to the Museum is now in Place de la Porte-Dorée. The museum building, in neo-Classical style, has a portico and a monumental bas-relief (by Alfred Janniot) on the façade depicting the contributions made by France's overseas colonies to the motherland and to civilisation.

The museum is devoted to the art of the Maghrebine (North African) states (Morocco, Algeria, Tunisia), Africa and Oceania (Polynesia, Australia).

On the lower floor is an aquarium with fossils, amphibians and brightly coloured fish from exotic waters.

Among the exhibits from Africa are fertility figures of the Dogon people of Niger, fantastic masks and fetishes expressing man's dependence on nature from Ghana and Ivory Coast, artistically decorated everyday objects of the Akan tribes, precious metal articles of the Ashantio, a people enriched by the trade in gold, bronzes from Benin, traditional costumes and magic utensils from Cameroun and royal masks from Zaire. The art of the Maghreb is distinguished by its richly inventive ornament, displayed in delicate embroidery, filigree jewellery and marvellously decorated furniture.

Among the examples of Oceanian art, with an air of magic about them, are woven masks from New Guinea, drums in the form of statues from Ambrym and Malekula (New Hebrides), bizarre dolls and sculpture full of symbolic meaning from Vanuatu and pictures on eucalyptus bark from northern Australia of a type still painted today.

★★Musée Picasso   K 5

The undoubted creator of the Picasso Museum was André Malraux. It was on his initiative, when Minister of Culture, that a law was passed enabling important works of art to be accepted in payment of estate duty. Thus after the death of Pablo Picasso the State became the owner of 203 paintings, 159 works of sculpture, 30 reliefs, 16 paper collages, 88 ceramic pieces and over 3000 sheets of drawings and printed graphic art, as well as illustrated manuscripts and correspondence. Further paintings, mainly from his later years, were added in 1990 under a bequest from his daughter.

The collection is displayed in the Hôtel Salé, a magnificent town mansion with semicircular wings built for Albert de Fontenay by Jean Boullier and lavishly decorated by Martin Desjardin and the Marsy brothers. As Fontenay was a salt-tax collector his house became known as the Hôtel Salé ("Salt House").

The interior of the Hôtel Salé (carefully restored by Roland Simounet) has rich stucco decoration. The visit begins with Picasso's "Man with a Lamb". In harmony with the architecture and rich ornament of the mansion, the old figurative decoration and the furniture by Diego Giacometto, the twenty rooms of the museum illustrate Picasso's development from his Blue Period to his latest work such as "Old Man, Seated" (1970–71).

In the selection of the works to be shown, in which Dominique Bozo took the leading place, the aim was to display the whole spectrum of Picasso's creative work and at the same time to reveal all the various artistic styles which he practised and influenced in the course of his life. In no other museum in the world is such a wide range of an artist's work to be found and the course of his development illustrated in such a complete and balanced manner.

The Picasso collection is complemented by a selection of works by artists who influenced him, including Cézanne, Renoir, Matisse, Derain, Braque, Miró and Rousseau.

Location
Hôtel Salé,
5 rue de Thorigny
(3rd arr.)

Métro stations
St-Sébastien-
Froissart, Chemin
Vert, Saint-Paul

Buses
29, 96

Opening times
Daily except Tue.
9.15am–5.15pm,
Wed. to 10pm

**Admission
charge**

Youthful years, Blue Period (1881–1903)   Room 1
Barely 14 years old, Picasso paints the morose portrait "Barefoot Girl" – and still signs with his paternal name, Pablo Ruiz. In his self-portrait of 1901 Picasso's use of blue monochrome finally asserts itself, blue being the colour of mourning and sorrow.

From the Pink Period to "Les Demoiselles d'Avignon" (1904–07)   Room 2
Gradually Picasso changes to grey, ochre and pink tones. The delicate "Seated Female Nude" (1905) belonged to the American authoress Gertrude Stein, a friend of Picasso and keen collector of his work. His sculpture "The Fool" (1905) heralds the subject of artistes and travelling entertainers, which appear again and again in his work. The famous "Les Demoiselles d'Avignon" (1907) has hung since 1939 in the Museum of Modern Art in New York. The Musée Picasso itself owns a number of preliminary studies which show how the final picture developed.

From "Les Demoiselles d'Avignon" to Cubism (1907–17)   Rooms 3 and 4
Picasso now breaks with tradition and uses harsh contrasts of colour and extreme simplification of form, as exemplified in "Mother and

Child" (1907). The geometric "Landscape with Two Figures" (1908) shows a clear link with Cézanne. In the years that follow shapes become unrecognisable and broken up into small flat pieces, and Cubism comes into being with "Man with a Mandolin" (1911) and "Man by the Fireside" (1916). A quasi-revolution sees the introduction of collage, with actual objects being used as media as well as paint, as in his series of constructions and reliefs between 1912 and 1914.

Room 5

Picasso bequest
Picasso's own private collection of works by other artists was, at his request, left to the French state. The inheritance includes works by Degas, Cézanne, Renoir, Rousseau, Matisse, Derain, Braque and Miró.

Room 6

Classical Period (1918–24)
The years 1920 to 1923 are known as the Classical Period, as the subjects of the paintings – unclothed or draped females with Greek profiles (e.g., "Three Women at the Well", 1921) – are clearly drawn from

Pablo Picasso

Born in Malaga in 1881, Picasso unquestionably belongs to the truly great artists of the modern age – for almost eight decades his work had a profound influence on the art of the 20th century. After learning the basics from his father, the painter and art-teacher José Ruiz Blasco, Picasso entered La Lonja art college in Barcelona when he was 14 years old and from 1896 studied at the Madrid Academy. This was followed by a sojourn of several years in Paris, and in 1904 he finally made France his adopted home.

Initially his work comprised mainly gracefully melancholic pictures, divided into his Blue Period (1901–03) and the brighter Pink Period (1906), so named because of the colours which dominated his paintings. With his epoch-making key work, "Les Demoiselles d'Avignon", completed in 1907, Picasso paved the way for himself and Georges Braque, later to be joined by Juan Gris and Fernand Léger, to develop analytical Cubism. After the First World War, while still occupied with cubistic and geometric forms, he also turned to the portrayal of figures. Now he was coming closer to Surrealism. Whereas previously his use of form had been geometric, now it was more organic, and his pictures were dominated by movement and figures of rounded plasticity. Towards the end of the 1920s he also turned more to sculpture. His main subjects now were illustrations based on ancient texts, works expressing his horror of the destruction caused by the Spanish Civil War and war in general – these included "Guernica" (1937), paintings of bull-fights, portraits and "artist and model" groups.

As a parallel to his artistic protests against the brutality of war he also became engaged in politics, leading to his becoming a member of the Communist party between 1944 and 1956. After the Second World War Picasso became extremely interested in ceramics and lithography. Thus, right up to the time of his death, the wide range of his work, methods and technique gained him a unique place in the history of art.

ancient art which the artist studied intensively during his stay in Rome.

Picasso and the theatre

Room 6

The world of travelling theatre, concert-cafés and circus people is one of Picasso's favourite subjects; through his acquaintance with Jean Cocteau he provides the set and costumes for the ballet "Parade" in 1915, followed by sketches for "Cuadro Flamenco" in 1921 and "Mercury" in 1924.

On the fringes of Surrealism; a period of change (1925–29)

Room 7

Picasso distorts, transposes and disfigures the human form without actually destroying it completely: "The Kiss" (1925), "The Artist and his Model" (1926), "A Woman Seated" (1929).

Portrait of Dora Marr

Picasso as a graphic artist

Room 8

Picasso completes more than 2000 graphic and lithographic works, employing all possible techniques, especially etching, engraving, wood-carving and lino-cuts, including "The Meagre Meal" (zinc etching, 1904), "Woman Weeping" (copper etching, 1937) and "David and Bathsheba" (pen-and-ink drawing on zinc, 1947).

Women Bathing (1927–37)

Room 9

Women bathing or on the beach – for example, "Figures on the Seashore" (1931) – are found again and again in Picasso's work after 1918, when he spends almost every summer by the sea – in Dinard, Juan-les-Pins or Cannes.

Boisgeloup (1930–35)

Room 10

In June 1930 Picasso acquires the chateau at Boisgeloup near Gisors. In his studio he works almost solely on sculptures, his model clearly being Marie-Thérèse Walter.

Bullfighting, Crucifixion, Fighting the Minotaur (thirty years)

Room 11

Picasso deals with the subject of the Crucifixion in 1930 and 1932 by means of drawings inspired by Matthias Grünewald's "Isenheim Altar", and in the 1950s he uses it again in conjunction with the theme of bullfighting. The Spanish bullfight, the slow ritual of killing, pitiless attack and defence by man and animal, remains present in Picasso's work until the end, for example, in "Death of the Female Torero" (1933) – the women being modelled on Marie-Thérèse Walter. Without doubt the most heavily symbolic figure in Picassos in the 1930s is the Minotaur, a creature born on the island of Crete from the forbidden love of a woman and a bull, symbol of the painful duality of man, a pitiful yet lovable animal which does not know how to tame its brutal instincts.

Musée Picasso

Room 12   *"Women at their Toilet" (1938)*
This gigantic collage (30 x 4.5m/98 x 15ft) in Cubist style was the pattern for a wall-hanging, but this did not materialise until 30 years later on instructions from André Malraux.

Sculpture Garden   *Sculptures*
Sculptures in iron and bronze, including "Woman in the Garden" (1929) and "Woman with Pushchair" (1950).

Room 13   *The Muses (1936–37)*
Through Paul Eluard, one of the poets of the Surrealist movement, Picasso gets to know the young photographer Dora Maar, who becomes his new companion through life. After 1936 the elegant brunette appears in a number of his colour-intensive likenesses which take the place of earlier pastel portraits of Marie-Thérèse.

Room 14   *Ceramics*
Picasso's friendship with Suzanne and Georges Ramié, who own a ceramics studio in Vallauris, awakens an interest in pottery. He makes small figures and vases and paints terracotta and glazed tiles, including "Roof Tile Decorated with Child and Dove" (1950) and "Spanish Shawl with Eye and Bulls" (1957).

Room 15   *From "Guernica" to the Second World War (1935–39)*
On April 26th 1937 German aircraft bomb the little Basque town of Guernica – the pointless slaughter of the civilian population shakes the world. More than 50 preliminary studies go into the painting of Picasso's "Guernica" canvas for the Spanish Pavilion at the 1937 World Exhibition.

Room 16   *War and Liberation (1940–47)*
In 1941 Picasso returns to Paris, where in 1943 he meets Françoise Gilot who remains his lover for ten years. Contemporary events are reflected in the realistic bronze sculpture "Death's Head" (1943), and in 1942 Picasso magics his "Bull's Head" out of an old leather saddle and some rusty handlebars.

Room 17   *Picasso and Literature (1947–54)*
Writers and poets such as Max Jacob, Louis Aragon, Paul Eluard, René Char and André Breton numbered among Picasso's lifelong friends. He illustrated their books but also wrote himself, as evidenced by the numerous documents, manuscripts and letters in the Museum.

"Maiden Skipping" (1950)

Vallauris (1947–54)

Sculpture plays a leading role in Picasso's work in Vallauris, including "Young Girl Skipping" (1950) and "Pregnant Woman" (1950–59). The portrait "Jacqueline with Folded Hands" (1954) is of Picasso's new wife Jacqueline Roque to whom he stays married until his death.

Room 18

Cannes, Vauvenargues (1955–61)

After 1955 Picasso works in his "Studio in La California" (1956) in Cannes, and in 1958 he buys the chateau at Vauvenargues near Aix-en-Province – here he produces in 1960 his impressively interpretative work "Breakast in the Open Air after Manet".

Room 19

Mougins – The Final Years (1961–73)

In 1961 Picasso and Jacqueline move to the Notre-Dame-de-Vie country estate in Mougins, where he works intensively on graphic drawings. Even in his last years love and eroticism govern his work, as seen in "The Kiss" (1969). With incredible energy Picasso continues even in extreme old age to use brush, pencil or engraving tool, producing inter alia the richly contrasting "Matador" (1970) and the almost pathetic painting "Old Man Seated" (1971). Picasso dies on April 8th 1973 in Mougins, but his grave lies in Vauvenargues.

Room 20

★Musée Rodin

G 5

In 1916 Auguste Rodin bequeathed to the State his own collections, his personal archives, his estate in Meudon and, above all, his complete works. In 1919 Rodin's previous home, the Hotel Biron, was opened to the public as a museum.

The magnificent gardens alone are worth a visit. Here will be found full-size copies of his world-famous monumental works. On the right, in front of the silhouette of the Eglise du Dome des Invalides, stands the aesthetic figure of the "Thinker" ("Le Penseur"), designed for the upper part of the bronze doors known as the "Gates of Hell". The first bronze casting of the dramatic sculptured group the "Burghers of Calais" (Les Bourgeois de Calais"), one of eleven copies in existence, was made in Calais in 1895. From 1880 until his death Rodin worked on the fascinating "Gates of Hell" ("Porte d'Enfer"), an extraordinary work of sculpture displaying traces of Art Nouveau. To the right of it a covered gallery houses various marble studies including "Ariane", a large funerary figure which remained unfinished because of the First World War. The monumental "Three Shadows" ("Trois Ombres") opposite dates from 1898.

Location
77 rue de
Varenne (7th arr.)

Métro station
Varenne

Buses
28, 49, 69, 82, 92

Opening times
Daily except Mon.
Winter:
9.30am–4.45pm
Summer:
9.30am–5.45pm

Admission charge
(Reduced charge
on Sun.)

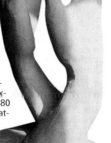

◄

A study of hands: "The Cathedral"

The works inside the museum include several studies of hands, among them the "Hand of God" ("La Main de Dieu"), a composition comprising the hand of God modelling the first beings on Earth from clay, together with the hand of the artist himself. Because of the skilful juxtaposition of the fingers, very few observers notice that "The Cathedral" ("La Cathédrale") comprises two identical right hands, the

Sculptures in the museum

Auguste Rodin

This gifted sculptor was born in the 5th arrondissement of Paris on November 12th 1840. He soon displayed a talent for drawing, and in 1854 his gift earned him a place in a renowned art college, the Ecole Impériale Speciale de Dessins et de Mathématiques. Rodin made three unsuccessful attempts to enter the Ecole des Beaux-Arts in Paris – his friend, the sculptor Dalou, later congratulated him for having thus avoided being trained along traditional lines. There followed years of employment as a plasterer and "figuriste" with firms of Parisian decorators, while practising carving busts in his spare time. In 1864 he met the beautiful seamstress Rose Beuret, who remained his loyal partner until the day she died, even though he refused to acknowledge their son Auguste, who was born in 1868. For seven years he worked with Carrier-Belleuse in Brussels, collaborating with the latter in some of the decorations for the Brussels Bourse. In the winter of 1875 he travelled to Italy where he studied the work of Michelangelo and other masters with great enthusiasm.

Artistic recognition came in 1880 when he was commissioned to design the "Gates of Hell" (La Porte d'Enfer), and he was engaged on this mammoth task on and off for the rest of his life. In London in 1881 his friend, Alphonse Legros, familiarised him with etching techniques. Rodin produced thirteen etchings in London which received enthusiastic acclaim in the British "Magazine of Art". A year later he met Camille Claudel, 24 years his junior. The stormy relationship between these two artists was to last ten years, during which time she was his colleague, pupil and model as well as his lover. Lack of money, expensive materials and rent for his rooms obliged Rodin to take on several commissions at the same time, including the "Burgers of Calais" (Les Bourgeois de Calais) in 1884 and the Claude Lorrain Memorial (1892). Thanks to the sponsorship of Emile Zola, Rodin obtained the contract for a statue of Balzac in 1891, although the rather unflattering result created quite a scandal, while his marble creation "The Kiss" (Le Baiser), carved in the same studio, was greatly admired. In the 1880s and 1890s he produced illustrations for some major texts such as Baudelaire's "Flowers of Wickedness" (Les Fleurs du Mal) in 1887. In 1889 Rodin was on the judging panel of the Paris World Exhibition, at which he was able to present his own exhibition of 170 sculptures in a building specially erected for the purpose in the Place d'Alma. This was followed by international exhibitions in Vienna (1901), Prague (1902), Dusseldorf and Leipzig (1904), important commissions and triumphant tours.

During the last ten years of his life Rodin devoted himself to smaller sculptures and subtle water-colours, received honorary doctorates from the universities of Jena and Oxford, and was designated a "Grand Officier" of the French Légion d'Honneur. Between 1905 and 1906 the poet Rainer-Maria Rilke worked as his secretary and persuaded him to purchase the Hotel Biron (built 1728–31) where he housed his personal collections and held receptions. The final days of his life were spent mainly in the Villa des Brillants in Meudon where, on January 29th 1917, now an old man, he finally married his lover Rose – two weeks later she died, and on November 17th of that year he succumbed to a lung infection. They are both laid to rest under a bronze "Thinker" in the garden of the villa.

"The Thinker" in the garden of the Rodin Musuem

silhouette of which is reminiscent of a church spire. Such frequent use of objects in pairs enabled Rodin to express varying shades of sensuousness and delicate feeling, such as the pure enthusiasm displayed by the dancers in "The Waltz" ("La Valse") and the reckless abandon of the "Eternal Spring" ("L'Eternelle Printemps"). The artistic embrace in "The Kiss" ("Le Baiser") – originally designed as part of the doors for his "Gates of Hell" and depicting the unhappy passion felt by Paolo Malatesta for his sister-in-law Francesca of Rimini – is a major work of erotic art. "The Eternal Idol" ("L'Eternelle Idole") has its admirers as part of the cult of female beauty and a certain indifference to womanhood, while the female nude "The Prayer" ("La Prière") is in homage to ancient sculpture. The first full-sized human figure Rodin sculpted was the bronze "Eve" which, together with an Adam, was also intended for the "Gates of Hell". In Room 9 can be seen the complex studies for the "Gates of Hell", inspired by Dante's "Divina Commedia", the allegorical poem describing the three kingdoms of the hereafter – Hell, Purgatory and Paradise. In the centre of the room stand "The Prodigal Son" ("L'Enfant Prodigue") and the "Thinker" in its original size. The quasi-animal concept of "Ugolino" a tyrant from Pisa who, after eating his own children, was condemned to be walled up and left to die, was a popular subject in the 19th century.

After Rodin's trip to Italy he sculpted "The Age of Bronze" ("L'Age d'Airain"), taken from a living model and showing the influence of the Italian Renaissance. In "Aurora" ("L'Aurore") the melancholy features of Camille Claudel emerge from the raw marble. "Call to Arms" ("L'Appel aux Armes") is the name given to a moving sculpture of a dying soldier which Rodin submitted in 1879 as his entry in a competition for a memorial to the defence of Paris during the war of 1870. Also worthy of note are the bust of Clémenceau and that of "Mozart" in marble, the latter actually a conversion of a 1909 portrait of Gustav

Mahler, as well as studies of Rodin's life-long companion Rose Beuret, Lady Sackville-West, the Japanese dancer Hanako, Balzac and Victor Hugo. There are also numerous drawings, pen and pencil sketches, Rodin's furniture and works by Camille Claudel (including "The Age of Maturity") and Van Gogh ("Father Tanguy"), as well as a female nude by Renoir.

Two other internationally famous figures lived for a time in the Hotel Biron, without getting to know each other well – the young Jean Cocteau (see Famous People) and the German poet Rainer Maria Rilke, who worked as Rodin's secretary.

★★Notre-Dame   J 5/6

Location
Ile de la Cité
(4th arr.)

Métro station
Cité

RER station
St-Michel-
Notre-Dame

Buses
21, 24, 38, 47, 81,
85, 96

Opening times
Daily 8am–
6.45pm

The foundation-stone of the Cathedral of Notre-Dame de Paris was laid in 1163. Louis IX (St Louis) and Bishop Maurice de Sully, its founders, wanted to build on the Ile de la Cité (see entry) a church which should resemble in style and beauty the first Gothic church which the Abbot of Saint-Denis (see entry) had begun to build in 1135. The building of Notre-Dame extended over 150 years, during which all the various phases of Gothic architecture – partly taken over from the great cathedrals of Chartres, Reims and Amiens – were reflected in its structure. (On the development of the Gothic style, see Saint-Denis.) The choir was built between 1163 and 1182, the nave between 1180 and 1200, both in Early Gothic style. The transition to High Gothic can be seen in the west front (1200–20) and the nave as altered between 1230 and 1250, pure High Gothic in the transepts (1250–60) and the choir as altered between 1265 and 1320.

Here, as later at Saint-Denis, the great 19th century restorer Viollet-le-Duc carried out an admirable restoration (1841–64) of the Cathedral, then badly dilapidated. Further restoration work started in 1992 and is expected to take until the year 2005 to complete.

Place du Parvis Notre-Dame

★Crypte
Archéologique
(open Apr.–Sept.
10am–4.45pm;
Oct.–Mar.
10am–5.45pm;
admission
charge)

There is an unobstructed view of the west front of Notre-Dame, even when there are crowds of tourists, from the Parvis Notre-Dame, the square in front of the cathedral. Under the square is the 117m/384ft long Crypte Archéologique, opened to the public in 1980, which contains the remains of houses of the 16th–18th centuries (see Cité), the Merovingian church of Saint-Etienne and Gallo-Roman buildings discovered during the construction of an underground car park. The entrance to the excavations, which are clearly laid out, with explanatory notes, is at the staircase leading to the underground car park.

In the centre of the square is a bronze plaque marking the official geographical centre of Paris, from which all distances are measured.

Exterior

★West front

The monumental and finely balanced west front of Notre-Dame reveals on closer examination the sequence of building phases and hence the development of the High Gothic style. The doorway (c. 1200), the window level (c. 1220), the traceried balustrade above the rose window and the unfinished towers (1225–50) illustrate the progressive refinement of the formal language of Gothic. The tripartite vertical articulation reflects the tripartite division of the interior into nave and aisles. The five horizontal sections (the doorway level, the Gallery of Kings, the windows, the traceried gallery, the towers) also correspond to different levels in the interior (the doorway zone to the arcading, the gallery of kings to the internal galleries, the window zone to the high windows in the interior).

Outstanding Gothic on the banks of the Seine: the Cathedral of Notre-Dame

The identity of the figures in the Gallery of Kings was for long uncertain, since their heads had been struck off during the Revolution. The discovery of 21 of the original heads in 1977 established that they were not kings of Judah, as had at one time been thought, but kings of France from Childebert I (511–588) to Philippe Auguste (1180–1223). The heads are now in the Musée de Cluny (see entry).

Gallery of Kings

The right-hand doorway is the magnificent Portail de Sainte-Anne (1210–20). The lower register of the tympanum depicts the story of Joachim and Anne, the Virgin's parents (the annunciation of Mary's birth, the meeting at the Golden Gate and the marriage of Mary and Joseph); in the middle zone are Mary in the Temple, the Annunciation and Nativity of Christ, the Annunciation to the Shepherds and Herod with the Three Kings; and above this again is the Virgin enthroned with the Infant Christ, surrounded by the heavenly host, to left and right of which are the kneeling figures of a king and a bishop, presumably Louis IX and Maurice de Sully, founders of the Cathedral. The sculptures in the upper and middle sections, carved between 1165 and 1175 for a different doorway, are the oldest in the Cathedral. On the intrados is the heavenly choir, on the central pier St Marcellus, bishop of Paris (19th century copy), and on the side walls are French kings and saints. The four figures in the recesses between the buttresses represent (from left to right) St Stephen, the Church triumphant, the Synagogue defeated and St Dionysius (see Saint-Denis).

Doorways

In the tympanum of the central doorway, the Portail du Jugement Dernier (originally 1220–30, destroyed in 18th c., restored by Viollet-le-Duc), is a representation of the Last Judgment: at the top, Christ the Judge (original); below this, the Archangel Michael directing the righteous to heaven and the damned to hell; below this again, the resurrection of the dead. On the intrados are (left) the choir of the blessed being received by Abraham in paradise and (right) hell, with grotesque demons; on the central pier is a figure of Christ (19th c.). On the door jambs are the wise (left) and foolish (right) virgins; on the side walls are the twelve Apostles (19th c.); and the reliefs along the base depict virtues (above) and vices (below); the figures on the right are original.

In the tympanum of the left-hand doorway, the Portail de la Vierge (1210–20), are (top) the Assumption of the Virgin, (middle) the Burial of the Virgin, with Christ and the Apostles, and (bottom) the Ark of the Covenant, with three prophets and three Old Testament kings.

In the archivolts are angels with censers and torches, patriarchs, prophets and the Forefathers of Christ, and on the jambs and the sides of the central pier, which bears a figure of the Virgin (by Viollet-le-Duc, 19th c.), are the symbols of the months and the signs of the zodiac. On the side walls are (left) St Dionysius (Denis) and kings and (right) John the Baptist, St Stephen, St Genevieve and a Pope.

Side walls

Both sides of Notre-Dame display the richness of High Gothic form. On the north front (1250–60) Jean de Chelles completed the transept in 1250, with the Portail du Cloître, which led into the former cloister. The doorway in the south transept, the Portail de Saint-Etienne (St Stephen's), was the work of Pierre de Montreuil. The acute-angled pediments over the doorways, reaching almost up to the rose windows, the dissolution of the transept walls into a profusion of stained glass and the bold thrust of the flying buttresses give the side walls of Notre-Dame the typical aspect and the charismatic power of the High Gothic cathedral.

Side doorways

In the tympanum of the Portail du Cloître (1250) are representations, in the bottom register, of a scene from the childhood of Christ and in the two upper registers of the popular medieval legend of St Théophile (Theophilus): (middle) the saint making a pact with the devil and being saved by the Virgin, and (top) the bishop showing the pact to the people. On the door piers is a 13th century statue of the Virgin (original), and in the rose window (1270) the Virgin is surrounded by Old Testament figures.

To the east of the Portail du Cloître is the small Porte Rouge (Red Door), the work of Pierre de Montreuil. In the tympanum the Virgin is represented between Louis IX and his wife Marguerite de Provence.

In the tympanum of the Portail de Saint-Etienne are representations of St Stephen preaching and being arrested (bottom), his martyrdom and burial (middle) and his resurrection (top). On the central pier is a figure of the saint.

**Tower
Opening times:**
Oct.–Mar.,
9.30am–5pm;
Apr.–Sept.,
9.30am–6.30pm

**Admission
charge**

The ascent of the tower (70m/230ft) involves climbing 387 steps, but the view from the top is one of the great experiences of a visit to Paris. Unlike other famous Paris viewpoints (the Eiffel Tower, the Sacré-Cœur, the Tour Maine-Montparnasse), the tower of Notre-Dame offers a close-up view of the historic centre of the city, with the Cité, the Hôtel de Ville, the Louvre, the Sorbonne, the Panthéon and the Ile Saint-Louis, as well as panoramic views of the modern city extending as far as the tower blocks of La Défense.

Interior

Dimensions

The five-aisled Cathedral of Notre-Dame is 130m/427ft long by 48m/157ft wide, with vaulting reaching up to a height of 35m/115ft. It can accommodate a congregation of 9000, 1500 in the galleries alone. Accordingly the cathedral has frequently been the setting of great official occasions (e.g. Napoleon's coronation as first Emperor of the French). The powerful unity of the interior with its 75 round pillars is impressively enhanced by indirect lighting.

Notre-Dame de Paris

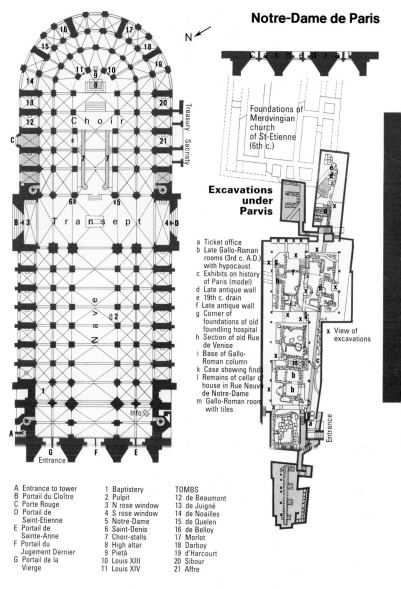

N

Cathedral

Foundations of Merovingian church of St-Etienne (6th c.)

Excavations under Parvis

a Ticket office
b Late Gallo-Roman rooms (3rd c. A.D.) with hypocaust
c Exhibits on history of Paris (model)
d Late antique wall
e 19th c. drain
f Late antique wall
g Corner of foundations of old foundling hospital
h Section of old Rue de Venise
i Base of Gallo-Roman column
k Case showing finds
l Remains of cellar of house in Rue Neuve de Notre-Dame
m Gallo-Roman room with tiles

x View of excavations

Entrance

Choir

Treasury

Sacristy

Transept

Nave

Info

Entrance

		TOMBS
A Entrance to tower	1 Baptistery	12 de Beaumont
B Portail du Cloître	2 Pulpit	13 de Juigné
C Porte Rouge	3 N rose window	14 de Noailles
D Portail de Saint-Etienne	4 S rose window	15 de Quelen
E Portail de Sainte-Anne	5 Notre-Dame	16 de Belloy
F Portail du Jugement Dernier	6 Saint-Denis	17 Morlot
G Portail de la Vierge	7 Choir-stalls	18 Darboy
	8 High altar	19 d'Harcourt
	9 Pietà	20 Sibour
	10 Louis XIII	21 Affre
	11 Louis XIV	

Ausgrabungen unter dem Vorplatz (Parvis) s. rechts

30 m

© Baedeker

A special feature of the interior is the reworking of the Early Gothic side walls of the nave, which already had a gallery over the arcading, on the model of Saint-Denis. The gallery was preserved instead of being replaced by a triforium as in other High Gothic churches. Above this were double pointed windows surmounted by rose windows – a feature borrowed from Chartres.

In the first bay of the nave Viollet-le-Duc had begun, in the course of his restoration work, to change the tripartite division of High Gothic back into the quadripartite division of Early Gothic. Fortunately he did not proceed with this, and it is now possible to recognise, in comparison with his alteration, the greater elegance of the High Gothic solution.

It is also interesting to note the change from the Romanesque acanthus and leaf ornament of the capitals in the choir to the Gothic foliage capitals in the nave.

Particularly fine is the rose window in the north transept (c. 1255), with 80 Old Testament scenes centred on the Virgin. The large rose window in the south transept depicts Christ surrounded by apostles, martyrs, the wise and foolish virgins and the story of Matthew. On the south-east pier at the crossing is the best known and most revered image of the Virgin in the cathedral – Notre Dame de Paris, a slender figure of around 1330 which was set up here in 1855. Of the medieval furnishings of the church there remain the choir screens (begun by Pierre de Chelles c. 1300), with 23 stone reliefs (1319–51, by Jehan Ravy and his nephew Jehan de Bouteiller), painted and partly gilded, depicting scenes from the life of Christ up to the Passion. In the south-east choir chapel is the tomb (showing Burgundian influence) of Jean Juvénal des Ursins (d. 1431), who as prévot des marchands established the freedom of shipping on the Seine and the Marne. Here too is the elaborate monument, in black and white marble, of the Comte d'Harcourt (d. 1718), by J.-B. Pigalle. Other notable features of the interior are the fine carved choir-stalls, a Pietà by Nicolas Coustou and the Baroque high altar.

The famous Cavaillé-Coll organ, completely restored by the firm of Boisseau in 1992, is one of the largest and most powerful in France, with 8500 pipes and some 110 stops. Every Sunday evening at 5.45 there are free and well attended organ recitals. High Mass is celebrated daily at 10am.

Trésor (Treasury)

Opening times:
Wed., Sat., Sun.,
2.30–6pm
(except Easter)

Admission charge

In the Treasury (entrance in choir, on right) is a reliquary designed by Viollet-le-Duc (1862) containing one of Christ's nails, a thorn from the crown of thorns and a fragment of the True Cross. The Sainte-Chapelle (see entry) was originally built by Louis IX to house the crown of thorns. Also on display are valuable manuscripts, precious monstrances, crosses, chalices and Napoleon's coronation robes.

Opéra de la Bastille

See Bastille

★Opéra-Garnier   H 4

Location
Place de l'Opéra
(9th arr.)

The Paris Opera House (officially the Académie Nationale de Musique et de Danse) was intended to establish a "Napoleon III style". The result was a sumptuous neo-Baroque building, grander and more elaborately decorated than any contemporary building of the kind in Europe. The winner of the architectural competition for the design of the Opera House was a previously unknown architect, Charles Garnier (1825–98), and the Opera was built to his design between 1862 and 1875. It was then the largest opera house in the world, covering an area of 11,000sq.m/13,000sq.yds, but had seating only for 2200 people.

The façade is divided horizontally into three. The ground floor has seven round-headed arches, which are flanked by eight allegorical figures: (from left) Poetry (by Jouffroy), Music (Guillaume), Idyll (Aizelin), Recitation (Chapu), Song (Dubois), Drama (Fabuière), Dance (a masterpiece by Carpeaux; original in Musée d'Orsay) and Lyric Drama (Perraud). Above the four central figures are medallions with the heads of Cimarosa, Haydn, Pergolesi and Bach. The loggia, with 16 tall and 14 small Corinthian columns, has busts of Halévy, Meyerbeer, Rossini, Auber, Spontini, Beethoven and Mozart. Above this is the attic storey, with four gilded groups glorifying Poetry and Fame.

On the side facing Rue Scribe is the Pavillon d'Honneur, which formerly gave the President of the Republic direct access to his box. It now contains a small library and a museum of opera props (open: Mon.–Sat. 11am–5pm).

The auditorium itself (restored in 1995/6) can be seen only at certain times, but the magnificent grand staircase (Escalier d'Honneur) of multi-coloured marble can be seen at any time. In the foyer are allegorical paintings (1864–74) by Paul Baudry. The auditorium, which is decorated entirely in red and gold, has a large ceiling painting by Chagall (1964).

Since the opening of the new opera house in Place de la Bastille (see Bastille) the Opéra-Garnier is used only for performances by visiting companies and ballet.

Métro station
Opéra

RER station
Auber

Buses
20, 21, 22, 27, 29, 31, 39, 42, 52, 53, 66, 68, 81, 95

Opening times
Daily 10am–5pm

Guided Tours
Tue.–Sun. 1pm

Ticket office
Tel. 40 01 25 14
40 01 20 82

The Opéra-Garnier – a sumptous neo-Baroque building designed by Charles Garnier (1825–98)

★Palais-Bourbon   G 5

Location
Quai d'Orsay
(7th arr.)

Métro station
Assemblée
Nationale

Buses
24, 63, 83, 84, 94

Opening times
For a conducted
visit or admission
to visitors'
gallery, apply in
writing to
Questure de
l'Assemblée
Nationale,
33 Quai d'Orsay,
75007 Paris

The former Palais-Bourbon is directly in line with the Madeleine and the obelisk in Place de la Concorde. It is now the seat of the National Assembly (Assemblée Nationale), the first chamber of the French Parliament; the second chamber, the Senate, meets in the Palais du Luxembourg (see entry). Until 1946 the country's legislative body was known as the Chambre des Députés.

The palace was built in 1722–28 for Duchesse Louise-Françoise de Bourbon, a legitimised daughter of Louis XIV and Madame de Montespan. During the French Revolution it was confiscated and reconstructed for parliamentary use. It has been the seat of the first chamber of the French Parliament since 1827.

The imposing colonnaded front added in the Napoleonic period was designed to be a counterpart to the Madeleine (see entry) on the opposite side of the Seine, which is also in classical style, with columns and a triangular pediment. The monumental figures in front of the ten-column portico of the Palais are of ministers of various French kings: from left to right Sully (Henri IV's minister), Michel de l'Hospital (François I), Henri II d'Agnesseau (Louis XV) and Colbert (Louis XIV). The allegorical figures in the pediment, representing France flanked by Freedom and Order, are by Cortot.

To left and right of the steps in front of the building are Minerva, symbolising Wisdom, and Themis, symbolising Justice.

To the rear of the Palais-Bourbon is Place du Palais-Bourbon, which gives an excellent impression of an 18th century square in the fashionable Faubourg Saint-Germain (see entry). The 18th century façade of the Palais on this side has been preserved. On this side too, is the entrance used by members of the National Assembly.

The semicircular chamber of the National Assembly, constructed in the time of the Directoire (1796–99) and remodelled by Jules de Joly in 1826, can be seen on prior application even when the Assembly is sitting. The decoration of the Library, with ceiling paintings depicting the history of civilisation, was the work of Delacroix (1838–47); it contains more than 350,000 volumes, including the original records of the trial of Joan of Arc.

On the west side of the Palais is the Hôtel de Lassay, built by the Prince de Condé in 1722–24 and now the official residence of the President of the National Assembly. A short distance away, on the Quai d'Orsay, is the French Foreign Ministry (Ministère des Affaires Etrangères).

Hôtel de Salm

A little way east of the Palais-Bourbon, at 64 rue de Lille, is the Hôtel de Salm, headquarters of the Légion d'Honneur.

★Palais de Chaillot   E 5

Location
Place du
Trocadéro
(16th arr.)

Métro station
Trocadéro

Buses
22, 30, 32, 63, 82

The austere but imposing Palais de Chaillot with its two curving wings stands on high ground above the Seine. It was built in 1937 (architects Jacques Carlu, Louis-Auguste Boileau and Léon Azème) on the site of the old Palais du Trocadéro. The broad main terrace linking the two wings, flanked on both sides by gleaming bronze statues, offers a spectacular view of the Eiffel Tower on the other side of the Seine. This was the entrance to the 1937 Exhibition.

The extensive wings of the Palais house four museums. In the west wing are the Musée de l'Homme and Musée de la Marine, in the east wing the Musée des Monuments Français and the Musée du Cinéma.

Musée de la Marine: a majestic three-masted French naval ship

The Musée de la Marine (Maritime Museum) documents the history of the French navy and merchant navy from the galley to the nuclear submarine. Its 13 rooms of pictures and models of ships and port installations, nautical equipment, old charts, figureheads, diving apparatus and much else present an excellent survey of seafaring history. Items of particular interest are a model of Columbus's "Santa Maria" (Room 1); the "Louis XV", a toy boat which belonged to the young king (Room 2); the "Valmy", the last sailing ship in the French navy, made of ebony, ivory and silver (Room 5) and some of the first steamships (Room 5) and "La Gloire", the world's first ironclad, launched in 1859 (Room 6).

★ **Musée de la Marine**

Opening times:
Mon. and Wed.–Sun.
10am–6pm

Admission charge

The Musée de l'Homme (Museum of Man) devotes a third of its area of 10,000sq.m/108,000sq.ft to its prehistoric and ethnographic collections; the rest of the area is occupied by rooms for special exhibitions and a library of over 180,000 volumes on the top floor. On the first floor is the prehistoric material, including such notable items as Menton Man, a cast of the Hottentot Venus and the famous Venus of Lespugue, carved from a mammoth's tusk. The section of the ethnographic department on the first floor is devoted to Africa (including rock drawings from the Hoggar district in the Algerian Sahara, medieval frescoes from Abyssinia and sculpture from West Africa). On the second floor are collections of ethnographic material from the Arctic regions, Asia and America (in particular the art of the Mayas and Aztecs).

★ **Musée de l'Homme**

Opening times:
Mon. and Wed.–Sun.
9.45am–5.15pm

Admission charge

The Musée des Monuments Français (Museum of French Monuments) in the east wing, founded in 1880 on the initiative of Viollet-le-Duc, the great restorer of historical monuments, displays reproductions and full-size models of major French monuments of art and architecture. The museum offers a vivid survey, presented chrono-

★ **Musée des Monuments Français**

Palais de Chaillot

Opening times:
Mon. and Wed.–
Sun. 9am–6pm

Admission
charge

logically, of the development of French styles in sculpture, painting and architecture over twelve centuries, from the Early Romanesque to the Neo-Classical period. To the right of the entrance hall are the wall paintings, distributed over three floors; to the left, in the east wing of the Palais, is the sculpture department.

On the ground floor are works of the Early Romanesque period (c. 800–1000) and crypt paintings from Auxerre (life of St Stephen, c. 850). On the first floor is Romanesque art of c. 1000–1200, including the fine paintings of Biblical scenes (Genesis to the Apocalypse) from the abbey church of Saint-Savin-sur-Gartempe in Vienne. The second floor is devoted to Early and High Gothic art (c. 1200–1400), the third floor to Late Gothic (c. 1400–1550).

Notable items in the sculpture collection, in chronological order, are Early Romanesque sarcophagi (6th–7th c.), the earliest grave-slab with relief decoration (11th c.; Room 1), Romanesque sculpture and reliefs from door arches and church doorways of the 11th century (Rooms 2–6), Crusader architecture in Palestine (12th–13th c.; Room 7), Early Gothic reliefs and sculpture, from originals in the cathedrals of Chartres, Reims, Paris and Strasbourg (12th–13th c.; Room 8), the High Gothic burial chapel of the Dukes of Burgundy (14th c.; Rooms 14 and 15), work of the High and Late Gothic periods (14th–15th c.; Rooms 16–18) and of the Late Gothic and Early Renaissance periods (15th–16th c.; Rooms 19–21). The Renaissance (16th–17th c.) is represented by works by Jean Goujon (1510–68), Ligier Richier (1500–66) and Germain Pilon (1536–90; Rooms 22–24); the French classical period (Baroque, 17th–18th c.) by François Girardon (1628–1715), Antoine Coysevox (1640–1720), the brothers Nicolas (1658–1753) and Guillaume Coustou (1677–1746; Room 25); the Rococo period (18th c.) by Maurice-Etienne Falconet (1716–91), Edme Bouchardon (1698–1762), Jean-Antoine Houdon (1741–1828) and Jean-Baptiste Pigalle

Austere but imposing: The Palais de Chaillot

(1714–85), with fine busts of Voltaire, Mirabeau and Rousseau (Rooms 26 and 27). The early Neo-Classical period of the 19th century is represented, among other works, by the "Marseillaise" carving from the Arc de Triomphe (Room 28).

The Museum of the Cinema covers the development of film from the first "pantinoscope" and the work of the Lumière brothers to the cult films of the present day. It was created by Henri Langlois, who began in the 1930s to collect anything and everything connected with photography and the cinema, including posters, film sets, film scripts and costumes. Film buffs will be thrilled by the props from famous films of the past – costly dresses from "Gone with the Wind", John Wayne's hat from "Stagecoach", bizarre street scenes from Robert Wiene's expressionist silent film "The Cabinet of Dr Caligari", Fritz Lang's robots from "Metropolis".

★**Musée du Cinéma**

Conducted tours:
Mon. and Wed.–Sun. 10am, 11am, 2pm, 3pm, 4pm

Admission charge

In 1936 Henri Langlois also founded the Cinémathèque Française (entrance in Avenue Albert-de-Mun), which has daily shows of three or four noted films of the past selected from its extensive holdings.

Cinémathèque Française

Below the terrace of the Palais de Chaillot, at the foot of which during the summer months youthful roller-skaters and skateboarders display their skill, is the Théâtre National de Chaillot, which has two houses with seating for a total of 3000 spectators. After the Second World War such illustrious actors and actresses as Gérard Philippe and Maria Casarès appeared here under the direction of Jean Vilar. Since 1981 the director has been Jérome Savary, who is noted for his avant garde productions.

Théâtre National de Chaillot

★Palais de Justice (Law Courts)

J 5

On the site now occupied by the Palais de Justice, on the Ile de la Cité (see entry), the Gauls, followed by the Romans and later the Merovingians, built their fortiified settlements and strongholds. This was the cradle of French royal authority. In the reign of Louis IX (St Louis; 1226–70) the royal residence, with the newly built Sainte-Chapelle (see entry), reached the peak of its magnificence. After the storming of the palace in 1358 by the rebellious merchants of Paris under the leadership of Etienne Marcel (see Hôtel de Ville), however, the court moved to the Louvre (see entry). From the 16th century onwards the palace was the seat of the Parlement de Paris, the highest French court of justice, whose assent was necessary for all laws promulgated by the king. This privilege was abolished by the young king Louis XIV after the Fronde (1648–52), a revolt against the royal authority. The French Revolution later removed both the king and the Parlement, sending all its members to the scaffold. The new citizens' courts moved into the old palace, which now became known as the Palais de Justice. Thereafter the building suffered much damage and destruction by fire and in the course of time was much altered, until finally at the turn of the century the Palais de Justice took its present form. The south wing was added in 1911–14. The Palais houses the civil and criminal courts, with the criminal investigation department in the south wing on the Quai des Orfèvres.

At the entrance to the Palais de Justice, in the Cour de Mai (where the maypole used to be set up), is a magnificent wrought-iron gate dating from the time of Louis XVI (1787). From here a flight of steps leads up to the Galerie Marchande (Merchants' Hall), which in the time of Louis IX was a passage between the royal palace and the Sainte-Chapelle; before the Revolution it was crowded with merchants offering their wares. This leads into the Salle des Pas Perdus

Location
4 boulevard du Palais (1st arr.)

Métro station
Cité

Buses
21, 24, 27, 38, 81, 85, 96

Opening times
Mon.–Fri.
9am–6pm

173

("Hall of the Lost Steps") – an allusion to the time wasted here by hopeful litigants. The hall is situated directly above the Salle des Gens d'Armes in the C nciergerie (see entry), the old Grande Salle of the royal palace, in which the king signed important treaties and held official receptions. The Neo-Classical decor is a reproduction of the oriiginal decoration by Salomon de Brosse, restored after a fire in 1871. From the Galerie Duc, named after the architect and restorer of ancient monuments Eugène-Emmanuel Viollet-le-Duc (1814–79), there is a view of the Sainte-Chapelle and, at the other end, of the Cour des Femmes of the Conciergerie. In the Vestibule de Harlay are statues of Charlemagne, Philippe Auguste, Louis IX and Napoleon, monarchs who were particularly concerned with law-making.

Opening off the S 'e des Pas Perdus is the Chambre Dorée, the Première Chambre le, which was originally Louis IX's bedroom and in 1793 became the Salle de la Liberté, seat of the revolutionary tribunal which passed over 2000 sentences of death, including that of Marie-Antoinette. The neo-Renaissance decor dates from the 19th century.

Palais de Tokyo   E 4

Location
13 avenue
Président-
Wilson (16th arr.)

Métro stations
Iéna,
Alma Marceau

Buses
32, 42, 63, 72, 80

The Palais de Tokyo, formerly called the Palais d'Art Moderne, was built for the Paris Exhibition of 1937. It now houses the Musée d'Art Moderne de la Ville de Paris (east wing) and the Centre National de la Photographie (west wing). Designed by Aubert, Dastugne, Dondel and Biard, it is a functional building in the Bauhaus tradition, like the neighbouring Palais de Chaillot (see entry). Both buildings show classical influences. The allegorical figures in the peristyle ("Strength" and "Victory") and the figure of "France" (1927) by the pool are by Antoine Bourdelle (1861–1929). The building will be in process of reconstruction until 1999.

Centre National de la Photographie

The Centre National de la Photographie (CNP), with a media library, was installed in the Palais de Tokyo in 1984. Its founder, Robert Delpire, a high-profile publisher of books on photography, has since organised a series of renowned exhibitions of international photography. The Centre also publishes well-regarded photographic books, including works by Henri Cartier-Bresson, Robert Doisneau, Lartigue, Newton and Duane Michals. During the reconstruction work the CNP's exhibits are housed in the Fondation Rothschild (11 rue Berryer: open: Mon., Wed.–Sat., noon–7pm).

★Musée d'Art Moderne de la Ville de Paris (MAM)

Opening times:
Tue.–Fri.
Sat., Sun.
10am–6.45pm

Admission charge

The city's Museum of Modern Art has occupied the east wing of the Palais de Tokyo since 1961. It offers a comprehensive survey of modern European art, complemented by interesting special exhibitions of contemporary art.

Among major Post-Impressionist works in the collection are pictures by Paul Cézanne, André Dunoyer de Segonzac and Maurice Utrillo, watercolours (1905–07) by Georges Rouault, landscapes by Raoul Dufy and his monumental "Fée Électricité", an allegory of the power of electricity painted for the 1937 Exhibition. Part of the collection, including works by Toulouse-Lautrec and Odilon Redon, was taken over from the Musée d'Orsay in 1986. Other notable items are Picasso's "Evocation" (1901), the first painting of his Blue Period; still lifes by Georges Braque; Fernand Léger's "Les Disques" (1918); Robert Delaunay's large painting, "L'Equipe de Cardiff" (1913; a number of pictures by the Fauves, including Matisse's "Pastorale" (1905) and Derain's "Phare de Collioure" (1905); and works by Albert Marquet, Maurice de Vlaminck, Suzanne Valadon and Amedeo Modigliani. The sculpture on display includes works by Jacques Lipchitz, Chavigné and a wood figure of "Orpheus" by Ossip Zadkine.

*Functional architecture in the best Bauhaus tradition –
the Palais de Tokyo*

Palais-Royal

H 4/5

The Palais-Royal (Royal Palace) is now occupied by the Conseil d'Etat, the supreme administrative court, and the Secrétariat de la Culture et de la Communication.

The palace, situated close to the Louvre (see entry), was built between 1634 and 1639 for Cardinal Richelieu (1585–1642), who on his death bequeathed it to the king. After Louis XIII's death his widow Anne of Austria moved into the palace, which then became known as the Palais-Royal. Her son, Louis XIV, returned to the Louvre in 1652, but soon afterwards, after a brief stay in the Château de Vincennes (see entry), transferred the court to Versailles (see entry). Thereafter the king granted the palace to the House of Orléans. Louis-Philippe d'Orléans – who supported the principles of the Revolution and accordingly became known as Philippe Egalité, though this did not save him from the guillotine – gave the palace its present form and surrounded the gardens with colonnades, shops and apartments.

On July 13th 1789 Camille Desmoulins, a lawyer and journalist, addressed a revolutionary crowd under these colonnades, and this was followed on the next day by the storming of the Bastille (see entry). Before and during the Revolution and under the First Empire the Palais-Royal was a popular meeting-place, with restaurants, cafés, gaming houses and brothels. It is said that when the Allies occupied Paris in 1814 Marshall Blücher lost 6 million francs in the gaming houses of the Palais-Royal. They, like the brothels, were closed down in 1830.

Notable residents in the Palais-Royal apartments have included Colette and Jean Cocteau.

Location
Place du Palais-Royal (1st arr.)

Métro station
Palais-Royal-Musée du Louvre

Buses
21, 27, 39, 48, 67, 69, 72, 74, 81, 85, 95

The courtyard of the Palais Royal – a favourite place for roller-skating between Buren's striped "columns"

Colonnes du Palais-Royal

A passage between the Palais-Royal and the Comédie Française leads into the inner courtyard, which since 1986 has been patterned by the controversial "colonnes" of the sculptor Daniel Buren. These black-and-white striped "columns", no more than a few inches high, are set in geometrically precise rows over the whole area of the courtyard. This is now a favourite spot with youngsters on roller-skates, who treat the columns as an obstacle course.

★Panthéon J 6

Location
Place du Panthéon
(5th arr.)

Métro station
Cardinal Lemoine

RER station
Luxembourg

Buses
84, 89

Opening times
Daily 10am –
6.15pm

Admission charge

The Panthéon, originally built as a church, is the national memorial and burial-place of France's great men. In 1756 Louis XV commissioned the architect Jacques-Germain Soufflot (1713–80) to build a magnificent new church on the site of a ruined abbey of Sainte Geneviève (patron saint of Paris; see Saint-Etienne-du-Mont). The church was completed in 1790, ten years after Soufflot's death. In 1791 the National Assembly resolved to convert it into a French Pantheon (a pantheon in classical Greece being a temple dedicated to the country's gods). Forty-two of the church's windows were walled up, giving the building the appearance of a mausoleum, with its cold outer aspect and dark interior.

The architecture of the Panthéon marks a clear break with the playful Rococo of the Louis XV style, as seen for example in the Hôtel de Soubise in the Marais (see entry), which in turn was a reaction against the clear, "classical" French Baroque of Louis XIV's reign. The Panthéon was the first building in Paris in the neo-Classical style which sought to return to the architectural simplicity and monumentality of classical antiquity. It set the standard for the period before and after Napoleon, as is shown by such massive structures as the Arc de Triomphe, the Madeleine and the Bourse (see entries).

Although Soufflot took St Paul's Cathedral in London as his model, he sought to put his own stamp on the building. Accordingly he gave it a portico projecting some considerable distance in front of the façade, so that an observer could not see the base of the dome, which would thus appear to hover above the building. On the triangular pediment borne on 18 Corinthian columns are the inscription "Aux grands hommes la Patrie reconnaissante" ("To great men, their grateful country") and a relief by David d'Anger showing France presenting laurels to her great men (among them Mirabeau, Voltaire and Rousseau to the left and Napoleon and his generals to the right).

The interior was designed by Soufflot to achieve visibility and clarity, with numerous windows and slender columns – even those supporting the dome. However constructional defects made it necessary to use massive piers, and the conversion of the building to serve as a mausoleum involved sacrificing many of the windows. While the Panthéon was in use as a church for a brief period during the reign of Napoleon the dome was decorated with a fresco, "Assumption of St Genevieve" (1811). On the side walls are frescoes by Puvis de Chavannes depicting the life of the saint, while others show Charlemagne, Louis IX and Joan of Arc.

Among the great men buried in the Panthéon, in addition to the philosophers already mentioned, are the writers Victor Hugo and Emile Zola, the great mathematician Gaspard Monge and the Resistance fighter Jean Moulin and the writer and Minister of Culture André Malraux, whose remains were transferred to the Panthéon in 1990.

Since Umberto Eco's best-selling novel "The Foucalt Pendulum". the self-same pendulum, which the scientist Foucalt used to prove that

Foucalt
Pendulum

The classical aspect of the Pantheon, burial place of many great Frenchmen

the earth rotates, has aroused interest. It can at present be seen in the Pantheon, but when the old church of Prieuré Saint-Martin-des-Champs has been renovated the pendulum will return there.

Paristoric   G 4

Location
11 bis rue Scribe
(9th arr.)

Métro stations
Opéra, Chausée
d'Antin

Opening times
Daily 9am–6pm
or 9pm

**Admission
charge**

"Paris, how can I get to know you?" – "By letting me tell you my secrets." This poetic dialogue is the prelude to the Paristoric multi-vision show lasting 45 minutes, which offers an unusual introduction to the fascinations of Paris. With the help of 30 computer-controlled slide projectors and the accompaniment of taped music ranging from Verdi by way of Ravel to Edith Piaf it presents the 2000-year history of the French capital on a screen 14m/46ft wide. Starting from Gallo-Roman Lutetia, it illustrates events in different historical periods, the architectural styles associated with different rulers and the build-ings that remain to exemplify them, coming right down to President Mitterand's ultra-modern *grands projets*. The film, initiated by Charles and Michel Ruty in 1990, is accompanied by a commentary in seven languages and quotations from great writers and philosophers who have been inspired by Paris. Whether you are new to Paris or know it well, you will find the Paristoric show a rewarding experience.

★Pavillon de l'Arsenal   K 6

Location
21 boulevard
Morland (4th arr.)

Métro station
Sully Morland

Opening times
Tue.–Sat.
10.30am–6.30pm,
Sun. 11am–7pm.
Documentation
Centre and
Photothèque:
Tue.–Sat. 2–6pm

Originally designed in 1878 as a private museum for a collection of watercolours, the Pavillon de l'Arsenal was opened in December 1988 as a documentation and information centre on the history of Paris.

With 1600sq.m/17,200sq.ft of exhibition space, the centre illustrates the development of the city and its architecture. The central feature of the permanent exhibition on "Paris, the City and its Projects", which occupies half the area of the centre, is a large model (40sq.m/430sq.ft) of the city on the scale of 1:2000. Special exhibitions, changing every three months, are devoted to particular themes in the history of Paris, often with comparisons between Paris and other European cities, and another exhibition illustrates new projects currently under way.

Excellent informative material on French architectural history is supplied by the Documentation Centre and Photothèque.

Père-Lachaise

See Cemeteries

★Petit Palais   F 4

Location
Avenue Winston-
Churchill (8th arr.)

Métro station
Champs-Elysées-
Clemenceau

Buses
28, 49, 72, 73, 83

Built, like the Grand Palais, for the Paris Exhibition of 1900, the Petit Palais shows the same architectural features as its larger neighbour. It has a magnificent main doorway with rich sculptural decoration, with a dome soaring above it.

In addition to interesting temporary exhibitions the Petit Palais has housed since 1902 the valuable art collections of the city of Paris, which have been much enhanced by private donations: the Dutuit brothers, for example, bequeathed to the city in 1902 a collection of ancient, medieval and Renaissance art, with pictures (including works by Rembrandt and Rubens), drawings, books, majolica, enamels and ceramics, while the Tuck collection, presented to the city in 1930, consists mainly of 18th century furniture, tapestries and sculpture. The Galerie Zoubaloff displays 19th century painting from Neo-Classicism to the Impressionists, including pictures by Gros, Géricault, Ingres, Delacroix, Millet, Corot, Courbet, Cézanne, Monet and Pissarro. There are also some attractive pieces of sculpture by Jean-Baptiste Carpeaux.

Opening times
Daily except Mon.
10am–5.40pm
Thur., 8pm

Admission charge

Place Charles-de-Gaulle

See Arc de Triomphe

★★Place de la Concorde   G 4

The spacious Place de la Concorde, at the intersection of two main axes (Louvre-Arc de Triomphe and Madeleine-Palais-Bourbon), is recognised as one of the finest squares in the world. Originally called Place Louis-XV, with an equestrian statue of the king in the centre, it was laid out by the architect Jacques-Ange Gabriel, who between 1755 and 1775 built two magnificent buildings on the north side of the square, flanking Rue Royale: to the right the Ministère de la Marine (since 1792; originally the Garde-Meuble de la Couronne, the royal furniture store), to the left the elegant Hôtel Crillon.

Location
8th arr.

Métro station
Concorde

Buses
24, 42, 72, 73, 84, 94

During the French Revolution the statue of the king was destroyed, the square was renamed Place de la Révolution and the guillotine was set up here. Among the many thousands executed in this square were

One of the two fountains by Hittorft in the Place de la Concorde

Louis XVI and Marie-Antoinette, Madame Dubarry, Charlotte Corday, Danton and finally Robespierre and his supporters.

The square was given its present name in 1795, under the Directoire.

Obelisk

In the centre of the square is an Egyptian obelisk, 22m/72ft high and weighing 220 tons, which was set up here in 1833. Dating from the time of Rameses II (13th century B.C.), it came from Luxor (the ancient Thebes) and was a gift to King Louis-Philippe by Mehmet Ali, Viceroy of Egypt.

Fountains and statues

Between 1836 and 1854 Jacob Ignaz Hittorff, a native of Cologne, gave the square its final form by erecting two fountains (the one to the north decorated with allegories of agriculture and industry, the one to the south with allegorical figures representing seafaring and fishing) and eight female figures (restored 1988) personifying France's eight largest cities (clockwise: Marseilles, Bordeaux, Nantes, Brest, Rouen, Lille, Strasbourg, Lyons). The lodges in the bases of the statues were formerly occupied by municipal employees (gardiens).

Place de l'Etoile

See Arc de Triomphe

★Place des Vosges
K 5

Location
East central
(4th arr.)

Métro stations
St-Paul, Bastille

Buses
20, 29, 65, 69, 76, 96

The Place des Vosges, in the eastern part of the Marais (see entry), is Paris's oldest public square, spaciously laid out in harmoniously uniform style, which provided a model for other squares such as Place Dauphine by the Pont Neuf, Place Vendôme and Place de la Concorde. The construction of the square, then known as Place Royale, between 1605 and 1612 confirmed the position of the Marais as an elegant aristocratic residential quarter. Designed by an unknown architect in the symmetrical form favoured by Renaissance architecture, with uniform houses of red brick and light-coloured stone faced with stucco, the square was a magnificent setting for festive occasions – tournaments, splendid state receptions, court weddings. It was also a favourite spot for duels, in spite of Cardinal Richelieu's ban on duelling. At No. 11 lived Marion Delorme, a celebrated courtesan of Louis XIII's reign whose salon attracted renowned men of letters of the day. At No. 1 the future Madame de Sévigné was born in 1626. At the end of the 17th century the great preacher Bossuet lived at No. 17.

In the centre of the north side of the square, standing higher than the other houses, is the Pavillon de la Reine, and in the corresponding position on the south side is the Pavillon du Roi, bearing the initials of Henri IV. Under each of these royal residences is an arch giving access to the square from outside. The other 38 houses in the square were privately owned.

In the reign of Louis XIV the Place Royale suffered a decline in status. In 1800 it was renamed Place des Vosges in honour of the département of the Vosges, which had been the first département to pay its taxes to the French Republic.

Carefully restored in 1987–89, the Place des Vosges, with its trees and fountains, now serves mainly as a children's playground and a pleasant meeting-place for the people of the Marais. In the arcades round the square are small antique shops, galleries and cafés. In the small restaurants such as "La Guirlando de Julie" (No. 25) visitors can enjoy a pleasant snack on a summer's day.

In the centre of the square is a small public garden with a marble equestrian statue of Louis XIII (by Dupaty and Cortot, 1819).

Statue of Louis XIII

Victor Hugo lived at No. 6, at the south-east corner of the square, from 1832 to 1848. The house is now a museum, with many mementoes of the great writer, including his manuscript of "Les Miserables", a gun with his portrait on the barrel, the decoration of the Chinese Room, which he designed himself, architectural sketches and drawings, as well as furniture which belonged to Juliette Drouet, Hugo's mistress. The museum is open Tue.–Sun. 10am–5.40pm.

Musée Victor Hugo

Place du Tertre

See Montmartre

★★Place Vendôme   G/H 4

To the north of the Tuileries (see entry) is the Place Vendôme, a magnificent square built in the late 17th and early 18th century which has preserved its original form.

Location
West central
(1st arr.)

The square, then called Place Louis-le-Grand, was laid out by Jules Hardouin-Mansart, one of the leading architects of the "Grand Siècle" under Louis XIV. The façades of the houses were built between 1686 and 1701, but the houses themselves were not completed until 1720. The original intention was that the royal academies (see Institut de France), the Mint (see Monnaie), the Royal Library and a hotel for

Métro stations
Madeleine,
Opéra, Concorde

The 44m-high column in the centre of the Place Vendôme commemorates Napoleon's glorious deeds

Place Vendôme

Bouquinistes' stalls on the banks of the Seine

Buses
21, 24, 27, 29, 42,
52, 68, 72, 84, 94,
95

foreign envoys should be installed in the square; but the king's financial difficulties forced him to make over the leases to the city of Paris, which then sold them to nobles and wealthy citizens. The new owners built houses behind the façades with courtyards and gardens in the style of the noble mansions of the day (see Marais).

The charm of the Place Vendôme, one of the finest examples of harmonious urban architecture in Europe, is that it has retained, unspoiled, the consistency of the overall design, successfully combining regal ostentation with civic simplicity. Following careful restoration in the early nineties it has recovered all its old splendour. Here, as in the Rue de la Paix, which runs north from the square to the Opéra, are to be found such famous jewellers as Boucheron, Van Cleef & Arpels and Cartier. Ernest Hemingway, Scott Fitzgerald and Gertrude Stein were habitués of the Bar Américain in the Ritz Hôtel which sadly hit the headlines in 1997 as the hotel where Princess Diana had stayed prior to her tragic death shortly afterwards in the accident near the Pont d'Alma (see Seine Bridges, Pont Alma). In No. 12 the composer Frédéric Chopin died in 1849 at the age of 39.

Colonne de la Grande Armée

In the centre of the square is the Colonne de la Grande Armée, with a spiral bronze relief recalling the glorious deeds of the French army. The column replaces an equestrian statue of Louis XIV which was destroyed in 1792 during the French Revolution. The present monument, 44m/144ft high, was erected by Napoleon in imitation of Trajan's Column in Rome. It is topped by a statue of Napoleon in the garb of a Roman emperor. In 1814 the original statue was melted down and the metal used for the statue of Henri IV on the Pont Neuf, to be replaced by a new one in 1833. In 1871, during the Paris Commune, the column was pulled down but was later re-erected with a copy of the statue of Napoleon.

Quais (Quays, Embankments)   H–K 5/6

It used to be possible to walk along the Quais de la Seine on two
levels, but now the lower level on the whole of the right bank and part
of the left bank has been taken over by an expressway to speed the
movement of traffic. Nevertheless a walk along the upper level, with
surging traffic on both sides, offers ample compensation in the magnificent panoramic view of central Paris, round the islands in the
Seine. The finest of all the riverside walks, however, are on the Ile
Saint-Louis and the Ile de la Cité (see entries).

Location
Centre (banks of
Seine between
Pont d'Austerlitz
and Pont des Arts

Métro stations
Cité, St-Michel

Booklovers too will enjoy browsing along the *quais*, lined by the stalls
boîtes, "boxes") of the *bouquinistes* who sell all manner of books old
and new, prints, posters and so on. Some of them specialise – in the
French classics, old engravings, books on Paris, art books, thrillers,
posters advertising exhibitions, etc. Until the middle of the 19th
century the bouquinistes usually took their *boîtes* home with them
every evening, but now most of them open up around noon and lock
up at dusk.

Bouquinistes

Responsibility for the quays and bridges on the Seine, which formerly
rested with the State, was transferred in 1988 to the city of Paris,
which has launched a comprehensive programme of renovation of
the quays (declared by UNESCO in 1991 a world heritage site).

Renovation

★Quartier Latin   H/J 6/7

The Quartier Latin, a colourful meeting place for young people from
all over the world, is bounded on the north by the Seine, on the south
by the Boulevard de Port-Royal and on the east by the Boulevard
Saint-Marcel and Boulevard de l'Hôpital. On the west it merges into
the Saint-Germain quarter (see entry) around the Odéon Métro station. In this area, in addition to the Sorbonne (see entry), now known
as the Université de Paris IV, are most of the *grandes écoles* (elite
colleges, separate from the University) such as the Ecole
Polytechnique and Ecole Normale Supérieure, the Université Censier
(Université de Paris III) and the Université Jussieu (Universités de
Paris VI and VII), the Collège de France (see entry) and old-established
lycées such as the Lycée Henri-IV adjoining the Panthéon, the Lycée
Louis-le-Grand behind the Sorbonne and the Lycée Saint-Louis on the
Boulevard Saint-Michel.

Location
Centre (5th arr.)

Métro stations
St-Michel,
Cardinal
Lemoine,
Monge

Buses
63, 84, 86, 89

Towards the end of the Middle Ages lack of space forced the schools
of Latin and theology on the Ile de la Cité (see entry) on to the left bank
of the Seine, where there then grew up the Quartier Latin or Latin
Quarter (so called because Latin was the language of scholars and
students).

The student quarter of Paris is now also a great tourist attraction,
with numerous cinemas, discothèques and restaurants (largely offering Arab, Greek and Asian cuisine). Some of the little restaurants
have a basement in which patrons can enjoy music, theatre or poetry
readings after their meal.

The Théâtre de la Huchette (23 rue de la Huchette), is a tiny theatre
which has staged the same programme – Eugène Ionesco's two
famous one-act plays, "La Cantatrice Chauve" ("The Bald Prima
Donna") and "La Leçon" ("The Lesson") – every evening for over 40
years, usually to full houses.

Théâtre de la
Huchette

Rue de Rivoli

Shakespeare
& Company

In Square Réne-Viviani is a legendary second-hand bookshop – George Whiteman's very individual Shakespeare & Company, which sells old editions of everything from Shakespeare to James Joyce.

Saint-Julien-
le-Pauvre

The church of Saint-Julien-le Pauvre, on the Quai Saint-Michel beyond Square Viviani, now belongs to the Greek Orthodox community. It was built, in High Gothis style, between the mid 12th and mid 13th century. In the 15th and 16th centuries the Rector of the University was elected in this church, and its bell was rung to announce the beginning of lecures. The interior of the church is dominated by an iconostasis installed in 1901.

★Rambouillet

Location
56km/35 miles
SW of Paris
(N 10 and N 306)

Rail service
from Gare
Montparnasse

Opening times
Château:
Mon. and Wed.–
Sun.
10am–11.30am
and 2–4.30pm
Park:
Daily 7am to 6pm

Admission
charge

Although it is the summer residence of the President of the Republic, the Château de Rambouillet is open to visitors.

In 1706 the château, built on the site of an old manor-house, was bought by the Comte de Toulouse, a legitimised son of Louis XIV and Madame de Montespan. Gothic, Renaissance and Baroque features in the structure show that the château has undergone considerable extension and renovation. In 1783 it was acquired by Louis XVI, who, like his predecessors and successors, used it as a hunting lodge. He had a dairy in the form of a Greek temple, the Laiterie de la Reine, built for Marie-Antoinette and established a sheep farm, on which merino sheep are still reared. Napoleon made the Château his residence, and since 1959 it has been the summer residence of the President and has occasionally been used for ministerial meetings.

The rich and elegant interior appointments include fine Delft tiles and period furniture. Notable features are the Marble Hall (Salle de Marbre; 1556), the 18th century Council Chamber, the bathrooms installed by Napoleon in 1809 and the Ballroom, with Aubusson tapestries.

There is pleasant walking in the park and forest of Rambouillet.

★Rue de Rivoli   G–J 4/5

Location
Between place de
la Concorde and
the Marais

Métro stations
Concorde, Palais-
Royal-Musée du
Louvre, Tuileries,
Châtelet

Buses
21, 67, 69, 74, 75,
81, 85

The Rue de Rivoli, on the right bank of the Seine, links Place de la Concorde with the Marais, from which it is continued by Rue Saint-Antoine to Place de la Bastille.

The oldest and most interesting part is the stretch between Place de la Concorde and Place du Louvre, skirting the whole of the north side of the Tuileries and the north wing of the Louvre (see entries). This section was given its present form in the time of Napoleon, who also gave the street its name, after his victory over Austria in the battle of Rivoli, near Verona, in 1797. The planning of the new street took several years (1802–11), and building work continued until 1833, twelve years after Napoleon's death, combining the traditional (uniform façades and round-arched arcades) and the contemporary (multi-storey buildings with metal roof structure). In 1853 the creator of modern Paris, Baron Haussmann, continued the Rue de Rivoli and Rue Saint-Antoine to Place de la Bastille.

During the French Revolution, when the area was still a maze of narrow streets and lanes, there stood between Place des Pyramides and Rue de Castiglione a riding school in which the Constituent Assembly met in 1789. A plaque on 230 rue de Rivoli records that the First French Republic was proclaimed here in 1792. At No. 210 the

Russian novelist Ivan Turgenev wrote his "Fathers and Sons" in 1862. The French diplomat and writer René de Chateaubriand lived at No. 194 from 1812 to 1814.

The arcades of the Napoleonic section of the street have long attracted strollers and window-shoppers with their jewellers' shops, art galleries, antique dealers, cafés and tearooms. Between the Louvre and the Hôtel de Ville (see entry) are three of Paris's largest department stores, the Samaritaine, the Belle Jardinière and the Bazar de l'Hôtel de Ville.

An equestrian statue of Joan of Arc (1410–31), heroine of France, stands in the centre of the Place des Pyramides. The work of Emmanuel Fremiet, it was re-gilded in the mid 1990s. The strictly religious daughter of a simple rural family from the Vosges, Joan of Arc believed that "voices" had called upon her to liberate France from the English during the Hundred Years War which had been going on since 1339. Her great military victory at Orleans was the turning point in the war. Shortly after, she was taken prisoner and burned at the stake in Rouen in 1431. Since she was canonized in 1920 the "Maid of Orleans" has been France's second patron saint.

France's heroine and patron saint
Joan of Arc

Joan of Arc
memorial

Rue Mouffetard   J 6/7

Rue Mouffetard is a narrow street running down from the Montagne Sainte-Geneviève, near the Panthéon and the church of Saint-Etienne-du-Mont (see entrier), to Place des Gobelins. The little street, lined by small restaurants (in the upper part of the street mainly Greek), has preserved something of its medieval character. As far back as Gallo-Roman times this was the route which the inhabitants took when travelling to the south. The street was occupied in the past by butchers and tanners and must have been a rather malodorous area, as its name suggests (from *mouffette*, a term applied to something evil-smelling). It is now a picturesque little street of old-established shops, wind-battered houses of the 16th-18th centuries and cosy bars, among them the popular "Pomme de Pin" in Place de la Contrescarpe which was frequented in the 16th century by Rabelais and the poets of the Pléiade, Du Bellay, Ronsard and Ponthus de Tyard.

The colourful market in the lower part of the "Mouffe", which sells everything from fresh fruit and vegetables by way of an excellent selection of cheeses to fish and poultry, is particularly lively on Sunday mornings.

Location
5th arr.

Métro stations
Cardinal Lemoine,
Place Monge,
Censier Daubenton, Les Gobelins

Buses
27, 47, 67, 83, 91

The steps of the Sacré-Cœur, a meeting-place for young people of all nations

★Sacré-Cœur   H 2

Location
35 rue du
Chevalier
de la Barre
(18th arr.)

Métro stations
Anvers, Abbesses

Buses
30, 54, 80, 85,
Montmartrobus
(55)

Opening times
Basilica
Daily 7am–11pm:
Tower and crypt:
daily
9am–6pm

**Admission
charge**

The Basilique du Sacré-Cœur (Basilica of the Sacred Heart) is one of
the great Paris landmarks, its domes gleaming high above the city on
the Butte Montmartre (see entry).

After France's defeat in the Franco-Prussian War and the repression
of the Commune (1871) the Catholics of France vowed to erect a
church on the hill of Montmartre as a symbol of contrition and hope.
The National Assembly approved the proposal in 1873 and work
began under the direction of the architect Paul Abadie in 1876. Because
of the porous sandstone on which it was built, however, construction
was difficult and protracted, and the church was completed only in
1911 and dedicated in 1919.

The Romanesque/Byzantine style of the church, often dismissed as
"wedding-cake" architecture, was modelled on the church of Saint-
Front in Périgueux. The interior, which seems heavy and over-ornate,
is notable for its size (100m/330ft long, 50m/165ft wide). In the choir is
a large mosaic of Christ with a flaming heart, flanked by the Archangel Michael and Joan of Arc on the right and Louis XVI and his family
on the left.

From the top of the tower (to the left of the main entrance; admission charge) there are superb panoramic views of Paris. From the
broad flight of steps in front of the church, thronged in summer with
young people and street entertainers, there is one of the finest prospects in Paris, with views, in clear weather, of Notre-Dame straight
ahead, with the Centre Pompidou in front of it, to the right the Opéra-
Garnier and beyond this the Dôme des Invalides.

★★Saint-Denis

The basilica of Saint-Denis was the burial-place of St Denis (Dionysius), the patron saint of France, and the French kings. Here the royal insignia and banner, the *oriflamme*, were preserved and the royal chronicles were kept. Several abbots of Saint-Denis acted as Regents of the kingdom. For twelve centuries almost all the French kings, from Dagobert I (d. 639) to Louis XVIII (d. 1824), were laid to rest in this splendid necropolis.

The building of the choir and west front of Saint-Denis marked the beginning of Gothic architecture, providing a model which was followed by Chartres, Senlis and Meaux cathedrals. The Gothic style of central and northern Europe, given expression in architecture, painting and sculpture, was born in France, in the province of Ile-de-France with Paris as its centre. Coming between Romanesque and Renaissance styles, it was predominant from the 12th to the early 16th century. The term Gothic stems from the Italian art historian Giorgio Vasari (1511–74), who, considering the style from the point of view of the Renaissance, regarded it as a barbaric (i.e. northern) form of art and associated it with the Goths. In the 19th century the Romantic movement's enthusiasm for history led at first to an uncritical and extravagant overvaluation, later followed by a more rational and balanced assessment of Gothic, now regarded as one of the high points of medieval architecture.

Saint-Denis has been an important place of pilgrimage since early Christian times. The legend of St Dionysius – missionary, first bishop of Paris and martyr – has it that after his beheading on the Butte Montmartre (see entry) the saint carried his head in his hands to the place where he desired to be buried. A church was built on the spot in the 5th century, followed in the 7th century by the foundation of an abbey. In the reign of Abbot Suger (1081–1151), in the 12th century, work began on the conversion of the church from Romanesque to Gothic. The Early Gothic west front and narthex were built between 1137 and 1140, the choir in 1140–43. A hundred years later the surviving central part of the earlier church was pulled down and replaced by a High Gothic high choir, transepts and nave under the direction of Pierre de Montreuil (d. 1264), Louis IX's architect (see Sainte-Chapelle). Over the centuries the church fell into disrepair. In the early 19th century restoration work began, and was later carried on by Viollet-le-Duc between 1858 and 1879 on the basis of historical records, giving the church the form in which we see it today.

Location
4.5km/3 miles N
(A 1)

Métro station
Saint-Denis-
Basilique

Buses
255, 256

Opening times
Oct. 1 to Mar. 31,
Mon.–Sat.
10am–5pm,
Sun. noon–5pm;
Apr. 1 to Sept. 30,
Mon.–Sat.
10am–7pm, Sun.
noon–7pm

The Early Gothic west front displays for the first time the characteristic features of Gothic architecture – clarity of structure (with some 19th century additions in a reproduction of the original style), the symmetrical disposition of the towers (the north tower was demolished in 1837 after being struck by lightning), the transition from round to pointed arches, the round window (later developed into the large rose windows of High Gothic) and the three doorways (symbolic of the Trinity).

Exterior

Of the sculpture on the doorways only the figures of the wise and foolish virgins on the central doorway, the Months (right) and the signs of the zodiac (left) are original.

In the tympanum of the central doorway is the Last Judgment (restored); to the right is the Communion of St Dionysius (reproduction), to the left his martyrdom with his companions Rusticus and Eleutherius (also a reproduction).

With its crenellations and its massive buttresses Saint-Denis has still something of the fortress-like character of the Romanesque churches, seen as "God's strongholds".

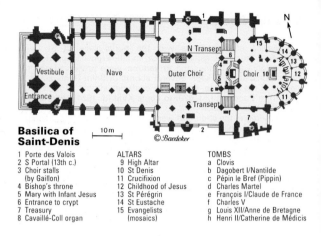

Basilica of Saint-Denis

10m

© Baedeker

N

1 Porte des Valois
2 S Portal (13th c.)
3 Choir stalls (by Gaillon)
4 Bishop's throne
5 Mary with Infant Jesus
6 Entrance to crypt
7 Treasury
8 Cavaillé-Coll organ

ALTARS
9 High Altar
10 St Denis
11 Crucifixion
12 Childhood of Jesus
13 St Pérégrin
14 St Eustache
15 Evangelists (mosaics)

TOMBS
a Clovis
b Dagobert I/Nantilde
c Pépin le Bref (Pippin)
d Charles Martel
e François I/Claude de France
f Charles V
g Louis XII/Anne de Bretagne
h Henri II/Catherine de Médicis

Interior

The interior of the church (108m/355ft long, almost 30m/100ft high) is of impressive effect, with its soaring columns and 37 windows, each 10m/33ft high. It is divided into the narthex, the nave, flanked by aisles, the high choir, the crossing, the transepts and the choir.

Here we find the final and perhaps the most important feature of Gothic, fully developed in High Gothic – the "architecture of light", by which is meant light not only in its literal sense but as an element in the structure and spatial articulation of the building. It is only through the incidence of light – determined in qualitative terms by the angle of incidence and in quantitative terms by the amount of light – that the height and depth of the interior space take on life and can be appreciated. The wall, no longer a load-bearing element in the structure, is dissolved into great expanses of window, and the load-bearing function is performed by the ribbed vaulting, which transmits the load to the pillars and columns, with the external buttresses providing stability. The use of pointed arches makes for higher vaulting and greater spatial freedom.

Apart from its combination of Early Gothic (narthex and choir) and High Gothic, the church also has the special feature that the triforium, the wall-passage between the arcading and the high windows in the aisles and transepts which is usually windowless, here also has windows.

Royal tombs

With only a few exceptions, all the kings and queens of France and their children, together with some particularly faithful servants of the Crown, are buried in Saint-Denis. Their tombs were plundered during the Revolution, but their remains were returned in 1817.

There are two separate parts in the crypt, one for the house of Bourbon to which Louis XVI belonged, the other for the remains of some 800 members of the Merovingian, Capetian, Orléans and Valois dynasties. Some of the tombs are masterpieces of French Renaissance art, in particular the sumptuous marble and bronze mausoleum of Louis XII (d. 1515) and his wife Anne de Bretagne (d. 1514), constructed between 1517 and 1531 (in north transept); the tomb of Henri II (d. 1559) and his wife Catherine de Médicis (d. 1589), by Germain Pilon, completed in 1573 (also in north transept); the 13th century sarcophagus of Dagobert I, with statues of his queen, Nanthile, and his son Clovis II (to right of high altar); and the tomb of François I (d. 1547), by Philibert Delorme (in south transept).

★★Sainte-Chapelle   J 5

A palace chapel on two levels, the Sainte-Chapelle is the great jewel of Paris's Gothic architecture. It is only rarely, on very special occasions, used for worship, but is very frequently in use for concerts. To reach the chapel, turn left immediately inside the large iron gate at the main entrance to the Palais de Justice (see entry).

This marvel of High Gothic architecture was built for Louis IX in less than 33 months in 1245–48, probably by Pierre de Montreuil. The chapel was built to house the very precious Christian relics which Louis had acquired from the Byzantine Emperor – and which had cost him two and a half times as much as the building of the chapel. The chapel then stood in the main courtyard of the royal palace, the site of which is now occupied by the Palais de Justice. During the 18th century one side of the chapel was joined up with a wing of the Palais de Justice. For more than 30 years (1802–37) the chapel was used for the storage of records, before being restored between 1841 and 1867.

The chapel stands in the large inner courtyard to the left of the entrance to the Palais de Justice. It is 33m/110ft long by 17m/55ft wide, 76m/250ft high to the tip of the spire and 42m/140ft to the top of the gable.

The Chapelle Basse (Lower Chapel) was originally for the court servants. Its vaulted roof, only 6.60m/22ft high, is borne on fourteen columns set close to the walls.

The Upper Chapel (Chapelle Haute) is the Sainte-Chapelle proper. It was dedicated to the Holy Relics and was reserved for the king, the royal family and high dignitaries of the court. The relics – a splinter of the True Cross, a fragment from the crown of thorns and a nail from the Cross – are now preserved in the Treasury of Notre-Dame (see entry). Visitors entering the chapel are first struck by the brilliance of the light, which seems to cancel out the force of gravity on the masonry. The beautiful vaulting is borne on fourteen 22m/70ft high buttresses which provide the framework for the windows, 15m/50ft high by 4m/13ft wide. Apart from a low blind arcade decorated with scenes of martyrdom round the base, the chapel has no walls as such. Its great beauty lies in the stained glass, depicting more than 1000 different Biblical scenes, which fill the Sainte-Chapelle with all the colours of the rainbow. A third of the total area of stained glass (the

Location
4 boulevard du Palais (1st arr.)

Métro station
Cité

Buses
21, 24, 27, 38, 81, 85, 96

Opening times
Daily 10am–5pm

Admission charge

Chapelle Basse

Chapelle Haute

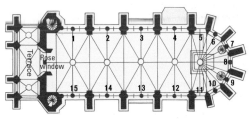

STAINED GLASS (about 615sq.m/2020sq.ft; partly restored)

1 Creation
   Adam and Eve, Noah, Jacob
2 Exodus; Joseph
3 Pentateuch
   Levi; Moses receives the Law
4 Deuteronomy
   Joshua, Ruth and Boaz
5 Judges: Gideon, Samson

6 Isaiah, Tree of Jesse
7 John the Evangelist, Life of
   the Virgin, Childhood of
   Christ
8 Christ's Passion
9 John the Baptist; Daniel
10 Ezekiel's prophecies
11 Jeremiah; Tobias

12 Judith; Job
13 Esther
14 Samuel, David, Solomon
15 Legend of the True Cross;
   discovery of the Cross;
   acquisition of relics by Louis IX
   and their deposition;
   consecration of Sainte-Chapelle

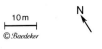

Sainte-Chapelle

10 m

© Baedeker

N

CHAPELLE HAUTE
UPPER CHAPEL

The brilliant light in Sainte-Chapelle comes from the beautiful stained glass

lower levels) has been faithfully restored; all the rest are original 13th century work. The Late Gothic rose window, depicting scenes from the Apocalypse, dates from the reign of Charles VIII (1493–98). Against the buttresses in the nave are statues of the twelve Apostles, though only half of them are original (3, 4, 6, 11, 12 and 13 on plan). In the third bay, on the left, are two recesses for the king and the queen. From his oratory in the 12th bay, on right, Louis IX could hear mass without being seen. In the apse is a small dais under a wooden baldachin, once occupied by the reliquary containing the sacred relics. Two flights of wooden steps lead up to it; the one on the left is original. Only the French king had the key to the reliquary, the contents of which he displayed to the assembled royal household on Good Friday.

★Saint-Etienne-du-Mont   J 6

Location
Place Ste-
Geneviève (5th
arr.)

Métro stations
Cardinal Lemoine,
Maubert Mutualite

RER station
Luxembourg

Buses
47, 84, 89

The church of Saint-Etienne-du-Mont was founded in 1492 for the servants of the Benedictine monastery which once stood on this site. Although it is dedicated to St Stephen, Paris's patron saint, St Geneviève, who saved the city from destruction by Attila the Hun, is also venerated here. The area round the church is named the Montagne Sainte-Geneviève after her.

The building of the church extended from the Late Gothic period to the Renaissance, and this is reflected in its architecture. The choir and transepts were completed in 1540, the nave in 1610. The ground-plan of the church and the stellar vaulting over the crossing with its pendant keystone 5.50m/18ft long, the "Lamb of God", are still Gothic, but the undecorated round pillars already show the influence of the

Renaissance. The richly decorated west front (by Claude Guérin, 1610–18) is in pure Renaissance style; the turret at the right-hand end is probably a survival from an earlier 13th century building.

An unusual feature for a Renaissance church is the triforium (normally found only in Gothic churches), which runs round the nave half way up the wall like a gallery. The church is famed for its rood-screen (by Philibert de l'Orme, 1530–41), with a marble central section and a spiral staircase at each end. To the right of this, at the entrance to the Lady Chapel, are the epitaphs of the philosopher Blaise Pascal (1623–62) and the dramatist Jean Racine (1639–99), who are buried in the church. To the left, in front of the next side chapel but one, is a sarcophagus which is said to contain a stone from the tomb of St Genevieve. There are stained glass windows dating from the construction of the church in the north aisle (Apocalypse, 1614) and the south aisle (Parable of the Marriage Feast, 1586).

Saint-Eustache   J 5

Saint-Eustache, the parish church of the Halles district, is dedicated to the Early Christian martyr Eustachius or Eustathius (Eustace), patron saint of hunters. Paris's last church in Gothic style, it already shows the influence of the developing Renaissance.

The foundation-stone of the church was laid in 1532, during the reign of François I, but it was not completed until 1640. Following the model of Notre-Dame (see entry), the cruciform ground-plan, the double aisles flanking the nave, the triforium (the wall-passage under the windows) and the net vaulting are Gothic features. The hybrid character of the church is seen most clearly in the piers supporting the vaulting: although the piers themselves follow Gothic models they are faced with Renaissance columns and pilasters.

The church is of impressive dimensions, matching the size and importance of the parish – 88m/289ft long, 44m/144ft wide, 34m/112ft high to the top of the vaulting.

The windows in the choir (by Philippe de Champaigne, 1631) depict the Apostles, the Fathers of the Church and St Eustachius. Over the left-hand doorway is a painting of the saint's martyrdom by Simon Vouet (c. 1635).

In a recess in the choir, to the left of the apse, is the tomb of Jean-Baptiste Colbert, Louis XIV's minister of finance (by Coysevox, after a design by Le Brun). On the nearby pedestrian area (formerly the market Halls, see Les Halles), Raymond Mason's colourful sculpture (1969) reminds passers-by of the "removal of the fruit and vegetable market from the heart of Paris", and depicts a market scene shortly before daybreak, when the markets opened up.

Saint-Eustache is famed for its large Ducroquet/Gonzalès organ (replaced in 1989 by a new one by Jan van den Heuvel) and for its concerts and recitals (on Sundays and public holidays at 11am). The first performances of Berlioz's "Te Deum" (1855) and Liszt's "Gran Mass" (1866) were in Saint-Eustache. An annual event is the performance of "St Hubert's Mass" to mark the opening of the hunting (shooting) season.

Location
Rue Rambuteau
(1st arr.)

Métro station
Les Halles

RER station
Châtelet-
Les Halles

Buses
29, 67, 74, 85

Concerts and
recitals

Saint-Germain-des-Prés   H 5/6

The Saint-Germain-des-Prés quarter could effectively be described as a galaxy of a number of small planets, with the residences of many top managers, high-ranking politicians and film stars, and visitors can

Location
6th arr.

Little art galleries, crowded jazz bars, amusing designer shops all can be found in Saint-Germain-des-Prés

Métro stations
St.-Germain-des-
Prés, Mabillon,
Odéon

Buses
39, 48, 63, 70, 86,
87, 95, 96

wander around for hours on end without getting bored if they enjoy the better things in life, art, culture and that popular sport which Parisians practise with such subtle discretion – to see and be seen. Collectors of antique books fill the shops in rue de l'Odéon, where Adrienne Monnier once lived at No. 7 and translated into French James Joyce's "Ulysses". Every third Parisian publishing house has an office here in the 6th arrondissement– the ladies' bookshop at 74 rue de Seine belongs to the popular publishers Editions des Femmes, while "La Hune", the art-book shop at 170 Boulevard Saint-Germain, specialising in books on films, architecture and design, stays open until midnight. In Saint-Germain-des-Prés one can find some excellent jazz-bars, amusing designer shops, colourful markets and cosy bistros. Like the neighbouring Quartier Latin (see entry) the cinemas offer excellent film programmes all the year round – foreign films are nearly always the original version. Galleries and antique shops rub shoulders along rue des Saints Pères, rue du Bac and rue de Seine, high-class boutiques such as Sonia Rykiel and Yves Saint-Laurent are found mainly in the Boulevard Saint-Germain and rue de Granelle. Barthélemy's is a veritable paradise for lovers of fine cheeses, while the little market street named rue de Buci offers fresh fruit and vegetables for sale in a charming Paris atmosphere.

The Saint-Germain-des-Prés became celebrated in the forties and fifties as the rendezvous of the existentialist circle which included Jean-Paul Sartre and Simone de Beauvoir (for both see Famous People) and other renowned writers and artists. In a host of small art galleries, the Ecole des Beaux-Arts (rue Bonaparte) and a series of legendary cafés and restaurants something of the quarter's artistic and intellectual milieu still remains. Sartre and Simone de Beauvoir were habitués of the Café de Flore on the Boulevard Saint-Germain, where they read, worked and talked with other leading figures in the intellectual life of Paris. Round the corner are two other famous literary cafés – the Deux Magots, once frequented by André Gide, Jean Giraudoux, Ernest Hemingway and André Breton, and the Brasserie Lipp, where Picasso, Man Ray, Max Ernst and Joan Miró used to meet for a *petit noir* (see Baedeker Special, pp.146–147). At No. 14 rue Jacob Richard Wagner completed his "Flying Dutchman", and in the 1920s the famous spy Mata Hari used to dance for the guests at Nathalie Clifford Barney's soirées. Biting sarcasm and macabre mockery were the trademark of Boris Viam, the uncrowned "prince of Saint-Germain", novelist, singer, trumpeter and jazz fan. Together with his wife Michelle, Jacques Prévert, Raymond Queneau and Juliette Gréco, Vian spent his nights in the crowded jazz-cellars of Saint-Germain such as the Tabou in rue Dauphine or the Club Saint-Germain. His scandalous writings attracted the attention of the censor and made him a best-seller. In 1959, when only 39 years of age, Vian died during the filming of his controversial novel "I'll Spit on Your Grave".

Meeting-place of existentialist bohemians

On a stroll through the Saint-Germain quarter the visitor will feel something of the inimitable charm of Paris, "city of dreams". Beside the old abbey church there is a charming little garden planted with nut-trees where it is tempting to linger. It contains a piece of sculpture by Picasso (whose studio was near here), "Hommage à Apollinaire".

★ Tour

Near here lies rue de Fürstenberg, which opens out into a romantic little square shaded by plane-trees. Named after Wilhelm Egon, Count of Fürstenberg, it occupies the site of the abbey of Saint-Germain-des-Prés, around which were stables and coach-houses. At 6 rue de Fürstenberg stands the house once occupied by Eugène Delacroix; it is now a museum with mementos and documents relating to the great Romantic painter (open: Mon. and Wed.–Fri. 9.30am–5pm). Opposite, at No. 5, is a house in which the playwright Jean Anouilh lived for a time. His play "Antigone" was given its first performance in 1944, with the permission of the German occupation authorities – although, camouflaged under its antique subject-matter, it was a clear call for resistance.

Place de Fürstenberg

A short distance away, at 13 rue de l'Ancienne-Comédie, can be found the oldest café-restaurant in Paris, the elegant Procope (a tip – try their speciality fish dishes). Founded by a Sicilian named Francesco Procopio dei Coltelli in 1686, it soon developed into the meeting-place of the Paris intellectuals, frequented by the *philosophes* of the Enlightenment and later by the hotheads of the Revolution and the poets of the Romantic period (tel. 01 43 26 99 20).

★ Procope

At the rear of the Procope the cobble-stoned Passage Cour de Commerce has been lovingly restored, and now contains some small shops and the "La Jacobine" bistro.

★ Passage Cour de Commerce

L'Eglise Saint-Germain-des-Prés, in the square of that name, belonged to a wealthy Benedictine abbey founded on this site in the 8th century and destroyed during the French Revolution. It bears the name of Germanus (Germain), a bishop of Paris who was canonised in 754. As early as the 6th century there was a church here, in the

★ Church of Saint-Germain-des-Prés

Le Procope, Paris's oldest café-restaurant

meadows (*prés*) bordering the Seine, containing the tombs of the Merovingian kings Childéric I, Clotaire II and Childéric II, which were plundered during the Revolution. Destroyed several times by the Norsemen, the church was rebuilt around the year 1000 in Late Romanesque (the nave) and Early Gothic (choir, completed 1163) styles. Of the conventual buildings there survive only the abbot's palace (16th–17th c.), the prior's lodgings and remains of the destroyed Lady Chapel. In the south transept is the tomb (by Kaspar Marsy) of King John Casimir Vasa of Poland (d. 1672), who became abbot of Saint-Germain after his abdication, and a marble statue of St Francis Xavier by Guillaume Coustou. In the second chapel on the south side of the choir can be seen the grave-slabs of the philosopher René Descartes (d. 1650) and two learned Benedictines, Jean Mabillon (d. 1707) and Bernard de Montfaucon (d. 1719). In the Lady Chapel (Chapelle de la Vierge) is a statue of the Virgin by Dupaty (1822).

★Musée Maillol

At 59–61 rue de Grenelle visitors can gain an insight into the life and work of Aristide Maillol (1861–1944), whose sculptures, drawings and engravings form the private collection of Dina Vierny. The museum, opened in 1995, also contains paintings and sculptures by Matisse, Degas, Picasso, Ingres, Bonnard, Cézanne, Rodin, Pollakoff, Kandinsky and Raoul Dufy (open; Mon., Wed.–Sat. 11am–6pm).

★Saint-Germain-en-Laye

Location
20km/12½ miles
W of Paris

In Saint-Germain-en-Laye, the birthplace of the composer Claude Debussy, is one of the many royal residences in the Ile-de-France. Here, on a plateau above the Seine, Louis VI built a castle in the 12th century. It was pulled down and rebuilt by François I, leaving only the

Sainte-Chapelle (predecessor of the one in Paris) and the keep of the old castle. The Renaissance château built by François I, which had fallen into disrepair during the 18th century, was restored, along with the Chapel, in the reign of Napoleon III, between 1862 and 1867.

Louis XIV was born in the château of Saint-Germain-en-Laye in 1638. In 1919 the peace treaty between France and Austria was signed in the first room of what is now the Museum of National Antiquities.

The Chapel, probably designed by the architect of the Sainte-Chapelle (see entry) on the Ile de la Cité, Pierre de Montreuil, was begun in 1245 – one of the earliest High Gothic buildings in the Ile-de-France. Saint-Germain is also famed for its terraces and park (laid out by the great landscape architect Le Nôtre) (in 1668–73). From the terraces there is a magnificent view across the Seine towards Paris.

The château of Saint-Germain-en-Laye has housed since 1867 the Museum of National Antiquities, which has a fine collection of archaeological material from all over France, ranging from the Palaeolithic (e.g. the Venus of Brassempouy) to the Bronze Age and Celtic and Gallo-Roman times.

RER station
St-Germain-en-Laye

Opening times
Château and Museum:
Daily except. Tue.
9.00am–5.15pm

Admission charge

Musée des Antiquités Nationales

Saint-Germain-l'Auxerrois   H 5

On Place du Louvre, at the east end of the Louvre (see entry), are the Mairie of the 1st arrondissement and the former royal parish church of Saint-Germain-l'Auxerrois, dedicated to St Germanus, bishop of Auxerre.

The present church shows a mixture of styles, with a Romanesque tower (12th c.), from which the bells tolled to signal the Massacre of St Bartholomew on August 24th 1572, a Gothic choir (13th c.), a nave and porch in Flamboyant (Late Gothic) style and a Renaissance doorway (1570). The finest feature is the porch (1435–39), a striking example of Late Gothic architecture. In the interior, note the fine stalls (by Le Brun, 1684) for the royal family.

Many artists who worked for the French kings of the 17th and 18th centuries are buried in this church, among them the architects Louis Le Vau and Robert de Cotte, the painters François Boucher, van Loo, Jean-Siméon Chardin and Jean-Marc Nattier and the sculptors Antoine Coysevox and the brothers Nicolas and Guillaume Coustou.

Location
2 place du Louvre (1st arr.)

Métro stations
Louvre, Pont Neuf

Buses
21, 67, 69, 72, 74, 81, 85

★ Saint-Séverin   J 6

In the lower part of the Quartier Latin (see entry) is the church of Saint-Séverin (named after a hermit named Severinus who lived here in the 6th century), one of the finest examples of the Flamboyant style of Late Gothic architecture. A visit to the church could be combined with one of the fine organ recitals regularly given here.

The church stands on the site of an early chapel and a small church which was destroyed by the Norsemen. The present church was begun at the beginning of the 13th century, partly destroyed, apparently by fire, in the 15th century, and was finally completed in Late Gothic style between 1450 and 1520.

The first three bays of the nave are in the simple style of the 13th century; then beyond this are slender pillars with elaborately carved capitals and fanciful keystones. The choir, surrounded by a very beautiful double ambulatory, is a masterpiece of Late Gothic architecture with its wonderfully intricate net vaulting. The stained glass in the first three bays, with figures of Apostles (14th c.), came from the choir of the church of Saint-Germain-des-Prés (see entry). The

Location
1 rue des Pràtres-St-Séverin (5th arr.)

Métro station
St-Michel

RER station
St-Michel-Notre-Dame

Buses
21, 24, 27, 38, 85, 96

other windows in the nave date from the 15th century. In sharp contrast are the modern windows in the choir (by Jean Bazaine, 1966). The little garden on the site of the old graveyard is surrounded by ossuaries.

★Saint-Sulpice   H 6

Location
Place St-Sulpice
(6th arr.)

Métro station
St-Sulpice

Buses
39, 48, 58, 63, 70,
84, 86, 87, 89, 96

Saint-Sulpice was founded in 1634 by the abbey of Saint-Germain-des-Prés (see entry) as a new parish church, but financial difficulties meant that it was not finished until 1766, when the façade was completed. No fewer that six architects were involved in the work.

The original plan by the Florentine architect G. N. Servandoni (1695–1766) to lay out in front of the church a square with a semi-circular range of uniform houses was not carried out. The square in its present form dates from 1808. In the centre of the square is the Fountain of the Four Bishops (by Louis Visconti, 1844), with figures of the four great French preachers Bossuet, Fénelon, Massillon and Fléchier.

The plain façade, modelled on Wren's St Paul's Cathedral in London, was the work of Servandoni. With its double row of columns (the upper ones Ionic, the lower ones Doric) it is a rare example of simple, unadorned classicism. The 73m/240ft high north tower was built by J.-F. Chalgrin (1777); the south tower (68m/223ft high) remained unfinished. The nave, begun by Christophe Gamard in 1646 and continued by Louis Le Vau from 1655 onwards, has a barrel-vaulted roof. The impression of spaciousness is enhanced by the tall windows which secure a uniform diffusion of light.

Interior

The two holy-water stoups at the entrance were originally gifts to François I from the Venetian Republic, and were bequeathed to the church by Louis XV. In the first side chapel on the right are three frescoes (1861) by the Romantic painter Eugène Delacroix depicting the Archangel Michael's fight with the dragon, the expulsion of Heliodorus from the Temple and Jacob wrestling with the angel. The ten statues on the pillars of the choir (by Edme Bouchardon, begun 1734) are of Christ, the Virgin and eight of the Apostles. The Lady Chapel (Chapelle de la Vierge), at the east end of the church, has four paintings by Carle van Loo (1705–65), a ceiling painting by François Lemoyne (1699–1737) and a marble figure of the Virgin by Jean-Baptiste Pigalle (1714–85). The mighty Cliquot organ (1781) was rebuilt and enlarged by Cavaillé-Coll in 1860. Organ recitals draw appreciative audiences.

In Saint Sulpice in 1822 the marriage took place between Victor Hugo and Adèle Foucher, and in 1841 the German poet Heinrich Heine married the shop assistant Cresencia Eugénie Mirat.

Saint-Vincent-de-Paul   J 3

Location
Place Franz-Liszt
(10th arr.)

Métro station
Poissonnière

Buses
32, 42, 43, 49

Saint-Vincent-de-Paul (1844), the most important church to be built in the reign of Louis-Philippe (1830–48), was designed by the Cologne-born architect Jacob Ignaz Hittorf (1792–1867), who combined the Christian architectural form of a five-aisled basilica with Roman and Greek elements (a Roman triumphal arch, Ionic and Corinthian columns). Notable features in the sumptuous interior are the fresco "Procession of the Saints" (1849–53) by Hippolyte Flandrin and the sculpture by François Rude (1784–1855) on the altar.

A bold iron construction of the Belle Epoque: the 107m-long Pont Alexandre III

Seine Bridges

The Seine bridges were scheduled by UNESCO in 1991 as international cultural monuments. Most of them are to be the subject of extensive restoration work by the end of the millennium.

Within the city of Paris the Seine is spanned by 35 bridges, 13 of them in the central area providing links to and between the Ile de la Cité and Ile Saint-Louis. These are the city's oldest bridges; those farther upstream or downstream mostly date from the 19th century. The bridges of medieval Paris served as promenades and meeting-places where people could gossip and do business. They were lined with shops, with the owners' living quarters above them. Then in modern times, when the bridges became important as traffic arteries, the old shops and houses were swept away.

The city's latest bridge is the Pont Genty near Pont d'Austerlitz between the Gare de Lyon and Gare Austerlitz.

Avenue Alexandre-III runs south between the Grand Palais and the Petit Palais to the Pont Alexandre-III (107.5m/118yds long), built 1896–1900 for the Exhibition of 1900. Richly decorated with allegorical statues (regilded 1989), it affords fine views, particularly of the Dôme des Invalides. The bridge was named after Tsar Alexander III in recognition of the Franco-Russian Alliance of 1892.

★Pont Alexandre-III
F 4/5

Some unknown person has sprayed the words "scene of the three sacrifices" on the parapet of the bridge over the road-tunnel near the Place d'Alma in which Princess Diana, her boyfriend Dodi Al-Fayed and the driver Henri Paul were killed on August 31st 1997. The scene of the tragic accident has become a place of pilgrimage, and visitors

Pont de l'Alma
F4/5
Scene of Princess Diana's accident

from all over the world remember the "English Rose" with flowers, candles and personal dedications. Since 1987 a replica of the flame of the Statue of Liberty in New York has burned in the centre of a little square as a symbol of Franco-American friendship.

★Pont des Arts
H 5

The cast-iron Pont des Arts, a pedestrian bridge known as the Passerelle, has since 1802 provided a link between the Louvre and the Institut de France.

Pont de la Concorde
G 4/5

The Pont de la Concorde, opposite the Palais-Bourbon, links Place de la Concorde with the left bank of the Seine. The bridge was built between 1787 and 1791, using stone from the demolished Bastille.

The view from the bridge on the right bank is of Place de la Concorde with its obelisk and beyond this the Madeleine. Farther downstream, on the same side of the Seine, are the Tuileries and the Louvre. Beyond this is the Ile de la Cité, with the towers of Notre-Dame . On the left bank can be seen the Dôme and Hôtel des Invalides and the Eiffel Tower.

Pont Marie
J 5/6

The five-arched Pont Marie runs from the Ile Saint-Louis to the right bank of the Seine. Built in 1614–35 on the orders of Louis XIII, it bears the name of its architect, Christophe Marie. Part of the bridge collapsed during a catastrophic flood in 1658 and 121 people lost their lives. In 1740, when there was another severe flood, all those living in the houses which lined the bridge were safely evacuated. In the following year a decree was issued that no more houses should be built on the bridge, and the remaining houses were gradually demolished. In the 19th century the "hump" of the bridge was levelled out to ease the passage of traffic.

★Pont Neuf
H 5

A favourite catch-question on the history of Paris is "Which is the city's oldest bridge?" The answer is the "New Bridge" – the Pont Neuf, which was built between 1578 and 1607 (restored in 19th c.). It is one of the handsomest of the Seine bridges and also the longest (330m/360yds), spanning both arms of the river at the western tip of the Ile de la Cité. (The Square du Vert-Galant was built up later.)

The Pont Neuf was equipped from the outset with the attributes of a modern bridge, a carriageway for traffic and pavements for pedestrians.

In 1985 the "packaging" artist Christo shrouded the twelve arches of the bridge for two weeks in 40,000sq.m/48,000sq.yds of champagne-coloured material, converting it into a work of "sculpture".

Pont Royal
G/H 5

After a number of unsuccessful attempts to build a flood-resistant bridge downstream from the Ile de la Cité, opposite the Tuileries, the public exchequer was exhausted, and when the bridge was finally built (by Jules Hardouin-Mansart, 1685–89) it was paid for by Louis XIV from his private purse: hence its name, the "Royal Bridge". Its "hump" was removed in 1850.

Sorbonne   H/J 6

Location
Rue des Ecoles, place de la Sorbonne (5th arr.)

The influential cathedral canons of medieval Paris had the reputation of being greedy for power and possessions, but Canon Robert de Sorbon, Louis IX's confessor, seems to have been an exception. In 1257, with the king's support, he founded a college (known after its founder as the Sorbonne) in which poor students of theology could live and study at his expense. The college soon developed into a leading school of theology and became a university, only to decline in importance in the late Middle Ages. Cardinal Richelieu, as Rector of the University, saved its buildings from falling into ruin and had it

partly rebuilt by Jacques Lemercier between 1624 and 1642. In the reign of Napoleon the Sorbonne was considerably enlarged and was given the status of a State university. The present buildings were erected between 1885 and 1901 (architect, Nénot), with 22 large lecture theatres, 38 tutorial rooms, 37 lecturers' rooms, 240 laboratories, a library, an observatory amd administrative offices.

In May 1968 the Sorbonne was one of the centres of the student unrest which spread throughout France and led to a general strike. A subsequent university reform split the Sorbonne into four universities. These all have their headquarters and some departments here, but most departments are scattered throughout the city and suburbs. Altogether there are now 13 universities in the Paris region.

The main front of the Sorbonne on Rue des Ecoles is decorated with allegorical representations of the sciences. To the right of the main entrance is the Secrerariat, where visitors can apply to see the principal lecture theatre, the Grand Amphithéâtre, which has seating for 2700. Here too can be seen a famous mural by the neo-Classical painter Puvis de Chavannes, "The Sacred Grove".

The chapel in the courtyard of the Sorbonne was built between 1635 and 1684. In the south transept is the tomb of Cardinal Richelieu (d. 1642), by François Girardon (1628–1715) after a design by Charles Le Brun (1619–90).

Chapelle de la Sorbonne

(If the chapel is closed, apply to the porter at 1 rue de la Sorbonne, under the arch.)

Métro stations
Odéon, Cluny-La Sorbonne, Maubert Mutualité

RER station
Cluny-La Sorbonne

Buses
21, 27, 38, 63, 85, 86, 87

Opening times
Mon.–Fri.
8am–8pm

Théâtre Français   H 5

The Théâtre Français, France's oldest national theatre, is the home of the Comédie Française, the national theatrical company.

The Comédie Française, founded by Louis XIV in 1680, originated from the troupe headed by Molière until his death in 1673. In 1812 Napoleon issued a decree making it a State company whose director was – and still is – appointed by the government.

The company's theatre was built between 1700 and 1790 and occupied by the Comédie Française in 1792. After being burned down in 1799 it was rebuilt in 1807. The present façade dates from 1867, the interior from the turn of the century, following thorough restoration and enlargement from 1900 onwards. In the foyer are Molière's chair, in which he died after suffering a haemorrhage, and Jean-Antoine Houdon's well-known bust of the ageing Voltaire (1781).

The Comédie Française confines itself mainly to the classical French repertoire, including the dramas and comedies of Corneille, Racine, Molière, Marivaux and Beaumarchais, together with such modern classics as Paul Claudel, Jean Giraudoux, Jean Anouilh and Samuel Beckett.

Location
Place André-Malraux (1st arr.)

Métro stations
Palais-Royal-Musée du Louvre

Buses
21, 27, 39, 48, 69, 72, 81, 95

Opening times
Advance bookings:
Daily 11am–6pm
Tel. 40 15 00 15

Thermes de Cluny

See Musée de Cluny

The Magician in Iron

At the end of March 1899 a cool wind was blowing over Paris when the genial and effervescent engineer and builder Alexandre Gustave Eiffel and his 300 workmen in overalls drank a glass of champagne 80m/260ft up above the French capital to celebrate the completion of one of the craziest, most pointless and yet most beautiful buildings in the world – the Eiffel Tower. During the two years it took to build this great iron construction had already become the talking point of the whole of Paris, a symbol of progress, of the glitter of the young French Republic, the very peak of contemporary technical achievement.

Born in Dijon in 1832, Eiffel founded the "Société Eiffel" metal-working company in 1868 and soon earned an international reputation as a designer of bridges and viaducts such as the Maria Pia bridge over the Douro river near Oporto in Portugal (1875) and the Truyère viaduct near Garabit, two bold examples of new and exciting industrial design. Eiffel was obsessed by bridges, the linking of separate locations, solving problems of distance, and mastery by the scientist of natural forces such as wind and water. His contributions to the architectural debates of the time regarding form and function also included industrial buildings such as the Western Railway Station in Budapest (1877), the copper-plated steel framework for the Statue of Liberty in New York and the massive dome of the Nice Observatory which, at over 22m/72ft in diameter, was in 1881 the largest in the world. Iron, the "new" material of the Industrial Revolution, was no longer something to be hidden behind walls; rather, its supporting and aesthetic functions were now to be appreciated in, for example, transparent edifices of metal and glass.

After retiring from his company in 1893 Eiffel devoted himself until his death in 1923 to aerodynamic research – and became a legend in his own right. He recorded his success story in an unbiased and precise way in the "Biographie Industrielle et Scientifique" – while not mentioning his failures. The "magician in iron", as his friends called him, was indebted for the idea of constructing the Eiffel Tower to two of his engineering colleagues, Maurice Koechlin and Emile Nougier. They suggested erecting a spectacular memorial to the French Revolution, the centenary of which was to be marked by the Paris Exhibition of 1889. Eiffel only really became enthusiastic about the idea when the architect Stephen Sauvestre gave the tower a greater degree of formal transparency by dividing it into three sections and including large arches in the lower section. Eiffel successfully superintended and completed the construction. The tender for this unique iron edifice, symbolic of the ideals of liberty engendered by the Revolution, of the new era of confidence and man's mastery of materials, won official approval in 1887.

★★Tour Eiffel (Eiffel Tower)   E 5

Despite oft-repeated doubts as to its stability, the Eiffel Tower celebrates its 110th birthday in 1999. In 1932 it lost its title as the world's highest man-made structure to the Empire State Building in New York (a title now held by the CN Building in Toronto with a height of 553.35m/1815ft). The Eiffel Tower has long been, and still is, the great landmark of Paris.

Standing 307m/1007ft high (320.75m/1052ft to the tip of the aerial), the tower consists of 15,000 steel sections held together by 2½ million rivets. Eiffel designed the tower in such a way that even under extreme wind pressure the structural weight is sufficient to prevent it from being blown over. Moreover the lattice construction reduced the pressure on the structure by about half, thus giving a double insurance against collapse. Originally the structure's total weight of 7500 tons was distributed in such a way that at ground level the pressure exerted was only 4 kilograms per sq. centimetre (57 lb per sq. inch), roughly the pressure exerted by a normal-sized adult on the seat of a chair. As individual sections are not replaced by a similar section but by a heavier concrete section, however, the total weight has increased to 11,000 tons. In the course of the recent renovation in 1996 many concrete sections were replaced by steel plates.

When the tower was being built there were vigorous public protests, and the construction company was obliged to give an undertaking to meet any claims for damage in the event of the tower collapsing on to surrounding buildings. Thanks to the double safeguards in the structure this has not happened, and the "cleaning-up" during the restoration work of the 1980s and 1990s has still further increased the security of the tower.

Location
Quai Branly
(7th arr.)

Métro stations
Ecole Militaire,
Bir Hakeim,
Trocadéro

RER station
Champ de Mars-
Tour Eiffel

Opening times
daily 9.30am–
11pm (lift)
8.30am–6.30pm
(stairs)

Admission charge

The Eiffel Tower, showpiece of the 1889 International Exhibition

Since the recent modernisation the top platform, at a height of 274m/900ft (orientation table), can be reached by lift. From this platform there are panoramic views extending in fine weather for some 70km/45 miles. The views from the first and second platforms, at 57m/187ft and 112m/367ft, are less extensive but have the advantage that surrounding districts of the city can be seen in more detail. At these levels there are restaurants, a post office (with a special franking, "Tour Eiffel") and a cinema, with an audiovisual show on the history of the Eiffel Tower. After dark the tower is impressively illuminated.

In spite of the controversy which it engendered in its early days, the Eiffel Tower has inspired numerous artists, including Signac, Seurat, Dauzat, Dufy, Utrillo, Chagall, Legrand and Robert Delaunay, who sought in a whole series of oil paintings to capture the dynamic of the tower's filigree-like structure.

★Tuileries G/H 4/5

Location
Between Louvre and Place de la Concorde (1st arr.)

Métro stations
Tuileries, Concorde

One of the largest and best known parks in Paris is the Tuileries (Jardin des Tuileries). When Catherine de Médicis had a palace built in 1563 on a site extending along the whole length of what is now Avenue du Général-Lemonnier, close to the Louvre (see entry), she named it the Tuileries after the tile-works which had previously occupied the site. In 1664 Colbert, Louis XIV's minister of finance, employed André Le Nôtre, later to be responsible for laying out the park at Versailles (see entry). to design the Tuileries Gardens. The palace itself was burned down during the Paris Commune in 1871 and was never rebuilt.

Relaxing midday break in the Tuileries Gardens

Coysevox's Baroque statues of winged horses guard the entrance on Place de la Concorde (see entry), which leads down, by way of terraces and ramps, to the large octagonal pond surrounded by busts and statues by the 18th century sculptors Coustou and Coysevox. On the steps leading up to the Jeu de Paume (see entry) is a bust of Le Nôtre (copy).

From the central avenue, the Grande Allée, there are fine views of the obelisk on Place de la Concorde, the Champs-Elysées and the Arc de Triomphe in one direction and of the Arc de Triomphe du Carrousel and the glass pyramid of the Louvre in the other.

For those who would appreciate a rest after their sightseeing there are tree-shaded benches on either side of the central avenue, near the sculptures by Maillol and the bronze statue of Dreyfus by Tim; or they can take some refreshment in one of the open-air cafés or watch a game of boules.

In the northern half of the gardens there are also cafés, a puppet theatre and donkey rides for children, who can also sail their boats in the large pond at the other end of the central avenue.

Buses
24, 42, 52, 68, 69, 72, 73, 84, 94

Opening times
Daily 9am to dusk

★UNESCO F 6

The UNESCO Building is the headquarters of the United Nations Educational, Scientific and Cultural Organisation, to which over 170 countries now belong. Designed by an international team of architects – Marcel Breuer (USA), Pier Luigi Nervi (Italy) and Bernard Zehrfuss (France) – the building represents a piece of modern architectural history. The main hall of the conference building (1955–58), trapezoid in shape, has a mural by Picasso, "The Victory of Light and Peace over Darkness and Depth" and two walls (the "Moon Wall" and the "Sun Wall") with ceramic decoration by Joan Miró. The building also contains bronze reliefs by Hans Arp and tapestries by Le Corbusier. Outside there are a "Recumbent Figure" by Henry Moore (UK) and a black steel mobile by Alexander Calder (USA). In the Japanese garden is an angel's head, a relic of a church in Nagasaki destroyed by the atom bomb.

Opening times: Visits by prior arrangement: tel. 01 45 68 03 71, fax 01 45 67 30 72.

Location
7 place de Fontenoy
(7th arr.)

Métro stations
Ségur,
Ecole Militaire

Buses
28, 49, 87

Val-de-Grâce H/J 7

The imposing Baroque church of Val de Grâce is part of a well preserved 17th century convent, now a military hospital. Anne of Austria, Louis XIII's wife, had purchased the conventual buildings and presented them to a house of Benedictine nuns, vowing at the same time to give them a church if she gave birth to an heir to the throne. In 1638 she had a son, the future Louis XIV, and in 1645 she fulfilled her vow, commissioning Jacques Lemercier to build the church, which was completed by Gabriel Le Duc in 1667. It was the only Baroque church in Paris so strongly influenced by Rome, the great centre of 17th century Baroque architecture.

Lemercier modelled the west front on the church of Santa Susanna in Rome with its double row of columns, but in a more vigorous and upward-striving form. The dome, modelled on St Peter's in Rome, is of livelier effect with its sculptured vases, windows and a relief frieze of the royal fleurs-de-lys and the initials A and L; while the drum is given a strongly plastic form, with projecting pilasters, overhanging cornices and deeply set windows.

The interior of the church is also marked by the plastic approach

Location
277 rue St-Jacques
(5th arr.)

Métro station
St-Jacques

RER station
Port-Royal

Buses
21, 27, 38, 83, 91

which governs its architecture and decoration as a whole. The barrel-vaulted nave consists of three bays, in each of which are side chapels. On the round-headed arches are reliefs of the Virtues, and in the medallions are the Forefathers of Christ. The crossing is given greater emphasis by a stepped dais bearing a baldachin supported on columns – again modelled on Bernini's baldachin in St Peter's. In the dome (height 40m/130ft, diameter 17m/55ft) is a huge fresco (by Pierre Mignard, 1665) of God the Father surrounded by saints and martyrs. The chapel on the left of the choir has a fresco portrait of Anne of Austria in the dome; the chapel on the right, formerly the nuns' choir, is dedicated to St Louis (Louis IX).

★Vaux-le-Vicomte

Location
55km/35 miles
SE of Paris
(A 4, A 6)

Rail service
from Gare de
Lyon/
Melun

Opening times
Apr. 1–Oct. 31,
10am–6pm;
Nov. 1–Mar. 31,
11am–5pm

**Admission
charge**

6km/4 miles north-east of Melun is Vaux-le-Vicomte, one of the finest châteaux in France, which served as a model for the château and park of Versailles (see entry).

The story of the château began in 1641, when the young Nicolas Fouquet, later Louis XIV's minister of finance, acquired the property. After making a great deal of money by shrewd speculation, he pulled down the old château in 1656 and employed the architect Louis Le Vau, the painter Charles Le Brun and the landscape gardener André Le Nôtre to build a new one. The magnificent new château, set in a beautiful park, was completed in the relatively short time of five years, costing Fouquet the enormous sum of 10 million livres. Three villages had to be removed to make room for the park, and at times there were over 18,000 workers employed on the task. Fouquet's enjoyment of the property, however, was short-lived. Ignoring all warnings, he entertained Louis XIV at a spectacular celebration at Vaux-le-Vicomte on August 17th 1661, a lavish event for which Molière had written a new comedy, "Les Fâcheux"; but only three weeks later he was arrested for enriching himself from his office and condemned to imprisonment for life, and Vaux-le-Vicomte was confiscated.

The splendour of Vaux-le-Vicomte led Louis XIV to resolve that he must himself possess the finest château in France. For this purpose he took over many of Fouquet's confiscated treasures, including costly vases, statues and even trees and plants. He also took over Le Vau, Le Brun and Le Nôtre, who created for him at Versailles the palace of palaces, the splendid centre and symbol of absolutist power.

Vaux-le-Vicomte survived the Revolution largely unscathed. Both the buildings and the park were thoroughly restored between 1975 and 1980. Fouquet's private apartments on the upper floor have been largely preserved in their original state. In the basement are the kitchen, the servants' dining room and the wine-cellar. Le Nôtre's park is a masterpiece of French landscape gardening: the strict regularity of its plan, with main, transverse and diagonal axes, is relieved by elaborate fountains, imposing sculptural groups and over-lifesize statues (e.g. of Hercules). In the old stables is a coach museum.

The château is seen at its finest on Saturdays between May and September, when it is illuminated from 8.30pm onwards by over a thousand candles. The fountains play from 3 to 6pm on the second and last Saturdays of the month from April to October.

Versailles   K6

Versailles (pop. 98,000), once the splendid residence of the French kings, is now chief town of the département of Yvelines. The town's

The fairytale Palace of Versailles – the life work of Louis XIV

main traffic artery is the broad Avenue de Paris, which meets the Avenue de Saint-Cloud and Avenue de Sceaux in the Place d'Armes. To the south of the Place d'Armes is the Salle du Jeu de Paume (the jeu de paume was a ball game similar to tennis), built for the king and the court in 1686, in which the National Assembly met in 1789. Farther south is the 18th century Cathedral of Saint-Louis. West of the Place d'Armes, in Rue de l'Indépendance-Américaine, are the former Grand Commun (by Mansart, 1682), now a military hospital, and the handsome Bibliothèque Municipale. In the northern part of the town are the church of Notre-Dame (by Mansart, 1684–86) and the 18th century Musée Lambinet (furniture, pictures, prints, weapons, etc.). On the east side of the spacious Place d'Armes are Mansart's Écuries Royales (Royal Stables, 1679–85; now a barracks), which could accommodate 2500 horses and 200 carriages.

The main attraction of Versailles, however, is the Château de Versailles, listed by UNESCO as a world heritage monument, which with its beautiful park and gardens is one of the most fascinating and historic sights in Europe. Its architecture and interior decoration, its park and the whole way of life of the French kings in the 17th and 18th centuries were taken as a model by many royal and princely courts in Europe.

Location
20km/12¹/₂ miles SW of Paris (A 13, N 10)

RER station
Versailles Rive Gauche (Line C 5)

Rail service
from Gare Montparnasse or Gare St-Lazare

★★Château de Versailles

Chapelle Royale, Grands Appartements du Roi et de la Reine, Galerie des Glaces, Musée de l'Histoire de France: Tue.–Fri. 9am–5.30pm Sat., Sun. 10am–5.30pm (admission free). Appartements et Cabinets Intérieurs du Roi, Opéra Royal: Tue–Sun. 9.45am–6.30pm; conducted tours 1.30pm (admission charge; entrance C). Appartements de Mad-

Opening times, conducted tours

ame de Pompadour et de Madame de Berry: Tue.–Fri. 11am–2pm; conducted tours (admission charge; entrance C 2). Cabinets Intérieurs de la Reine et de la Dauphine: conducted tours Wed.–Fri. 3.30pm (admission charge; entrance C 2).

History

A small hunting lodge, originally built for Louis XIII by Philibert Le Roy in 1631–34, was transformed by Louis XIV into the present huge and magnificent palace between 1661 and 1710. First Louis Le Vau (d. 1670) extended the original building by adding two wings on the east side, enclosing the Cour de Marbre. Then Jules Hardouin-Mansart, appointed court architect in 1676, added an additional storey to Le Vau's wings and built the Galerie des Glaces (Hall of Mirrors) and the long north and south wings on the garden front. Finally came the two neo-Classical pavilions flanking the Cour Royale, by Gabriel (18th c.) and Dufour (1820). The whole gigantic building is said to have cost 500 million gold francs in addition to the compulsory labour of the peasants, and up to 36,000 men were employed on its construction. Charles Le Brun was responsible for the interior decoration, André Le Nôtre for the landscaping of the park and gardens. When complete the Château accommodated a population of 10,000.

Louis XIV's successors made no major changes or additions to the Château: Louis XV had some rooms decorated in Rococo style and built the neo-Classical Petit Trianon, and the gardens were extended by Louis XV and XVI. For something over a century (1682–1789) Versailles was the residence of the French kings. The principles of absolutism required that the high nobility should be in constant attendance at court, and Versailles – the Château and the park – provided a splendid setting for the display of the absolute power of the French monarchy.

In 1789 the States-General of France were summoned to meet at Versailles, and the third estate (the ordinary people) joined the other two (nobility and clergy) to form a National Assembly. It was the first step on the road to revolution. On October 5th–6th Louis XVI was carried off from Versailles and compelled to take up his residence in the Tuileries Palace. Thereafter Versailles lost its former importance. During the Franco-Prussian War (1870–71) Versailles was occupied on September 19th 1870 and remained the German headquarters until March 6th 1871. On January 18th 1871 the German Empire was proclaimed in the Hall of Mirrors. After the First World War the Treaty of Versailles was signed on June 28th 1919, again in the Hall of Mirrors. In June 1978 a bomb attack by Breton separatists caused serious damage to the Château.

Exterior

The exterior view of the Château from the town is immensely impressive. Three broad avenues meet in the Place d'Armes at the entrance to the forecourt. Flanking the central avenue, the Avenue de Paris, are the former Royal Stables (Ecuries Royales; Mansart, 1679–85). The forecourt is entered through an iron gate. On the far side, at the entrance to the Royal Courtyard (Cour Royale), is an equestrian statue of Louis XIV (1835). At the far end of the Cour Royale, which could be used only by the royal family, is the narrower Marble Courtyard (Cour de Marbre), which until 1830 was on a slightly higher level and had coloured marble paving. The entrance to the Château, which also gives access to the park, is on the right-hand side of the Cour Royale.

The parts of the building enclosing the Cour de Marbre are the oldest in the Château, dating back to Louis XIII's hunting lodge. Here, on the first floor, are the royal private apartments. Along the two sides of the hunting lodge Le Vau built on another range of rooms for the state apartments (Grands Appartements, on the first floor) and the apartments of the heir to the throne on the ground floor. Mansart linked these two suites of rooms by building the Hall of Mirrors (Galerie des Glaces) along the park front of the building and added the north and

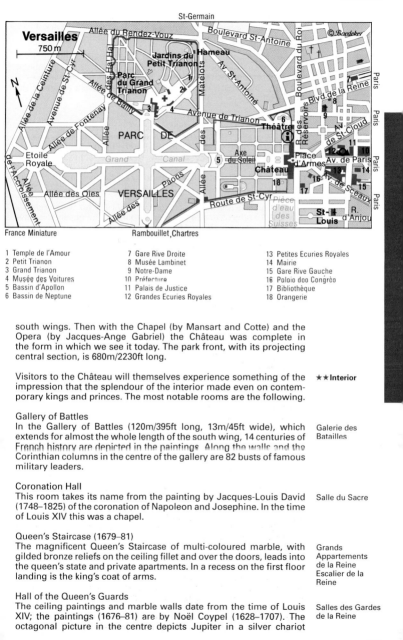

south wings. Then with the Chapel (by Mansart and Cotte) and the Opera (by Jacques-Ange Gabriel) the Château was complete in the form in which we see it today. The park front, with its projecting central section, is 680m/2230ft long.

Visitors to the Château will themselves experience something of the impression that the splendour of the interior made even on contemporary kings and princes. The most notable rooms are the following.

★★Interior

Gallery of Battles

In the Gallery of Battles (120m/395ft long, 13m/45ft wide), which extends for almost the whole length of the south wing, 14 centuries of French history are depicted in the paintings. Along the walls and the Corinthian columns in the centre of the gallery are 82 busts of famous military leaders.

Galerie des Batailles

Coronation Hall

This room takes its name from the painting by Jacques-Louis David (1748–1825) of the coronation of Napoleon and Josephine. In the time of Louis XIV this was a chapel.

Salle du Sacre

Queen's Staircase (1679–81)

The magnificent Queen's Staircase of multi-coloured marble, with gilded bronze reliefs on the ceiling fillet and over the doors, leads into the queen's state and private apartments. In a recess on the first floor landing is the king's coat of arms.

Grands Appartements de la Reine Escalier de la Reine

Hall of the Queen's Guards

The ceiling paintings and marble walls date from the time of Louis XIV; the paintings (1676–81) are by Noël Coypel (1628–1707). The octagonal picture in the centre depicts Jupiter in a silver chariot

Salles des Gardes de la Reine

207

Versailles

drawn by two eagles. The four pictures in the arches represent divine virtues in examples from antiquity.

Antichambre de la Reine

Queen's Antechamber
In this antechamber visitors waited to be presented to the queen in the audience chamber or in her bedroom. The ceiling paintings, which date from the time of Louis XIV, depict celebrated women of antiquity (by Claude Vignon, 1673). The four tapestries are of the same period.

Salon de la Reine

Queen's Audience Chamber
Only the ceiling paintings (allegories of the arts and sciences; by Michel Corneille, 1671) date from the time of Queen Maria Theresa of Austria (Louis XIV's wife: not to be confused with the Austrian Empress of that name), since the room was altered by Marie-Antoinette in 1785. The large Gobelins portrait of Louis XV (1770) was the work of P.-F. Cozette after a design by Michel van Loos.

Chambre de la Reine

Queen's Bedroom
In the Queen's Bedroom, created in 1671–80 for Queen Maria Theresa, 19 princes and princesses were born. The queen also gave private audiences in this room.

The Rococo ceiling is later (1729–35); it has four grisaille paintings by François Boucher (1703–70), from designs by Robert de Cotte, depicting the four virtues of a queen (compassion, generosity, wisdom, fidelity). The Gobelins medallions with portraits of the Empress Maria Theresa of Austria, the Emperor Joseph II and Louis XVI date from the time of Marie-Antoinette. The little jewellery cabinet (by Schwerdtfeger, 1787) to the left of the bed was a gift to Marie-Antoinette from the city of Paris two years before the Revolution.

Petits Appartements de la Reine

Queen's Private Apartments
The queen's private apartments, in the style of Marie-Antoinette's time (1770–81), can be reached from her bedroom.

Salon de la Paix

Hall of Peace
The Salon de la Paix was created in 1680–86 as a counterpart to the Salon de la Guerre at the other end of the Hall of Mirrors. The ceiling painting is by Le Brun, the portrait of Louis XVI over the chimney by Lemoyne.

Galerie des Glaces

Hall of Mirrors
After the annexation of Lorraine Louis XIV also acquired the dukedom of Burgundy under the Peace of Nijmegen in 1678, thus consolidating France's supremacy in Europe. In the same year he resolved to build a gallery which, with the Salon de la Guerre and Salon de la Paix at each end, should add to the magnificence of the palace and glorify the king, in a series of allegorical representations, as lord of both war and peace.

The world-famed Hall of Mirrors (73m/246ft long, 10m/33ft wide and 12m/40ft high) was designed by Jules Hardouin-Mansart (1646–1708); the interior decoration was by Charles Le Brun (1619–90). Like similar galleries in the châteaux and mansions of the time, the Hall of Mirrors served as a passage between the king's and the queen's apartments, and it was here that the courtiers waited upon the king and queen. It was rarely used for great ceremonies or entertainments. The room gets its name from the 17 arched mirrors (each made up of 10 segments – i.e. a total of 306 segments), corresponding to the 17 round-headed windows in the outer wall. In this historic room the German Empire was proclaimed in 1871 and the Treaty of Versailles was signed in 1919. Since the restoration work which was completed in 1980 it has been fitted out with genuine or reproduction period

The Hall of Mirrors connecting the King's and Queen's apartments

furniture, statuary and chandeliers (much of all this in gilded plastic material). The paintings on the barrel-vaulted ceiling, which add up to the most monumental ceiling painting in France, tell the story of Louis XIV's reign down to the Peace of Nijmegen.

King's Antechamber
This room (1701), named after the oval "ox-eye" window over the fire-place, originally contained pictures by Veronese, later replaced by portraits of the royal family. A notable feature is the 53m/174ft long frieze of children's games, which, like the group of putti in the park, reflects the ageing king's desire for "more youth and less seriousness".

Salon de l'-Œil-de-Bœuf

King's Bedroom
Louis XIV's bedroom (1701), in which he died on September 1st 1715, was the principal room in Louis XIII's hunting lodge. It was here that the famous ceremonies of the "Lever du Roi" in the morning and the "Coucher du Roi" in the evening took place, when the king granted audiences. After long and costly work the room was restored to its original state in 1980.

Chambre du Roi

Council Chamber
During the reigns of Louis XV and XVI all important State decisions were taken in this room. The decoration (by Jacques-Ange Gabriel, 1755) is a masterpiece of French Rococo.

Cabinet du Conseil

King's Private Apartments
The king's private apartments are reached from the Council Chamber. They were decorated in Rococo style by J.-A. Gabriel (1755 onwards) for Louis XV, who liked to relax here, away from the ceremonial eti-quette of the court. Louis died in the first room (the bedroom) in 1774.

Petits Appartements du Roi

Versailles

Salon de la Guerre — **Hall of War**
From this room there are extraordinary views in one direction along the Hall of Mirrors to the Salon de la Paix at the other end (which dates from the same period), and in the other through the long suite of the Grands Appartements. On the west wall is a large oval stucco relief by Antoine Coysevox (1640–1720) glorifying Louis XIV.

Grands Appartements Salon d'Apollon — **Apollo Saloon**
The Apollo Saloon, its walls hung with valuable tapestries, was originally the Throne Room. The ceiling painting of "Apollo in the Chariot of the Sun accompanied by the Seasons" by Charles de la Fosse, a pupil of Le Brun's, expresses the central allegorical theme from which Louis XIV's style of the "Roi Soleil" ("Sun King") was derived. Over the fireplace is the well-known portrait of the king in a robe trimmed with ermine.

Salon de Mercure — **Mercury Saloon**
Of the original appointments (1670–80) of the Salons d'Apollon, de Mercure and de Mars only the ceiling paintings in their magnificent frames remain: the marble has been replaced by wood and the walls covered with fabric. The Grands Appartements were the state apartments in which the king held court from 6 to 10 every morning. The names of the rooms and the representations of classical deities were designed to relate Louis XIV's reign to the history of the western world.

Salon de Mars — **Mars Saloon**
This room, with a ceiling painting by Audran, was formerly the Guard Room. In it is the famous painting of Marie-Antoinette and her three children (1787) by Madame Vigée-Lebrun.

Salon de Diane — **Diana Saloon (1675–80)**
The ceiling painting of Diana with her attributes is by Gabriel Blanchard, the bust of Louis XIV (1665) by Bernini.

Salon de Vénus — **Venus Saloon**
The Salon de Vénus, like the Salon de Diane, has preserved the austere, cold marble decor of the 1660s. Originally all seven of the Grands Appartements were in this style, which reflected the young Louis XIV's striving for power, glory and a great name to leave to posterity – always with the model of antiquity in mind. This is seen in the marble walls and columns, the statues in the antique style, including one of Louis XIV as a Roman Emperor, and the ceiling paintings with their representations of Titus and Berenice, Anthony and Cleopatra, Jason and Medea, Theseus and Ariadne, Europa and Jupiter, Amphitrite and Poseidon.

Salon d'Abondance — **Hall of Abundance (c. 1680)**
The ceiling painting of the goddess of abundance with her cornucopia is by R.-A. Houasse, a pupil of Le Brun. In this room supper was served at receptions.

Salon d'Hercule — **Hercules Saloon (1710–36)**
The ceiling painting, "The Triumph of Hercules" (1733–36), is by François Lemoyne. The two paintings by Veronese, "Eliezer and Rebecca" (over the fireplace) and "The Meal with Simon the Pharisee", were gifts to Louis XIV from the Venetian Republic.

Chapel
The Chapel was begun by Jules Hardouin Mansart in 1699 and completed by his brother-in-law Robert de Cotte in 1710. Mass is celebrated here at 5.30pm on the first Sunday in the month, Easter Day, Pentecost and November 1st. The gallery reserved for the royal family, with a tall Corinthian colonnade, was on a level with the royal

apartments. Every Tuesday at 5.30pm there are concerts in the chapel by the Centre for Research in Baroque Music, which was installed in Versailles in 1988.

The Museum on the History of France displays pictures and sculpture illustrating French history from the Crusades to the 19th century. The works by Laurent de la Hyre, Philippe de Champaigne and Noël Hallé (16th and 17th c.) are of particular interest.

Musée d'Histoire de France

The Royal Opera House (seen only on conducted tours) was built by Jacques-Ange Gabriel for Louis XV. It was completed in 1770, after only two years' work, in time for the marriage of the future Louis XVI with Marie-Antoinette. Like the palace chapel and the east front of the Louvre (see entry), it has a colonnade of Ionic columns. Its elegant decoration, using gilded bronze, marble and mirrors, matches the rest of the Château.

Opéra Royal

★★Parc de Versailles

The Château and the Park of Versailles form a unity: without the Château the park would lack a focal point and lose its function as an extension of the grand state apartments within the Château, while without the park the Château would seem pent up within itself, with no room to expand into a wider setting. This is borne out by the fact that the plans for the park were completed before the final plans for the Hall of Mirrors and the side wings of the Château had taken shape.

The Park of Versailles, covering an area of more than 800 hectares/ 2000 acres, is the finest example of 17th century French landscape gardening. Its creator, André Le Nôtre (1613–1700), son of a gardener at the Tuileries, had previously worked in the Tuileries Gardens and designed the park at Vaux-le-Vicomte (see entry), but Versailles was his masterpiece. The characteristic features of the French gardens of the 17th century, their symmetry and their taming of nature into geometric forms, were in tune with the ideals of the French classical period, which saw in such creations an expression of man's dominance over nature. The relationship between the palace and the park, conceived as a wider area for the display of royal power, is seen here in its fundamental significance: the monumental Château symbolises the monarch's absolute power over men, while the park reflects his image as the master of nature. This is at its most apparent in the Bassins and the Grand Canal, where artificial means are used to ensure that the water is always still.

In the 18th century, during the reign of Louis XVI, the gardens round the Petit Trianon were laid out in the English style. The contrast between the two styles is very marked: the English-style park was an artificial arrangement of "unspoiled" nature, offering the possibility of acting out "real" rural life in the setting of a miniature village.

The Grand and Petit Trianons, miniature palaces set in gardens, were the only places where the French kings could have any privacy. Elsewhere in the park and in the Château they were subject, like everyone else at court, to the rules of etiquette and ceremonial.

Opening times
Daily from
sunrise
to sunset

The Bosquets
(Salle de Bal,
Colonnade,
Dômes,
Bains d'Apollon)
can be visited
during the main
fountain displays,
the grandes eaux
(May 3–Oct. 4, on
1st, 3rd and 4th
Sun. in month at
11.15am and
3.30pm.)
Information:
Office
du Tourisme,
7 rue des
Réservoirs,
tel. 01 39 50 36 22

The Bassin de Neptune is an artificial pool created by Le Nôtre in 1679–84, with sculptured figures (by Adam, Bouchardon and Lemoyne, 1740 onwards) of Neptune with his trident and his wife Amphitrite with a sceptre, flanked by Oceanus on a unicorn and Proteus with sea creatures and plants.

Bassin de Neptune

The Parterres (open terraces) extend in front of the stone terrace a few steps higher, on which are four bronze statues of Bacchus, Apollo, Mercury and Silenus and two handsome marble vases with reliefs by

Parterres

Antoine Coysevox depicting the war with Turkey and the peace treaties of Aix-la-Chapelle and Nijmegen.

On the Parterre du Nord are 24 statues, in groups of four, representing cosmic forces – the seasons of the year, the times of day, the elements, the continents, the humours, the genres of literature. On the middle parterre, the Parterre d'Eau, are two pools with 24 bronze figures personifying the rivers of France. The southern part of the Parterre du Midi has sumptuous displays of flowers. Below the Parterres is the Orangery (1684–86), the central gallery of which is 155m/170yds long. Beyond it is the Pièce d'Eau des Suisses, a lake constructed by the royal Swiss Guard. On the Parterre de Latone is a pool with a sculpture group depicting Latona or Leto, Zeus's wife, and her children Diana and Apollo fleeing from the wicked Lycian peasants, whom Zeus punishes by turning them into frogs.

Salle de Bal

The Bosquet de la Salle de Bal (Ballroom), a kind of amphitheatre for acting and dancing, can be seen only when the *grandes eaux* are on.

Allée Royale

The Allée Royale, also known as the Tapis Vert ("Green Carpet"), links the Bassin de Latone and the Bassin d'Apollon along the main longitudinal axis of the park.

Colonnade

The Colonnade (1685) is a circular arcade of marble Ionic columns designed by Jules Hardouin-Mansart as an elegant setting for festivities. It can be seen only on a conducted tour.

View from the Bassin d'Apollon up the Allée Royale to the Château

The figure of Apollo on the chariot of the sun (by Jean-Baptiste Tuby, 1670) is an allegorical allusion to Louis XIV, the Sun King.

Bassin d'Apollon

In the time of Louis XIV gilded gondolas presented to the king by the Venetian Republic sailed on the waters of the Grand Canal and the Petit Canal at right angles to it.

Grand Canal

The Grand Trianon was built between 1678 and 1688 for Louis XIV by Jules Hardouin-Mansart and Robert de Cotte. Here the king had a private space, free from court etiquette. The little palace has two wings, one for Louis and the other for his favourite Madame de Maintenon. The Grand Trianon, which had fallen into disrepair, was restored by Napoleon. The interior is partly Baroque and partly Empire (furniture).

Grand Trianon (daily except Mon. and pub. hols. 9.45am–noon and 2–5pm)

The Petit Trianon was built by Jacques-Ange Gabriel in 1763–67 for Louis XV's favourites.
    Louis XVI later presented it to Marie-Antoinette.

Petit Trianon (daily except Mon. and pub. hols. 2–5pm)

An English-style garden was laid out for Marie-Antoinette on the site of Louis XV's botanical garden, and in it was built a miniature hamlet, with a farm, a dairy, a mill and a dovecot. In this area too are the Temple de l'Amour (Temple of Love, 1778), the Belvédère (an octagonal pavilion of 1777), the Théâtre de la Reine (1780) and the Pavillon Français (by Jacques-Ange Gabriel, 1750).

Hameau de la Reine

La Villette

Bosquet des Dômes

Of the handsome pavilions in the Bosquet des Dômes there remain only foundations, statues and reliefs. In the centre of the little wood is a group by Gaspard Marsy, "The Titans".

Bosquet des Bains d'Apollon

The romantic setting of the famous Apollo group was a later addition. On the north-western edge of this bosquet is the Ile des Enfants, with a group of children playing (1710) which dates from the time of the ageing Louis XIV, who wanted to see "more youth" around him.

Musée des Voitures

The Carriage Museum contains a collection of state coaches, sleighs, sedan chairs and harness of the Baroque period.

Vidéothèque de Paris

See Les Halles

★★La Villette   M 2

Location
North-eastern Paris (19th arr.)

Métro stations
Porte de Pantin (W), Porte de la Villette (E)

On a 35 hectare/85 acre site in north-eastern Paris there has been developed since the mid eighties, under the direction of the architects Bernard Tschumi and Adrian Fainsilber, a new recreation and leisure park with a cultural objective. Two factors influenced the choice of the site: one was that a large abattoir built during the de Gaulle era closed down in 1974; the other was the presence on the site of a 19th century market hall of cast-iron construction which it was desired to preserve. After reconstruction work lasting six years the Cité des Sciences et de l'Industrie – 270m/885ft long and 47m/154ft high, with a glass front and four huge blue-painted steel girders supporting the roof – was opened in March 1986.

Buses: 139, 150, 152, PC. Information: Tel. 01 36 68 29 30.

Cité des Sciences et de l'Industrie

In the words of its director, Maurice Levy, the Cité des Sciences et de l'Industrie is a large communications centre rather than a museum. The object is to make science and technology accessible to ordinary people and to explain to visitors their development in France, the present state of the art and the prospects for the future. The Cité is also designed as a platform for the exchange of ideas between all French firms working in these fields.

Opening times: Tue.–Sat. 10am–6pm. Sun., 10am–7pm. Information: tel. 01 40 05 80 90. Admission charge.

Explora

Over the central concourse of the museum, where the visit begins, are spherical domes through which sunlight is transmitted into the museum through a system of movable mirrors. The interior is in the form of a full-size replica of an American space station, from which escalators convey visitors to the "Explora" exhibition. The exhibition, which covers an area of some 30,000sq.m/323,000sq.ft, is in four sections: "Language and Communication" (language, information science, mathematics, sound, light, the brain, art and technology), "From the Earth to the Universe" (astronomy and space travel), "The Adventure of Life" (the biosphere, construction, transport, technology, science, archaeology) and "Matter La Villette and the Work of Man" (the earth and its resources, energy, structure of matter, manufacture of basic materials and products). In addition there are 10,000sq.m/108,000sq.ft available for special exhibitions (e.g. on man-made materials, telecommunications, transport technology, fashion, nutrition, the Eureka projects) and conferences. Other facilities are photographic, film, video and sound libraries. Visitors can

Parc de la Vilette

watch video films, carry out scientific experiments and work interactively with a computer. In all this the aim is to motivate and intensify the learning process by making the first contacts as lively as possible and by involving as many of the five senses as possible. Afterwards visitors can relax over a cup of coffee or something to eat, with a view of the "Ariane" rocket or the demonstrations of soil-free farming and high-tech agriculture.

The Aquarium in the basement shows Mediterranean flora and fauna in a reconstruction of the Mediterranean biotope.

Aquarium

The Inventorium is designed to interest children in science and technology at an early age. It is in two sections, for three- to six-year-olds and six- to twelve-year-olds. By building a house on a "building site" children learn team work and leadership, while working at a computer terminal gives a training in logical thinking. Finally for the older ones the Minitel offers an introduction into the information age.

Inventorium

The Médiathèque (Media Library) in the basement caters for ordinary people with an interest in science and technology. In addition to over

Médiathèque

215

La Villette

The new scenic café in the Cité de la Musique with a view of the Grande Halle and the concert stage

300,000 volumes, 5000 journals and 1000 learning programmes in the Paul Painlevé Hall, it has a collection of international documentary films on video cassette.

Cinaxe, 3D cinema, Planetarium

Other features are the Cinaxe, a movable projection room borne on three pairs of cylinders for speed experiments (entrance from outside); the Louis Lumière Cinema (3D), on level 0; and the Planetarium, near the Explora exhibition.

"Argonaute"

In front of the south entrance to the Cité is a French submarine built in 1957, the "Argonaute", with a record of 400,000km/250,000 miles under water.

Géode

Shows Tue.–Sun. every hour 10am–9pm.

Information: tel. 01 40 05 80 90

Admission charge

The south front of the Cité is reflected in the pool which surrounds it and in the Géode, the huge shining sphere opposite it which seems to be floating on the water in another pool. This futuristic structure, 36m/ 118ft in diameter, has a skin of polished chromium-nickel steel. At night it is illuminated from below, creating its own star-lit firmament. The Géode is actually a cinema. Inside, the audience recline comfortably in bucket seats, surrounded by the hollow sphere of wafer-thin aluminium sheets, now transformed into a screen. On this screen, with a total area of 1000sq.m/10,750sq.ft, documentary films are projected at an angle of 172°, with 12-channel stereo sound and 12,000 watts. The films are shot specially for the Géode, using a camera on the Canadian "Omnimax" system. The giant computer-controlled projector uses a 15 kilowatt lamp (normal projectors usually have only a 1½ kilowatt lamp), and the 70mm film produces frames almost ten times the size of the usual 35mm format. Since demand for tickets is high, it is advisable to book in advance.

The old rotunda at the Porte de la Villette entrance to the park, once occupied by veterinary staff, now houses material on local history (open: Tue.–Sun. 10am–6pm).

Maison de la Villette

On the east side of the park is the Zénith concert hall (by Philippe Chaix and Jean-Paul Morel), with seating for 6400, which is used mainly for rock concerts and variety shows. It is named after the red Zénith aircraft which stands nearby.

Zénith

The Grande Halle, formerly a cattle hall (Halle aux Bœufs), is notable for the elegance of its cast-iron architecture (1867). After two years' conservation and alteration work (architects Bernhard Reichen and Philippe Robert) it was officially opened by President Mitterand in 1985. With a total area of 20,000sq.m/215,000sq.ft, it can accommodate exhibitions, concerts, theatrical productions and other events of every kind.

Grande Halle

Opening times:
Tue.–Fri. and Sun. 10am–7pm, Sat. 10am–10pm

Admission charge

Scattered about in the spaciously laid out park are a number of decorative little buildings (folies, "follies") which provide refreshments.

Folies

At the south end of the park is the Théâtre Paris-Villette, remodelled as a municipal theatre by Bernard Guillaumot, with seating for 300. It puts on mainly plays by contemporary authors.

Théâtre Paris-Villette

Near the Théâtre Paris-Villette is the Cité de la Musique (by Christian de Portzamparc, 1991). In the western half of the building are the teaching rooms of the new Conservatoire de Musique, while in the eastern half are a concert hall with seating for 1200 and other rooms for public performances and events. Also in the complex are the Musée de la Musique (formerly in Rue de Madrid; over 4500 musical instruments, open: Tue.–Sat., noon–6pm, Thur. to 9.30pm, Sun. 10am–6pm) a sound studio and the Institut de Pédagogie Musicale.

Cité de la Musique

★Vincennes   N/O 7/8

★Bois de Vincennes

The Bois de Vincennes, on the eastern edge of Paris, is the counterpart of the Bois de Boulogne (see entry) at the other end of the city and is roughly the same size. It lies just outside the Boulevard Périphérique and is bounded on the east and south by the river Marne.

In the 13th century, during the reign of Philippe Auguste, the forest was surrounded by a 12km/7½ mile long wall to form a hunting reserve for the king and his guests. By the 17th century it had become a popular place of resort for the citizens of Paris and six openings had been made in the walls to allow them access. The area was replanted in the reign of Louis XV. In 1798 it became an artillery training ground. Napoleon III had the Bois redesigned in the style of an English park, the Lac de Gravelle and a riding track were laid out by Baron Haussmann and the Bois was presented to the city of Paris as a public park. With its footpaths and bridle-paths and its beautiful lakes (Lac de Saint-Mandé, Lac Daumesnil), it is now an attraction in its own right, drawing large numbers of people in quest of recreation as well as those who come for the Château de Vincennes and the Zoo. Also in the Bois de Vincennes are the Cartoucherie (a former gunpowder factory), with the Théâtre du Soleil (see Practical Information, Theatres), the Hippodrome de Vincennes (see Practical Information, Sport) and the Musée National des Arts Africains et Océaniens (see entry).

Location
South-eastern outskirts (12th arr.)

Métro stations
Porte Dorée, Château de Vincennes

RER station
Vincennes

Buses
46, 86, PC

Opening times
Summer, 9.30am–8pm; winter, 9.30am–5pm

Vincennes

Lac Daumesnil	There is a footpath round the Lac Daumesnil, and a bridge gives access to the little islands in the lake (café-restaurant). Rowing boats can be hired, as can bicycles.
Parc Floral	On the Esplanade du Château is the Parc Floral (area 31 hectares/77 acres), a botanic garden with magnificent displays of flowers and rare plants. It was originally laid out for the 1969 Flower Show by D. Collin, and is still used for flower shows and art exhibitions. Also in the park are an "exotarium" (exotic fishes and reptiles), a sculpture garden, a lake, a children's playground and a restaurant.
Ecole du Breuil, Jardin Tropical, Lac des Minimes	Visitors interested in landscape architecture will want to see the Ecole d'Horticulture du Breuil, at the south-east corner of the Bois de Vincennes (Route de la Pyramide). To the north is the Jardin Tropical (45 bis Avenue de la Belle-Gabrielle). Close to this is the Lac des Minimes (boat hire, café-restaurant).

★Zoo de Vincennes

Location Near Porte Dorée	The Zoo de Vincennes, near Lac Daumesnil at the west end of the Bois, was established for the Colonial Exhibition of 1931. Laid out on a spacious scale, it fits harmoniously into the landscape of the Bois de Vincennes. Within its 17 hectares/42 acres it houses some 600 mammals and 1200 birds in numerous large enclosures, with heated cages for winter. From the 72m/236ft high artificial (concrete) crag in the centre of the Zoo there are views of the Bois de Vincennes, with the Château, and (in clear weather) eastern Paris.
Métro station Porte Dorée	
Buses 87, PC	
	Opening times: Daily 9am–5.30pm. Admission charge.

★Château de Vincennes

Location Avenue de Paris, 94300 Vincennes	The history of the Château de Vincennes can be traced in its architecture, which shows a combination of a medieval fortified castle with a Baroque palace. The walls of the castle, with their nine towers and the magnificent keep, enclose a spacious courtyard with four 17th century pavilions.
Métro station Château de Vincennes	The story of Vincennes begins in the 11th century, when the French crown acquired the forest of Vincennes, which belonged to the abbey of Saint-Maur. Thereafter the Bois de Vincennes belonged to the French kings, who built a hunting lodge here in the 12th/13th century. In the 14th century this was enlarged into a fortified castle, and in the 15th century it became the favourite residence of the royal family. After the defeat of the Fronde in 1652 the castle became a prison for opponents of the absolutist monarchy, including the Prince de Condé, the Prince de Conti and Cardinal de Retz; in the 18th century state prisoners included Diderot, Mirabeau and the Marquis de Sade, who spent some years of his life in prison here.
RER station Vincennes	
Bus 56	
Opening times Summer, daily 10am–6pm; winter, daily 10am– 4.15pm	
Admission **charge**	In the 17th century Cardinal Mazarin commissioned Le Vau to build two symmetrical ranges of rooms, the Pavillon du Roi and the Pavillon de la Reine, in which the 22-year-old Louis XIV and his bride Maria Theresa of Austria spent their honeymoon in 1661. In the early 18th century a porcelain manufactory was installed in the Tour du Diable (Devil's Tower) on the east side of the château; later in the century, however (1759), this was transferred to Sèvres. After being used by Napoleon I as an arsenal the château was renovated under Napoleon III by Viollet-le-Duc. Further extensive restoration was required after 1944 to make good the damage caused by German forces during their retreat.

The imposing keep, completed about 1330, served both as a watch-tower and as living quarters. Standing 52m/170ft high, with five sto-reys, it has walls 3m/10ft thick, further reinforced by four round corner towers, a circuit of outer walls, a wall-walk and a moat. The cells which once housed prisoners have since 1934 been occupied by a museum.

Keep

On the ground floor are the kitchen and store-rooms, on the first floor reception rooms and a business room, on the second the king's bed-room and the chapel, on the third the apartments of the royal family and the treasury, on the fourth rooms for members of the household and on the fifth the armoury. From the roof terraces there are fantastic panoramic views.

Rooms

The Sainte-Chapelle (1379–1552), modelled on the Sainte-Chapelle (see entry) in the royal palace on the Ile de la Cité, has preserved its Gothic character (openwork gable, walls made up entirely of windows, variety of Late Gothic forms) in spite of the fact that it was completed only in the Renaissance period (magnificent Renaissance windows in choir). In the northern oratory is the tomb of the Duc d'Enghien, the last Prince de Condé, shot by Napoleon in Vincennes in 1804. A column outside the castle walls below the Tour de la Reine commemorates his execution.

Sainte-Chapelle

The two Pavillons Royaux, the Pavillon du Roi and the Pavillon de la Reine, were built by Louis Le Vau (1654–61). The Pavillon de la Reine was the residence of Anne of Austria, mother of Louis XIV. Cardinal Mazarin died in the Pavillon du Roi on March 9th 1661.

Pavillons Royaux

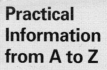

**Practical
Information
from A to Z**

Practical Information

Air Travel

Airports

Aéroport Roissy Charles de Gaulle (CDG)

23km/14 miles north-east of the city centre; TGV connection.
Information: tel. 01 48 62 22 80; daily 7am–11pm.
Getting to and from Paris: A1 motorway, 40–60 minutes.
Free shuttle bus between the airport and the nearest RER station, then Line B3 to the city centre (40 minutes; departures every 15 minutes).
Air France shuttle buses between Etoile air terminal (Charles de Gaulle/Etoile, 16th arr.) and the airport (20 minutes; departures every 15 minutes), between Porte Maillot air terminal and the airport (30 minutes; departures every 20 minutes), and between Gare Montparnasse (TGV Atlantique) and the airport (1 hour).
RATP buses: Line 350 (Gare de l'Est, 10th arr.), 50 minutes; Line 351 (place de la Nation, 12th arr.), 40 minutes; departures every 15 minutes.
Roissybus: runs to l'Opéra (9th arr.), departures every 15 minutes.
Roissyrail: trains to Gare du Nord (35 minutes; departures every 15 minutes).
Hélifrance helicopters: information, reservations: tel. 01 45 54 95 11.

Aéroport Orly (Sud/Ouest)

14km/9 miles south of the city centre.
Information (24-hour service): 01 49 75 15 15
Getting to and from Paris: A6 motorway, 30–50 minutes.
RATP buses: Line 215 (place Denfert-Rochereau, 14th arr.), 25 minutes; Line 183A (Porte de Choisy, 13th arr.), 50 minutes.
Air France shuttle buses between Les Invalides air terminal (Aérogare des Invalides, 7th arr.) and the airport, 40 minutes. Departures: Orly Sud every 15 minutes; Orly Ouest every 20 minutes.
ORLYVAL (RER line B; automatic Métro) to Gare d'Antony, 29 minutes to Châtelet, departures every 4–7 minutes; RER Line C2 to city centre, departures every 15 minutes.
Orlybus: runs to Denfert-Rochereau, departures every 12 minutes.
Orlyrail: trains to Gare d'Austerlitz, 35 minutes, departures every 15 minutes.
Air France shuttle buses to Charles de Gaulle airport every 20 minutes.
Hélifrance helicopters: information, reservations: tel. 01 45 54 95 11.

Aéroport Le Bourget

Paris's smallest airport, 40km/25 miles north of the city.
Information: tel. 01 48 34 93 90.
Getting to and from Paris: A1 motorway, 40–70 minutes.
RATP buses: Line 350 (Gare du Nord, Gare de l'Est, 10th arr.) 30 minutes; Line 152 (Porte de la Villette, 19th arr.) 25 minutes.

Airlines

Air France

Reservations (daily 7am–9pm): tel. 08 02 80 28 02
Charles de Gaulle airport: tel. 01 48 64 13 48
Orly airport: tel. 01 49 75 15 15
2 esplanade des Invalides (7th arr.); tel. 01 43 17 21 00
49 avenue Hoche (9th arr.); tel. 01 44 09 52 61

◀ *A street café*

12 rue Castiglione (1st arr.); tel. 01 47 78 14 14	British Airways
4 place de Londres, Roissy-en-France 95700; tel. 01 47 42 30 62	British Midland
47 avenue de l'Opéra (2nd arr.); tel. 01 47 42 12 50	Aer Lingus
10 rue de la Paix (2nd arr.); tel. 01 44 50 20 20	Air Canada
109 rue du Faubourg St-Honoré (8th arr.); tel. 01 42 99 99 01	American Airlines
tel. 01 47 68 92 92	Delta Airlines
13–15 boulevard Madeleine (8th arr.); tel. 01 44 55 52 01	Qantas Airways

Antiques

Le Louvre des Antiquaires
2 place du Palais-Royal (1st arr.); tel. 01 42 97 27 00
Métro: Palais-Royal; open Tue.–Sun. 11am–7pm
Three floors holding 250 antique dealers offering antiques of all kinds and all periods.
Le Village Suisse
78 avenue de Suffren (15th arr.); tel. 01 43 06 69 90
Métro: La Motte-Picquet; open Thur.–Mon. 10.30am–7pm
About 100 upmarket shops.
Antique shops in the arcades around the place des Vosges.

Shops

Under the arcades of the Place des Vosges – antiques and curios

Boat Trips

Quarters	Carré Rive Gauche rue du Bac, rue de Beaune, rue de Lille, rue de l'Université, rue des St-Pères, quai Voltaire Métro: Bac. Open Mon. afternoon–Sat. 10–12am, 2–7pm Village Saint-Paul Numerous shops in the rues St-Paul, des Jardins St-Paul, de l'Ave-Maria, and quai des Célestins Métro: Sully-Morland; open daily Tue.–Sat. 11am–7pm
Auction house	Hôtel des Ventes Drouot Richelieu 9 rue Drouot (9th arr.); tel. 01 48 00 20 20 Métro: Richelieu-Drouot, Le Peletier Open Mon.–Sat. 11am–6pm; auctions from 2pm. 17 rooms on three floors.

Boat Trips

Bateaux-Mouches (rive droite)	Pont de l'Alma (8th arr.); tel. 01 42 25 96 10; Métro: Alma-Marceau Departure: daily 10am–11pm (every half hour but 10.30, 11.30, 1.30, 5.30–8 and 10–11pm departures not guaranteed). Lunch daily 1pm, afternoon coffee, with music, 3.45pm, and dinner 8.30pm.
Bateaux Parisiens	Eiffel Tower: Pont d'Iéna (7th arr.); tel. 01 44 11 33 44 Métro: Trocadéro, Bir-Hakeim Departure: high season, daily every 20 minutes from 9.30am–10.30pm; low season, every 30 minutes from 10am–5pm.
Vedettes du Pont-Neuf	Pont-Neuf, Square du Vert Galant (1st arr.); tel. 01 46 33 98 38 Métro: Pont-Neuf Departure: 10.30, 11, 12, 1.30–5pm (every 30 minutes)
Vedettes de Paris Ile-de-France	Port de Suffren (7th arr.); tel. 01 47 05 71 29 Métro: Bir Hakeim Departure: daily 10am–5.30pm (every 30 minutes)
Canauxrama	Voyages of discovery on the Paris canals; tel. 01 42 39 15 00 Breakfast cruise on Canal Saint-Martin (booking essential) Departure: Mon.–Sat. 9.15 from Bassin de la Villette (19th arr.), quai de la Loire Métro: Jaurès Arrival: Bassin de l'Arsenal (Paris's new marina). Métro: Bastille Afternoon trip in opposite direction: 2pm Day trip on the Canal de l'Ourcq and Canal St-Denis Departure: Sun., Thur. 8.45am from Bassin de la Villette (19th arr.), quai de la Loire Métro: Jaurès "La Villette d'hier et de demain" (La Villette of yesteryear and tomorrow). Reservations: tel. 01 46 24 86 16 Departure: Mon., Tue., Wed. 9.15, 10.45am, 2, 3.20pm from Bassin de la Villette (19th arr.), quai de la Loire. Métro: Jaurès Arrival: Parc or Bassin de la Villette
Paris Canal	Cruise on the Seine and Canal Saint-Martin; tel. 01 42 40 96 97 Departure: May–November 9am–12.30 from Quai Anatole-France Métro: Solferino, Jaurès Arrival: Bassin de la Villette. Métro: Porte de Pantin Return trip in the afternoon.

From May to September the Batobus provides a riverbus shuttle
service, leaving at 25 minute intervals between 10am to 7pm and
operating between the Louvre and the Eiffel Tower, with stops at
Hôtel de Ville, Notre-Dame, St-Germain des Prés and Musée d'Orsay;
tel. 01 44 11 33 99.

Batobus

Cafés, Salons de Thé and Brasseries

French cafés have little in common with their
English namesakes. They are more like
bars or pubs since they stay open well
into the night and also serve all
kinds of alcoholic and non-alcoholic
drinks. With their typical little marble
tables and wicker chairs Paris's cafés,
brasseries and salons de thé are ideal
places to enjoy a drink and a snack
while taking a break from sightseeing
to watch the world go by. If you simply
order "un café" you get a small black
espresso coffee. For coffee with milk ask
for "café crème", "grand crème" or "café au
lait". Tea-drinkers might like to try one of the popular French versions
of herbal tea, in which case ask for an "infusion" or "tisane".

Meeting places
for all Paris

Angelina
226 rue de Rivoli (1st arr.); tel. 01 42 60 82 00
Open daily 10am–7pm
An elegant establishment with Louis Quinze seating.

Cafés
(a selection)

★La Coupole
102 boulevard du Montparnasse (14th arr.); tel. 01 43 20 14 20
Open daily 8am–2am
This famous Art Deco café was renovated in 1988/1989 and as in the
days of Hemingway, Sartre and Picasso is a rendezvous for artists,
professionals and politicians.

Dalloyau
101 rue de Faubourg Saint-Honoré (8th arr.); tel. 01 42 99 90 00
Open Mon.–Sat. 9.30am–7.15pm, Sun. 8.45am–1.45pm
2 place Edmond-Rostand (6th arr.); tel. 01 43 29 31 10
Open Mon.–Sat. 9.30am–7.15pm, Sun. 9am–7pm
The very best cakes and pastries for the very best people.

★Les Deux Magots
170 boulevard Saint-Germain (6th arr.); tel. 01 45 48 55 25
Open daily 8am–2am
The haunt of such famous literati as Jean Paul Sartre and Simone de
Beauvoir (see Baedeker Special, pp. 146–147).

★La Flore
172 boulevard Saint-Germain (6th arr.); tel. 01 45 48 55 26
Open daily 7.45–1.45am
Where the new young generation of literati hang out.

Hard Rock Café
14 boulevard Montmartre (9th arr.); tel. 01 53 24 60 00
Open daily 8am–2am
Hamburger or spare ribs to a rock 'n roll accompaniment surrounded
by memorabilia of such rocking greats as Buddy Holly, Jim Morrison,
Madonna, Jimi Hendrix and Prince.

As in the golden era, "La Coupole" is still today a rendezvous for artists and writers

Lipp: see Restaurants

★Procope
13 rue de l'Ancienne Comédie (6th arr.); tel. 01 43 26 99 20
Open daily 12–2am
Opened in 1686 and lovingly renovated in 1989, this historic café has at various times included La Fontaine, Molière, Racine, Diderot, Victor Hugo and Alfred de Musset among its regulars.

Salons de thé
(a selection)

Some salons de thé – a more stylish version of the café – serve light meals as well as tea and cakes, etc.

A la Cour de Rohan
59/61 rue Saint-André-des Arts (6th arr.); tel. 01 43 25 79 67
Open Wed.–Fri. 12–7pm, Sat. 3–7pm
A superior blend of fine teas and antiques.

★Aux Delices
39 avenue de Villiers (17th arr.); tel. 01 47 63 71 36
Open Mon.–Sun. 9am–6.45
A favourite haunt of Sarah Bernhardt and Mistinguett, Aux Delices lives up to its name with its very special chocolate mousse.

L'Escale
25 rue de Miromesnil (8th arr.); tel. 01 42 89 59 72
Open: Sun.–Fri. 6.30am–8.30pm
Reputedly the best sandwiches in Paris.

Au Priori Thé
35/37 Galerie Vivienne (2nd arr.); tel. 01 42 97 48 75
Open Mon.–Sat. 12–8pm
Specialities include American brownies and apple pie.

Camping

The Paris tourism office (see Information) can supply a full list of all the camp sites in the Ile-de-France region.

Site guides

Fédération Française de Camping et de Caravaning
78 rue de Rivoli (4th arr.); métro: Hôtel de Ville
tel. 01 42 72 84 08, fax 01 42 72 70 21
Open Mon.–Fri. 9am–12.30, 1.30–5.30pm

Car Rental

See Driving in Paris

Chemists

See Health Care

Children

A bustling capital city like Paris may at first sight not appear particularly child-friendly but on closer inspection it has a great deal to offer its younger visitors, including special attractions and concessionary rates. Children under five travel free on the bus and metro and then pay half-fare up to the age of ten. Many of the museums and other attractions have reduced rates for children and families. Some museums also have facilities specially for children.

Paris for children

A real outdoor pleasure for adults and children alike is to look down on the city from above, whether it be on a visit to the Eiffel Tower, Arc de Triomphe, Notre Dame or Sacré Coeur. Children also enjoy seeing Paris from the top of a bus – the open topped Balabus and lines 29 and 56 are just right for this – or from a boat on the Seine. The "Ferme de Georges Ville" (12th arr.), Paris's only farm and complete with all the usual farm animals, is good value for kiddies as is the "Jardin d'Acclimatation", their special park in the Bois de Boulogne. Most Parisian parks have puppet shows and some, like the Jardin du Luxembourg, also have pony rides and roundabouts. Green spaces like these have plenty of room to run and play, as well as play areas and in some cases, such as the Jardin des Halles, adventure playgrounds. The terrace of the Trocadéro is the place for rollerblading and skateboarding where you can join in – if you can! – or watch others doing their party tricks.

Fun and games outdoors

If you plan to go to an afternoon puppet show or children's theatre in the park remember that, outside the school holidays, these and other children's programmes are only on Wednesdays, Saturdays and Sundays.

Children

Information

Kiosque Paris-Jeunes, 25 boulevard Bourdon (4th arr.); tel. 01 42 76 22 60: Mon.–Fri. 10am–5.30pm – what's on information for young people.

Museums and other attractions

A visit to a museum can be entertaining as well as instructive and nearly all the large museums have an "atelier d'enfants", a children's workshop where youngsters can familiarize themselves with the exhibits through supervised creative play and experimentation. One of the most interesting museums for children is the "Cité des Sciences et de l'Industrie" at La Villette, a science museum full of hands-on interactive displays and gadgets, which you can get to by boat – an added inducement for children. The Palais de la Découverte, which also has a planetarium, falls into the same category. Other children's favourites are a visit to the circus (see entry) or the zoo at Vincennes, plus of course the theme parks around Paris, especially Disneyland and Parc Astérix (see Parks, Gardens and Theme Parks).

Eating out with children

There are not many restaurants with children's menus, although "Hippotamus", the local 15-strong steak-house chain (tel. 01 53 77 51 77), is an honourable exception and Paris also has plenty of other fast food outlets.

Some restaurants do put on an occasional Sunday brunch for children. These include Méridien-Montparnasse, 19 rue du Commandant-Mouchotte (16th arr.); tel. 01 44 36 44 00, and Le Niel's, 27 avenue des Termes (17th arr.); tel. 01 47 66 45 00.

Smart outfits for youngsters

Agnès Bolita, 10 rue du Jour (1st arr.); métro: Les Halles. Enchanting creations by the top designer.

The Place des Vosges with its play area is a suitable place for a children's picnic

Catamini, 23 boulevard de la Madeleine (1st arr.); métro: Madeleine. Imaginative children's collections and play-space for tiny tots; 7 other branches in Paris.

*Du Pareil au Même, 7 rue Saint-Placide (6th arr.). Everything from baby things to teenage clothes, and at reasonable prices; 16 other branches in Paris.

*Le Nain Bleu (the Blue Dwarf), 408 rue Saint-Honoré (8th arr.); métro: Madeleine. The finest toy store in Paris – and the most expensive.

Pain d'Epice (Gingerbread), 29 passage Jouffroy (9th arr.); métro: Rue Montmartre. Everything for the doll's house.

Allo Service Maman; tel. 01 42 67 99 37: 24-hour service Baby-Sitting Service, 18, rue Tronchet (8th arr.); tel. 01 46 37 51 24: daily 7am–10pm	Babysitting agencies
Hôpital Necker Enfants Malades 149–151 rue des Sèvres (15th arr.); tel. 01 44 49 42 90	Children's clinic
See Theatres	Children's theatre

Cinemas

Parisian filmgoers are truly spoilt for choice, with over 300 films screened every week. Dedicated movie buffs can also revel in "hommages" and retrospectives of actors, directors, etc. put on by art cinemas and "cinémathèques" such as Accatone and Champo (see also Facts and Figures, Film). Tickets are up to 30% cheaper one day a week (Monday or Wednesday, depending on the cinema). Do not forget a 10% tip for the usherette – that is her only income.

There are more than 100 cinemas and their programmes usually change on Wednesdays. A complete list can be found in magazines such as Pariscope, 7 à Paris and L'Officiel des Spectacles. Many cinemas stay open round the clock.

What's On

Accatone
20 rue Culas (5th arr.); tel. 01 46 33 86 86
Art-house cinema with first-rate retrospectives.

Outstanding cinemas (a selection)

Champo
51 rue des Ecoles (5th arr.); tel. 01 43 54 51 60
Film festivals and special programmes featuring silver-screen idols from the Marx brothers to Mizoguchi.

Dôme IMAX
Parvis de la Défense; tel. 01 46 92 45 60
Dôme IMAX opened in the ultra-modern high-rise district of La Défense in 1992 to compete with La Géode as Paris's second wrap-around cinema. The images projected on the grandest of scales (image maximale, i..e. IMAX) onto the vast screen of this spherical cinema, 27m/89ft in diameter, are ten times the size of the normal 35mm film.

La Géode: see A to Z, La Villette

★Grand Rex
1 boulevard Poissonière (2nd arr.); tel. 01 36 68 70 23
This palatial movie palace, with seating for 3000, took two years to build and was opened in 1932 by wealthy film producer Jacques Haïk. The finest showcase in Parisian cinema history (it was scheduled as a national monument in 1981) it has screened everything over the years from Hollywood westerns to the very latest French productions.

Max Linder Panorama
24 boulevard Poissonière (9th arr.); tel. 01 48 24 88 88
This ultra-cool modern film theatre on three floors can seat around 700. Many of the films it screens are shown in their original version (i.e. not dubbed) and its visitors' book features celebrities ranging from Serge Gainsbourg and Sting to Wim Wenders.

La Pagode
57bis rue de Babylone (7th arr.); tel. 01 36 68 75 07
Scheduled a national monument in 1990, La Pagode was built in 1896 by Alexandre Marcel for Monsieur Morin, a director of Bon Marché, the famous department store. Although not every single part of the building was imported from Japan, the timber framework certainly was, and for many years the "Pagoda" was where the smart set of Paris came to see and be seen. It was converted into a cinema in 1931 with the coming of sound, and many great movies had their French premières here. It continues to show top films by top directors.

Cinémathèques	See A to Z, Palais de Chaillot See A to Z, Centre Pompidou
Vidéothèque	See A to Z, Les Halles
European Film Centre	The new European Film Centre, on the place d'Italie, was built between 1989 and 1993 by the Japanese architect Kenzo Tange. It has a main auditorium with seating for 800 and a screen 20x10m/66x33ft, and two smaller cinemas, each seating 150.

Circus

Le Cirque de Paris	Avenue de la Commune de Paris, 92000 Nanterre; RER: Nanterre Season: November–June
★Cirque d'Hiver Bouglione	110 rue Amelot (11th arr.); métro: Filles-du-Calvaire A wonderful Belle Epoque circus building, opened in 1852 by Napoleon III.

Information in Pariscope about circus performances is in the section for young people headed "Pour les jeunes". Information

Currency

The unit of currency is the French franc (F) made up of 100 centimes. There are bank notes for 20, 50 100, 200 and 500 francs, and coins in denominations of 5, 10, 20 and 50 centimes and 1, 2, 5, 10 and 20 francs. Unit of currency

On 1 January 1999 the euro became the official currency of France, and the French franc became a denomination of the euro. French franc notes and coins continue to be legal tender during a transitional period. Euro bank notes and coins are likely to start to be introduced by January 2002.

Banks are usually open on weekdays from 9.30am–noon and from 2.30–4pm, and close on Saturdays or Mondays; they also close at midday on the eve of public holidays. Banks

All banks will take Eurocheques and travellers' cheques. Eurocheques can be cashed up to a maximum of 1400 francs. If you lose your cheque card telephone your bank immediately so that it can be stopped. Travellers' cheques should be kept separately from your receipt and the list of numbers. Cheques and Eurocheques

Although banks, car hire firms and many hotels, restaurants and shops will take credit cards, they are less likely to accept Eurocheques. Credit cards can also be used in many cash dispensers, and can be used to pay motorway tolls. Again, if you lose your card inform the issuing agency immediately by telephone. Credit cards

Money can be changed in banks and official exchange bureaux but not as a rule in savings banks (caisses d'épargne). Remember that many banks are closed on Mondays. Changing money

At airports:
Orly: 6.30am–11pm daily
Roissy Charles de Gaulle: 6.30am–11.30pm daily Late-night money changing

At railway stations:
Gare de Lyon: 6.30am–11pm
Gare de l'Est: 6.45am–10pm in summer, 6.45am–7pm in winter
Gare d'Austerlitz: 7am–9pm daily
Gare Saint Lazare: Mon.–Sat. 8am–7pm, Sun. 9am–6pm
Gare du Nord: daily 6.15am 10.00pm
Gare de Montparnasse: daily 8am–8pm (summer), 8am–7pm (winter)
Porte Maillot (Société Générale): Mon.–Fri. 9.30am–12.30pm, 2.15–4.20pm

Banks with late-night opening:
U.B.P., 154 Champs-Elysées (8th arr.), Mon.–Fri. 9am–5pm, Sat., Sun. 10.30am–1pm, 2–6pm
C.C.F., 127 Champs-Elysées (8th arr.), daily 9am–7.30pm

Customs Regulations

Member States of the European Union (EU), which includes France, the United Kingdom and Ireland, form a common internal market, and there is theoretically no limit to the amount of goods that can Allowances between EU countries be taken from one EU country to another provided they have been purchased tax paid in an EU country, are for personal use and not intended for resale. Customs authorities have, however, issued guidelines as to the maximum amounts considered reasonable for persons over 17 years of age. These are: 1.5 ltr of spirits or 20 litres fortified wine or sparkling wine (port, sherry, etc.), 90 litres of table wine, no limit on beer; 300 cigarettes or 150 cigarillos or 75 cigars or 400g smoking tobacco. There is no limit on perfume or toilet water.

The allowances for goods purchased in duty-free shops – due to be phased out in 1999 – at airports and on aircraft and ferries are the same as for entry from non-EU countries (see below).

Entry from non-EU countries

For visitors coming from a country outside the EU, or who have arrived from an EU country without having passed through customs control with all their baggage, the allowances for goods obtained anywhere outside the EU for persons over the age of 17 are: 1 litre spirits or 2 litres of fortified wine, plus 2 litres table wine; 60g perfume, 250cc toilet water, 200 cigarettes or 100 cigarillos or 50 cigars or 250g smoking tobacco.

Re-entry to other countries

For other English-speaking countries the duty-free allowances are as follows: Australia 250 cigarettes or 50 cigars or 250g tobacco, 1 litre spirits or 1 litre wine; Canada 200 cigarettes and 50 cigars and 900 g tobacco, 1.1 litres spirits or wine; New Zealand 200 cigarettes or 50 cigars or 250g tobacco, 1 litre spirits and 4.5 litres wine; South Africa 400 cigarettes and 50 cigars and 250g tobacco, 1 litre spirits and 2 litres wine; USA 200 cigarettes and 100 cigars or a reasonable quantity of tobacco, 1 litre spirits or 1 litre wine.

Disabled Access

Information

Comité National Français de Liaison pour Réadaptation des Handi-capés (CNFLRH)
236bis rue de Tolbiac, F-75013 Paris; tel. 01 53 80 66 66
The CNFLRH leaflet contains detailed listings of accommodation, transport and public places adapted for disabled access.
Another useful publication is Access in Paris, an access guide for the disabled; for further information contact Access Project (PHSP), 39 Bradley Gardens, London W13 8HE, United Kingdom.

The annual French hotel guide, the Guide National Officiel de l'Hôtellerie Française — Les Hôtels de France, indicates hotels that cater for the disabled by using the wheelchair logo.

Information about hotels and restaurants with wheelchair access is also available from the APF (Association des Paralysés de France), 17 boulevard Auguste Blanqui, 75013 Paris; tel. 01 40 78 69 00, fax 01 45 89 40 57.

Driving in Paris

Go with the flow!

Driving in Paris is not for the fainthearted, and given the excellent public transport system and the problems of trying to park and cope with French drivers it – may be as well – to leave the car at home. If you do decide to drive in Paris, though, you need to concentrate but also go with the flow – watching what other drivers are doing can often be more important than any road sign. When entering a large boulevard from a minor road this can mean slipping into the stream of traffic rather than insisting on the official priority you may have when coming from the right. Apart from this, the general rules of the road are drive on the right, overtake on the left, and give way to vehicles coming from the right.

The French speed limits are: 50kph/31mph in built-up areas; 80kph/50 mph on the Paris ring-road; 90kph/56mph on main roads; 110kph/ 68mph on dual carriageways; 130kph/80mph (110kph/70mph in bad weather) on motorways (autoroutes/péage).

Speed limits

The larger streets in Paris have bus and taxi lanes which may not be used by other vehicles until after 8.30pm. If you do venture into these lanes you risk a chorus of hooting by angry bus and taxi drivers as well as a hefty fine.

Bus and taxi lanes

If you opt to park anywhere except an official parking space or in a multi-storey car park be sure, when parking on the level, to leave the car in neutral with the handbrake off. That way it should survive being shunted back or front by other drivers.

On-street parking

Yellow lines along the kerb mean that parking is forbidden and if you do park there you run the risk of having your car towed away since the police are very strict about illegal parking. It also costs a great deal to recover your car once it has been towed away, not to mention all the trouble involved. This of course does not arise if you use official on-street parking spaces (the maximum pay and display or metered period is usually two hours). If you do use pay and display make sure that the ticket you get from the machine ("horodateur") is easy to see inside the windscreen.

Paris has a number of multi-storey car parks which are open round the clock. These include underground car parks such as those below the place Vendôme, place des Invalides and avenue des Champs-Elysées.

Multi-storey car parks

The legal blood alcohol limit is 0.5.

Drinking and driving

For Paris: tel. 01 47 05 90 01
For France: tel. 01 48 94 33 33 and 08 36 68 20 00

Information on traffic conditions

Automobile Club de France (ACF), 6/8 place de la Concorde (8th arr.); tel. 01 43 12 43 12
ACIF, 14 avenue de la Grande Armée (17th arr.); tel. 01 40 55 43 00

Automobile Clubs

24-hour breakdown services are available from:
Automobile Club Secours; freefone 0800 05 05 24
SOS Dépannage; tel. 01 47 07 99 99
SOS Help; tel, 01 47 23 00 00 (English-speaking)

Breakdown services

Police: tel. 17 (police secours)

Emergencies

Petrol stations open round the clock include:
Garage Saint-Honoré, 58 place du Marchee Saint-Honoré (1st arr.)
Shell, 109 rue de Rennes (6th arr.)
Esso, 1 avenue Matignon (8th arr.)
Total, 53 rue Marcadet (18th arr.)

Petrol stations

To rent a car you will need to show your driving licence. You will often also be required to produce a major credit card.

Car rental

Car rental firms in Paris include:

Tel. 01 46 10 60 60

Avis

Electricity

Budget France	Tel. 01 46 86 65 65
Europcar/Interrent	Tel. 01 30 43 82 82
Hertz	Tel. 01 47 88 51 51
Inter Touring Service	117 boulevard Auguste Blanqui (13th arr.); tel. 01 45 88 52 37 Vehicles specially adapted for use by people with disabilities.

Electricity

Most electricity supply in Paris is 220 volts, but some hotels still have 110 volts. If in doubt, ask. British and non-European appliances will usually require two-pin Continental-type adaptors

Embassies and Consulates

Australia	Embassy and consulate: 4 rue Jean-Rey; tel. 01 40 59 33 00, fax 01 40 59 35 38
Canada	Embassy: 35 avenue Montaigne; tel. 01 44 43 29 16, fax 01 44 43 29 93
Ireland	Embassy: 12 avenue Foch (entrance 4 rue Rude); tel. 01 44 17 67 00, fax 01 44 17 67 50
New Zealand	Embassy: 7 rue Léonardo-da-Vinci; tel. 01 45 00 24 11, fax 01 45 01 26 39
South Africa	Consulate: 59 quai d'Orsay; tel. 01 53 59 23 23, fax 01 47 53 99 70
United Kingdom	Embassy: 35 rue du Faubourg-Saint-Honoré; tel. 01 44 51 31 00 Consulate: 16 rue d'Anjou; tel. 01 44 51 31 02, fax 01 44 51 31 27
United States	Embassy: 2 avenue Gabriel; tel. 01 43 12 22 22 Consulate: 2 rue St Florentin; tel. 01 43 12 22 22, fax 01 42 66 05 33

Emergency Services

Police	Tel. 17
Fire	Tel. 18
Ambulance	Tel. 15 (SAMU) or 01 45 67 50 50
Medical aid	See Health Care
Chemists	See Health Care
Breakdowns	See Driving in Paris

Events

Calendar of Events

Last Sunday: Prix d'Amérique horse race, Hippodrome de Vincennes (see Sport) — *January*

Palm Sunday: Prix du Président de la République horse race, Hippodrome d'Auteuil (see Sport) — *March*
Festival International du Son (international festival of sound)
Salon des Indépendants (art exhibition) in the Grand Palais
La Foire du Trône (big fair in the Bois de Boulogne until June)

Foire Internationale (international trade fair), Parc des Expositions, Porte de Versailles (until May) — *April*

Festival de Poésie (late April/early May) — *April/May*

International tennis championships, Stade Roland Garros (see Sport) — *May*
Festival de l'Ile de France: concerts, open buildings (until July)
Nuits de Sceaux (music festival in Sceaux), see Excursions (until June)

June 21st: La Fête de la Musique (concerts and balls in every Paris district) — *June*
Festival du Marais (music and drama in the Marais quarter; until July)
International rose-growers' contest at Bagatelle (see A to Z)

July 14th (Quatorze Juillet): Fête Nationale. Celebration of France's national day starts the evening before with a grand ball on the place de la République and smaller street parties throughout the city. The morning of July 14th is marked by a parade along the Champs-Elysées and the day ends with a giant firework display on the place du Trocadéro. — *July*
Festival de Paris (Paris summer festival): classical and contemporary music (until September)
Final stage of the Tour de France cycle race; finishing line on the Champs-Elysées.

Salon d'Automne (autumn art exhibition) in the Grand Palais. — *September*
Internationale des Antiquaires (biennial antiques fair on even-numbered years; until October)
Biennale de Paris: exhibitions and installations by young International avant-garde artists (even numbered years, until November)
Festival International de Danse: major international ballet festival (until mid-December)
Festival d'Automne (autumn festival): modern music, jazz, drama, folk (until December)
Festival de l'Ile-de-France (until December)
Festival de Musique de Chambre de Paris (Paris chamber music festival)

Salon de l'Automobile (international motor show): Parc des Expositions, Porte de Versailles; (every other year). — *October*
International film festival
Festival de Jazz
Vendanges de Montmartre: celebration of the wine harvest of Montmartre's last remaining vineyard on the first Saturday in October (cnr. rue des Saules/rue de l'Abreuvoir), parade, music, dancing, etc.
Prix de l'Arc de Triomphe horse race, Hippodrome de Longchamp (see Sport).

Fashion in Paris – a reawakening

They come from London, Antwerp and New York. They are called John Galliano, Alexander McQueen and Stella McCartney, Martin Margiela and Alber Elbaz. These "enfants terribles" have reawakened the world of Paris fashion. The haute couture scene of Christian Dior, Givenchy, Chloé, Hermès and Guy Laroche had become very quiet. Hand-sewn luxury fashions costing between £10,000/$16,000 and £100,000/$160,000 scarcely cater for today's breed of customers and therefore it is hardly surprising that only 15 of the largest fashion houses have survived, compared with the 100 which existed fifty years ago. As to whether the new avant-garde with their modern slant will be able to rescue the legendary world of haute couture remains to be seen.

The world of fashion descends on Paris four times a year: in January and July there are collections of haute couture; in March and September it is the turn of prêt-à-porter (ready to wear). In 1997 the Belgian Martin Margiela celebrated his autumn show for Hermès as fashion without models: the clothes were hung flat and gathered up on iron clothes hangers and were displayed by people in white hospital coats. The English eccentric John Galliano (b. 1961) who succeeded Gianfranco Ferré at the house of Dior, aroused the hoped-for storm with his innovations; a former punk Alexander McQueen (b. 1970) now creates fashion for Givenchy. "Tough and tender" are the designs made by Stella McCartney (b. 1971) for Chloé: sensuous fashion for confident ladies. At Guy Laroche the New Yorker Alber Elbaz (b. 1962) runs a successful operation and shows flair in combining American marketing with French style.

But Paris's claim to be the leading world centre for fashion does not date just from the present century. Louis XIV succeeded in getting the whole of Europe's aristocracy to don jerkins, breeches and full-bottomed wigs. Even rococo fashion with its protruding farthingales, heavily laced corsets and powdered wigs was created at the French court; while these self-same

symbols of silk and satin were then abolished by the French revolutionaries. The history of French fashion is told in a lively, gripping and lucid way at the **Musée de la Mode et du Textile**, re-opened in 1997 in the renovated Rohan wing of the Louvre. Those wishing to find out about current fashion need to take a look at the show-rooms in the main streets of "haute couture", the avenue Montaigne, rue du Faubourg St Honoré, boulevard de la Madeleine and rue Cambon.

It was an Englishman, in fact, who founded **haute couture** in France. Charles Frederick Worth had settled in Paris around the middle of the 19th century. He introduced the idea of a model to display individual clothes and the "collection" became part of his considerable commercial success. Worth was the first to use a mannequin, his wife Marie, to model his clothes, and he used his signature as a trademark, something which was also new. 1868 saw the setting-up of the "Chambre Syndicale de la Couture Française" which drew up strict rules to regulate the rights and obligations of those fashion houses taking part in the scheme. Worth exerted a powerful influence on international fashion for a period of over thirty years, from the crinoline through to the cul de Paris, until finally Paul Poiret freed women from corsets and hoop skirts at the beginning of the 20th c. The person who really master-minded a radical reform of the world of fashion was **Coco Chanel**. After the First World War she saw that the new generation of women had undergone a fundamental change, now taking on new jobs and roles with a new-found confidence and no longer accepting their traditional sexually inferior position. Professional women now had just as little use for long, restricting and heavy clothes as they did for long showy hair styles. "True elegance", as Coco Chanel put it, "requires unrestricted freedom of movement". Men's clothes and working clothes provided her with a host of new ideas for creating functional, comfortable and uncomplicated garments for women. She did not see her models as being totally exclusive, but always as a suggestion which could be imitated, whether for home dressmaking or for factory production.

Her shirtwaisters and jersey ensembles with straight jackets and pullovers became standard items. In this way Coco Chanel made a decisive impact on women's fashions in the 1920s. The arrival of her "Chanel No. 5" on the market – still highly successful even today – was like a revolution. Like her clothes, this scent was intended to be appropriate for every occasion. Ernest Beaux, a perfumer of genius, had presented Chanel with 10 different creations, numbered from 1 to 5 and 20 to 24. Her choice fell on the No. 5, partly

fashion houses were opened in Paris in the 1920s and 1930s: Vionnet, Grès, Schiaparelli, Rochas, Lanvin... A real sensation was created, however, by the appearance of Christian Dior's first collection on February 12th 1947. To counter the drab fashions of wartime he came up with the elegant "Ligne Corolle" (corolla line), which was designated the "New Look" in the international press and today is admired as a museum piece. A "Dior dress" – this dream of countless women in the post-war period became a symbol of

Elegant costumes and the "little black dress" made Coco Chanel famous

because it was her lucky number and also because she wanted to be able to introduce the perfume with her new collection on May 5th. A limpid freshness and a colourless crystal cube with a white label underline the simple elegance of the scent, which soon became the most widely sold perfume in the world and ushered in the great era of "designer scents". And it was no less a person than Marilyn Monroe who breathed the words: "When I go to bed all I wear is a few drops of Chanel No. 5."

A large number of haute couture

everything that was desirable and yet out of reach for the ordinary person. To be fashionably dressed was a sign of mystique and social standing and wealthy private customers, crowned heads of state and film stars formed the financial backbone of French haute couture, which in turn set the tone for fashion world wide. Notwithstanding Chanel's scornful comment: "Dior? He doesn't clothe women, he carpets them", luminaries such as Marlene Dietrich and Eva Perón went to Dior's studio in the avenue Montaigne to have their dresses made, while the British Princess Margaret wore the "new look" during a state visit to France. In 1952 **Hubert de Givenchy** was suddenly catapulted to world fame when he designed Audrey Hepburn's wardrobe for the Billy Wilder film "Sabrina". Hepburn again wore clothes by Givenchy in the cult picture "Breakfast at Tiffany's", while Grace Kelly and Jacqueline Kennedy were among his customers. In 1953 Coco Chanel decided to reopen the house of Chanel in the rue Cambon and in the following year the Chanel costume in her summer collection acquired classic status.

An entirely new commercial situation developed in the 1960s. Young people were setting the standards and they had no time for the exclusive and dictatorial world of haute couture. For the first time the mature woman had to give up her dominant rule in world fashion and make concessions to youth. However, these changes were not recognised in Paris, but in London. At the end of the war a training course for fashion designers had been established at the Royal College of Art and by the end of the fifties the beneficiaries of this scheme were beginning to make their names with unconventional ideas – first and foremost Mary Quant, who launched the mini-skirt and with the opening of boutiques led fashion away from the exclusivity of made-to-measure haute couture. By now even Paris was forced to recognise the changing market. The couturiers began to design collections for the younger generation. In 1965 the first "Salon du **prêt-à-porter**" was set up in Paris and in 1973 the "Chambre Syndicale du Prêt-à-porter des Couturiers et Créateurs de Mode", responsible just for prêt-à-porter, was established. New fashion creators arrived on the scene: Louis Féraud presented his first collection in 1960; **Yves Saint Laurent** went independent in 1962 and during the 1970s and 1980s was considered one of the leading couturiers, along with the houses of Dior, Cardin, Laroche, Scherrer, Castelbajac, Courrèges, Rykiel and Chanel. The most notable of the 1980s avant-garde was **Jean-Paul Gaultier**, who worked first as a designer at Cardin and then presented his first collection in

1976. "My strongest muscle is my eye", avers Gaultier, always on the hunt for arresting images. He became well-known because his fashion, inspired by the world of the streets and by other cultures, always treads the thin dividing-line between originality and bad taste. Gaultier combined the ballerina's dress with leather jacket and trainers, and with his "high-tech" collection parodied the classic Chanel costume by using artificial fur and a shower hose as a belt. He was the first to introduce the pattern-mix used by haute couture into prêt-à-porter, he moved from the "oversized look" to the skin-tight line and launched the naked waist beneath square protruding tops. He selects his models personally and will send a woman from the street onto the catwalk, as well as friends, dancers, punks and older ladies. Gaultier's turnover is derived from prêt-à-porter and perfumes, which alone account for half of it. And this despite the fact that his perfume bottle in the shape of a woman's corseted torso, met with resistance when it first appeared in 1993. The whole thing is marketed in a can. Since 1995 the sweet-smelling man has also been marketed in a can.

Strengthened by their country's economic boom, **Japanese fashion creators** have penetrated the French market. Kenzo Takada, Issey Miyake, Rei Kawakubo for Comme des Garçons and Johji Yamamoto invented the minimalist "Japanese" style: straight-lined collections with clear shapes, high-quality textiles and finely-conceived details which have been successfully varied right up to the present time. For the art historian **Christian Lacroix**, on the other hand, the motto is "If it pleases it's allowed": this master of pattern-mix delves deep into his chest of materials and combines fabrics which at first sight seem to conflict with one another but harmonize in the end. Plenty of colour, historical borrowings, Oriental and African influences: these are the elements to be found in the "neo-romantic " Lacroix. **Martina Sitbon** is another who turns historical costume into new old fashion. Her journey goes from the Middle Ages to the present, passing through every style. Stylistic elements are torn from their context and combined afresh: for example, she juxtaposed

Uncrowned king of French couturiers: Karl Lagerfeld

narrow floral-patterned drain-pipe trousers with buckled shoes from the time of Louis XIV. For years now **Yves Saint Laurent** has had little or no contact with the avant-garde. His clothes decorate but do not provoke. And yet it is he of all people who has discovered a future direction for the fashion world: in 1996, for the very first time, an haute couture display could be seen live on the internet on http://fashionlive.worldmedia.fr/YSL/. Internet users were able to peep behind the curtain before the couture countdown and experience the final preparations close up.

In order to reach even more people with prêt-à-porter fashion, the creative élite have recently been designing reasonably priced clothes for department stores and mail-order companies. And it is the latter, rather than internet selling, which has recently been used by **Karl Lagerfeld** to reach the masses. The Hamburg-born designer with the Mozart pigtail has been in charge of Chanel since 1983. In contrast with the furore caused by the "enfants terribles", Lagerfeld's fashions owe their styles to a classic modern concept: clear lines,

openly geometric patterns and an irresistible simplicity.

Fashion for the masses is also available at "Tati". In its nine branches around Paris this French chain of department stores sells all kinds of discontinued lines and leftover stock, bargains and designer fashion. The largest branch is located next to the Barbès-Rochechouart métro station and was opened as long ago as 1947. Its founder Jules Ouaki created the shop-window, invented self service shopping and the bargain counter. This, the biggest cut-price store in the whole country, today has a turnover of some £200 million/$350 million each year. Once past the polyester jerseys and household goods, shoppers will come to the store's own in-house designer label, "La rue est à nous", designed by Gilles Rosier and Claude Sabbah, who were previously employed at Dior and Gaultier. No item costs much more than £30/$50 and the smart clothes are particularly popular with young people. Even such a prestigious store as "Galeries Lafayette" has recently set up a special area for these sorts of fashions.

Excursions

November   November 11th: Armistice Day ceremony at the Arc de Triomphe
Festival d'Art Sacré (festival of sacred art; until December)

What's On Listings

Weekly listings magazines   Paris has several listings magazines. On sale everywhere and covering the week from Wednesday to the following Tuesday, they are: L'Officiel des Spectacles, Semaine de Paris, Pariscope and 7 à Paris.

Monthly listings   Paris Capitale and Nova are monthly periodicals with the very latest news on what's happening and where it's all at.

Office du Tourisme publications   The head office of the Office du Tourisme (see Information) stocks masses of up-to-date events leaflets, including "Paris sélection", a monthly publication with sections in other languages.

Maison d'Information Culturelle   26 rue Beaubourg (3rd arr.); tel. 01 42 74 27 07
Open daily except Sun. 10am–8pm
The cultural information centre provides free information about everything happening in Paris on the cultural scene.

Excursions

For visitors with time to spare there a number of places well worth visiting within easy reach of Paris, whether by public transport or on a sightseeing tour. Details of tour operators and tours of this kind are available from the Office du Tourisme (see Information).

Breteuil
Château and park   Location: 35km/22 miles south-west of Paris
The restored 17th c. château is an attractive setting for the concerts and other events in Paris's summer festival (see Events, Festival Estival). The park was designed by famous landscape gardener André le Nôtre

Champs
★Rococo château   Location: 20km/12½ miles east of Paris
The former village of Champs-sur-Marne holds the sumptuously appointed Rococo château built in the early 18th c. by Madame de Pompadour (née Jeanne Antoinette Poisson), Louis XV's official mistress. Acquired by the State in 1935, with its well preserved interior (fine wood panelling, Salon Chinois) it is a magnificent example of the Louis Quinze period. The park, laid out by Claude Desgots, a nephew of Le Nôtre, was lovingly restored early in the 20th c.

Chantilly   See A to Z, Chantilly

Compiègne   Location: 85km/53 miles north-east of Paris
The town of Compiègne (pop. 44,000), on the left bank of the Oise, was a favourite residence of the kings of France from Merovingian times onwards, and with its large château and extensive forest still attracts many visitors. Here in 1430 Joan of Arc was taken prisoner by the Burgundians and handed over to the English. In the Forest of
★Forest   Compiègne, now criss-crossed by footpaths and hiking trails, stood the railway carriage (now replaced by a replica) in which the armistice with Germany was signed on November 11th 1918. The classical-
★Château   style château, built for Louis XV by Jacques-Ange Gabriel between 1751 and 1788, now houses a museum and a carriage collection.
     The Hôtel de Ville (Town Hall, 1505–11) holds the Musée de la Figurine Historique. To the west of the Town Hall is the 18th c. Hôtel de Songeons, with the Musée Vivenel (sculpture, pictures, drawings,

Never out of fashion – an excursion to the country to sit in the sun and eat icecream

ceramics, enamels). There are two interesting churches, Saint-Antoine (13th/16th c.) and Saint-Jacques (early Gothic, with 15th c. alterations), which has a 49m/160ft high tower.

See A to Z, Disneyland · Paris

Disneyland · Paris

Location: 20km/12½ miles north of Paris
This charming little town (pop. 4500) is the location of the Château d'Ecouen (1541–55), now the Musée National de la Renaissance. The church of Saint-Accueil has a late Gothic choir and fine 16th c. windows.

Ecouen
★Musée de la Renaissance

See A to Z, Fontainebleau

Fontainebleau

See A to Z, Maisons Laffitte

Maisons Laffitte

See A to Z, Malmaison

Malmaison

Location: 9km/5½ miles south-west of Paris
An enjoyable way of getting to Meudon in fine weather is to go by boat on the Seine.
 The suburb of Meudon (alt. 30m/98ft–153m/502ft; pop. 52,000), situated on terraces above the left bank of the Seine, has been home in the past to illustrious artists, politicians and musicians. Poets and writers Ronsard and Rabelais, Balzac and Céline all lived here, Richard Wagner wrote his "Flying Dutchman" in 1841 at 17 Avenue du Château, and Hans Arp lived here from 1929 to 1941; his house in rue des Châtaigniers (Clamart) is now a museum (open Fri.–Sun. 2–6pm).

Meudon

Excursions

★Terrasse de Meudon

Above the old part of town to the west, at an altitude of 100m/330ft, is the Terrasse de Meudon (accessible until dusk), with a fine 16th–18th c. church. The terrace affords fine views of the Seine valley and Paris. At its south-west corner, in the Château de Meudon (destroyed 1871; later rebuilt with alterations), is the Astrophysical Observatory. To the west of the terrace, reached by way of a flight of iron steps and the château park, is the Bois de Meudon, with its beautiful little lakes (Etang de Villebon, Etang de Trivaux), a popular excursion for the Parisians.

Bois de Meudon

★Villa des Brillants, Musée Rodin

The Villa des Brillants, on Meudon's north-eastern outskirts, is where Auguste Rodin spent the last 20 years of his life; he is buried in the park with his lifelong companion Rose Beuret. The house is now a museum, with sketches, models and casts of the great sculptor's work (including Honoré de Balzac, 1891, Victor Hugo, 1890, Porte de l'Enfer, 1880).

At 11 Rue des Pierres is a house once occupied by Molière's wife, Armande Béjart, now a museum (history of the château; mementoes of notable residents of Meudon, including Wagner, Courbet and Rodin).

Bellevue

North-west of Meudon, also on a terrace above the Seine, is the residential suburb of Bellevue. The château which was built here in the mid 18th c. for Madame de Pompadour, Louis XV's favourite – in its day one of Europe's most famous summer palaces – was destroyed during the French Revolution.

Rambouillet

See A to Z, Rambouillet

Saint-Cloud

Location: 12km/7¹/₂ miles south-west of Paris
The suburb of Saint-Cloud (pop. 28,000) is in a lovely setting on the left bank of the Seine. The Parc de Saint-Cloud (area 450 hectares/1100 acres), laid out by André Le Nôtre in the 17th c., is on a plateau between Saint-Cloud and Sèvres. From the "Lanterne de Diogène", a terrace at the east end of the park, there are superb views of Paris and the Seine basin. Some 500m/550yds north of this are the fountains of the Grande Cascade (1734, by Antoine Lepautre and Hardouin-Mansart) and the Grand Jet, which on certain Sundays (alternating with Versailles, see A to Z) shoots up to a height of 42m/140ft. Below the plateau to the south-east is the Pavillon de Breteuil, headquarters of the International Weights and Measures Office, keeper of the standard measures (in platinum) of the metre and kilogram.

★Parc de Saint-Cloud

St-Germain-en-Laye

See A to Z, St-Germain-en-Laye

Sceaux
Château

Location: 10km/6 miles south-west of Paris
The château at Sceaux, nestling picturesquely on a hillside, was built in 1856 on the site of a house that belonged to Colbert, Louis XIV's minister of finance, and which fell victim to the French Revolution. Nowadays it contains the Musée de l'Ile de France (art, literature, folklore; see Museums). From July to October the Orangerie (by Jules Hardouin-Mansart, 1685) is the venue for recitals and concerts of chamber music. The park (area 228 hectares/563 acres) is one of André Le Nôtre's great masterpieces.

Senlis

Location: 50km/30 miles north-east of Paris
The trim little town of Senlis (pop. 15,3000) was the see of a bishop from the 3rd c. until 1790. The former Cathedral of Notre-Dame (1153–84), with a richly sculptured west doorway and a beautiful interior, is on the north-eastern edge of the old town. Near the cathedral are remains of the Gallo-Roman town walls and a ....teau (Hunting Museum), and there are the ruins of a P..... .eatre on the town's western outskirts.

★Notre-Dame

Location: 10km/6 miles west of Paris

The suburb of Sèvres (pop. 20,500) lies on the left bank of the Seine. On the north side of its Grande Rue, near the bridge over the Seine, is the famous Sèvres porcelain factory. Originally founded in 1738 at Vincennes, it was moved to Sèvres in 1756 and transferred to its present premises in 1876 (conducted tours; open Wed.–Mon. 10am– 5pm). The bottom two floors hold the Musée National de Céramique, established in 1824 by Alexandre Brongniart, with collections of earthenware, Oriental ceramics, faience, porcelain, etc. (including a 3.15m/10½ ft high Neptune vase, 1867).

★Porcelain factory

Musée Céramique

Location: 50km/30 miles west of Paris

The circular park around the delightful 17th c. château of Thoiry holds a zoo and the Réserve Africaine, a drive-through African safari park.

Thoiry
★Réserve Africaine

See A to Z, Vaux-le-Vicomte

Vaux-le-Vicomte

See A to Z, Versailles

Versailles

Food and Drink

French cuisine is world-famed both for its quality and its variety. Since the average Frenchman attaches importance to a well chosen menu and sets aside between one and two hours for his meals, eating plays an important part in daily life and has developed into an essential component of French culture.

French cuisine

A concern with the quality and variety of meals is believed to have been brought to the French court by Henri II's wife Catherine de Médicis, and like all courtly fashions to have spread from there to the ordinary French household. Henri IV, seeking to better the lot of the people of France, declared that he wanted every peasant to have a chicken for his Sunday dinner. The French Revolution brought with it not only civil liberties but also a higher standard of cuisine for ordinary people. In 1827 Anthelme Brillat-Savarin wrote his "Physiologie du Goût" ("Physiology of Taste"), which still provides a philosophical basis for the enjoyment of good food. In 1986 a University of Cooking was established in the Château du Vivier in Écully, where the most celebrated chefs in France teach the high art of French cuisine.

Characteristic features of the highest standard of French cooking (*haute cuisine*) are careful preparation, the use of fresh ingredients (anything canned or preserved is anathema), delicacies such as truffles, mushrooms and cognac, as well as butter and cream (*crème fraîche*). Herbs and spices are used on a large scale and in a variety of combinations. French sauces are famous.

Haute cuisine

In recent years there has been much talk of *nouvelle cuisine*, which avoids over-elaboration and seeks to bring out the natural taste of the finest and freshest ingredients.

Nouvelle cuisine

There are also various regional cuisines which are esteemed by the most discriminating palates.

Cuisine régionale

Visitors to France should not ignore this aspect of French culture, even though it may sometimes occupy a good deal of valuable sight-seeing time. Some experience of this essential element in the famous French *savoir vivre* is necessary for anyone who really wants to get to know France.

Meals

The simple French *petit déjeuner* (breakfast), with white or black coffee, tea or chocolate and croissants or rolls, is often taken in a café. Lunch (*déjeuner*) is served in restaurants between noon and 2.30pm, and may be either a set meal (*menu*) consisting of hors d'oeuvre, main course and cheese and/or dessert, followed by coffee, or an *à la carte* meal selected from the full menu (carte). The evening meal (*dîner or souper*) is similar to lunch, except that the hors d'oeuvre is usually replaced by soup. White bread is the usual accompaniment to a meal, cut either from the long crisp *baguettes* or the shorter *flûtes*. The fixed-price menu is cheaper than an *à la carte* meal, and the price will sometimes include wine. The *plat du jour* ("dish of the day") is also good value.

Drinks

The meal is accompanied by wine almost as a matter of course. Some French wines are, of course, world-famous, and correspondingly expensive. For everyday drinking, however, an ordinary country wine is recommended (a *petit blanc* or a *petit rouge*), in a carafe (about $1/2$ litre) or carafon ($1/4$ litre). When ordering wine in bottle – either a full bottle (*bouteille entière*) or half bottle (*demi-bouteille*) – it is a good idea to ask the waiter's advice.

There are also good French beers, now increasingly popular, from Alsace (Pêcheur, Kronenbourg, Kanterbräu, Mutzig) and Lorraine (Champigneulles, Vézélise). Beer is either in bottle (*cannette*) or draught (*bière pression*). A small glass of draught beer is called a *demi*.

France has a wide range of mineral waters, either still (*eau minérale non-gazeuse*) or containing carbonic acid (*eau gazeuse*). The best known brands are Perrier, Vichy, Evian, Vittel and Contrexéville.

Glossary of food terms

See Language, Food and Drink

Galleries

Paris has a great many art dealers and galleries. Most of them are located in and around Saint-Germain des Près, the Marais, Bastille and the Louvre.

The Galleries Association publishes a free monthly programme listing the current exhibitions which is obtainable from the galleries themselves or ordered from: Associations des Galeries; tel. 01 48 44 29 28, fax 01 42 38 63 54.

Beaubourg/
Les Halles

Bama
40 rue Quincampoix (4th arr.); tel. 01 42 77 38 87
Open Tue.–Sat. 2.30–7pm
Avant-garde art

Alain Blondel
4 rue Aubry-le-Boucher (4th arr.); tel. 01 42 78 66 67
50 rue de Temple (4th arr.); tel. 01 42 71 85 86
Open: Tue.–Fri. 11am–7pm, Sat. 2–7pm
Realism and Thirties art

Crousel-Hussenot
80 rue Quincampoix (3rd arr.); tel. 01 48 87 60 81
Open Tue.–Sat. 2.30–7.30pm
Avant garde art

Daniel Templon
30 rue Beaubourg (3rd arr.); tel. 01 42 72 14 10
Open Tue.–Sat. 10am–7pm
Famous artists from New York, Germany, France

Beaubourg
23 rue du Renard (4th arr.); tel. 01 42 71 20 50
Open Tue.–Sat. 10.30am–1pm, 2.30–7
Art by César and Yves Klein, Edouard Pignon and Joseph Beuys

Farideh Cadot
77 rue des Archives (3rd arr.); tel. 01 42 78 08 36
Open Tue.–Sat. 10.30–12, 2–7pm
French and foreign artists such as Wilden Salomé, Luciano Castelli,
Fischer, Hazzlitt and Sonneman

Durand-Dessert
3 rue des Haudriettes (3rd arr.); tel. 01 42 77 63 60
Open Tue.–Sat. 2–7pm
European avant garde, including Richter, Morellet, Tosani

Dina Vierny
36 rue Jacob (6th arr.); tel. 01 42 61 32 83
Open Tue.–Sat. 10–12, 3–7pm
Drawings by Maillol, Matisse, etc.

Saint-Germain
des Près

Denise René
196 boulevard Saint-Germain (7th arr.); tel. 01 42 22 11 02
Open Tue.–Sat. 10am–1pm, 2.30–7
Kinetic and neo-constructivist art

Albert Loeb
10/12 rue des Beaux-Arts (6th arr.); tel. 01 46 33 06 87
Open Tue.–Sat. 10–12.30, 5.30–6.30pm
French painting from the Sixties and Seventies

Karl Flinker
25 rue de Tournon (6th arr.); tel. 01 43 25 18 73
Open Tue.–Sat. 10–1pm, 2.30–7
Older generation of contemporary painters

Jaquester
153 rue Saint-Martin; tel. 01 42 78 16 66
Open Tue.–Sat. 2–7pm
Modern art

3rd
arrondissement

Galerie Art et Publicité
183/185 rue Saint Martin; tel. 01 48 87 46 28
Open Tue.–Sat. 2–7pm
Art and advertising, including old enamel signs

Bernheim Jeune
27 avenue Matignon; tel. 01 42 66 60 31
Open Tue.–Sat. 10.30—12.30, 2.30–6.30
Fin de siècle art

8th
arrondissement

Ariel
140 boulevard Haussmann; tel. 01 45 62 13 09
Open Mon.–Fri. 10.30–1pm, 2.30–6.30
Fifties art and works of the new "Ecole de Paris"

Artcurial
9 avenue Matignon; tel. 01 42 99 16 16
Open Tue.–Sat. 10.30am–7.15pm
Art market sponsored by L'Oréal cosmetics

Vitesse
48 rue de Berri; tel. 01 42 25 48 13
Art on the themes of toys and motor racing

11th
arrondissement

Art à la Bastille
27 rue de Charonne
Consortium of 25 galleries with modern Parisian art, including Nane
Starn, Leif Stähle, Galerie Keller

14th
arrondissement

Galerie des Colonnes (Ensemble Ricardo Bofill)
86 rue du Château; tel. 01 43 27 11 86
Open Mon.–Sat. 11.15–1.15pm, 2–7
Art of the Thirties

Photographic
galleries

Viviane Esders
12 rue Saint-Merri (4th arr.); tel. 01 42 71 03 12
Open Tue.–Fri. 2–7pm
Exclusive photoworks

Zabriski
37 rue Quincampoix (4th arr.); tel. 01 42 72 35 47
Open Tue.–Sat. 11am–7pm
One of the top international photograph galleries

Texbraun
12 rue Mazarine (6th arr.); tel. 01 46 33 14 57
Open Tue.–Sat. 2.30–7pm
Photography of the Seventies and Eighties

Agathe Gaillard
3 rue du Pont-Louis-Philippe (4th arr.); tel. 01 42 77 38 42
Open Tue.–Sat. 1–7pm
One of the oldest photograph galleries in Paris – top names at top prices

Getting to Paris

By air

The quickest way of getting to Paris is by air. There are scheduled
flights to Paris from London, New York, Toronto, Johannesburg, etc.
and plenty of charter flights and package deals to the city's two international airports (see Air Travel).

By car

With the opening of the Channel Tunnel Paris is now within easy
reach of London by road. The route by road is the M20 to Ashford
where cars are loaded on "le Shuttle". The journey through the
tunnel to Calais takes 35 minutes then the route continues on the
A15 motorway to Paris. The Shuttle operates throughout the year,
24 hours a day, with up to four departures an hour at peak times.
Advance booking is not required.
   There are still numerous car ferries across the Channel. The shortest
crossing is Dover to Calais (35 minutes by hovercraft, 75–90 minutes
by ferry). Folkestone–Boulogne by Seacat takes 55 minutes, Rams-
gate–Dunkirk 90 minutes, Newhaven-Dieppe 4 hours.

By coach

A number of coach services operate between London and Paris.
These include Eurolines, 52 Grosvenor Gardens, London SW1W 0AU;
enquiries: 01582 404 511, telesales 0990 143 219. The journey takes
about 9 hours.

By rail

The Channel Tunnel has brought Paris within three hours of London
by rail. The Eurostar service runs between London Waterloo and Gare

du Nord Paris up to 17 times a day. Passport and customs controls take place on the train. There are buffet coaches and a trolley service for light refreshments; the first-class fare includes a meal served at your seat.

Health Care

Nationals of EU countries are entitled to health care under the French health services on the same basis as the French. This means paying for treatment and medicines but being reimbursed between 70% and 80% of the cost by the local sickness insurance office (caisse primaire d'assurance maladie). Visiting EU nationals need to bring form E111 with them. To get a refund in Paris present your form E111, along with any certificates of treatment (feuille de soins) or receipts for medication, to Social Security (Securité sociale): Centre 461, Relations internationales, 173 rue de Bercy, F-75012 Paris; tel. 01 40 19 53 00.

Health insurance

However, to be on the safe side, both EU and non-EU nationals would be well advised to take out some form of short-term health insurance, if only to save time and ensure complete cover.

S.O.S. Médicin (24 hours); tel. 01 47 07 77 77
S.O.S. Docteur nuit (at night); tel. 01 43 37 77 77
SAMU (Service Aide d'Urgence)
tel. 01 45 67 50 50 or tel. 15

Emergency medical care

S.O.S. dentaire (8–12pm)
tel. 01 43 37 51 00

Dental emergency

Hôtel Cochin, 27 rue du Faubourg Saint-Jacques (14th arr.);
tel. 01 42 34 17 60

Burns

Hôpital Fernand Vidal; tel. 01 40 37 04 04

Poisons

Hôpital Necker Enfants Malades; 149/151 rue de Sèvres (15th arr.)
tel. 01 44 49 42 90

Children's clinic

Open round-the-clock:
Pharmacie Dhéry/Galerie des Champs-Elysées
84 avenue des Champs-Elysées (8th arr.)
tel. 01 45 62 02 41; Métro: George V

Chemists (pharmacies)

Pharmacie Européenne de la Place de Clichy
6 place de Clichy (9th arr.)
tel. 01 48 74 65 18; Métro: Place de Clichy

Open at night:
Pharmacie des Arts, 106 boulevard Montparnasse (14th arr.)
tel. 01 43 35 44 88; Métro: Vavin
Open Mon.–Sat. till midnight, Sun. 8pm–midnight

Pharmacie d'Italie, 61 avenue d'Italie (13th arr.)
tel. 01 44 24 19 72; Métro: Tolbiac
open Mon.–Sat. till midnight, Sun. 8pm–midnight

Pharmacie Opéra, 6 boulevard des Capucines (9th arr.)
tel. 01 42 65 88 29; Métro: Opéra and Madeleine
Open Mon.–Sat. till 12.30pm in summer, midnight in winter; Sun., pub. hols. 3pm–12.30am in summer, 3–11pm in winter

Hotels

Categories

Paris has over 1500 hotels, and a booklet listing them is available from French national tourist offices. They are officially classified according to a star system, but those listed here have been put into four categories based on price. The budget category, with one star (★), ranges between 180 and 350 francs for a double room, the next category up, with two stars (★★) and a greater degree of comfort, is from 350 to 700 francs, the next price range up, with three stars (★★★), is between 700 and 1200 francs, while top of the range hotels, with four stars (★★★★), are grand hotels charging between 1200 and 2500. The super de luxe hotels, though, are in a class of their own, charging 2500 francs and above, and warranting four stars and L for luxury (★★★★L). The number of rooms is denoted by "r". The rates that hotels charge must, by law, be posted up at the reception desk and in hotel rooms.

Reservations

Since Paris gets great numbers of visitors all year round, and even more in the peak holiday season, the fashion weeks and during the Tour de France, it is essential to book well in advance. Reservations can be made either with hotels direct or through a travel agent. The simplest way of booking direct is by fax with a credit card number. Some hotels expect a telephone booking to be confirmed with a cheque in payment for the first night. The official hotel reservation offices (see Information, Office du Tourisme) will only book rooms for immediate use.

Exclusive, discrete and luxurious – the Hotel de Crillon in the Place de la Concorde

List of Hotels (a selection)

★★★★L Bristol
112 rue du Faubourg Saint-Honoré (8th arr.), 200 r.
tel. 01 53 43 43 00, fax 01 53 43 43 01
A veritable palace of a hotel, in the super luxury class, with Louis Quinze and Seize furniture, oriental rugs and original paintings. All this has its price of course – 2500 francs and upwards. The swimming pool on the sixth floor has a wonderful panoramic view of Paris; the restaurant owes its magnificent ambience to crystal chandeliers, wood panelling and sumptuous neo-rococo decor, and the waiters even wear tailcoats. The cuisine is still top quality, thanks to the new head chef, Michel del Burgo, who can transform the most humble ingredients into exquisite culinary delights.

Super
luxury hotels

★★★★L Crillon (de)
10 place de la Concorde (8th arr.), 163 r.
tel. 01 44 71 15 00, fax 01 44 71 15 02
The Crillon is not just one of the best addresses in Paris, it is one of the top hotels in the world. Many of the rooms and suites in this grandest of grand hotels near the Champs-Elysées are fitted out with silk drapes, antique furniture and marble bathrooms. The superb reception rooms date from the 18th c., and there is nowhere to equal the Leonard Bernstein suite, with its penthouse terrace garden and view over the rooftops of Paris. Many VIPs, Michael Jackson and Yassir Arafat among them, have elected to stay at the Crillon.

★★★★L Inter Continental
3 rue de Castiglione (1st arr.), 450 r.
tel. 01 44 77 11 11, fax 01 44 77 14 60
This most perfectly run of establishments leaves nothing to be desired. Its Salon Imperial is a listed showcase in itself, and there are some lovely views of the Tuileries.

★★★★L, Plaza-Athénée
25 avenue Montaigne (8th arr.), 205 r.
tel. 01 53 67 66 65, fax 01 53 67 66 66
Located in the elegant haute couture district, just a few yards from Christian Dior and Chanel, this super de luxe hotel is where the fashion VIPs gather – models, couturiers and their celebrity clientele. The hotel's special feature is its lush green courtyard, and the adjoining rooms are sought after accordingly. The Bar Anglais is where Mata Hari, the legendary First World War spy, was arrested.

★★★★L Ritz
15 place Vendôme (1st arr.), 187 r.
tel. 01 43 16 30 30, fax 01 43 16 36 68
One of the bars at the Ritz is named after Ernest Hemingway, who celebrated the Liberation of Paris here. And the crème de la crème and other celebrities continue to frequent this world-famous luxury hotel up to the present day. Only recently once again named the European hotel of the year, the Ritz maintains its reputation for a certain style of service whereby its highly trained staff are seemingly able to respond to a patron's wishes before they are even uttered. Incidentally, César Ritz was the first hotelier to offer his guests their own bathroom.

★★★★Buci
22 rue Buci (6th arr.), 24 r.
tel. 01 43 26 89 22, fax 01 46 33 80 31
This completely renovated 16th c. hotel in the middle of Saint-Germain des Prés is within easy walking distance of Notre-Dame, the Louvre, Jardin du Luxembourg and top fashion outlets such as Dior and Yves Saint-Laurent.

Luxury hotels

★★★★Manoir (au)
153 boulevard Saint-Germain (6th arr.), 32 r.
tel. 01 42 22 21 65, fax 01 45 48 22 25
A very modern hotel in Saint-Germain des Prés, opposite Flore and
Les Deux Magots and near the famous Brasserie Lipp, Au Manoir has
rooms with antique furniture and sound insulation. Reception is
friendly and solicitous.

★★★★Pavillon de la Reine
28 places des Vosges (3rd. arr.), 55 r.
tel. 01 40 29 19 19, fax 01 40 29 19 20
This little hotel in one of Paris's loveliest squares is very quiet despite
its central location. Part of it dates back to the 17th c., including the
grand lobby in the style of Louis XIII. The rooms either look onto the
hotel gardens or the flower-filled courtyard.

★★★★Relais Christine
3 rue Christine (6th arr.), 51 r.
tel. 01 40 51 60 80, fax 01 40 51 60 81
Although this former Augustinian 16th c. abbey in the heart of Saint
Germain has been fully converted and renovated the Relais Christine
still has something of the tranquil air of the cloister. Breakfast is
served in a beautiful room with a vaulted ceiling.

★★★★Saint-Honoré
15 rue Boissy d'Anglais (8th arr.), 112 r.
tel. 01 44 94 14 14, fax 01 44 94 14 28
The Sofitel Group hotel is on the Place de la Concorde, close to the
Champs-Elysées. Most of the rooms look onto an inner courtyard and
are therefore pleasantly quiet.

★★★★Westminster
13 rue de la Paix (2nd arr.), 102 r.
tel. 01 42 61 57 46, fax 01 42 60 30 66
Part of the Warwick International hotel chain, the Westminster,
located between Opéra and Place Vendôme, is surrounded by exquisite jewellers and fashion boutiques; it has 18 suites and 84 extremely
luxurious rooms.

Upper range for
comfort and price

★★★Bretonnerie
22 rue Sainte-Croix-de-la-Bretonnerie (4th arr.), 29 r.
tel. 01 48 87 77 63, fax 01 42 77 26 78
This 17th c. town-house in the heart of the Marais combines
modern comfort with a strong sense of the past that lingers on in
the timber beams and wooden furniture of the bedrooms as well as
the lounge and intimate little breakfast room. The standard of care
is excellent.

★★★Chevaliers (des)
30 rue de Turenne (3rd arr.), 24 r.
tel. 01 42 72 73 47, fax 01 42 72 54 10
Right in the historic Marais quarter, close to the Place des Vosges, the
Chevaliers has airy rooms in soothing colours, friendly reception and
breakfast served in a 17th c. vaulted crypt.

★★★Collège de France (du)
7 rue Thénard (5th arr.), 29 r.
tel. 01 43 26 78 36, fax 01 46 34 58 29
Hotel in the Latin Quarter with small unpretentious rooms plus double doors and windows for soundproofing; there is a lovely view over
the rooftops of Paris from the fifth floor.

Fantastically beautiful and wickedly expensive – a suite in the legendary Hotel Ritz

★★★Deux Iles
59 rue Saint-Louis-en-l'Ile (4th arr.), 17 r.
tel. 01 43 26 13 35, fax 01 43 29 60 25
The rooms in this very popular little hotel on the Ile Saint-Louis may not be large but are beautifully decorated. A former 17th c. mansion, the Deux Iles is particularly prized by its guests for the quiet location, intimate atmosphere and extremely good breakfasts. Early reservation is essential.

★★★Etoile-Pereire
146 boulevard Pereire (17th arr.), 25 r.
tel. 01 42 67 60 00, fax 01 42 67 02 90
Nearly all the rooms give onto a quiet courtyard; modern in style and facilities, they vary in size. Breakfast is outstanding, with 40 kinds of jam, and the location is particularly handy for getting onto the Périphérique or to the Air France Terminal.

★★★Gaillon Opéra Best Western
9 rue Gaillon (2nd arr.), 26 r.
tel. 01 47 42 47 74, fax 01 47 42 01 23
The rooms, with their timbered ceilings, have a rustic air about them and, although not particularly spacious, are extremely comfortable. The location is good – near the Opera and shops.

★★★Grands Hommes
17 place du Panthéon (5th arr.), 32 r.
tel. 01 46 34 19 60, fax 01 43 26 67 32
A hotel since it was first established in the 18th c., the Grands Hommes has superbly furnished rooms, two of them with a terrace. At one time the favourite haunt of the Surrealists, André Breton in particular, it has great views from the 5th and 6th floor rooms over the rooftops of Paris.

★★★Lenox
9 rue de l'Université (7th arr.), 34 r.
tel. 01 42 96 10 95, fax 01 42 61 52 83
This hotel is tastefully decorated in the English style. The pleasant staff deserves a mention and room service is available until 2am. It is worth trying for a room on an upper floor as these are quieter and more spacious. The surrounding University Quarter offers a chance for browsing in the bookshops and visiting the antique dealers.

★★★Lutèce
65 rue St-Louis-en-l'Ile (4th arr.), 23 r.
tel. 01 43 26 23 52, fax 01 43 29 60 25
Like the Deux Iles the Lutèce is in an old mansion on the idyllic Ile Saint-Louis. Here too the rooms are quite compact but quiet and stylishly decorated. This is a hotel with real charm.

★★★Marroniers
21 rue Jacob (6th arr.), 37 r.
tel. 01 43 25 30 60, fax 01 40 46 83 56
Although in an area bustling with life, the Marroniers itself is a haven of quiet and pleasurable comfort. The bedrooms are extremely attractive as are also the lounge and the breakfast room. In summer breakfast is served under the chestnut trees in the delightful garden.

★★★Montalembert
3 rue de Montalembert (7th arr.), 56 r.
tel. 01 45 49 68 68, fax 01 45 49 69 49
Top of the range hotel, with a touch of luxury, where gentle tones predominate with the odd splash of colour. The superb suites on the 8th floor are the work of celebrated designer Christian Liaigre. The cosy lounge holds a library for the benefit of guests.

★★★Novotel Paris Halles
8 place de M.-de-Navarre (1st arr.), 285 r.
tel. 01 42 21 31 31, fax 01 40 26 05 79
Close to the Pompidou Centre and Forum des Halles – modern architecture in glass and metal – this Novotel has rooms overlooking Les Halles.

★★★Perle (La)
14 rue des Canettes (6th arr.), 38 r.
tel. 01 43 29 10 10, fax 01 46 34 51 04
Although La Perle is on one of the busiest little streets in the heart of Saint-Germain des Prés, thanks to double glazing its comfortable rooms afford peace and quiet; most overlook the inner courtyard.

★★Alizé Grenelle
87 avenue Emile Zola (15th arr.), 50 r.
tel. 01 45 78 08 22, fax 01 40 59 03 06
Well set-up rooms with bath and minibar, and double-glazing to ensure a good night's sleep.

Middle range for comfort and price

★★André Gill
4 rue André Gill (18th arr.), 32 r.
tel. 01 42 62 48 48, fax 01 42 62 77 92
Directly on the Pigalle, this is a quiet and comfortable little place, and above all relatively good value.

★★Arts (des)
7 Cité Bergère (9th arr.), 26 r.
tel. 01 42 46 73 30, fax 01 48 00 94 42
Comfortable hotel in quiet location with its own car parking; close to such shopping meccas as Galeries Lafayette.

★★Brésil (du)
10 rue Le Goff (5th arr.), 30 r.
tel. 01 43 54 76 11, fax 01 46 33 45 78
This Latin Quarter hotel is unspectacular but the rooms are immaculate. Sigmund Freud stayed here in 1885.

★★Esméralda
4 rue Saint-Julien-le-Pauvre (5th arr.), 19 r.
tel. 01 43 54 19 20, fax 01 40 51 00 68
The rooms are small but this is no surprise given that this delightful little hotel behind the abbey of Saint-Julien-le-Pauvre is 300 years old. However their compactness is more than compensated for by the artistic decor, homely atmosphere and an unforgettable view of Notre Dame.

★★Grand Hôtel Joan of Arc
3 rue de Jarente (4th arr.), 36 r.
tel. 01 48 87 62 11, fax 01 48 87 37 31
In a quiet street that only gets noisy when July 14th is celebrated on the nearby Place Ste-Cathérine, the hotel has rooms furnished in Louis Quinze style.

★★Itinéraires
19 rue Salvador Allendé (92000 Nanterre), 137 r.
tel. 01 47 25 91 34, fax 01 47 21 84 21
A great barn of a place, and out of town, so what is its advantage? The price! It has rooms with up to 8 beds, ideal for families or small groups. All rooms up to 4 beds have shower and WC. And there's an excellent métro service from Nanterre into Paris.

★★Timhotel Jardin des Plantes
5 rue Linne (5th arr.), 33 r.
tel. 01 47 07 06 20, fax 01 47 07 62 74
Flowers are everywhere – on the carpets, curtains, bathroom tiles, etc. – and real ones in all the rooms and in the botanical gardens opposite. Then the weather is fine breakfast is served in the roof garden, where there is a superb view.

★★La Louisiane
60 rue de Seine (6th arr.), 80 r.
tel. 01 44 32 17 17, fax 01 46 34 23 87
La Louisiane has long been a favourite with writers, actors and musicians, numbering among its most famous guests Jean-Paul Sartre and Simone de Beauvoir.

★★Place des Vosges (de la)
12 rue Birague (4th arr.), 16 r.
tel. 01 42 72 60 46, fax 01 42 72 02 64
In a very quiet location, this pretty little 17th c. mansion is an ideal base for exploring the Marais. The lounge may have rustic charm but the bedrooms have every modern comfort.

★★Prima Lepic
29 rue Lepic (18th arr.), 38 r.
tel. 01 46 06 44 64, fax 01 46 06 66 11
Right in Montmartre, the Prima Lepic furnishes its rooms with a mixture of old and new so that each one is different, not too big but extremely comfortable.

★★Vieux Marais (du)
8 rue du Plâtre (4th arr.), 30r.
tel. 01 42 78 47 22, fax 01 42 78 34 32
Small, unpretentious hotel with a great welcome – this is a real find.

Information (Renseignements)

Budget hotels	★Centre (du) 112 rue de Charenton (12th arr.), 22 r. tel. 01 43 43 02 94, fax 01 43 43 51 52 Pleasant hotel with simple comfort. ★Ermitage 42bis rue de l'Ermitage (20th arr.), 24 r. tel. 01 46 36 23 44, fax 01 46 36 89 13 Small and simple, highly recommended for budget travellers. ★Saint André des Arts 66 rue Saint André des Arts (6th arr.), 31 r. tel. 01 43 26 96 16, fax 01 43 29 73 34 This hotel in the heart of Saint-Germain is particularly popular with young people. The rooms may be small but they can sleep up to four people.
Disneyland · Paris	Disneyland · Paris has seven themed hotels: ★★★★Disneyland (fairy-tale theme with magic castle etc.), ★★★★New York (like a New York skyscraper), ★★★★Newport Bay Club (smart resort style), ★★★Sequoia Lodge (modelled on a lodge in a National Park), ★★Cheyenne (Wild West theme), ★★Santa Fé (American south-west desert hotel), ★★Davy Crockett Ranch (trapper-style log cabins). Bookings: Disneyland Paris, Central Booking Office, B.P.153 F-77777 Marne-La-Vallée Cedex; fax 01 60 30 60 65
Private accommodation	Paris Accueil, 23 rue de Marignan (8th arr.); tel. 01 42 56 37 47 Locaflat, 63 avenue de la Motte Picquet (7th arr.); tel. 01 40 56 99 50

Information (Renseignements)

French tourist offices abroad

Australia	25 Bligh Street, Sydney NSW 2000 tel. (2) 9231 5244, fax (2) 9221 8682
Canada	1981 Av. McGill College, Suite 490, Montreal, Quebec H3A 2W9 tel. (514) 288 4264, fax (514) 845 4868 30 Patrick Street, Suite 700, Toronto, Ontario M5T 3A3 tel. (416) 593 4723, fax (416) 979 7587
Ireland	10 Suffolk Street, Dublin 2 tel. (1) 679 0813, fax (1) 679 0814
South Africa	c/o Air France, 196 Oxford Road, 1st Floor Oxford Manor, Illovo 2196, P.O. Box 41022, Craighall 2024; Johannesburg 20000; tel. (11) 880 8062, fax (11) 880 7772
United Kingdom	178 Piccadilly, London W1V 0AL tel. (0891) 244 123, fax (0171) 493 6594
United States	444 Madison Avenue, 16th floor, New York, NY 10022 tel. (212) 838 7800, fax (212) 838 7855 676 North Michigan Avenue, #3360, Chicago, Illinois 60611 tel. (312) 751 7800, fax (312) 337 6339 9454 Wilshire Boulevard, Suite 715, Beverly Hills, CA 90212 tel. (310) 271 6665, fax (310) 276 2835

In Paris

The French tourist office in Paris acts as a visitors' bureau which can help plan a visit and find a hotel. It also provides a number of leaflets about Paris, what's on listings, maps of the city, museum guides, etc.

Office du Tourisme et des Congrès de Paris

Bureau d'Accueil Central
127 avenue des Champs-Elysées;
tel. 01 49 52 53 54,
fax 01 49 52 53 00
Open daily 9am–8pm
(closed on May 1st)

Central office
8th arr.

Arrivée grandes lignes;
tel. 01 45 84 91 70
open Mon.–Sat. 8am–3pm

Gare d'Austerlitz
13th arr.

Hall d'arrivée;
tel. 01 46 07 17 73
open Mon.–Sat. 8am–9pm in high season, 8am–8pm in off season

Gare de l'Est
10th arr.

Sortie grandes lignes; tel. 01 43 43 33 24
open Mon.–Sat. 8am–9pm in high season, 8am–8pm in off season

Gare de Lyon
12th arr.

18 rue de Dunkerque; tel. 01 45 26 94 82
open Mon.–Sat. 8am–9pm in high season, Mon.–Sat. 8am–8pm in off season

Gare du Nord
10th arr.

15 boulevard de Vaugirard, Arrivée grandes lignes; tel. 01 43 22 19 19
open Mon.–Sat. 8am–9pm in high season, 8am–8pm in off season

Gare de Mont-parnasse15th arr.

Champs-de-Mars; tel. 01 45 51 22 15
open daily 11am–6pm May–Sep.

Tour Eiffel 7th arr.

Bureau d'acceuil, 29 rue de Rivoli; tel. 01 42 76 43 43
open Mon.–Sat. 9am–6pm

Mairie de Paris
4th arr.

127 avenue des Champs-Elysées (8th arr.)
tel. 01 49 52 53 91, fax 01 49 52 53 00

Bureau des Congrès

RATP (see Public Transport), the Paris transport authority, has two offices which give out general information and also sell tourist tickets for travel in Paris by bus, métro and RER:
53bis quai des Grands-Augustins (6th arr.); tel. 01 40 46 42 17
place de la Madeleine (8th arr.); tel. 01 42 65 31 81

RATP Services Touristiques

SITU is an electronic system to help you find your way around. Key in the address required and get a print-out of the best way of getting there by public transport.

SITU

Comité Régional de Tourisme, 26 avenue de l'Opéra (1st arr.)
tel. 01 42 60 28 62, fax 01 42 60 20 23

Région Ile-de-France

Espace Tourisme Ile-de-France du Carrousel du Louvre, 99 rue de Rivoli (1st arr.)
tel. 01 42 44 10 50, fax 01 42 44 10 59; open Wed.–Mon. 10am–7pm, closed January 1st, May 1st, December 25th.

Centre d'Information et de Documentation de la Jeunesse (CIDJ)
101 quai Branly (15th arr.); tel. 01 44 49 12 00
Métro: Bir-Hakeim; open Mon.–Sat. 9am–7pm
All kinds of information about accommodation, what's on, jobs, etc.

Information for young people

Service Parisien d'Accueil aux Etudiants Etrangers
6 rue Jean Calvin (5th arr.); tel. 01 40 79 91 00
Métro: RER Luxembourg; open Mon.–Fri. 9am–6pm
Bureau for welcoming foreign students; general information about
accommodation, what's on, studying in France.

Language

The French language developed out of the Vulgar Latin which was
spoken by the Celtic peoples of France during the Roman occupation,
and although in the course of history it has assimilated many words
of Celtic and later of Germanic origin it has preserved its Romance
character. For centuries it was the most important of the Romance
languages, widely spoken by educated people and in diplomatic inter-
course. Although it is the mother tongue of only some 80 million
people, it is taught in schools around the world and used as a language
of trade and communication over large areas of the globe, and
remains, therefore, one of the world's most important languages.

English is widely spoken in France, particularly in hotels, restaurants and sights frequented by visitors.

Pronunciation

Characteristic features are the placing of the stress towards the end of
the word and the frequent nasalisation of vowels.

Vowels (always pronounced without the diphthongisation found in
English): *ai* like English *ay*; *ais* an open *e* as in "bed"; *é* like *ay*; *è* and *ê*
an open *e*; *an*, *en*, *em* at the end of a syllable like a nasalised *on* (*not*
quite *ong*); *un*, *im*, *in*, *ein* at the end of a syllable like a nasalised *un*
(not quite *ung*); *eu* a little like the *u* in "*fur*"; *oi*, *oy* like *wa*; *ou* like *oo*;
u a sound obtained by pronouncing *ee* with rounded lips.

Consonants: *c* before *e*, *i* or *y* and *ç* before other vowels, like *s*; *c*
before *a*, *o* or *u* like *k*; *j*, and *g* before *e*, *i* or *y*, like *zh*; *g* before *a*, *o* or *u*
like a hard English *g*; *ch* like *sh*; *gn* usually like *ny* in "canyon"; *h*
always silent; *ll* between vowels often palatalised to a consonantal *y*
sound, but sometimes a light *l* (e.g. in *elle*); *q*, *qu* like *k*.

The following letters are usually silent at the end of a word (and
often also at the end of a syllable): *d*, *e*, *r* (only after *e*), *s*, *t*, *x*, *z*.

Numbers

0	zéro	22	vingt-deux
1	un, une	30	trente
2	deux	40	quarante
3	trois	50	cinquante
4	quatre	60	soixante
5	cinq	70	soixante-dix
6	six	71	soixante et onze
7	sept	80	quatre-vingt(s)
8	huit	81	quatre-vingt-un
9	neuf	90	quatre-vingt-dix
10	dix	91	quatre-vingt-onze
11	onze	100	cent
12	douze	101	cent un
13	treize	153	cent cinquante trois
14	quatorze	200	deux cent(s)
15	quinze	300	trois cent(s)
16	seize	400	quatre cent(s)
17	dix-sept	500	cinq cent(s)
18	dix-huit	1000	mille
19	dix-neuf	1001	mille un
20	vingt	2000	deux mille
21	vingt et un	1,000,000	un million

1st	premier		7th	septième	Ordinals
	première		8th	huitième	
2nd	deuxième		9th	neuvième	
	second(e)		10th	dixième	
3rd	troisième		11th	onzième	
4th	quatrième		12th	douzième	
5th	cinquième		100th	centième	
6th	sixième				

Half	demi(e)	Fractions
Third	tiers	
Quarter	quart	
Three-quarters	trois quarts	

When addressing anyone it is usual to add the polite Monsieur, Madame or Mademoiselle, and any request or enquiry should be accompanied by s'il vous plaît ("please").

Useful expressions

Good morning, good day!	Bonjour!
Good evening!	Bonsoir!
Good night!	Bonne nuit
Goodbye	Au revoir
Do you speak English?	Parlez-vous anglais?
I do not understand	Je ne comprends pas
Yes	Oui
No	Non
Please	S'il vous plaît
Thank you	Merci

Yesterday	Hier
Today	Aujourd'hui
Tomorrow	Demain
Help!	Au secours!
Have you a single room?	Avez-vous une chambre à un lit?
Have you a double room?	Avez-vous une chambre à deux lits?
Have you a room with private bath?	Avez-vous une chambre avec bain?
How much does it cost?	Combien (est-ce que) ça coûte? Quel est le prix de . . .?
Please wake me at 6	Veuillez me réveiller à six heures
Where is the lavatory?	Où sont les toilettes?
Where is the chemist's?	Où est la pharmacie?
Where is the post office?	Où est la poste?
Where is there a doctor?	Où y a-t-il un médecin?
Where is there a dentist?	Où y a-t-il un dentiste?
Is this the way to the station?	Est-ce le chemin de la gare?

January	Janvier	Months
February	Février	
March	Mars	
April	Avril	
May	Mai	
June	Juin	
July	Juillet	
August	Août	
September	Septembre	
October	Octobre	
November	Novembre	
December	Décembre	

Language

Days of the week	Sunday	Dimanche
	Monday	Lundi
	Tuesday	Mardi
	Wednesday	Mercredi
	Thursday	Jeudi
	Friday	Vendredi
	Saturday	Samedi

Festivals	Day	Jour, journée
	Public holiday	Jour de fête
	New Year	Nouvel An
	Easter	Pâques
	Ascension	Ascension
	Whitsun	Pentecôte
	Corpus Christi	Fête-Dieu
	Assumption	Assomption
	All Saints	Toussaint
	Christmas	Noël
	New Year's Eve	La Saint-Sylvestre

Road and traffic signs	Attention!	Caution
	Au pas!	Dead slow
	Bouchon	Tailback
	Brouillard	Fog
	Centre ville	To town centre
	Chantier	Road works
	Danger (de mort)	Danger (of death)
	Déviation	Diversion
	Douane	Customs
	Fin de limitation de vitesse	End of speed restriction
	Frontière	Frontier
	Garage	Parking; passing place
	Gravier, gravillons	Loose stones, gravel
	Halte!	Stop
	Impasse	No through road; cul-de-sac
	Limitation de vitesse	Speed restriction
	Passage interdit!	No entry, no thoroughfare
	Passage protégé	You have priority at junction ahead
	Poids lourds	Heavy loads
	Priorité à droite	Traffic coming from right has priority
	Prudence!	Drive with care
	Ralentir, ralentissez!	Reduce speed now
	Route barrée	Road closed
	Sens unique	One-way street
	Serrez à droite	Keep in to the right
	Sortie de camions	Trucks crossing
	Tenez vos distances!	Keep your distance
	Toutes directions	All directions
	Travaux	Road works
	Verglas	Black ice
	Virage (dangereux)	(Dangerous) bend
	Voie unique	Single-lane traffic
	Zone blue	Parking only with parking disc
	Zone rouge	"Red zone" (parking prohibited)
	Mise en fourrière immédiate	Parked cars may be towed away

Rail and air travel	Airport	Aéroport
	All aboard!	En voiture!
	Arrival	Arrivée
	Baggage	Bagages
	Baggage check	Bulletin de bagages
	Bus station	Gare routière

Couchette	Couchette	
Departure	Départ	
Flight	Vol	
Halt	Arrêt	
Information	Information, renseignements	
Lavatory	Toilette(s)	
Left luggage office	Consigne	
Line (railway)	Voie	
Luggage	Bagages	
Non-smoking	Non-fumeurs	
Platform	Quai	
Porter	Porteur	
Restaurant-car	Wagon-restaurant	
Sleeping-car	Wagon-lit	
Smoking	Fumeurs	
Station	Gare	
Stewardess	Hôtesse (de l'air)	
Stop	Arrêt	
Ticket	Billet, ticket	
Ticket collector	Contrôleur	
Ticket window	Guichet	
Timetable	Horaire	
Train	Train	
Waiting room	Salle d'attente	
Window seat	Coin fenêtre	
Address	Adresse	At the post office
Express	Exprès	
Letter	Lettre	
Letter-box	Boîte à lettres	
Parcel	Paquet, colis	
Postcard	Carte postale	
Poste restante	Poste restante	
Postman	Facteur	
Registered	Recommandé	
Small packet	Petit paquet	
Stamp	Timbre (-poste)	
Telegram	Télégramme	
Telephone	Téléphone	
Telex	Télex	
Abbaye	Abbey	Topographical terms
Arènes	Amphitheatre	
Autoroute	Motorway	
Avenue	Avenue	
Bain(s)	Bath(s)	
Banlieue	Suburb(s)	
Basilique	Church (usually one of particular dignity)	
Bassin	Dock; ornamental lake, pond	
Belvédère	Viewpoint	
Bibliothèque	Library	
Bois	Wood	
Boulevard	Boulevard, avenue	
Bourse	(Stock) exchange	
Butte	Low hill, bluff	
Camping	Camping site	
Carrefour	Road or street intersection	
Cascade	Waterfall	
Cathédrale	Cathedral	
Champ	Field	
Chapelle	Chapel	

Château	Castle, country house, manor-house
Château-fort	(Fortified) castle
Chemin	Road, track
Chemin de fer	Railway
Cimetière	Cemetery
Cité	City (often the old part of a town)
Cité universitaire	University residence(s)
Clocher	(Bell-)tower
Cloître	Cloister
Colonne	Column
Côté	Side
Cour	Courtyard
Cours	Avenue
Dôme	Dome
Donjon	Keep
Ecole	School
Ecole normale	Teachers' training college
Escalier	Staircase
Est	East
Faubourg	Suburb, outer district of town
Fleuve	River (flowing into sea)
Fontaine	Fountain
Forêt	Forest
Funiculaire	Funicular
Gare	Railway station
Golf	Golf-course
Halle	Market hall
Hameau	Hamlet
Hippodrome	Racecourse
Hôpital	Hospital
Horloge	Clock
Hôtel	Hotel; aristocratic mansion
Hôtel de ville	Town hall
Hôtel-Dieu	Hospital
Ile	Island
Impasse	Cul-de-sac
Jardin	Garden
Jardin des plantes	Botanic garden
Lac	Lake
Lycée	Grammar school
Mairie	Town hall
Maison	House
Marché	Market
Monastère	Monastery
Monnaie	Mint
Mont	Mount(ain)
Montagne	Mountain
Moulin	Mjll
Musée	Museum
Nef	Nave (of church)
Nord	North
Oratoire	Oratory
Ouest	West
Palais	Palace
Palais de justice	Law courts
Parc	Park
Passerelle	Footbridge
Piscine	Swimming pool
Place	Square
Pont	Bridge
Porcho	Porch

Port	Port, harbour
Portail	Doorway
Porte	Door
Poste	Post office
PTT	Post office
Quai	Quay; embankment
Quartier	Quarter, district (of a town)
Rivière	River (not flowing into sea)
Rond-point	Roundabout
Route	Road
Ru	Stream
Rue	Street
Salle	Hall, room
Square	Public square with gardens
Stade	Stadium
Sud	South
Tapisseries	Tapestries
Temple	Temple; Protestant church
Thermes	Baths
Tombe, tombeau	Tomb
Tour	Tower
Trésor	Treasure, treasury
Tribunal	Law court
Trottoir	Pavement
Université	University
Village	Village
Ville	Town

Food and Drink

Couvert place-setting (knife, fork, spoon, etc.). – Knife *couteau*; fork *fourchette*; spoon *cuiller*; glass *verre*; cup *tasse*; napkin *serviette (de table)*; corkscrew *tire-bouchon*.
Table-setting

Artichauts artichokes; *huîtres* oysters; *bouchées* pasties; *canapés* small open sandwiches, canapés; *cornichons* pickled gherkins; *foie gras* goose liver; *crudités* a selection of salad vegetables; *jambon cru* raw ham; *saumon fumé* smoked salmon.
Hors d'oeuvres

Bouillon clear meat soup; *consommé* clear soup; *potage* soup containing a variety of ingredients.
Soup

Œufs au plat fried eggs; *œufs pochés* poached eggs; *œufs brouillés* scrambled eggs; *œufs à la coque* soft-boiled eggs; *omelette* omelette; *omelette aux champignons* mushroom omelette; *omelette aux fines herbes* omelette with mixed herbs; *omelette au fromage* cheese omelette; *omelette au jambon* ham omelette.
Egg dishes

Aiglefin haddock; *anchois* anchovy; *anguille* eel; *barbeau* barbel; *barbue* brill; *brochet* perch; *cabillaud* cod; *carpe* carp; *carrelet* plaice; *colin* hake; *congre* conger-eel; *féra* dace; *flétan* halibut; *hareng* herring; *limande* dab; *maquereau* mackerel; *merlan* whiting; *ombre* grayling; *ombre chevalier* char; *perche* perch; *plie* plaice; *raie* ray, skate; *sardine* sardine; *saumon* salmon; *sole* sole; *tanche* tench; *thon* tunny; *truite* trout; *turbot* turbot. – *Crevettes* shrimps; *écrevisses* crayfish; *homard* lobster; *huîtres* oysters; *langouste* spiny lobster; *moules* mussels; *palourdes* clams; *clovisses* cockles; *oursin* sea-urchin. – *Cuisses de grenouille* frogs' thighs; *escargots* snails; *tortue* turtle.
Fish (poisson)

Agneau lamb; *boeuf* beef; *cochon de lait* sucking pig; *mouton* mutton; *porc* pork; *veau* veal.
Meat (viande)

Cuts of meat: *Ballotine* meat roll, galantine; *cervelle* brain; *côte* rib; *entrecôte* steak cut from the ribs; *escalope* fillet (of veal); *filet* fillet (of beef); *foie* liver; *gigot* leg of mutton; *jambon* ham; *langue* tongue; *pieds* feet; *poitrine* breast; *ris* sweetbread; *rognons* kidneys; *selle* saddle (of mutton), baron (of beef); *tête* head; *tournedos* fillet steak; *tripes* tripe.

Methods of cooking: *Carbonnade* meat grilled on charcoal; *cassoulet* stew made in an earthenware dish; *chaudfroid* in aspic; *civet* stew (of venison, etc.: *civet de lièvre* jugged hare); *émincé* thinly sliced meat served in sauce; *pâté* pâté; *rôti* roast; *soufflé* soufflé; *terrine* potted meat, pâté.

Poultry (volaille)

Bécasse woodcock; *caille* quail; *canard* duck; *caneton* duckling; *coq* cock; *dindonneau* turkey; *faisan* pheasant; *oie* goose; *perdreau* partridge; *pigeon* pigeon; *pintade* guineafowl; *poulet* chicken; *poularde* fattened pullet.

Game (gibier)

Cerf venison (red deer); *chevreuil* roe-deer; *lapereau* rabbit; *lièvre* hare; *sanglier* wild boar.

Vegetables (légumes)

Ail garlic; *artichaut* artichoke; *asperges* asparagus; *betterave* beetroot; *cardon* cardoon; *carotte* carrot; *céleris* celery; *chicorée* endive; *chou (blanc)* cabbage; *chou rouge* red cabbage; *choux de Bruxelles* Brussels sprouts; *chou-fleur* cauliflower; *chou-rave* kohl-rabi; *concombre* cucumber; *endive* chicory; *épinards* spinach; *fenouil* fennel; *haricots verts* French beans; *laitue* lettuce; *lentilles* lentils; *oignon* onion; *poireau* leek; *petits pois* peas; *salade verte* green salad; *salsifis* salsify; *tomate* tomato.

Potatoes and rice

Pommes de terre potatoes; *pommes frites* chips; *purée de pommes* potato purée, mashed potatoes; *pommes-croquettes* potato croquettes; *pommes à la dauphine* dauphine potatoes; *riz* rice.

Mushrooms (champignons)

Cèpes boletus mushrooms; *champignons de Paris* mushrooms (cultivated in the Loire valley); *chanterelles, girolles* chanterelles; *helvelles* turban-top mushrooms; *morilles* morels; *truffes* truffles.

Methods of cooking

Braisé braised; *farci* stuffed; *frit* fried; *glacé* glacé; *gratiné* gratiné; *grillé* grilled; *(à la) meunière* fried in butter; *poché* poached; *sauté* sauté.

Sweets (desserts)

Biscuits biscuits; *coupe glacée* ice-cream sundae; *crème* cream; *crème Chantilly* whipped cream; *crêpes* pancakes; *crêpes Suzette* dessert pancakes, flambé; *flan* custard; *gâteau* cake; *gaufrettes* waffles; *glace* ice; *mousse* mousse; *petits fours* fancy biscuits, petits fours; *sorbet* water ice; *tarte* tarte; *vermicelles à la Chantilly* chestnut mousse with whipped cream.

Fruit (fruits)

Abricot apricot; *amandes* almonds; *avelines* filberts; *cerises* cherries; *citron* lemon; *fraises* strawberries; *framboises* raspberries; *melon* melon; *noisettes* hazelnuts; *noix* walnuts; *orange* orange; *pastèque* water-melon; *pêche* peach; *poire* pear; *pomme* apple; *prune* plum; *raisin* grapes.

Cheese (fromage)

Only a selection from the enormous range of French cheeses can be given here. *Roquefort* a ewe's-milk cheese from Roquefort (Aveyron); *Camembert* a famous soft cheese from Normandy; *Brie* a delicate soft cheese from the Ile-de-France; *Munster, Géromé* strong-smelling soft cheeses made in Alsace and Lorraine; *Pyrenean cheeses* ewe's-milk cheeses with a light-coloured rind and cow's-milk cheeses with a black rind; *Bleu de Bresse* a mild creamy blue cheese from the

Lyonnais; *nut cheese* a soft cheese containing walnuts or almonds, made in various parts of the country (particularly Savoy) which is increasingly popular.

Milk products

From Normandy and Brittany come very good salt butter (*beurre salé*) and *crème fraîche*, a sourish-tasting cream with a fat content of 40%. *Yaourt* yoghurt; *fromage blanc* cream cheese.

Libraries

Bibliothèque Nationale
58 rue de Richelieu (2nd arr.); tel. 01 47 03 81 26
Métro: Pyramides; open Mon.–Sat. 12–6pm
To date the old national library has housed the national collection representing the entire French output of documentation in every field. Its holdings include valuable books, periodicals, prints, maps and plans, coins and Oriental manuscripts. Since 1997, however, these are gradually being transferred to the new French national library (BNF, see below). The Bibliothèque Nationale also mounts major temporary exhibitions on the history of art and bibliography.

Bibliothèque Nationale

The ultra-modern Bibliothèque Nationale de France (see A to Z) in the 13th arrondissement, built to relieve the pressure on the old national library, was opened in 1996.

Bibliothèque Nationale de France (BNF)

Bibliothèque Sainte-Geneviève
10 place du Panthéon (5th arr.); tel. 01 43 29 61 00
Métro: Cluny La Sorbonne; open Mon.–Sat. 10am–10pm
With over 3 million volumes the Bibliothèque Sainte-Geneviève, in the University quarter, is second only to the Bibliothèque Nationale.

Bibliothèque Sainte-Geneviève

See A to Z, Marais

Archives Nationales

Bibliothèque de l'Arsenal
1 rue de Sully (4th arr.); tel. 01 53 01 25 25
Métro: Sully-Morland
Mainly French literature; also medieval manuscripts and works on the history of the cinema

Bibliothèque de l'Arsenal

See A to Z, Marais

Bibliothèque Forney

See A to Z, Marais

Bibliothèque Historique de la Ville de Paris

Bibliothèque Marguerite Durand (women's library)
21 place du Panthéon (5th arr.); tel. 01 45 70 80 30
Métro: Censier-Daubenton; open Tue.–Sat. 2–6pm
A reference library, founded by feminist journalist and author Marguerite Durand in 1931, with over 25,000 volumes on the history of women in society and the women's movement.

Bibliothèque Marguerite Durand

See A to Z, Institut Français

Bibliothèque Mazarine

See A to Z, Centre Pompidou

Bibliothèque publique d'information

Lost Property

Lost property office	Bureau des Objets Trouvés 36 rue des Morillons (15th arr.); tel. 01 55 76 20 20 Métro: Convention; open Mon., Wed., Fri. 8.30am–5pm, Tue.–Thur. 5–8pm (except July, August and Christmas)

Markets

Paris has almost a hundred markets, with at least one in every arrondissement, so the markets listed here can only be just a small selection. Some are general markets, selling fresh produce such as fruit and vegetables, while others specialise in flowers, clothes, birds, postage stamps, books, etc. And of course there are the flea markets which sell just about anything.

Covered markets as a rule are open Tue.–Sat. 8am–1pm and 4–7.30pm, Sun. 8am–1pm. Street markets operate on different days of the week, usually between 7am and 1.30pm.

Street markets (rues commerçantes)	Rue de Buci (6th arr.), rue Cler (7th arr.), rue de Poteau (13th arr.), rue Legendre (17th arr.), rue Lepic (18th arr.), rue Montorgueil (1st arr.), rue Mouffetard (5th arr.); boulevard de Belleville (20th arr.)
Covered markets (marchés couverts)	Marché d'Aligre, place d'Aligre (12th arr.); Marché Daumesnil, boulevard de Reuilly (12th arr.); Marché Batignolles, 96 rue Lemercier (17th arr.); Marché Château-d'Eau, rue Château-d'Eau (10th arr.); Marché Enfants Rouges, 39 rue de Bretagne (3rd arr.); Marché Saint-Quentin, boulevard de Magenta (10th arr.)
Flea markets (marchés aux puces)	Porte de Clignancourt, see A to Z, Marché aux Puces Porte de Montreuil (20th arr.), open Sat., Sun., Mon. 7am–7.30pm Porte de Vanves (14th arr.), open Sat., Sun. 7am–7.30pm
Flowers (marchés aux fleurs)	Place Louis-Lépine (4th arr.), open daily (except Sun.) 8am–7.30pm Place de la Madeleine (8th arr.), open daily (except Mon.) 8am–7pm Place des Ternes (17th arr.), open daily (except Mon.) 8am–7pm
Postage stamps (marché aux timbres)	Carré Marigny Cnr. avenue Gabriel/avenue Marigny (8th arr.); open Thur., Sat., Sun., public holidays 10am–6pm
Clothing (marché de la friperies)	Carreau du Temple 1 rue Dupetit-Thouars (3rd arr.), open Tue.–Sun. 9am–12, Mon. 9am–7pm
Birds (marchés aux oiseaux)	Place Louis-Lépine (4th arr.), open Sun. 8am–7pm Quai de la Mégisserie (1st arr.) open daily (except Sun.) 9am–7pm A wide selection of birds and pets for sale on the banks of the Seine
Fabrics (marché aux tissus)	Marché Saint-Pierre Place Saint-Pierre (18th arr.), open daily (except Sun.) 9am–7pm The fabrics market at the foot of the butte de Montmartre has everything from silks and satins to printed cotton and curtains, bedlinen and table cloths, mostly at affordable prices. The restored market hall also holds the Museum for Naive Art.
Marché international de Rungis	Open for visits Mon.–Fri. 12–3pm; information: tel. 01 46 87 60 00 Buses: 216 (Denfert-Rochereau), 185 (Porte d'Italie) Train: from Gare d'Austerlitz to Pont-de-Rungis

Since Les Halles, the market halls in the city centre, were dismantled in 1969, the "belly of Paris" has been located on a 600ha/1482 acre site in the southern suburb of Rungis, from where it provides the city and its region with daily supplies of fresh fruit and vegetables, meat and other foodstuffs. Rungis holds about 30 million hectolitres of wine in reserve, 7 million of them destined for Paris alone. Some 3 million tonnes of provisions account for a turnover here of over 50 billion francs a year.

Museums

Paris has over 150 museums. For information about museums and exhibitions call: Allô-Musées: tel. 01 42 76 66 00.

Admission to many museums is cheaper on Sundays, and is free for the national museums run by the State. To visit a number of museums on weekdays buy a Paris museums pass (see below, carte musées et monuments). This saves money – Paris museums are expensive! – and avoids having to queue. And don't forget – most museums are closed on Mondays and Tuesdays!
Admission charges

The "carte musées et monuments" is a museums pass allowing admission to over 70 museums and monuments in and around Paris. It can be for 1, 3 or 5 days and is on sale at main métro and railway stations, tourist offices (see Information), through Minitel (code 3615 FNAC) and from participating museums and monuments.
Carte musées et monuments

Tickets for museums and special exhibitions can also be bought in advance from:
FNAC/Boutique Musée & Compagnie, 49 Rue Etienne Marcel; tel. 01 40 49 00
Advance ticket sales

List of Museums

See A to Z, Centre Pompidou
Centre de Création Industrielle

25 rue d'Estienne d'Orves, 93502 Pantin; Métro: Hoche
Open Tue.–Fri. 11am–4pm, Sat., Sun. 11am–8pm
Exhibition of cars on a grand scale
Centre International de l'Automobile

See A to Z, Centre Pompidou
Centre Pompidou

See A to Z, La Villette
Cité de la Musique

See A to Z, La Villette
Cité des Sciences et de l'Industrie

17 quai Malaquais, 14 rue Bonaparte (6th arr.)
Métro: Saint-Germain-des-Prés
Open Mon.–Fri. 8am–8pm (except Aug.), library 1–6pm
Collections of the 17th c. Royal Academy of Art and the Ecole des Beaux Arts; alternating art exhibitions.
Ecole Nationale Supérieure des Beaux Arts

See A to Z, Les Halles
Espace Grevin

See A to Z, Montparnasse
Fondation Cartier

Museums

Fondation Le Corbusier	Villa La Roche, 10 square du Docteur Blanche (16th arr.); Métro: Jasmin, Ranelagh, Porte d'Auteuil; open Mon.–Thur. 10–12.30, 1.30–6pm, Fri. 10–12.30, 1.30–5pm (except Aug.) The villa, built by Le Corbusier in 1925, represents the experimental architectural style of the golden Twenties; gallery of Cubist paintings.
Galeries Nation. du Grand Palais	See A to Z, Grand Palais
Galerie Nationale du Jeu de Paume	See A to Z, Jeu de Paume
Maison Honoré de Balzac	47 rue Raynouard (16th arr.); Métro: Passy, Muette; RER: Kennedy Radio France; open Tue.–Sun. 10–5.40pm; library: daily (except Sun.) 10am–6pm Home of author Honoré de Balzac (see Famous People) with manuscripts, documents and a library of works by and about Balzac.
Maison Victor Hugo	See A to Z, Place des Vosges
Manufacture Nationale des Gobelins	42 avenue des Gobelins (13th arr.) Métro: Gobelins; guided tours: Tue., Wed., Thur. 2, 2.45pm State factory where tapestries are still woven by centuries-old techniques.
Monnaie de Paris	See A to Z, Monnaie
Musée Jacque- mart-André	158 boulevard Haussmann (8th arr.); Métro: Miromesnil, Saint-Philippe-du-Roule; RER: Charles-de-Gaulle-Etoile; open daily 10am–6pm Re-opened in 1996 and owned by the Institut de France, the museum's art collections are housed in a sumptuous Second Empire mansion commissioned from the architect Parent in the late 19th c. by Protestant banker Edouard André and his wife Nélie Jacquemart. The audio-guide is in six languages. The collection includes works by Bellini, Uccello, Tiepolo, Botticelli and Della Robbia from the Italian Renaissance, by Flemish masters such as Rembrandt, Franz Hals, Ruysdaâl and Van Dijk, plus French 18th c. painters, among them Boucher, Chardin, Fragonard and Chattier. The Andrés' love of the decorative arts is evident from magnificent furniture and tapestries from the royal factory of Beauvais. The tearoom with a terrace on the courtyard has a ceiling fresco by Tiepolo and walls covered in priceless hangings.
Musée Baccarat	30bis rue de Paradis (10th arr.), Métro: Gare de l'Est, Château d'eau, Poissonière; RER: Gare du Nord; open Mon.–Sat. 10am–6pm Over 1200 items of Baccarat glass tracing its development from 1828 to the present.
Musée Henri Bouchard	25 rue de l'Yvette (16th arr.); Métro: Jasmin; RER: Boulainvilliers Open Wed., Sat. 2–5pm, closed last two weeks of every quarter Studio of sculptor Henri Bouchard (1894–1960)
Musée Bourdelle	16 rue Antoine Bourdelle (15th arr.); Métro: Montparnasse-Bienvenue, Falguière; open Tue.–Sun. 10am–5.40pm Works by the sculptor Antoine Bourdelle, a pupil of Rodin, plus exhibitions of modern sculpture.
Musé Bricard	See A to Z, Marai, Hôtel Libéral Bruand

63 rue de Monceau (8th arr.); Métro: Villiers, Monceau; open Wed.–Sun. 10am–5pm
  Rococo furniture and tapestries (second half of 18th c.); costume exhibitions. Collection endowed by Count Moïse de Camondo in 1935 on behalf of his son Nissim, one of the fallen in 1917.

Musée Nissim de Camondo

See A to Z, Musée Carnavalet

Musée Carnavalet

7 avenue Vélasquez (8th arr.); Métro: Villiers, Monceau
Open: Tue.–Sun. 10am–5.40pm
  Municipal museum of Chinese art from the 14th c. to the present in the Parc Monceau.

Musée Cernuschi (Musée d'Art Chinois de la Ville de Paris)

See A to Z, Marais, Hôtel de Donan

Musée Cognacq-Jay

See A to Z, Chantilly, Grand Château

Musée Condé

11 rue Pierre et Marie Curie (5th arr.); open Mon.–Fri. 1.30–6pm
  The Radium Institute which opened here in 1914 in its new clinker building was originally headed by twice Nobel Prize winner Marie Curie – in 1903 she shared the Nobel Prize for physics with her husband and Becquerel, and won the prize for chemistry on her own in 1912 – then by her daughter Irène and finally by son-in-law Frédéric. The entire laboratory was decontaminated in 1981 so today's visitor can safely view the Nobel Prizewinner's laboratory apparatus, white coat and the extremely thick glasses she had to wear because of cataracts. The leaflet obtainable from the museum "Parcours des Sciences. Les pionniers de la radioactivité du Musée au Collège de France" guides the visitor along a trail through the Jardin des Plantes, bd. Saint-Michel and Panthéon between the places where the pioneers of radioactivity worked.

Musée Curie

11 rue Poulbot, Espace Montmartre (18th arr.); Métro: Abbesses, Anvers; open daily 10am–6pm.
  Sculptures and paintings by Salvador Dali

Musée Dali

50 avenue Victor Hugo (16th arr.); Métro: Victor Hugo, Kléber; open daily 11am–7pm
  Pre-colonial African art and temporary exhibitions.

Musée Dapper

22bis rue Gabriel Péri, 932 Saint-Denis; Métro: Saint-Denis; bus: 156 (from Porte de la Chapelle); open Mon., Wed.–Sat. 10am–5.30pm, Sun., holidays 2–6.30pm
  Housed in a former Carmelite convent dating from the time of Louis XIII, the museum has exhibits ranging from collections on the Carmelite order and the Paris Commune of 1871, to archaeological material and modern art.

Musée d'Art et d'Histoire de la Ville de Saint-Denis

42 rue des Saules (18th arr.); Métro: Lamarck-Caulaincourt; open Sun.–Thur. (except Aug., Jewish holidays) 3–6pm
Museum of Jewish art with adjoining library.

Musée d'Art Juif

See A to Z, Palais de Tokyo

Musée d'Art Moderne de la Ville de Paris

See A to Z, Musée de Cluny

Musée de Cluny

Museums

Symbol of eternal love: "The Kiss" by Auguste Rodin

Musée de la Chasse et de la Nature
See A to Z, Marais, Hôtel de Guénégaud

Musée de la Contrefaçon
16 rue de la Faisanderie (16th arr.); Métro: Porte Dauphine; open Mon.–Thur. 2–5pm, Fri. 9.30–12
Over 300 fake perfumes, foodstuffs, designer labels, cars, etc.

Musée de la Femme et Collection d'Automates de Neuilly
12 rue du Centre, 92 Neuilly; Métro: Pont-de-Neuilly; open daily (except Tue., holidays, July, Aug.) 2.30–5pm
Collection of antique automata, with explanatory film at 3pm daily; Museum of Woman.

Musée de l'Air et de l'Espace
Aéroport du Bourget; RER: line B to Le Bourget then bus 152; open daily except Mon. May–Oct. 10am–6pm, Nov.–April 10am–5pm
Aerospace and aviation museum

Musée de la Marine
See A to Z, Palais de Chaillot

Musée de la Mode et du Costume
Palais Galliéra, 10 avenue Pierre 1er de Serbie (16th arr.)
Métro: Iéna; open daily (except Mon.) 10am–5.40pm
Museum of fashion plus costumes and uniforms from 1735 to the present day.

Musée de la Mode et du Textile
107 rue de Rivoli (1st arr.), on three floors in the renovated Rohan wing of the Louvre; Métro: Palais-Royal –Musée du Louvre, open Tue., Wed.–Fri. 11am–6pm, Tue. till 10pm, Sat., Sun. 10am–6pm
The recently re-opened costume museum, with a collection of over 80,000 items of clothing to draw on from the 16th c. to the present, ranks among the best in the world. Visitors can trace the evolution of both the male and female silhouette from 1700 to 1980 and follow the vicissitudes of fashion from the whalebone corset to the very latest Nineties look. The oldest garment is a 7th c. Coptic tunic. The rest of the collection ranges from the fabulous creations of the court of the Sun King and iron-hooped crinolines from the mid-19th c. to haute couture by Chanel, Dior, Cardin, Worth, Schiaparelli, Courrèges and Guy Laroche.

Cité de la Musique, 221 avenue Jean-Jaurès (19th arr.)
Métro: Porte de Pantin; open Tue., Fri. and Sat. 12–7.30pm, Sun.
10am–6pm, Thur. till 9.30pm
Recently re-opened museum with a collection of 900 musical instruments from the Renaissance to the present.

Musée de la Musique

9 rue Scribe (9th arr.); Métro: Opéra, Chaussée d'Antin; RER: Aubder;
open daily 9am–5.30pm, closed Oct.–March, Sun.
History of perfume from ancient Egypt to the 20th c. (perfume flasks, etc.).

Musée de la Parfumerie Fragonard

34 boulevard de Vaugirard (15th arr.); Métro: Montparnasse-
Bienvenue, Pasteur; open daily except Sun. 10am–6pm
History of postal services and philately; library and photo archive.
Closed for renovation during 1999.

Musée de la Poste

Impasse Berthaud, 22 rue Beaubourg (3rd arr.)
Métro: Rambuteau; open daily except Mon. 10am–6pm
A collection of 300 porcelain dolls made in France between 1860 and 1960.

Musée de la Poupée

1 bis rue des Carmes (5th arr.); Métro: Maubert-Mutualité, St-Michel;
open Mon.–Sat. 9am–5pm
   Housed in the police station of the 5th arrondissement this museum
of crime, founded in 1909 and with about 2000 items, is a very special
kind of black museum – on his first visit to Paris Alfred Hitchcock is
said to have rated it well above the Louvre. The historic collection
documents assassinations, revolutions and crimes that kept all of
France in suspense. Exhibits include the blade of a guillotine, weighing almost 9kg/18lbs, from the French Revolution, a model of the
"estrapade", an 18th c. instrument of torture, the warrant for
Voltaire's arrest "for impertinent utterances" about the monarchy,
documents about the necklace affair and France's most notorious
female poisoner, the Marquise de Brinvilliers, sentenced in 1676, as
well as famous items of evidence such as the casing of the bomb that
Felice Orsini hurled at Napoleon III in 1858 and the book that the anarchist Gorguloff used to hide the weapon with which he shot the President Paul Doumer on May 6th 1932.

Musée des Collections Historiques de la Préfecture de Police

See A to Z, Saint-Germain-en-Laye

Musée de la Préhistoire

107 rue de Rivoli (1st arr.)
Métro: Palais Royal, Tuileries; open Mon., Wed.–Sun. 12.30–6pm
Poster museum; temporary exhibitions.

Musée de la Publicité

See A to Z, Musée de l'Armée

Musé de l'Armée

Quai Saint-Bernard (5th arr.)
Métro: Austerlitz; open in daytime
Sculpture park with works by Arman, Brice, César, Etienne-Martin,
Schoffer, Stahly, Zadkine etc.

Musée de la Sculpture en plein Air de la Ville de Paris

See A to Z, Marais, Musé Bricard

Musée de la Serrure

See A to Z, La Défense

Musée de l'Automobile

See A to Z, Montmartre

Musée de la Vie Romantique

See A to Z, Marais, Hôtel de Rohan-Soubise

Musée del'Histoire de France

Museums

Musée de l'Histoire de Paris	See A to Z, Musée Carnavalet
Musée de l'Homme	See A to Z, Palais de Chaillot
Musée de l'Ile-de-France	Château de Sceaux, 92330 Sceaux RER line B: Parc de Sceaux; open daily except Tue. 2–5pm, in summer 6pm The history of the Ile de France in documents, pictures, coins, ceramics and other objets d'art; Sat., Sun. audio-visual guided tour in Pavillon de l'Aurore
Musée de l'Institut du Monde Arabe	1 rue des Fossés Saint-Bernard (5th arr.) Métro: Jussieu; open Tue.–Sun. 10am–6pm Arabic-Islamic civilisation from the 8th to the 19th c.
Musée de l'Orangerie des Tuileries	Jardin des Tuileries, Place de la Concorde (1st arr.) Métro: Concorde; open Mon., Wed.–Sun. 9.45–5.15; closed one week in September. Jean Walter and Paul Guillaume collection. Works by the Impressionists and Post-Impressionists, including Renoir, Cézanne, Matisse, Derain, Soutine, Picasso and "Les Grandes Nymphéas" by Claude Monet.
Musée de Radio-France	Maison de Radio-France, 116 avenue du Président Kennedy (16th arr.) Métro: Ranelagh, Passy, Mirabeau; RER: Kennedy, Radio-France Guided tours daily (except Sun.) 10.30, 11.30, 2.30, 3.30, 4.30 History and daily workings of Radio-France's radio and TV station; studio tours.
Musée des Antiquités Nationales de France	See A to Z, Saint-Germain-en-Laye
Musée des Arts Décoratifs	Pavillon de Marsan, Palais du Louvre 107 rue de Rivoli (1st arr.); Métro: Palais-Royal, Tuileries; open daily except Mon. 12–6pm Applied and decorative art from the Middle Ages to the 18th c.; temporary exhibitions. Musée des Arts Décoratifs is currently under renovation, some collections may not be viewed until 2000. Ring for details.
Musée des Instruments de la Musique Mécanique	Impasse Berthaud (3rd arr.); Métro: Rambuteau; open Sat., Sun., holidays 2–7pm Music boxes, old gramophones, Limonaire organs and clockwork pianos from 1840 to the present.
Musée des Monuments Français (closed until 1999)	See A to Z, Palais de Chaillot
Musée des Plans-Reliefs	See A to Z, Musée de l'Armée
Musée d'Orsay	See A to Z, Musée d'Orsay
Musée du Cinéma Henri Langlois	See A to Z, Palais de Chaillot

"Horses" by Guillaume Coustous in the courtyard of the Louvre, sculpted for Marley Park in 1745

See A to Z, Louvre	Musée du Louvre
See A to Z, Luxembourg	Musée du Luxembourg
See A to Z, Petit Palais	Musée du Petit Palais
See A to Z, Montmartre	Musée du Vieux Montmartre

5 square Charles Dickens (16th arr.)
Caveau des Echansons; Métro: Passy; open daily except Mon. 10am–6pm
The former wine cellars of the 13th/14th c. abbey of Passy are on the right bank of the Seine, quite close to the Eiffel Tower. The wines from the vines planted here on the heights of Chaillot had an excellent reputation and were highly prized by Louis XIII. A tour of the exhibition in the medieval vaults can be followed by wine-tastings in the wine bar, open till 6pm.

Musée du Vin

12 rue Surcouf (7th arr.); Métro: Latour-Maubourg, Invalides; RER: Invalides; open daily (except Sun., holidays) 11am–7pm
Museum of the State tobacco industry with exhibits from the history of tobacco and its uses, including pipes, snuff boxes etc.

Musée-Galerie de la SEITA

10 boulevard Montmartre (9th arr.); Métro: Montmartre; RER: Auber; open daily 1–7pm, from 10am in school holidays
Fun for young and old – a popular waxworks, founded in 1882, with historical tableaux and famous people.

Musée Grévin

Museums

Musée Guimet	See A to Z, Musée Guimet (closed for renovation during 1999)
Musée Kwok On	41 rue des Francs-Bourgeois (4th arr.); Métro: Saint-Paul; open Mon.–Fri. 10am–5.30pm Traditional Asian crafts and theatre.
Musée Maillol	See A to Z, Saint-Germain-des-Près
Musée Maréchal Leclerc et de la Libération de Paris, Musée Jean Moulin	Allée de la 2e Division Blindée, Bâtiment Nord-Parc, Dalle jardin Atlantique (15th arr.) Métro: Montparnasse-Bienvenue; open Tue.–Sun. 10am–5.40pm Museum about Maréchal Leclerc de Hauteclocque, Resistance fighter Jean Moulin (interred in the Panthéon), his partner Mme Sasse and the French Resistance movement.
Musée Marmottan	See A to Z, Musée Marmottan
Musée National d'Art Moderne	See A to Z, Centre Pompidou
Musée National de Céramique	See Excursions, Sèvres
Musée National de la Légion d'Honneur et des Ordres de Chevaleries	Hôtel de Salm, 2 rue de Bellechasse (7th arr.) Métro: Solférino; RER: Gare d'Orsay; open daily (except Mon., holidays) 2–5pm Decorations and medals of the orders of chivalry and the Royal, Imperial and Republican orders from the Middle Ages to the present.
Musée National de la Renaissance	See Excursions, Ecouen
Musée d'Ennery	59 avenue Foch (16th arr.); Métro: Dauphine; open Sun., Thur. 2–6pm Collection of oriental art.
Musée National des Arts Africains et Océaniens	See A to Z,
Musée National des Arts et Traditions Populaires	6 avenue du Mahatma Gandhi, Jardin d'Acclimatation (16th arr.) Métro: Sablons, Porte Maillot; Bus: 73; open daily (except Tue., Jan 1st, May 1st, Dec. 25th) 9.30am–5pm Museum of French folk art.
Musée National des Techniques	292 rue Saint-Martin (3rd arr.); Métro: Réaumur-Sébastopol; RER: Châtelet-Les Halles; open daily (except Mon. and school holidays) 10am–5.30pm Unique collection tracing the history of science and technology from the 16th to 20th c.
Musée National Eugène Delacroix	See A to Z, Marais
Musée National Jean-Jacques Henner	43 avenue de Villiers (17th arr.); Métro: Malesherbes, Wagram, Monceau; open Tue.–Sun. 10am–12, 2–5 Works by the Alsace painter Jean-Jacques Henner (1829–1905)
Musée National Gustave Moreau	14 rue de la Rochefoucault (9th arr.); Métro: Trinité; open Thur.–Sun. 10–12.45, 2–5.15, Mon., Wed. 11am–5.15pm Museum in the former home and studio of the Symbolist painter Gustave Moreau (1826–1898), with around 1000 paintings and some 5000 drawings.

10 rue du Cloître (4th arr.); Métro: Cité; RER: Châtelet-Les Halles; open Wed., Sat., Sun. 2.30–6pm
History of the Ile de la Cité.

Musée Notre-Dame de Paris

See A to Z, Belleville and Ménilmontant

Musée Edith Piaf

See A to Z, Musée Picasso

Musée Picasso

See A to Z, Musée Rodin

Musée Rodin

See A to Z, Chantilly, Grandes Ecuries

Musée Vivant du Cheval

100 bis rue d'Assas (6th arr.)
Métro: Vavin, Notre-Dame-des-Champs, Port-Royal; RER: Port-Royal
open Tue.–Sun. 10am–5.30pm
Works by the Russian sculptor Ossip Zadkine on show in the garden house and studio where he worked from 1910 to 1928.

Musée Zadkine

See A to Z,

Muséum National d'Histoire Naturelle

Muséum National d'Histoire Naturelle

Jardin des Plantes

See A to Z, Grand Palais

Palais de la Découverte

See A to Z, Pavillon de l'Arsenal

Pavillon de l'Arsenal

Bibliothèque Polonaise de Paris, Societé Historique et Litteraire Polonaise, 6 quai d'Orléans (4th arr.); Métro: Pont-Marie; guided tours Thur. 2, 3, 4 and 5pm
All kinds of memorabilia of the gifted composer.

Salon Chopin

Music

Paris is world renowned for music and its audiences can look forward to classical concerts with internationally famous soloists, conductors and orchestras, the top ballet companies, and the hit musicals. After a number of years in the doldrums the jazz scene is very much alive and kicking again in what used to be one of its real strongholds. Rock, pop, funk, soul, techno plus salsa and other tropical rhythmns all have many fans here too, while the Afro-beat which is taking the hit parade by storm in many countries actually evolved in this multicultural metropolis on the Seine. And what of the chanson, the witty yet sentimental cabaret number that is so typically French? It may not be so much in vogue these days but it still has an important role to play in the musical psyche of the Parisian (see Baedeker Special, pp.276–277).

Opera, ballet and concerts

Thanks to its many fine concert halls Paris has some kind of musical event to offer almost every day. To find out when and where consult the what's on listings in the daily press or in L'Officiel des Spectacles, 7 à Paris or Pariscope.

Salles de concert

Music

Auditorium des Halles
Forum des Halles, Port Saint-Eustache (1st arr.); tel. 01 42 33 00 00
Métro/RER: Châtelet-Les Halles

Radio France
116 avenue du Président Kennedy (16th arr.); tel. 01 45 24 15 16
Métro: Ranelagh, Passy, Mirabeau

Salle Cortot
78 rue Cardinet (17th arr.); tel. 01 49 24 80 16; Métro: Courcelles

Salle Gaveau
45 rue La Boâtie (8th arr.); tel. 01 45 63 20 30; Métro: Saint-Augustin

Salle Pleyel
252 Faubourg Saint-Honoré (8th arr.); tel. 01 45 61 53 00
Métro: Ternes, Charles de Gaulle-Etoile

Centre International de Paris, Palais des Congrès
Porte Maillot (17th arr.); tel. 01 47 58 13 03; Métro: Porte Maillot

Théâtre des Champs-Elysées
15 avenue Montaigne (8th arr.); tel. 01 49 52 50 50
Métro: Alma-Marceau

Palais de Chaillot
Place du Trocadéro (16th arr.); tel. 01 47 27 81 15
Métro: Trocadéro

Church concerts

Church concerts are mainly given in Notre-Dame, Saint-Eustache, Saint-Sulpice, Sainte-Chapelle, Madeleine, Saint-Germain-des-Près and Saint-Louis-des-Invalides, which is part of the Hôtel des Invalides (see A to Z).

Opera houses

Opéra National de Paris Bastille
Place de la Bastille (12th arr.); tel. 01 40 01 17 89, fax 01 40 01 16 16
Métro: Bastille
This new opera house, opened in 1989, has taken over opera from the Palais Garnier (see A to Z, Bastille).

Opéra Comique (Salle Favart)
5 rue Favart (2nd arr.); tel. 01 42 44 45 46
Métro: Richelieu-Drouot
Mainly French operas and operettas.

Théâtre Musical de Paris (TMP)
1 place du Châtelet (1st arr.); tel. 01 42 61 19 83
Métro: Châtelet

Ballet and musicals

Opéra National de Paris Palais Garnier
Place de l'Opéra (9th arr.); tel. 01 40 01 25 14, fax 01 40 01 20 82
Métro: Opéra
Re-opened in February 1996 this is now the home of ballet (see A to Z, Opéra-Garnier).

Péniche Opéra
Quai de Jemappes (10th arr.); tel. 01 42 45 18 20
Métro: Jaurès
Musicals and lyrical drama.

Espace Marais
23 rue Beautreillis (4th arr.); tel. 01 42 71 10 19
Métro: Place de la Bastille
Modern ballet in a small theatre in the Marais.

Bataclan
50 boulevard Voltaire (11th arr.); tel. 01 47 00 30 12
Métro: Oberkampf (see also Rock, folk, Latin below)

Bobino
20 rue de la Gaîté (9th arr.); tel. 01 43 27 75 75
Métro: Edgar-Quinet

Olympia
Entrance: 18 rue Caumartin (9th arr.); tel. 01 47 42 25 49
Métro: Madeleine, Opéra
This famous music hall was rebuilt in 1997/1998 not far from its original location on the Boulevard des Capucines.

Zénith
211 avenue Jean-Jaurès (19th arr., see La Villette); tel. 01 42 08 60 00
Métro: Porte de Pantin

Nightlife

Paris, like New York, is a city that never sleeps. It throbs with life by day and by night, when there is something for everyone, whatever the hour. To find out what is on consult Pariscope or L'Officiel des Spectacles, which come out every Wednesday. The most popular places for night-owls are around Saint-Germain-des-Prés, the Latin Quarter, Marais, Montparnasse, the rue de Lappe in the Bastille and the rue Fontaine near Pigalle – just remember that nightlife in Paris doesn't really get going until midnight.

Some Parisian bars have made history and become regular institutions.

China Club
50 rue de Charenton (12th arr.); tel. 01 43 43 82 02
Popular meeting point, with three floors to choose from – a bar in the basement with red walls, flickering fire and soft music, an old colonial-style Chinese restaurant on the ground floor with subdued lighting and upholstered in red and black, and, on the first floor, a Chinese smoking lounge.

Le Dépanneur
27 rue Fontaine (9th arr.); tel. 01 40 16 40 20
American bar – chili con carne and tequila, plus regular techno-DJs – and the only bar in the city that stays open round the clock!

La Distillerie
50 rue du Faubourg St Antoine (12th arr.); tel. 01 40 10 99 00
Tropical nights in the heart of Paris. Elisabeth de Rozière serves all sorts of concoctions of rum accompanied by the appropriate Caribbean specialities.

*Harry's New York Bar
5 rue Daunou (2nd arr.); tel. 01 42 61 71 14
This is one of Paris's most famous nightspots – and one of the oldest, too, first established in 1911. This American bar whose regulars have included Hemingway and Scott Fitzgerald is where the legendary Bloody Mary and other cocktails are supposed to have been invented. The fifth "pétrifiant" – a cocktail whose name says it all – is free provided you're still upright of course!

Hot Jam Sessions
and Afro Beat

Well before the Second World War Paris had become the European centre for jazz, with Josephine Baker making the whole world hold its breath with her naked dancing in "negro music", and the legendary Django Reinhardt founding European jazz in the "Hot Club". In the 1940s and 1950s Paris was indisputably the capital of jazz. It was not just French stars, such as Juliette Gréco, Barbará, Boris Vian and Guy Béart who had a following here. American jazz greats such as Miles Davis and Billy Holiday also often appeared in the clubs of St Germain des Prés in front of enthusiastic audiences, and some even settled in the French capital for a number of years. In the 1970s, though, interest in jazz waned dramatically, particularly with the advent of discothèques, and many clubs had to close. Only midway through the 1980s was there a renaissance in Paris of the jazz scene, which many had thought was almost dead. The ups and downs of the Paris scene are nowhere to be found more clearly than in the fortunes of the **Club Montana** (28 rue Saint Benoît, 6th arr., tel. 01 45 48 93 08, métro: Saint Germain des Prés). Montana enjoyed its heyday in the 1950s. By the middle of the 1960s this had all gone, the place was sold and turned into a pizzeria. But with the jazz revival of the 1980s even the Montana made a comeback and the old French and American jazz stars returned to the club which remained the same smoke-filled, dimly-lit place, full to bursting, that they had known previously. In the last few years the Montana has become more and more a fashionable bar with smart furnishings, special lighting effects and disco sound. So does this mean farewell to jazz again? Perhaps at the Montana, but not in Paris as a whole! The enthusiasm for jazz in the French capital shows no signs of flagging. Lovers of the genre all want to come here, regardless of their stylistic preferences,

and enjoy the variety on offer. One place, in particular, has tour guides going into raptures – "the most important jazz club", "the best place in the whole of Paris for jazz" – but whether these superlatives are appropriate, the jazz fan should perhaps go and find out for himself: the place in question is **New Morning** (7–9 rue des Petites Ecuries, 10th arr., tel. 01 45 23 51 41, métro: Château d'Eau). What is a fact is that almost every big name in the world of jazz has appeared here at some time or another: Miles Davis, Chet Baker, Oscar Petersen etc. What is also true is that it not only has the largest stage and the finest acoustic but also the biggest range of concerts. Well-known artists from outside France still occasionally put in an appearance, but generally the soloists are young talented French musicians who seldom disappoint their audience. One word of warning, however: lovers of jazz and jazz alone are advised to check on the programme details in advance, e.g. in "Pariscope", as jazz is not the only music on offer – programmes also include blues, soul, Latin-American and African rhythms. Those who prefer the intimate setting of a jazz cellar will also be disappointed – New Morning is located in an old factory and can accommodate around 600 people. At least, tickets are easier to come by here than elsewhere.

For a more "creepy" atmosphere try the **Caveau de la Huchette** (5 rue de la Huchette, 5th arr., tel. 01 43 26 65 05, métro: Saint-Michel), a cellar vault which was used as a dungeon during the French Revolution. Heads even used to roll here too – the guillotine once stood where the loudspeaker boxes are now set up. But this venue is steeped in history in other ways: as the oldest jazz cellar in the student district of the Quartier Latin it was the meeting place of the existentialists, who met here to exchange ideas, while film directors of the 1950s used it as a setting for

Samba, salsa, reggae and zouk – all are performed at African and Caribbean nights

individual scenes. And just as the cellar ambience has remained the same since the year dot, so the programme of music on offer has changed very little: live music with dancing to traditional jazz of the forties and fifties, but also rock 'n' roll, boogie woogie and swing. Asthmatics and militant non-smokers would be well advised to give the place a wide berth, however!

Another jazz venue with an authentic ambience is **Le Petit Opportun** (15 ruc des Lavandières Ote Opportune, 1st arr, tel. 01 42 36 01 36, métro: Châtelet). This jazz cellar, one of the most famous in Paris, is reached through a bistro bar on the ground floor. It is an ideal place for jazz fans who have a preference for small groups, such as a quartet, rather than for big bands – the cellar, originally a 13th c. vault, would be far too small for larger forces. Indeed it is so tiny that the audience space is limited to 40 people at most. Not for claustrophobics then! Especially as it is always full. It is no surprise that lovers of New Orleans and contemporary jazz always have a really good time here. The owner is himself a musician and knows his stuff. Each week

two or three different groups appear and the patron is always willing to give a chance to young unknown talents, if he considers them promising.

One of the most delightful jazz clubs in Paris is without doubt **Le Petit Journal Montparnasse** (13 rue du Commandant Mouchotte, 14th arr., tel. 01 43 21 56 70, métro: Montparnasse). Its big stage surrounded by long tables plays host to the stars of French jazz. The acoustic is exceptional and the ambience is just right: wood panelled walls, a 10m/33ft long bar and lively staff. Its proprietor also owns **Le Petit Journal Saint Michel** (71 boulevard Saint Michel, 5th arr., tel. 01 43 26 28 59, métro: Luxembourg), a cosy and very intimate bar with small tables, which gets its name from a magazine which used to be widely read at the end of the 19th c. Some of these historic editions are on the wood-panelled walls and are worth looking at. In this long established club in the lively Quartier Latin the bands often change round and they do not perform on a stage but on the same level as their audience, which is made up of all ages. The programme of music on offer is also equally wide-ranging: New Orleans jazz, bebop, but also blues and Dixie. It is advisable to get there in good time before the start of a concert in order to be sure of getting a seat.

For enthusiasts of all post-1940 branches of jazz there is an excellent variety on offer at **Sunset** (60 rue des Lombards, 1st arr., tel. 01 40 26 46 60, métro: Châtelet): Sundays, jazz vocal; Mondays, Latin jazz; Tuesdays, talented newcomers; Wednesdays to Saturdays, a range of different styles. This tiny jazz cellar with its "métro" tiles and photos on the walls has space for around 100 people, although they have to sit on children's chairs, which is not conducive to comfort, in spite of the agreeable volume-level.

"These days, to have a career, you need to go to Paris." Johnny Clegg, the highly successful white musician from South Africa, knows what he is talking about: in France he enjoys superstar status. Many musicians come to Paris from black Africa, Latin America and the Caribbean because they hope to forge a career here. And many are in fact successful. David Byrne of the Talking Heads once declared Paris to be "the capital of world beat music". Indeed, Paris can boast many patrons and an informed public, while in the studios on the Seine, CDs of Afro beat and Latino sound are produced and specialist CD shops, as well as radio broadcasts bring these exotic sounds right into the people's midst. The musicians and singers whose sparkling rhythms whip up the atmosphere in the African and Latino night-clubs are big business. For years an absolute "must" in terms of the "alternative" Paris night life has been the **Chapelle des Lombards** (19 rue de Lappe, 11th arr., tel. 01 43 57 24 24, métro: Bastille). Here there is always plenty going on – and until well into the small hours. Go for the African, Caribbean and Latin American rhythms such as samba, salsa, reggae, tango and zouk. The bands, which are constantly changing, can sometimes be outstanding and the audience is totally mixed,

colourful and full of temperament. A visit to the "Chapelle", which resembles a dungeon rather than a chapel, is guaranteed to leave one perspiring – particularly as there is no space to let off steam dancing. It is always "standing room only" – don't expect to be able to sit down!

Another "must" is **Keur Samba** (79 rue de la Boétie, 8th arr., tel. 01 43 59 03 10, métro: Saint Augustin) – the last port of call for many night-birds! In this exotic disco the spectators are still heaving to the sounds of bands from all over the world (African, Cuban, West Indian, Latin-American) when the sun is starting to rise over Paris. The small dance area is normally occupied almost entirely by regulars: affluent Parisians of African or Latin American extraction. The drawback is the bouncers at the door, who brook no discussion: anyone in jeans or casual clothes will be turned away in no uncertain terms. To be acceptable a "gentleman" should be dressed in dark clothes and have an attractive lady at his side.

In the cellar of the **Café de la Plage** (59 rue de Charonne, 11th arr., tel. 01 47 00 91 60, métro: Ledru Rollin), which on the ground floor is always full to overflowing, there is always plenty going on: rhythms from Africa, Latin America and the West Indies, but also jazz and blues. To find out what is playing it is best to consult the entertainments programme "Pariscope".

Do not be led astray by the name! **Le Tango** (18 rue au Maire, 3rd arr., tel. 01 42 72 17 78, métro: Arts et Métiers) was indeed once a tango bar. Now, however, it is the place where a mixed black and white audience are whipped up into such a frenzy by the hot, pulsating African and West Indian rhythms that the humidity level in the by no means large dance bar approaches that of a sauna. Ladies need to be careful, however – there are often "over-attentive" men milling around here!

Paris can certainly still boast an active and vibrant music scene with traditions which stretch back over many years.

Juveniles
47 rue de Richelieu (1st arr.); tel. 01 42 97 46 49
In this wine bar, run by Englishman Tim Johnston, tasty delicacies are served along with great wines from all over the world, though the best are probably those from the south-west of France.

*Raphaël
17 avenue Kléber (16th arr.); tel. 01 44 28 00 28
Wonderful refuge from the masses – oriental carpets, peace and quiet but stylish decor as well. The bar closes at 11.30pm but is open in the late morning.

Cabaret, revues, floor-shows

The glamorous days of the Naughty Nineties are long gone, and night spots of this kind are largely kept going nowadays by foreign tourists. When these nude shows cannot be avoided though, it is as well to do without with expensive and usually poor food.

Crazy Horse Saloon
12 avenue George V (8th arr.); tel. 01 47 23 32 32
Reckoned to be the best striptease in Paris the Crazy Horse, founded in 1951, is famous for its polished acts and truly beautiful girls.

Folies Bergère
32 rue Richer (9th arr.); tel. 01 44 79 98 98
The oldest Parisian variety theatre, founded in 1867, has been directed since 1993 by the avant-garde Argentinian Alfredo Arias. He has brought flair, poetry and a touch of nostalgia to the revue "Fous des Folies" in modern music-hall style.

Lido
116 avenue des Champs-Elysées (8th arr.); tel. 01 40 76 56 10
A lavish spectacle with superb routines by the famous Bluebell Girls – glitter, feathers and lots of laser effects – and always to full houses.

Moulin Rouge
82 boulevard de Clichy (18th arr.); tel. 01 46 06 00 19
In the heart of the city's red light district around the Place Pigalle, the famous home of the can-can still delights the tourists with the traditional high-kicking routines.

Discos and clubbing

Most Paris discos only get going after midnight. When it comes to clubbing the doormen can be a problem: whether you get in or not can depend on how much they like the look of you!

*Les Bains
7 rue du Bourg-l'Abbé (3rd arr.); tel. 01 48 87 01 80
This former Turkish bath is where the celebrities of the fashion and film world come to see and be seen, a real institution among the Parisian discos. Difficult to get past the doorman though – hot music, lots of techno.

*Le Balajo
9 rue de Lappe (11th arr.); tel. 01 47 00 07 87
Nostalgic dance hall with Forties ambience in the trendy Bastille quarter. Monday, Friday and Saturday between 3.30 and 6.30 is tango time. And every evening there are long queues waiting to get into this swinging scene for the hot rhythmns of salsa and mambo.

La Locomotive
90 boulevard de Clichy (18th arr.); tel. 01 53 41 88 88
This enormous disco near the Moulin Rouge has three floors for dancing, and the occasional show by rock groups. Here young people predominate, and the doormen are less formidable than elsewhere.

La Casbah
18/20 rue de la Forge-Royale (11th arr.); tel. 01 43 71 71 89
Shades of Scheherazade here, with "Casablanca" a constant projected presence on the club walls, but the music is Seventies and
the clientele relatively civilized.

Café de l'Industrie
16 rue Saint-Sabin (11th arr.); tel. 01 70 01 35 33
Previously a low-life bar, now a star on the clubbing scene, this is half
bar, half restaurant – cheap and cheerful, popular with the young and
always busy.

Rock, folk,
Latin

Fans of modern music styles will be in their element in Paris where
you can find every kind of beat – be it jazz, afro, rock, folk or Latin – on
the clubbing scene.

La Java
105 rue du Faubourg-du-Temple (10th arr.); tel. 01 42 02 20 52
Swinging night-scene with Latin American music, especially Cuban
rhythmns and a Brazilian evening on Sunday – a rainbow coalition of
all colours, cultures and ages.

Hard Rock Café
14 boulevard Montmartre (9th arr.); tel. 01 42 46 10 00
They are all over the world, these Hard Rock Cafés, and Paris in no
exception – music to match, hard rock and loud!

Bataclan
50 boulevard Voltaire (11th arr.); tel. 01 47 00 30 12
Medium-sized music hall. Live music, especially rock, plus disco with
house and techno, alternating with theme scenes (striptease, gay
nights). Not for the fainthearted!

Le Saint
7 rue Saint-Séverin (5th arr.); tel. 01 43 25 50 04
Rock and soul from the Fifties to the Seventies in a 13th-c. crypt.

Opening Times

Shop opening hours are not regulated by law in France. Since museums and monuments such as châteaux often stop admitting visitors
up to half an hour before official closing time, the times given here are
only an indication. To be on the safe side allow up to an hour either
way when planning a visit. Alternatively anyone who shows interest
and some persistence may get a surprise by being admitted outside
normal hours and having a personal guided tour.

Shops

As a rule shops are open from 9.30am to 6.30pm. Food shops tend to
open earlier but the smaller ones often close for lunch from 12.30 to 2
or even 4 then stay open later in the evening. Shops normally close
on Sundays but bakers, butchers, wine merchants and florists are
open until noon or 1pm. All the shops which open on Sundays are
closed on Mondays and sometimes on Wednesdays.

Department
stores

Department stores and some of the larger retailers open during the
week from 9.30am to 6.30pm.

Shopping malls,
supermarkets

Shopping malls and supermarkets (centres commerciaux, super-
marchés) are usually open from 9am to 7pm or 9pm. Some open on
Sunday mornings, and many of them are closed on Mondays.

See Currency	Banks
See Postal Services	Post offices
Museum opening times in this guide are given either under the section for that museum in the A to Z, or in the entry in the Museums section in this part of the guide. All the State-run museums (Musée National de...) are closed on Tuesdays. Some museums are closed on public holidays.	Museums
Public parks and gardens are open until dusk. They open at 10am from October to March, and at 8am for the rest of the year.	Parks and gardens

Parking

See Driving in Paris

Parks, Gardens and Theme Parks

See A to Z, Bois de Boulogne	Bois de Boulogne
See A to Z, Vincennes	Bois de Vincennes
92 boulogne-Billancourt, 6 quai du 4 Septembre; Métro: Porte de Saint-Cloud, Porte d'Auteuil; buses: 52, 72; open 15 March–1 April and 1 Sept. to 15 Nov. daily 2–6pm, 1 April to 20 Aug. 2–7pm Different gardening styles in one large park.	Jardins Albert-Kahn
See A to Z, Bois de Boulogne	Jardin d'Acclimatation
Dalle Montparnasse – place des 5 Martyrs du Lycée Buffon (14th/15th arr.) Reached by lifts from the Gare Montparnasse this modern 6ha/15 acres of gardens has lawns, quiet places and tennis courts.	Jardin Atlantique
See A to Z, Luxembourg	Jardin de Luxembourg
See A to Z, Jardin des Plantes	Jardin des Plantes
See A to Z, Tuileries	Jardin des Tuileries
3 avenue de la Porte d'Auteuil (16th arr.); Métro: Porte d'Auteuil; open April–Sep. daily 9am–6pm, Oct.–March 10am–5pm The city's municipal nursery; visitors can look round the gardens and greenhouses.	Jardin Fleuriste de la Ville de Paris
Métro: Balard; 15th arr. Futuristic park with two large greenhouses, theme gardens and many water features on the former site of the Citroën car factory (landscape gardeners: Provost, Clément; 1992).	Parc André Citroën
Rue des Morillons (15th arr.); Métro: Convention A modern park with a scented garden, terraced vines and a babbling brook.	Parc Georges Brassens

Parks, Gardens and Theme Parks

Parc des Buttes-Chaumont
Métro: Buttes-Chaumont, Botzaris; 19th arr.
This park, on one of the highest points in Paris, was laid out by Adolphe Alphand for Napoleon III in 1866/67 on what was then a bare hill (*chauve*=bare, *mont*=hill, i.e. Chaumont). It was designed on the English model as a terraced natural park and has quite a large lake overlooked by a promontory crowned by a little Roman temple. Visitors can relax in the lakeside restaurant or hire a rowing boat on the lake.

★Parc Monceau
Boulevard de Courcelles (8th arr.); Métro: Monceau
The aristocrat among Paris's parks, the Parc Monceau was redesigned in 1862 by Adolphe Alphand. A favourite haunt of Marcel Proust, its sculpture and ruins still lend it a romantic air and many newlyweds come here for their wedding photographs.

Parc Montsouris
Boulevard Jourdan (14th arr.); Métro/RER: Cité Universitaire
Another idyllic place for an open-air outing, the Parc Montsouris is opposite the student residences of the Cité Universitaire Internationale. Laid out on the English model in 1862, it has winding paths, little waterfalls and children's play areas. The city's meteorological observatory is in the south-west corner.

Parc Zoologique de Paris
See A to Z, Vincennes

★Promenade Plantée (Bastille-Vincennes)
Métro: Gare de Lyon, Reuilly-Diderot; 12th arr.
Unusual 4.5km/2¹/₂ mile walk (and cycle path) over the redundant Daumesnil viaduct – the "Viaduc des Arts" – between the Place de la Bastille and Bois de Vincennes.

A colourful "folly" in the Parc de la Villette, a recreational and educational complex

Between Paris and Versailles, on the edge of the Marly forest, the Désert de Rez covers an area of some 40ha/100 acres. It was conceived in the late 18th c. by a certain Monsieur de Monville, whose dream it was to create a philosopher's park with walks that would stimulate contemplative thought. His architect, Le Rouge, was charged with shaping hillocks, diverting streams, and planting rare plants and shady trees, a task eventually completed in 1780. All this has long since reverted to nature, but the Désert de Rez remains a gem among Paris's green spaces.

★Le Désert de Rez

See Excursions, Saint-Cloud

Parc de Saint-Cloud

See A to Z, Villette

Parc de la Villette

See A to Z, Fontainebleau

Fontainebleau

See Excursions, Sceaux

Sceaux

See A to Z, Versailles

Versailles

★★Theme Parks

See A to Z, Disneyland · Paris

Disneyland • Paris

Off the A1 motorway, 38km/24 miles north of Paris in the Oise Département, Parc Astérix, opened in 1989, extends over 18ha/45 acres and recreates the comic-book world of that lovable little ancient Gaul, Asterix, and his large friend Obelix. The busy Via Antiqua will take you to visit their village and then on to ancient Rome and the Ave Caesar carousel. Other attractions include the dolphinarium, and the Paris street that takes you through a thousand years of French history. Two new attractions in 1998 are Le Forêt des Druids and Les Espions de César.

Parc Astérix

At Elancourt, just 10km/6 miles south-west of Versailles, is a hexagonal park (area 5 ha/12 acres; opened 1991) reproducing France in miniature. Broad paths take visitors through old rural villages and typical French countryside, passing by the châteaux of the Loire, imposing fortresses, famous cathedrals, etc., plus, of course, the sights of Paris. An audiovisual show featuring puppets from the Musée Grévin recounts highlights in the history of France.
RER: Line C Saint-Quentin-en-Yvelines, then bus 420; information: tel. 01 30 51 51 51

Le Pays France Miniature

Post

Post offices are open Monday to Friday from 8am to 7pm and Saturdays from 9am to noon. The head post office (Poste principale, 52 rue du Louvre, 1st arr.) is open every day round the clock; after 7pm for cash withdrawal, letters and telegrams only. The Champs-Elysées post office (71 Champs-Elysées, 8th arr.) is also open every day, but its opening hours are: 8am–7pm, Sun. 10am–12, 2–7pm.

Post offices

French postboxes are yellow and have two slits, one for local letters, within the département, and one for everywhere else.

Postboxes

Stamps (timbres) are sold in post offices, tobacconists (bureaux de tabac) and bars selling cigarettes.

Postage

Telegrams	Tel. 36 55 (24-hours)
Post codes	The last two numbers in the post codes for Paris refer to the number of the arrondissement (e.g. 75009 = 9th arrondissement).

Public Holidays

January 1st (Jour de l'An, New Year's Day)
May 1st (Fête du Travail, Labour Day)
May 8th (Fête de l'Armistice de 1945, VE Day)
July 14th (Fête Nationale, Bastille Day)
August 15th (Assomption, Assumption)
November 1st (Toussaint, All Saints)
November 11th (Fête de l'Armistice de 1918, Armistice Day)
December 25th (Noël, Christmas Day)
plus Ascension Day, Easter Monday, Whit Monday

Public Transport

Information

The métro, RER and bus services for Paris are operated by its own public transport authority, the Régie Autonome des Transports Parisiens (RATP). For general information about these services: tel. 01 43 46 14 14 (6am–9pm daily). There is also an English-speaking RATP infoline: 08 36 68 41 14.

Métro
(map pp.286–287)

With its excellent network of 15 lines covering the whole of Paris, and its relatively cheap fares, Paris's underground system, the Métro – short for Métropolitain – is the best way for visitors to get around the city.

When using the métro remember that although the lines each have their own number they are generally referred to by the name of the station at the end of the line. Thus if you want to get to *Montparnasse* from *Cité* you take the line which terminates at *Porte d'Orléans*. The signs for the "Direction" are blue and the connections (Correspondances) to other lines are given in white and yellow illuminated signs. Each station concourse carries maps of the whole system and each carriage has a map showing the route of that particular line. The first train leaves at 5.30am and the last train leaves the terminals at 12.30am. During peak hours trains run at 90 second intervals, otherwise, when demand is less, the time between them varies between 2 and 7 minutes.

Tickets can be bought at métro stations and from some tobacconists (with the "tabac" sign). You can get a single ticket (ticket/billet) for one journey anywhere within zone 1, a book (carnet) of 10 tickets (which works out about 40% cheaper – ask for "un carnet, s'il vous plaît"), a ticket for a day, week, or month, or a special "Paris Visite" travel pass (see below). To get on to the platform insert the ticket into a slot at the barrier which will automatically check and cancel it. Métro and bus tickets are interchangeable.

RER

The Réseau Express Régional (RER) has four lines in Paris: lines A and B are operated by RATP, lines C and D by SNCF (Société Nationale des Chemins de Fer – France's national railway company). A new line, Météore, is due to run from the south-east of the city on the right bank of the Seine up to the Madeleine. The sections of the RER in the city have the same fares and tickets as the métro, but changing from one RER line to another requires a new ticket. SNCF fares vary according to the length of the journey. As well as single tickets, which are obtainable from ticket offices and machines, there are SNCF season tickets for a week or a month: for information tel. 01 53 90 20 20 (6am–10pm). RER trains run from 5.30am until midnight or 12.30am, and are less frequent than the métro (during peak hours they run at between 2 and 7 minute intervals).

The RATP bus system has 60 lines in Paris alone (and over 150 in the suburbs) which makes it less easy to use than the métro, but buses do have the added advantage of letting you see more of Paris by exploring the city above ground.

Buses

The tickets are the same as for the métro, and tickets and carnets can be bought from the driver. A ticket is valid only for a single journey, without changing. Each ticket covers up to two stage (sections) within the city, and you need to get an extra ticket if you travel outside the central zone. Buses generally operate from 6.30am to 8.30pm, but some lines run until 1.30am. Apart from these there is the Noctambus service, which operates from 1am to 6am, leaving from Châtelet every 30 to 60 minutes (limited service on Sundays and bank holidays). Another special service is the Balabus which is a sightseeing bus that operates from April to September on Sundays and bank holidays from 12 midday to 8pm. Information about all these bus services is also available in English on the RATP infoline: tel. 08 36 68 77 14.

Paris Visite is an RATP travel card designed specially for visitors. It is a flat-rate travel ticket valid for 1, 2, 3 or 5 consecutive days which allows unlimited access to the métro, buses, RER network, Montmartre funicular, Montmartrobus, Noctambus, airport shuttle services and the SNCF trains in the Ile de France region. It also entitles the holder to reductions on admission charges for a number of Paris attractions. Paris Visite passes are half-price for children under 12 and obtainable from the main Métro and RER stations, SNCF stations in the Ile de France region, Paris's international airports and all tourist offices (see Information), including RATP's "Services Touristiques": 53ter quai des Grands-Augustins; tel. 01 40 46 42 17, and place de la Madeleine; tel. 01 42 65 31 18. *Formule 1* is a ticket for one day's unlimited travel on bus, métro and RER in 2 or 3 zones. The Carte orange, with the *Coupon jaune*, is for unlimited travel for a week or a month and needs a passport photograph to go with it.

Travel cards
(Paris Visite,
Formule 1,
Coupon jaune)

The six main-line railway stations are all linked by métro and have their own métro station. Each train station – Gare du Nord, Gare de l'Est, Gare de Lyon, Gare d'Austerlitz and Gare Montparnasse – has a City of Paris tourist information centre as well (see Information).

**Main-line
rail travel**

SNCF operates all France's main-line trains, including the TGV, the high-speed rail service.
For information about SNCF services within Ile-de-France: tel. 01 53 90 20 20.
For information about major TGV lines throughout France: tel. 08 36 35 35 35.

Information

In France, you must stamp your ticket before boarding the train, using one of the orange *composteur* machines in the station concourse or on the platform. You can be fined on the train if your ticket has not been properly stamped.

Tickets

Gare d'Austerlitz/Gare d'Orleans
55 quai d'Austerlitz (13th arr.); tel. 01 45 84 14 18
Trains for south-western France, Spain and Portugal.

Stations

Gare de l'Est
10 place du 11 Novembre 1918 (10th arr.); tel. 01 42 09 51 97

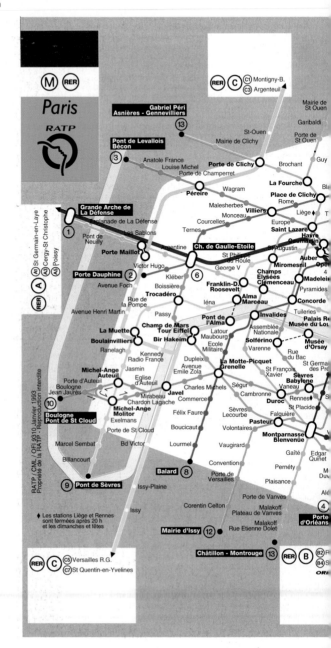

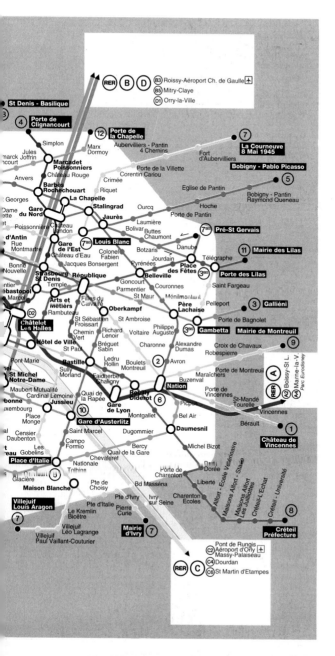

Trains for eastern France, Luxembourg, Germany, Austria, Switzerland and eastern Europe.

Gare de Lyon
20 boulevard Diderot)12th arr.); tel. 01 43 41 52 70
Trains for south-eastern France by TGV, Switzerland and Italy

Gare de Montparnasse
17 boulevard Vaugirard (15th arr.); tel. 01 43 22 57 96
Trains for Brittany and Aquitaine, including the TGV Atlantique

Gare du Nord
18 rue de Dunkerque (10th arr.); tel. 01 42 80 11 50
Trains for northern France, Scandinavia, Belgium, Holland, Germany and Great Britain, including Eurostar

Gare Saint-Lazare
13 rue d'Amsterdam (8th arr.); tel. 01 43 87 72 51
Trains for Normandy and connections for cross-Channel ferries

Rail Travel

See Public Transport

Restaurants

Gastronomy's undisputed capital

Paris sees itself as the undisputed capital of gastronomy – and with good cause, since it has restaurants – and cuisines – of every description, from the gourmet temples of haute cuisine to more informal bistros serving regional specialities, plus ethnic restaurants with food from all over the world.

In a Parisian restaurant the customer waits to be shown to a table by the head waiter and once seated is expected to order a three course meal, opting either for a set meal or choosing from the à la carte menu. Tax and service charges are included (usually shown by "s.c." – *service compris* – at the foot of the bill) but you may choose to leave a tip of perhaps 10% or add it under "extras" on the credit card slip (nowadays many restaurants accept credit cards).

Very few restaurants offer low-cost light meals or snacks. You are more likely to find these in a bistro or brasserie (see Cafés, Salons de Thé and Brasseries), or, for the bottom end of the market, try a fast-food outlet such as one of the self-service chains (see Children). If you are on a tight budget it is worth remembering that even the top restaurants charge less at lunchtime, and many places have good value set menus consisting of a main course with either a starter or a dessert, sometimes with wine as well.

Categories

Given that Paris has so many restaurants the following selection can only cover a fraction of what is on offer. The three price categories are intended as a guide for a meal à la carte, and obviously the cost is more if vintage wines or expensive specialities are chosen.

Category I   from 400 francs per person
Category II   from 250 francs per person
Category III   from 150 francs per person

Relaxing at Fouquet's Restaurant after a stroll in the Champs-Elysées

Restaurants with French cuisine

★Les Ambassadeurs (in Hôtel Crillon)
10 place de la Concorde (8th arr.); tel. 01 44 71 16 16 (open daily)
The grand dining room, glistening with mirrors and crystal chandeliers, is the epitome of luxury, against a background of marble mosaics, frescoes and midnight blue decor. And the creative cuisine exquisitely accords with these elegant surroundings, making this legendary de luxe Paris hotel a real gourmet mecca.

Category I
(famous for their
haute cuisine)

★L'Ambroisie
9 place des Vosges (4th arr.), tel. 01 42 78 51 45 (closed Sun., Mon.)
Simple, almost severe decor, under a high ceiling, but undoubtedly stylish. Since he opened his own restaurant in 1985 Bernard Pacaud has continued to rank as one of Paris's top chefs. You need to book weeks ahead to enjoy the very finest of French classical cuisine, with a view of Notre Dame thrown in for good measure.

★L'Assiette
181 rue du Château (14th arr.); tel. 01 43 22 64 86 (closed Mon., Tue.)
Looking at it from outside you would never think that this was one of Paris's top restaurants, frequented by VIPs such as fashion supremo Karl Lagerfeld, writer Françoise Sagan and France's late President, François Mitterrand, who, accompanied by his four bodyguards, used to lunch here most Saturdays. The food here, though, is of the very finest, presided over by the inimitable Lulu Rousseau, one-time militant Trotskyist and veteran of 1968 (hence the black Basque beret).

★Fouquet's
99 avenue des Champs-Elysées (8th arr.); tel. 01 47 23 70 60
(closed Sun. 1st floor)
Opened in 1901 this was the first restaurant on the Champs-Elysées
and was a grand place to dine from the outset, a kind of luxury
canteen for the theatre, film and art world. In 1988, after it had been
threatened with closure, all Fouquet's friends rallied round to secure it
listed status.

★Jules Verne
Champ de Mars, Eiffel Tower (2nd platform; 7th arr.); tel. 01 45 55 61
44 (open daily)
Certainly one of the most impressive rooms with a view in town –
here Paris is quite literally at your feet. The decor (black and shades of
mauve) is unobtrusive so as not to detract from the breathtaking
panorama of the city. Opened in 1983 the restaurant serves meals that
rank as highly as the view – and with prices to match. If it is full, try the
new restaurant "Altitude 95" on the Tower's first platform (tel. 01 45
55 00 21).

★Laurent
41 avenue Gabriel (8th arr.); tel. 01 42 25 00 39 (closed Sat. lunch,
Sun.)
The enchanting terrace is graced by 100-year-old trees. The menu is
also a delight – masterchef Philippe Braun was a pupil of Maître Joël
Robuchon. The service is excellent and the wine-list of a like quality,
with Philippe Bourguignon in charge of the wine and ever ready to
help you make the perfect choice. The prices are relatively reasonable
for such haute cuisine, but you need to book well ahead to be sure of
a table.

★Maxim's
3 rue Royale (8th arr.); tel. 01 42 65 27 94 (closed Sun.)
This legendary establishment, with its Art Nouveau decor, has always
been a favourite rendezvous of the famous, where international VIPs
rub shoulders with Paris's top people. The prices that patrons have
to pay for the name, the stylish interior and the excellent traditional
cuisine are as you would expect – 800 francs and upwards, and then
only after you have made your reservation long beforehand.

★Alain Ducasse
59 Avenue Raymond Poincaré (16th arr.); tel. 01 47 27 12 27
(closed Sat., Sun., July)
Joël Robuchon, the previous chef whose restaurant here opened in
1993, was adjudged chef of the century by Gault et Millau. When the
Master retired in 1996 his place in this magnificent establishment was
taken by Alain Ducasse, already a holder of three Michelin stars.
Try his turbot with calamares or poulet de Bresse with foie gras and
truffles. Needless to say, you have to book weeks ahead to get a table
in one of the three comfortable dining rooms.

★La Tour d'Argent
15/17 quai de la Tournelle (5th arr.); tel. 01 43 54 23 31 (closed Mon.)
One of the most famous gourmet restaurants in Paris, with its own
gourmet museum. Wonderful view of the Seine and Notre Dame,
luxurious setting, fastidious ambience, tables gleaming with top quality glassware and silver, outstanding service, fantastic wine list and
incredible traditional French cuisine – and all priced accordingly. You
need to book at least a month in advance to dine here in the evening,
but you may well get a table here at lunchtime, and at a more affordable price.

★Bofinger
5 rue de la Bastille (4th arr.); tel. 01 42 72 87 82 (open daily)
The oldest brasserie (1864) in Paris and a star restaurant in the Bastille quarter. It is worth a visit if only for the wonderful fin-de-siècle decor – tables under the glass dome are particularly at a premium. The food also has a great reputation; recommended fare – Alsace specialities with excellent sauerkraut or the wonderful oysters. One drawback: it's always packed.

Category II
(fine food at
more reasonable
prices)

★Carré des Feuillants
14 rue Castiglione (1st arr.); tel. 01 42 86 82 82
(closed Sat. lunch, Sun., August)
Just behind the Place Vendôme, top chef Alain Dutournier delights in experimenting with exquisite regional dishes from the south-west of France. There is a wine merchant's shop that goes with the restaurant.

★Le Dôme
108 boulevard du Montparnasse (14th arr.); tel. 01 43 35 25 81
(closed Mon.)
This wonderful fish restaurant is and always has been the place for oysters – especially when accompanied by savoury bread and wonderful butter, it stays open late into the night too.

★Aux Iles Marquises
15 rue de la Gaîtè (14th arr.); tel. 01 43 20 93 58 (closed Sat.–Sun. pm)
Still something of a find, here you can get very good fish and other culinary specialities but at much lower prices than in many other fish restaurants.

Lipp
151 boulevard Saint-Germain (6th arr.); tel. 01 45 48 53 91 (open daily)
For some time they have changed the specialities here every four years as compared with every 20 to 30 years previously. Since it opened in 1900, Lipp's has not been patronised for its food, which certainly has its ups and downs, but because it is Lipp's, the most famous brasserie in Paris, and certainly worth a look, with its listed fin-de-siècle interior. Every prominent French politician, writer and journalist has been here at some time or other. Its reputation is on the wane, though, and the food and service are probably not what they used to be.

★Michel Rostang
20 rue Rennequin (17th arr.); tel. 01 47 63 40 77 (closed Sat., Sun.)
Michel Rostang is an aesthete in the kitchen, creating dishes that are as exquisite as they are original. There is a feast for the eyes as well, in the wonderful glass sculptures in the Lalique room of this high-class restaurant.

Au Pied de Cochon
6 rue Coquillière (1st arr.); tel. 01 42 36 11 75 (open 24 hours)
Open round the clock, and has been since 6th December 1946. This is where early risers, late-night partygoers and the porters and traders from the provision market used to congregate for onion soup and breakfast, but since Les Halles transferred to Rungis in 1969 the early morning here has been much quieter. During the day tourists and the colourful denizens of the quarter still keep the place busy – try the excellent mussels, lobsters, etc. or the eponymous pig's trotters.

★Le Train Bleu
Gare de Lyon, 1st floor (12th arr.);
tel. 01 43 43 09 06 (open daily)
This elegant restaurant in the Gare de Lyon, built for the world fair in

Outside a brasserie on the banks of the Seine – French cooking combined with the Parisian zest for life

1900, is a relic from the Belle Epoque but owes its name to the famous Blue Train that from 1922 to 1960 ran between Paris and the Côte d'Azur. In the "finest station restaurant in the world" you dine under a ceiling depicting in vivid colour the stations the train passed through on its way to the Mediterranean. A word to the wise: the bar here is cheaper than in the neighbouring brasseries.

★Au Trou Gascon
40 rue Taine (12th arr.); tel. 01 43 44 34 26 (closed Sat., Sun.)
This little Belle Epoque restaurant serves excellent food with a sumptuous Gascon panache.

Category III
(good food and
good value)

Chartier
7 rue du Faubourg Montmartre (9th arr.); tel. 01 47 70 86 29
(open daily)
Chartier, which first opened in 1896, has from its earliest days served good food – traditional French dishes such as blanquette de veau – at surprisingly low prices. With its waiters in long white aprons, black waistcoats and bow ties, and a cheery atmosphere it is always crowded – and not only with the average diner. Celebrity regulars in the past have included Edith Piaf and Marcello Mastroianni.

★Chez Françoise
Entrance next to the Pont Alexandre III opposite 2 rue Fabert, in the Air France building below the car park for the Aérogare des Invalides (private parking in front of the restaurant); tel. 01 45 80 12 02
Not easy to find but well worth the effort, offering excellent traditional cuisine supplemented by a superb wine list – plus blues, jazz and chansons.

★Le Clocher
22 rue Guillaume Apollinaire (6th arr.); tel. 01 42 86 00 88 (open daily)
Jolly atmosphere and the best of regional recipes like Granny used to
make such as pot-au-feu, confit de canard and crème brûlé.

La Guirlande de Julie
25 place des Vosges; tel. 01 48 87 94 07
You can eat out here superbly under the arches of the delightful Place
des Vosges. Try the carte de jour of fresh seasonal foods.

★Le Petit Zinc
11 rue Saint Benoît (6th arr.); tel. 01 42 61 20 60
Opposite the Latitudes Jazz Club in the heart of Saint-Germain-
des-Prés – fine food and lovely art nouveau interior. Try the ravioli
à l'escargot, lamb cutlets in olive sauce or pheasant with pureed
celeriac and potato. Be sure to book!

★Polidor
41 rue Monsieur Le Prince (6th arr.); tel. 01 43 26 95 34 (open daily)
Always crowded out, this bistro (dating from 1845) serves generous
portions. Regulars have their own napkins, the service is friendly, the
prices moderate. Ernest Hemingway and André Gide are said to have
eaten here.

Le Roi du Pot-au-Feu
34 rue Vignon (9th arr.); tel. 01 47 42 37 10 (closed Sun., July)
You can still get pot-au-feu done the traditional way in this pleasant
little bistro. In summer it has tables out on the pavement.

Thoumieux
79 rue Saint Dominique (7th arr.); tel. 01 47 05 49 75
(open daily)
A Thirties brasserie attached to a hotel, Thoumieux serves simple
dishes at very reasonable prices and is always full right up to midnight. A popular place to eat, so book in advance.

★Ty Coz
35 rue Saint-Georges (9th arr.); tel. 01 48 78 42 95
(closed Sun., Mon. evening)
A breton decor with breton food – sweet and savoury crêpes, fish
specials, seafood, everything is "à la bretonne". Cheery place with
superb cuisine. Ten years ago its former owner and head chef,
Jacqueline Libois, founded the ARC (association of women restaura-
teurs and chefs) which has long since demonstrated that men are by
no means the only chefs with gourmet prowess. Mme Libois has
since retired and transferred the restaurant to her equally accom-
plished daughter.

Restaurants with ethnic cuisine

★Soleil d'Est chez Chen   Chinese
15 rue du Théâtre (15th arr.); tel. 01 45 79 34 34 (open daily)
Try the steamed ravioli or delicately spiced lobster, then be persuaded
to go onto the Peking duck, served, as it should be, in three parts (cat. II).

Nioullaville
32/34 Rue de l'Orillon (11th arr.); tel. 01 40 79 91 00 (open daily)
Vast Chinese restaurant with seating for 500. Here you can choose
what you want from little trolleys wheeled between the tables. Very
large menu; chefs from China, Vietnam, Thailand and Cambodia can
be seen working away diligently in the steamy kitchen (cat. III).

Salons de Thé

Indian	**★Kamal** 20 rue Rousselet (7th arr.); tel. 01 44 07 18 85 (open daily) This exquisite restaurant, in an obscure sidestreet, is very popular thanks to the extremely obliging service, lengthy menu with dishes from northern India, and painstakingly prepared and finely spiced food (cat. III).
Japanese	**★Benkay** 61 quai de Grenelle (15th arr.); tel. 01 40 58 21 26 (open daily) Benkay, in the Nikko Hotel, is one of the best Japanese restaurants in Paris. You can enjoy the house specialities – raw fish and kebabs – and other cunningly contrived dishes as well as a superb view of the Seine (cat. I).
Jewish	**★Jo Goldenberg** 7 rue des Rosiers (4th arr.); tel. 01 48 87 20 16 (open daily) You get to the restaurant through the delicatessen attached to it. Specialities include pastrami, gefilte fish, salt beef and strudel. Photos of celebrity guests decorate the walls (cat. II).
Portuguese	Saudade 34 rue des Bourdonnais (1st arr.); tel. 01 42 36 30 71 (closed Sun.) The walls of the Saudade, reckoned to be the best Portuguese restaurant in town, are covered with fine "azulejos", Portugal's own traditional tiles, and the speciality of the house is naturally that other traditional Portuguese favourite, bacalhau (salted cod), served up in a host of different ways. Needless to say the wine list covers the whole spectrum of Portuguese wines, from vinho verde to port (cat. II).
Russian	**★Dominique** 19 rue Bréa (6th arr.); tel. 01 43 27 08 80 (closed Sun., Mon. lunch) A shop and restaurant where you can eat out in style in the dining room at the back, or nibble little Russian delicacies at the bar from the shop around the corner. The restaurant with its nostalgic images of Mother Russia is not only a favourite haunt of Russians living in Paris but has often hosted visitors from the homeland such as Nobel prizewinner André Solzhenitsyn. Vast vodka selection! (cat. II)

Salons de Thé

See Cafés, Salons de Thé and Brasseries

Shopping and Souvenirs

Fashion capital and shopper's paradise

Think of shopping in Paris and immediately fashion springs to mind. After all, this is still the city of haute couture and the home of the great fashion houses. Those who can afford their one-off creations are very few and far between though, but even the fashion-conscious on a limited budget can still find a good buy in Paris so long as they settle for something less than a couturier label. Fashion apart, the French capital ranks alongside London and New York as one of the world's finest cities for shopping, and its department stores and boutiques can supply every need. Top of the list for most people, besides fashion and fashion accessories, comes exclusive perfumes, antiques, fine food and wine. Take care though, shopping in Paris may be a wonderful experience but it is very easy to spend a lot of money. Most things are more expensive here than in other European big cities. That is partly due to the high rents that many shops have to pay, but also

A glorious praline house – few can resist its chocolate and cakes

because the VAT here is higher than in most neighbouring countries (luxury goods, for example, carry a VAT rate of 20.6%, see VAT below). But even bargain hunters can still strike lucky. Away from the tourist beat are shops that always stock goods at reduced prices, even outside the sales season.

One feature of Paris is that so many shops of the same kind are grouped together in one particular street or district. The big couturiers are centred on the rue du Faubourg-Saint-Honoré, avenue Montaigne and place des Victoires, while Saint-Germain-des-Prés is the place for good fashion boutiques. Shoe shops are in the rue de Grenelle, rue de Cherche-Midi and rue de Rennes. Textile wholesalers are mainly in the rue de Sentier, d'Aboukir, de Clery, Réaumur and rue de Turenne. Luxury jewellers are to be found on the place Vendôme and in rue de la Paix. For crystal, porcelain and silver, look in the rue du Paradis, while around the place de Fuerstemberg is the area for table linen, cushions, vases, and other elements of interior design. Antique shops are mainly in the rue Saint-Paul and the 6th arrondissement. Art galleries and bookshops are grouped around the rue de Seine, furniture stores along the rue du Faubourg-Saint-Antoine. The best delicatessens are close to the place de la Madeleine.

Shopping districts

With VAT on luxury items – precious stones, perfumes, tobacco wares, CDs, etc. – at 20.6% it is worth claiming this tax back if you can. This is possible for visitors from outside the European Union who buy a minimum of 1200 francs worth of goods at the same time in the same shop. You need to get the sales staff to fill in a "bordereau de vente à l'exportation" which you then get stamped at customs on leaving France. Once back home send the duly stamped form to the shop within 3 months and you will get your VAT back. Your refund may take less time if you pay by credit card.

Value Added Tax (VAT)

Shopping and Souvenirs

Selection of shops

Antiques	See entry
Books	Boulinier, 20 boulevard Saint-Michel (5th arr.), comics.

Bouquinistes: See A to Z, Quais
★FNAC, in Forum des Halles, 1 rue Pierre-Lescot (1st arr.); France's largest chain of book and media stores, where books are slightly cheaper than elsewhere. CDs and photographic materials too. Branches: 136 rue de Rennes (6th arr.), 4 place de la Bastille (12th arr.), 26/30 avenue des Ternes (17th arr.).

Shakespeare & Company: see A to Z, Quartier Latin.

CDs and records

Crocodisc, 40/42 rue des Ecoles (5th arr.) – everything except classical music.

FNAC: see Books

★Virgin Megastore, 52/60 avenue des Champs-Elysées (8th arr.): mammoth stocks (from classical to contemporary music) in the concourse of the former National City Bank.

Children's things

See Children

Department stores

Bazar de l'Hôtel de Ville, 52/64 rue de Rivoli (4th arr.); smaller than giants like Lafayette and Printemps but consequently easier to look round. Particularly good for DIY and interior decorating.

Forum des Halles: see A to Z, Les Halles

Les 4 Temps: see A to Z, La Défense
Au Bon Marché, 22 rue de Sèvres/rue du Bac (7th arr.); the grand-father of modern department stores (since 1852) and the only one on the Rive Gauche.

★Les Galeries Lafayette, 40 boulevard Haussmann (9th arr.); elegant department store under a vast glass dome, where all the fashionable names are represented; has possibly the world's largest perfume department. A total of over 70,000 brand names.

★Le Printemps, 64 boulevard Haussmann (9th arr.); high fashion and exquisite perfumes under a Belle Epoque glass dome from the time of Napoleon. Café on a rooftop terrace with a view.

La Samaritaine, 19 rue de la Monnaie (1st arr.); rather old-fashioned – the 9th floor of the building with the lovely Art Nouveau façade has a viewing platform complete with café and great view of Paris.

Fabrics

Rodin, 36 avenue Champs-Elysées (8th arr.). Quality products – muslin, silk, wool, haute couture fabrics, plus special offers.

Wolff et Descourtis, 18 Galerie Vivienne (2nd arr.), mainly Italian and French silk and wool.

Fashions for men

★Bidermann, 114 rue de Turenne (3rd arr.); top men's fashions at half the usual price.

Sonia Rykiel, 194 boulevard Saint-Germain (6th arr.); men's outfitters from head to toe, women's fashions a few doors along at No. 175.

Bazar de l'Hôtel de Ville – Paris's temple to interior decorating also has a large perfumery department

★Paul Smith, 22 boulevard Raspail (7th arr.); classical English, casual and just a little "crazy".

Agnès B, 6 rue du Jour (1st arr.); shopping for the whole family from this successful woman designer – for baby, tot, teenager, mum and dad.

Fashions for women

Azzedine Alaïa, 7 rue de Moussy (4th arr.); in a converted warehouse – shapely clothes especially for the fuller figure.

★Christian Lacroix, 73 rue du Faubourg-St-Honoré (8th arr.); a tendency to favour the warm colours of his homeland of Provence.

★Kenzo, 3 place des Victoires (1st arr.); time and again refreshing new combinations of checks and colours, great casual classics for both men and women.

★Lolita Lempicka, 13 rue Pavée (4th arr.); divine bridal creations. Mendès, 65 rue Montmartre (2nd arr.); haute couture by Versace, Yves Saint Laurent and Christian Lacroix at half-price.

★Le Mouton à Cinq Pattes, 19 rue Grégoire-de-Tours (6th arr.); highlights of the Paris fashion scene at super-saver prices.

★Réciproque, 89/123 rue de la Pompe (16th arr.); couturier clothing at moderate prices.

At 64/122 rue d'Alésia (14th arr.); south of Montparnasse cemetery – ex-factory clothing by prêt-à-porter manufacturers like Cacherel, Kenzo and Daniel Hechter at half-price.

Glass-covered Nostalgia

Walter Benjamin thought of "les passages de Paris" as "the most important architecture of the 19th century", as "a phantasmagoria of a Utopian goal"; Louis Aragon named them "human aquaria" and "great glass coffins"; Julio Cortázar described them as "false skies of stucco and dirty roof-windows". The first "passages" or arcades date back to the end of the 18th century but the heyday of these glass-roofed streets came between 1800 and 1860. This was the time when everything had become too small and crowded in Paris; when in the narrow, unpaved streets the noise, filth and stench were getting more and more out of control; when, thanks to the invention of iron girders, street-long roofs of glass with skylights could be built. It was the time when wily speculators realized the economic advantages provided by such shopping arcades if located in an area such as that around the Palais Royal, where trade – and entertainments – had flourished previously. It was a time when that breed best described as the idle stroller or *flâneur* appeared on the scene, seeking refuge in these enclosed spaces from the dirt and din of the gutter and the vagaries of the elements, and proceeding at a speed which equated, as Benjamin wrote in his fragment "Oeuvres de Passages", with that of someone taking a snail for a walk. The German poet Heinrich Heine was also amazed when he took a walk down the first arcades in Paris to have gas lighting. In the end well over a hundred shopping arcades with restaurants and tea salons enjoyed a vibrant existence in the 1st, 2nd and 19th arrondissements. Their decline was completely sudden. From 1853 onwards boulevards with broad pavements and electric lighting were built under the direction of Baron Haussmann, the prefect of Paris, and along these wide new roads the first large department stores began to open. An open-air culture became established, causing the *flâneurs* to forsake for good the arcades which they had so delighted

in frequenting. Most of these then became mere passageways, short-cuts between the new boulevards, and quickly degenerated into gloomy, filthy, stinking places. Now, however, in the last few years many of these shopping arcades are enjoying a real renaissance, although the twenty or so which have been lovingly restored remain places of nostalgia rather than commercial activity.

This old-world charm is particularly in evidence at the **Galerie Véro-Dodat** in Les Halles, between rue J.-J. Rousseau 19 and rue Bouloi 2 (1st arr.). This 80m/88yd long arcade, which was built for two prosperous butchers, Véro and Dodat, and opened in 1826, has now been splendidly refurbished. Time seems to have stood still here. With its black and white tiles, wooden panelling on the walls and beautiful mirrors between the shop fronts, the discreetly lit gallery creates a peaceful, wonderfully old-fashioned ambience, inviting the visitor to be a *flâneur* of yesteryear. Those interested in antiques will be in raptures in the doll shop of Robert Capia, where porcelain dolls from two centuries – "those veritable fairies of the arcades" in the words of Benjamin – are stacked right up to the ceiling. The **Galerie Vivienne**, a few hundred metres further on, in rue des Petits Champs (2nd arr.), is more elegant still. This arcade, built in 1823 and restored in pastel tones with its bas-reliefs and beautiful mosaic floor in the neo-classical style, was once the most exclusive covered shopping street in Paris, along with the **Galerie Colbert**, which leads off it at the far end and has also been restored to new glory. The difference between these and the less grand examples of *passages* was also clear from their nomenclature – only the most prestigious shopping streets were given the title "galerie". Among the most important businesses occupying the 176m/190yd long Galerie Vivienne are the designer-second-hand shop "La Marelle", the oldest bookshop in Paris

Galerie Vivienne: one of the most distinguished shopping arcades

"Petit-Siroux" (opened in 1826), the futuristically designed shop of Jean-Paul Gaultier, the enfant terrible among fashion designers, the expensive wine merchants "Legrand", a "Galerie Satirique", designed to keep the window-shopper amused, and the smart, yet casual tea salon "A Priori Thé".

The atmosphere of a long forgotten age is also discernible in the **Passage Jouffroy** on boulevard Montmartre (9th arr.), which has hardly been restored at all. Browsing in front of the boxes of books, which are set out over a length of 40m/44yds outside an antiquarian bookshop, is rather like being in a reading room. Indeed this shopping street is above all a paradise for collectors of all kinds: photographs of film stars, books about the cinema, old metal toys, doll's-house accessories and old cameras. The "Musée Grevin" a museum of waxworks, also finds an appropriate setting here. Just opposite, on the other side of the boulevard Montmartre, is the entrance to the winding **Passage des Panoramas** (2nd arr.). The large sculpted scenes of European cities by the American artist,

Fulton, which were housed in large rotundas and gave the arcade its name, have long since gone – they were destroyed in 1831. The 350m/383yd long arcade, one of the first places to benefit from gas lighting in 1817, used to be a meeting place for polite society with its array of variety theatres, cafés and elegant shops and was where, at the Théâtres des Variétés, Jacques Offenbach celebrated his triumphs. Its fame is nowadays somewhat dimmed.

Many of these arcades have over the years lost some of their charm, for instance, the Passage des Princes (2nd arr.), which has been more and more taken over by video and souvenir shops. Other shopping arcades are also unfortunately becoming very run-down – for example the Passage Brady (10th arr.) and the Passage du Ponceau (2nd arr.), where small traders are struggling to survive. And others, which have only recently been restored at great expense, such as the Passage du Bourg-L'Abbé and the three-storey Passage du Grand Cerf (both 2nd arr.), have a strange stillness all of their own, as if something is stopping their new-found beauty being appreciated.

Shopping and Souvenirs

In the rue du Jour, not far from Forum des Halles, can be found unconventional youthful fashion by Agnès B, Toi du Monde and Jean-Paul Gaultier.

Fine foods

★Alléosse, 13 rue Poncelet (17th arr.); Roger Alléosse sells virtually every type of French cheese.

★Androuet, 41 rue d'Amsterdam (8th arr.); over 200 cheese specialities, plus a restaurant with cheese menus.

Caviar Kaspia, 17 place de la Madeleine (8th arr.); caviar, salmon, trout.

★Debauve et Gallais, 30 rue des Sts-Pères (7th arr.); previously a chemist's but from 1800 a superlative chocolate shop with the very best pralines and 40 kinds of bonbon. The oldest confectioners in Paris, with branches at: 33 rue Vivienne (2nd arr.), 107 rue Jouffroy d'Abbans (17th arr.).

Fouquet, 22 rue François 1er (8th arr.); house speciality bonbons but not exactly cheap.

Divay, 50 rue du Faubourg-Saint-Honoré (10th arr.); good value sausages and pasties.

★Fauchon, 26 place de la Madeleine (8th arr.); world-famous delicatessen, where you can get luxury snacks in the basement.

★Izraël, 30 rue François Miron (4th arr.); spices and spirits from all over the world, reckoned to be the best epicerie in Paris.

Poujauran, 20 rue Jean-Nicot (7th arr.); great bread, crispy on the outside, wonderfully fresh on the inside.

Tartine et Chocolat, 60 avenue Paul Doumer (16th arr.); exquisite shop with delicious chocolates, branches at: 105 rue du Faubourg-Saint-Honoré (8th arr.), 24 rue de la Paix (2nd arr.), 266 boulevard Saint-Germain (7th arr.).

Jewellery

★Cartier, 13 rue de la Paix (2nd arr.); the famous jeweller's original store founded in 1847 with several branches in Paris including 51 rue François Ier (8th arr.), 12 avenue Montaigne (8th arr.), 7 and 23 place Vendôme.

Artcurial, 9 avenue Matignon (8th arr.); contemporary creations.

Leather goods

Hermès, 24 rue du Faubourg-Saint-Honoré (8th arr.); elegant classical handbags, wallets and belts, not exactly cheap.
Louis Vuitton, 54 avenue de Montaigne (8th arr.); luxury luggage.

Lingerie

★Chantal Thomas, 1 rue Vivienne (1st arr.); elegant lingerie and other fashion wear for women.

Sabbia Rosa, 71 rue des Sts-Pères (6th arr.); lovely lacey lingerie, but expensive.

Markets

See entry

Marie Marcié, 56 rue Tiquetonne (2nd arr.); classic but quirky models.

Millinery

★Olivier Chanan, 6 rue des Rosiers (4th arr.); elegant, extravagant and crazy, for him and her; clients include Queen Elizabeth II.

House of Cartier: for over 150 years the top name for high-quality jewellery

Fragonard, 39 boulevard des Capucines (2nd arr.); includes a Musée de la Parfumerie (free admission). **Perfumes**

★Guerlain, 68 avenues des Champs-Elysées (8th arr.); famous family firm with a history of over 160 years, creating exclusive perfumes for the rich; the only one of the great French parfumiers that sells its products exclusively to its own clients in its own country.

★Jean F. Laporte, 5 rue des Capucines (1st arr.) and 84bis Rue de Grenelle (7th arr.); great fragrances for him and her.

Shu Uemura, 176 boulevard Saint-Germain (6th arr.); Japanese cosmetics, very good advice.

Robert Clergerie, 5 rue du Cherche-Midi (6th arr.); extremely elegant trendsetter models. **Shoes**
   The rue du Cherche-Midi in Saint-Germain-des-Prés is full of shoe shops and designers from classical to crazy.

★Stéphane Kélian, 6 Place des Victoires (2nd arr.); probably France's best known shoe designer, way-out creations.

See Glass-covered Nostalgia (Baedeker Special, pp.298–299) **Shopping arcades**
Passage Choiseul, rue St-Augustin (2nd arr.)
Narrow and not very chic but extremely busy covered arcade from 1825 with a wide selection of wares; this is where the locals come to shop. From here it is worth making a sortie to the Bouffes Parisiens theatre where Jacques Offenbach premiered his "Orpheus in the Underworld".

Shopping and Souvenirs

★Galerie Colbert, rue des Petits Champs (2nd arr.)
This arcade, one of the finest in Paris, belongs to the neighbouring Bibliothèque Nationale and joins directly onto the Galerie Vivienne. Complete with rotunda and corinthian columns, the arcade has a good assortment of art books in the Librairie Colbert. Its Art Nouveau restaurant Le grand Colbert is also worth a visit.

Passage du Caire, 2 place du Caire (2nd arr.)
The longest and the oldest shopping arcade in Paris, the Passage du Caire was opened in 1799 to commemorate Napoleon's Egyptian campaign – hence the hieroglyphs and busts of pharaohs at the entrances. This very busy arcade is the hub of Parisian ready-to-wear clothes.

Souvenirs and unusual presents

Anna Joliet, 9 rue de Beaujolais (1st arr.); unusual music boxes and small music automata.

★Arguence, 16 rue du Pont Louis-Philippe (4th arr.); wonderful old violin and cello shop.

Carrousel du Louvre, 99 rue de Rivoli (1st arr.); this subterranean shopping arcade has all kinds of presents, souvenirs and other paraphernalia – only a little kitsch, but not very cheap either.

Emilio Robba, 29 Galerie Vivienne (2nd arr.); artificial flowers made of silk and other materials.

★Maison de la Famille, 10 place de la Madeleine (8th arr.); tasteful country-house style interior design items.

A table display at Pavillion Christophe

Olivier Pitan, 23 rue des Saints-Pères (6th arr.); enchanting flower arrangements.

Papeterie Moderne, 12 rue de la Ferronerie (1st arr.); enamel street signs (copies and originals), menu cards, price tickets, etc.

★Pavillon Christofie, 24 rue de la Paix (2nd arr.); exquisite silver and other tableware.

★Simon, 36 rue Etienne Marcel (2nd arr.); specialist in kitchen utensils such as copper pans and fine china.

La Samaritaine: see Department stores | Sports goods

★Au Vieux Campeur, 48 rue des Ecoles (5th arr.); a shop selling just about anything, it dates from the early Forties.

See Children | Toys

Les Caves Taillevent, 199 rue du Faubourg-Saint-Honoré (8th arr.); over 25,000 bottles from the regions of France. | Wines

★Legrand Filles et Fils, 1 rue de la Banque (2nd arr.); superb top wines, and everything needed to go with them – wine glasses, carafes, corkscrews, etc.

★Maison de la Vigne et du Vin de France, 21 rue François Ier (8th arr.); grand wine merchant in an elegant 18th/19th c. mansion.

Sightseeing Tours

The Paris tourist office (see Information) is just one of the many agencies that organize guided tours of the city. It has also worked out five trails – De la République à la Villette, Les Grands Boulevards, La Nouvelle Athènes, Les Champs Elysées and Montmartre – which have been put together in the "Carnets de poche du piéton", the pedestrian's pocket guide.
Guided
city tours

Baedeker's suggestions for individual sightseeing in Paris: see pp.62.

The Caisse Nationale des Monuments Historiques in the Marais quarter (Hôtel de Sully, 62 rue Saint-Antoine; tel. 01 44 61 20 00) organizes guided walks on historic and art history themes. The programme is available from their office; there is no need to book, just be at the appropriate meeting point a few minutes before the walk is due to start. | Caisse Nationale des Monuments Historiques guided walks

82 rue Taitbout (9th arr.); tel. 01 45 26 26 77 (not Sun., pub. hols.)
Métro: Saint-Georges; organized excursions. | Paris et son Histoire

35 rue La Boâtie (8th arr.); tel. 01 45 63 99 11
Métro: Saint-Augustin, Miromesnil
Guides who will go with you in your car or on the bus; all languages. | Troismil

Restaurant Panam 2002; tel. 01 42 25 64 39 (reservation required)
You can dine and tour the sights of Paris at the same time (2hrs); dep. 1pm, 8pm, 10pm cnr. rue de Rivoli/rue de Castiglione (1st arr.). | Restaurant-bus

17 rue de Clichy (9th arr.); tel. 01 42 85 72 79 (reservation required)
Tour in Bel Ami, a luxurious vintage Mercedes restored to its Belle Epoque glory and fitted with air-conditioning and video screen. | Bel-Ami bus

Sightseeing Tours

City tours by bus	Paris Vision, 214 rue de Rivoli (1st arr.); tel. 01 42 60 30 01; Métro: Tuileries.
	Cityrama, 4 place des Pyramides (1st arr.); tel. 01 44 55 61 00; Métro: Palais Royal.
	Cityrama/Théâtres-Voyages-Excursions, 21 rue de la Paix (2nd arr.); tel. 01 47 42 06 47; Métro: Opéra.
	Balabus Balabus is a special RATP service that takes in all the major sights. It operates from April to September from noon to 8pm, between Puteaux-La Défense and Gare de Lyon, on Sundays and public holidays; tel. 01 43 46 13 13.
	Les Cars Rouges Red doubledeckers operated by Parisbus with 9 stops; tel. 01 42 30 55 50.
Excursions by minibus	Paris Bus, 22 rue de la Prévoyance, Vincennes; tel. 01 43 65 55 55 Excursions by minibus from the hotel.
Paris by bicycle	**Paris à Vélo** 9 rue Jacques Coeur (4th arr.); tel. 01 48 87 60 01; Métro: Bastille Guided cycle tours through the centre from the Louvre to Marais or around unknown corners of Paris, such as a ride along the Canal de L'Ourcq to Parc de la Villette, linked to a trip to the sleepy La Mouzaia quarter. Romantic souls can even explore the city by night. Departures: 10am, 3pm and 8.30pm.
	Paris à Vélo c'est Sympa 37 boulevard Bourdon (4th arr.); tel. 01 48 87 60 01; Métro: Bastille Unusual and topical commentated tours.
	Paris Vélo 2 rue du Fer à Moulin (5th arr.); tel. 01 43 37 59 22; Métro: Censier cycle hire and accompanied tours daily (daytime and night-time programme).
Vespa hire	Contact Location, 10bis avenue de la Grande Armée (17th arr.) tel. 01 47 66 19 19.
Sightseeing by helicopter	Seeing Paris from the air may be something of an extravagance but in fine weather it is certainly worth it.
Héli-France	Héliport de Paris, 4 avenue de la Porte de Sèvres (15th arr.); Métro: Balard; tel. 01 45 57 53 67.
Hélicap	Héliport de Paris, 4 avenue de la Porte de Sèvres (15th arr.); Métro: Balard; tel. 01 45 57 75 51. Helicopter flights over the Défense quarter and Versailles.
Balloon flights	Air Ballon Communication, 12 rue Bonaparte; tel. 01 43 29 14 13. France Montgolfière, 76 rue Balard; tel. 01 40 60 11 23.
Boat trips	See entry
Sightseeing trips in Ile de France	Some agencies that specialise in city sightseeing tours offer excursions further afield in the Ile de France as well. These can also be booked at the offices of RATP, Paris's public transport authority, and SNCF, the French State Railways:

Services Touristiques de la RATP
53bis quai des Grands-Augustins (6th arr.); tel. 01 43 46 42 03; Métro:
Pont-Neuf, Saint-Michel; open Mon.–Fri. 8.30am–noon, 1–4.45pm;
Sat., Sun., public holidays 8.30–noon, 2–4.45pm.
Place de la Madeleine (8th arr.); tel. 01 42 65 31 18; Métro: Madeleine;
open Mon.–Fri. 7.30am–6.45pm, Sat., Sun., public holidays 6.30am–
6pm

Bureaux de Tourisme de la SNCF: see Information

Smoking

Since 1992 all public buildings, restaurants, hotels and covered
places are officially no smoking areas; smoking is only permitted in
zones where signs proclaim these to be designated smoking areas.
Failure to comply with the smoking ban is punishable by a fine, but,
this being Paris, it is not likely to be strictly enforced.

Souvenirs

See Shopping

Sport

Allo-Sports; tel. 01 42 76 54 54   Sport information
Mon.–Thur. 10.30am–5pm, Fri. 10.30am–4.30pm
Allo-Sports is an information service covering all sporting events in
Paris and sports activities (information about the addresses of clubs,
what's on where, etc.).

Spectator sports

Football is very popular in France – and all the more so since France's   Football
victory in the World Cup '98. Rugby is another favourite game, and is   and rugby
almost as popular as in the United Kingdom.
Parc des Princes (24 Rue du Commandant-Guilbaud, 16th arr.),
Paris's largest stadium, holds 49,000 and is the home ground of Paris
St-Germain F.C. This is where France's Cup Final takes place, usually
in early June, and is also the French venue for rugby's five nations
tournament. Other events, such as large pop concerts, are also held
here.

The Marathon de Paris takes place late April/early May, starting at   Marathon
around 9am from the Champs-Elysées where it also finishes.

The French are passionate punters when it comes to horse-racing.   Racecourses
Paris probably has more race-meetings than any other city in Europe,
and more betting on the horses as well.

Hippodrome d'Auteuil
See A to Z, Bois de Boulogne
This is where the "Prix du Président de la République" is run on the
first Sunday in April.

Sport

Hippodrome de Longchamp
See A to Z, Bois de Boulogne
As elegant on occasions as Ascot, Longchamp is the home of the Prix de l'Arc de Triomphe, probably the world's greatest horse race.

Hippodrome de Vincennes, Bois de Vincennes
RER A: Joinville le Pont; Métro: Château de Vincennes

Trotting races

Hippodrome de Chantilly (see A to Z, Chantilly)
18 avenue du Général Leclerc, 60 Chantilly
Train: from Gare du Nord to Champs de Courses
Flat racing

Cycle racing

The Tour de France, which was first staged in 1903, takes place over three weeks in July every year and ends in the Champs-Elysées.

Tennis

Tennis is one of the most popular sports in France, where it has over 4 million players. This enthusiasm has quite a lot to do with the charisma surrounding the French Open, the Grand Slam tournament that takes place in Stade Roland Garros, France's premier tennis venue (2 avenue Gordon-Bennett, 16th arr.). Tickets for the Open, which takes place around the end of May, can be booked from February onwards.

Participatory sports

Sports centres

Aquaboulevard: see Swimming Pools

Espace Vit'Halles
48 rue Rambuteau (3rd arr.); tel. 01 42 77 21 71; Métro: Les Halles; Rambuteau
Keep-fit, gymnastics, body building, steam bath, sauna, aerobics

Thermes du Royal Monceau, 39 avenue Hoche (8th arr.)
tel. 01 42 99 85 66; Métro: Ternes
Luxury club with fitness centre, sauna, swimming pool, squash

Boule

Places where France's national sport is played include the Bois de Boulogne, the boulevard Richard Lenoir (11th arr.) and the Arènes de Lutèce (5th arr.).

Free climbing

La Samaritaine, 75 rue de Rivoli (1st arr.)
tel. 01 40 41 25 15; Métro: Châtelet
You can train on the 5m/16ft high climbing wall in the department store basement, for which there is no charge.

Centre Sportif Poissonnier, 2 rue Jean Cocteau (18th arr.)
tel. 01 42 51 24 68; Métro: Porte de Clignancourt
Beginners and experts practise on the 21m/75ft high climbing wall.

Golf

On weekdays many Paris golf clubs allow non-members to play.
Golf Club de l'Etoile, 10 avenue de la Grande Armée
tel. 01 43 80 30 79; Métro: Charles de Gaulle-Etoile
Golf lessons on seven courses and a putting green.

Riding

To go horse riding in the Bois de Boulogne or Bois de Vincennes it is necessary to belong to a riding club; information: La Société d'Equitation de Paris; tel. 01 45 01 20 06.

Roller skating

La Main Jaune, place de la Porte Chemperret (17th arr.)
tel. 01 47 63 26 47; Métro: Porte de Champerret
Roller-skating rink, with skate hire. Roller-disco Fri., Sat. from 10pm.

Paris has over 30 pools. See Swimming Pools.

Swimming

Squash Rennes-Raspail, 149 rue de Rennes (6th arr.); tel. 01 45 44 24 35
Métro: Montparnasse Bienvenue.

Squash

Stadium Squash Club, 66 avenue d'Ivry (13th arr.); tel. 01 45 85 39 06
Métro: Porte d'Ivry.

Paris has about 150 public tennis courts which cost very little and are
open to everyone. For information contact: l'Espace Information
Jeunesse et Sports; tel. 01 42 76 22 60.

Tennis

Tennis Action, 145 rue de Vaugirard (15th arr.); tel. 01 47 34 36 36;
Métro: Vaugirard. This club has ten different tennis centres in and
around Paris.

Centre de Tennis du Jardin du Luxembourg, Jardin du Luxembourg
(6th arr.); tel. 01 43 25 79 18; Métro: St-Sulpice. The tennis courts in
the Jardin du Luxembourg are very popular – the best time to go is
during working hours.

Swimming Pools (piscines)

Les Amiraux
6 rue Hermann, La Chapelle; Métro: Simplon
Open Mon. 2–7.30pm, Tue.–Sat. 7am–7.30pm, Sun. 8am–6pm

Outdoor

Cachan
2 avenue de l'Europe; buses 184, 187
Open Mon.–Sat. 10am–8pm (Wed. 10pm), Sun. 9am–6pm

Chatillon-Malakoff, Stade Nautique
57 rue Jean-Bouin; Métro: Chatillon – Etienne-Dolet
Open Mon.–Thur. 10am–8pm, Fri. 10am–10pm, Sat., Sun. 9am–7pm

Indoor

Georges Vallerey
148 avenue Gambetta; métro: Porte des Lilas
Open Mon., Wed., Fri.–Sun. 10am–8pm, Tue., Thur. 10am–10pm

Molitor
Porte Molitor; Métro: Michel-Ange Molitor
Open Mon., Thur. 12–1.45pm, 5.30–7.30, Tue. 12–1.45pm, 7.30–9pm,
Wed. 10am–7.30pm, Fri. 12–2pm, 7.30–9pm, Sat. 12–7.30pm

Butte-aux-Cailles
5 place Paul Verlaine; Métro: Place Italie. Open Tue.–Sun. 9am–7pm
    Aquaboulevard
4/6 rue Louis Armand; tel. 01 40 60 10 10
Métro: Balard; open: 9am–midnight daily
This is the leisure pool that has absolutely everything. Modelled on a
vast cruise liner it has giant waterslides, a heated pool with wave
machine, beaches indoors and out, Turkish baths, whirlpools, sauna,
solaria, restaurants, boutiques, fitness centre, golf, tennis, squash,
etc., etc....

Outdoor and
indoor

Edouard-Pailleron
30 rue Edouard-Pailleron; Métro: Bolivar
Open Mon.–Fri. noon–1.45pm, 5–7.30pm (Tue., Thur. 9pm); Sat.
noon–7.30pm, Sun. 8.30am–6pm.

Facilities for
the disabled

Bernard-Lafay
79 rue de la Jonquère; métro: Porte de Clichy
Open Tue., Thur., Fri., Sat. 7am–5.15pm, Sun. 8am–5.15pm.

Taxis

Paris has around 15,000 taxis in circulation – although there never seems to be one around when it is needed. Taxis can be hailed in the street and are for hire if the sign on the roof is lit up – or from one of the city's 470 taxi ranks. Taxis are hardest to come by between 7.30 and 9 at night when the drivers change shifts. Passengers are expected to sit in the back and drivers are within their rights to refuse to take more than three.

Fares
: Fares are made up of a minimum charge plus rates that vary according to the time of day and the distance covered. Within Paris the day rate ("Tarif A") which operates from 7am to 7pm on weekdays is 3.45 francs per kilometre (1998). You pay more at other times and there are also supplements for luggage, animals and journeys from train stations and airports. The journey from Charles-de-Gaulle airport to Paris, for example, should cost around 300 francs. The rates for the day tariff, night tariff (Tarif B) and journeys in the suburbs, etc. (Tarif C) are clearly indicated inside each taxi. The usual tip is around 10 to 15%.

Radio taxis
: Radio taxis include:
G7: tel. 01 47 39 47 39
Taxis Bleus: tel. 01 49 36 10 10
Alpha Taxis: tel. 01 45 85 85 85

Motorbike taxis
: Motorbike taxis (called Scooter Express) have no meters, so agree on the fare before starting.

Complaints
: Any complaints should be directed to: Préfecture de Police, Service des Taxis, 36 rue des Morillons (15th arr.); tel. 01 55 76 20 00; Métro: Convention.

Telephone

Phoneboxes
: Most public phoneboxes are operated by phonecards (télécartes). These can be bought as cards for 50 or 120 units from post offices, tobacconists and offices of France Telecom. The public phones in bistros and post offices still take coins or tokens ("jetons") which you can get at the cash-desk.

Dialling codes
: Within France to Paris and within Paris:
01 + eight-figure number

To Paris from abroad:
00 (international access code) 33 (code for France) 1 (code for Paris minus 0) i.e. 00 33 1 + eight-figure number

From Paris to:
Australia: 00 61 plus local code (minus 0) then number
Canada, United States: 00 1 etc.; Ireland: 00 353 etc.;
South Africa: 00 27 etc.; United Kingdom: 00 44 etc.

Theatres

Even theatre-lovers with little or no French should find something to their taste in the wide range of programmes that Paris has to offer in its 130 or so theatres. You can take in the classics by such greats as Racine and Molière at the Comédie Française, aim for lighter entertainment at one of the popular "théâtres de boulevard" or see what the experimental avant-garde café-theatres have to offer.

It pays to buy tickets in good time before the performance, since there is usually a crowd at the box office. If you speak French you can generally book theatre, ballet and opera tickets in advance ("location") over the telephone. Alternatively you can try one of the ticket agencies, most of which are located around the Opéra and on the Champs-Elysées. Most theatres sell some tickets for the same day's performance at half-price. The two ticket offices at 15 Place de la Madeleine and Châtelet-Les-Halles RER Station also sell half-price tickets for the same day from 12.30pm every day except Monday.

Tickets and ticket offices

Advance ticket sales abroad for theatre performances and exhibitions:
Cityrama; tel. 01 44 55 60 50, fax 01 42 60 33 71
Paris Vision Opéra Théâtre; tel. 01 40 06 01 00, fax 01 47 42 69 29

Information about what's on at the theatre is available in the publications by the Tourist Office (see Information) and in the weekly listings magazines, L'Officiel des Spectacles, Pariscope and 7 à Paris.

What's on

Comédie Française
2 rue du Richeliu (1st arr.); tel. 01 40 15 00 15
Métro: Palais-Royal (see also pp.175–176)

Classical

La Cartoucherie de Vincennes
Route de la Pyramide, Bois de Vincennes
Métro: Château de Vincennes then bus 112
Three theatres and one studio in a disused cartridge factory:
Théâtre du Soleil (Ariane Mnouchkine); tel. 01 43 74 87 63
Théâtre de la Tempàte; tel. 01 43 74 94 67
Théâtre de l'Epée de Bois; tel. 01 43 74 20 21
Atelier de Chaudron; tel. 01 43 28 45 08

Classical and modern

Odéon
1 place Paul-Claudel (6th arr.); tel. 01 43 25 70 32;
Metro: Odéon
Second stage of the Comédie Française and home of Giorgio Strehler's Théâtre de l'Europe.

Théâtre de la Ville
2 place du Châtelet (4th arr.); tel. 01 42 74 22 77;
Métro: Châtelet
Directors here include Patrick Chéreau.

Théâtre National de Chaillot
Place du Trocadéro (16th arr.); tel. 01 53 65 31 00;
Métro: Trocadéro

Théâtre National de la Colline
15 rue Malte-Brun (20th arr.); tel. 01 43 66 43 60;
Métro: Gambetta

Theatres

Amandiers de Paris
110 rue des Amandiers (20th arr.); tel. 01 44 62 85 40
Métro: Ménilmontant

Antoine–Simone Berriau
14 boulevard de Strasbourg (10th arr.); tel. 01 42 08 77 71
Métro: Strasbourg – Saint-Denis

Atelier
Place Charles-Dullin (18th arr.); tel. 01 46 06 49 24
Métro: Anvers

Bouffes Parisiens
4 rue Montsigny (9th arr.); tel. 01 42 96 92 42
Métro: 4 Septembre

Carré Silvia Montfort
106 rue Brancion (15th arr.); tel. 01 45 31 28 34
Métro: Porte de Vanves

Comédie des Champs-Elysées
15 avenue Montaigne (8th arr.); tel. 01 47 23 37 21
Métro: Alma-Marceau

Daunou
7 rue Daunou (2nd arr.); tel. 01 42 61 69 14
Métro: Opéra

Edouard VII
Place Edouard VII (9th arr.); tel. 01 47 42 57 49
Métro: Opéra

Le Dejazet
41 boulevard du Temple (3rd arr.); tel. 01 48 87 97 34
Métro: Fille du Calvaire, République

Fontaine
10 rue Fontaine (9th arr.); tel. 01 74 74 40
Métro: Blanche

Gaîté Montparnasse
28 rue de la Gaîté (4th arr.); tel. 01 43 20 60 56
Métro: Gaîté

Théâtre Grevin
10 boulevard Montmartre (18th arr.); tel. 01 42 46 84 47
Métro: Rue Montmartre

Gymnase Marie-Bell
38 boulevard de Bonne-Nouvelle (10th arr.); tel. 01 42 46 79 79
Métro: Bonne Nouvelle

Mathurins
36 rue des Mathurins (8th arr.); tel. 01 42 65 90 00
Métro: Havre-Caumartin, Madeleine, Auber

Michodière
4bis rue de la Michodière (2nd arr.); tel. 01 47 42 96 77
Métro: Opéra

Montparnasse
31 rue de la Gaîté (14th arr.); tel. 01 43 22 77 30
Métro: Montparnasse, Edgar-Quinet

Nouveautés
24 boulevard Poissonière (2nd arr.); tel. 01 47 70 52 76
Métro: Montmartre

Palais-Royal
38 rue Montpensier (1st arr.); tel. 01 42 97 59 81
Métro: Bourse, Palais Royal

Théâtre Renaud-Barrault
Avenue F. Roosevelt (8th arr.); tel. 01 42 56 60 70
Métro: Franklin Roosevelt

Théâtre de l'Est Parisien
159 avenue Gambetta (20th arr.); tel. 01 43 63 20 96
Métro: Saint Fargeau

Variétés
7 boulevard Montmartre (2nd arr.); tel. 01 42 33 09 92
Métro: Montmartre

Cafés-théâtres

Bec Fin
6 rue Thérèse (1st arr.); tel. 01 42 96 29 35
Métro: Palais Royal

Blancs-Manteaux
15 rue des Blancs-Manteaux (4th arr.); tel. 01 48 87 15 84
Métro: Hôtel de Ville, Rambuteau

Café d'Edgar
58 boulevard Edgar-Quinet (14th arr.); tel. 01 43 20 85 11
Métro: Edgar-Quinet

Café de la Gare
41 rue du Temple (4th arr.); tel. 01 42 78 52 51
Métro: Hôtel de Ville

**Experimental
theatre**

Petit Casino
17 rue Chapon (3rd arr.); tel. 01 42 78 36 50
Métro: Arts et Métiers

Athenée Louis-Jouvet
4 Square de l'Opéra Louis-Jouvet (9th arr.); tel. 01 47 42 67 27
Métro: Opéra

La Bastille
76 rue de la Roquette (11th arr.); tel. 01 43 57 42 14
Métro: Bastille

Cité Internationale Universitaire
21 boulevard Jourdain (14th arr.); tel. 01 45 89 38 69
Métro: Cité Universitaire

Théâtre de la Commune
2 rue Edouard-Poisson, 93 Aubervilliers; tel. 01 48 33 16 16
Métro: Fort d'Aubervilliers

Théâtre de Paris
Rue Blanche (9th arr.); tel. 01 48 74 16 82
Métro: Blanche, Trinité

Essaion
6 rue Pierre-au-Lard (4th arr.); tel. 01 42 78 46 42
Métro: Rambuteau

Theatres

Bouffes du Nord
37bis boulevard de la Chapelle (10th arr.); tel. 01 42 39 34 50
Métro: La Chapelle

Ouvert
4bis Veron cité (18th arr.); tel. 01 42 55 74 40
Métro: Blanche

L'Escalier d'Or
18 rue d'Enghien (10th arr.); tel. 01 45 23 13 10
Métro: Château d'Eau

Lucenaire-Forum Centre National d'Art et d'Essai with eight stages
53 rue Notre Dame des Champs (6th arr.); tel. 01 45 44 57 34
Métro: Vavin, Notre Dame des Champs

Théâtre des Amandiers
7 avenue Pablo Picasso, 92 Nanterre; tel. 01 47 21 18 81
RER/SNCF: Nanterre/Université

Théâtre Gérard Philipe
59 boulevard Jules-Guesde, 93 Saint-Denis; tel. 01 42 43 00 59

Théâtre de la Huchette
23 rue de la Huchette (5th arr.); tel. 01 43 26 38 99
Métro: Saint Michel
Since 1958 this theatre has staged performances of Eugène Ionesco's "La cantatrice chauve" and "La Leçon" every day except Sunday.

Children's theatre

Centre d'Animation des Batignolles
77 rue Trauffaut (17th arr.); tel. 01 47 37 30 75
Métro: Brochant; open daily 3pm
Musical clowns, conjurers, puppetry

La Magie des Automates
8 rue Bernard de Clairvaux (3rd arr.); tel. 01 42 71 28 28
Métro: Rambuteau; open daily (except Tue.) 10.30am–6.30pm

Théâtre Guignol Anatole
Parc des Buttes-Chaumont (19th arr.); tel. 01 43 87 13 12
Métro: Laumière; open daily 3.30, 4.30 pm
Punch and Judy

Théâtre Jerval
Relais du Bois, Croix Catalan, Bois de Boulogne (16th arr.)
tel. 01 47 37 30 75
Métro: Porte Maillot, Porte Dauphine, Sablons
open Wed., Sat., Sun. 2.30pm

Théâtre 3 sur 4
122 boulevard du Montparnasse (14th arr.); tel. 01 43 27 09 16
Métro: Vavin, Raspail; open Wed., Sun. 3pm

Puppet theatre

Jardin d'Acclimatation
Boulevard des Sablons, Bois de Boulogne (16th arr.)
Métro: Sablons
open Wed., Sat., Sun., pub. hols. 3, 3.15pm

Marionettes du Champs de Mars
Champs de Mars (7th arr.); tel. 01 46 37 07 87
Métro: Ecole Militaire; open Wed., Sat., Sun 3.15, 4.15pm

Marionettes du Luxembourg
Jardin du Luxembourg (6th arr.); tel. 01 43 26 46 47
Métro: Vavin, Notre Dame des Champs

Marionettes des Champs-Elysées
Square Marigny (8th arr.); tel. 01 42 57 43 34
Métro: Champs-Elysées Clemenceau

Marionettes du Parc Montsouris
Parc Montsouris, avenue Reilles/rue Gazan (14th arr.); tel. 01 46 65 45 95
Métro: Cité Universitaire, Glacière

See Music

Opera, ballet

Ticket Offices

See Theatres

Time

France is on Central European Time, one hour ahead of Greenwich
Mean Time. Summer Time, when clocks are advanced an hour (i.e.
GMT + 2 hours), is in force from late March to the end of September.

Tipping

In France it is not the general rule to tip in restaurants since the
service charge is usually included in the bill ("service compris"), but if
you do choose to tip leave it on the table rather than include it in
payment for the bill. Hotel staff will expect a tip, though, and so do
lavatory attendants, theatre and cinema ushers, and tour guides,
while the rate for tipping taxi drivers is 10 to 15%.

Travel Documents

Nationals from EU countries, Canada, New Zealand and the United
States only need a valid passport to enter France; Australians and
South Africans also require a visa. Children under 16 must have their
own passport or be entered in their parents' passport.

Personal papers

France recognizes national driving licences and vehicle registration
documents, and you should take these with you. It is sensible to have
a "green card" too, thus ensuring your car has international insurance cover. You will also need to display an oval nationality sticker.

Vehicle
documents

When to Go

Paris is a city for all seasons, but the best months are May and June,
and September and October. In July and August it can get very hot
and humid and, since this is when the Parisians leave town for their
summer holidays, many of the city's shops, restaurants and theatres

are closed. In winter the temperature seldom drops below freezing, but rain is more frequent.

Youth Hostels and Hotels

The following organizations specialise in accommodation for young people:

Acceuil des Jeunes en France (AJF)	12 rue des Barres (4th arr.); tel. 01 42 72 72 09 Métro: Hôtel de Ville
	Plateau Beaubourg (A.J.F.) 119 rue St-Martin (4th arr.); tel. 01 42 77 87 80 Métro: Châtelet
	Hôtel de Ville (A.J.F.) 16 rue du Pont Louis-Philippe (4th arr.); tel. 01 42 78 04 82 Métro: Hôtel de Ville
Union des Centres de Rencontres Internationales de France (UCRIF)	Centrale de Réservations et d'Information 20 rue Jean-Jacques Rousseau (1st arr.) tel. 01 42 36 88 18 Métro: Halles
Fédération Unie des Auberges de Jeunesse (FUAJ)	United Federation of Youth Hostels 27 rue Pajol (18th arr.) tel. 01 46 07 00 01
Hôtels de la Jeunesse (youth hotels)	The following youth hotels are located in old mansions and convents, with green courtyards, in the centre of Paris:
	Le Fauconnier 11 rue du Fauconnier (4th arr.); tel. 01 42 74 23 45 Métro: Pont-Marie, Saint-Paul
	Centre International Paris, Opéra 11 rue Thérèse (1st arr.); tel. 01 42 60 77 23 Métro: Pyramides
Auberges de Jeunesse (youth hostels)	Le D'Artagnan 80 rue Vitruve (20th arr.); tel. 01 43 61 08 75 Métro: Porte de Bagnolet; half-board compulsory
	Jules Ferry 8 boulevard Jules Ferry (11th arr.); tel. 01 43 57 55 60 Métro: République; no groups
Information	For further information about accommodation for young people see Information.

Index

Index

Index

The Principal Sights at a Glance

Imprint

130 illustrations, 16 maps and plans, 1 large map at end of book

German text: Dr Madeleine Reincke; contributions from Dr Irene Antoni-Komar, Achim Bourmer, Helga Cabos, Mechthild Haas, Wolfgang Liebermann

Editorial work: Baedeker-Redaktion (Dr Madeleine Reincke)

General direction: Rainer Eisenschmid, Baedeker Ostfildern

Cartography: Franz Huber, Munich; Mairs Geographischer Verlag GmbH & Co., Ostfildern (large map)

English translation: James Hogarth

Revised translation: Wendy Bell, David Cocking, Brenda Ferris, Crispin Warren

Source of illustrations: AP-Phot/Patrick Kovarick (1); Archiv für Kunst und Geschichte (5); IFA Bilderteam (5); Helga Lade (2); Laif (5); Mauritius (4); Dr Madeleine Reincke/Helga Cabos (83); Réunion des Musées Nationaux (7); Shapowalow (4); Anja Schliebitz (1); Schuster (3); Klaus Thiels (1); Transglobe (1); Ullstein (7).

Front and back cover: AA Photo Library (P. Kenward)

4th English edition 1999
Reprinted 2000 (×3)

© Baedeker Ostfildern
Original German edition 1998

© Automobile Association Developments Limited 2000
English language edition worldwide

Published by AA Publishing (a trading name of Automobile Association Developments Limited, whose registered office is Norfolk House, Priestley Road, Basingstoke, Hampshire RG24 9NY; registered number 1878835).

Distributed in the United States by:
Fodor's Travel Publications, Inc.
201 East 50th Street
New York, NY 10022

A CIP catalogue record of this book is available from the British Library.

Licensed user: Mairs Geographischer Verlag GmbH & Co., Ostfildern

Printed in Italy by G. Canale & C. S.p.A., Turin

ISBN 0 7495 1991 6